LETTERS TO A
TROUBLED
CHURCH

1 AND 2 CORINTHIANS

RAY C. STEDMAN

Discovery House Publishers

Books, music, and videos that feed the soul with the Word of God

Box 3566 Grand Rapids, MI 49501

Discovery House Publishers is affiliated with RBC Ministries,
Grand Rapids, Michigan.

Discovery House books are distributed to the trade exclusively by
Barbour Publishing, Inc., Uhrichsville, Ohio.

Interior design by Sherri L. Hoffman

Library of Congress Cataloging-in-Publication Data

Stedman, Ray C.
    Letters to a troubled church : studies in 1 and 2 Corinthians / Ray
    C. Stedman ; edited by James D. Denney.
        p.   cm.
    Includes bibliographical references and index.
    ISBN 978-1-57293-255-5 (alk. paper)
    1. Bible. N.T. Corinthians—Commentaries. I. Denney, James D. II.
    Title.
BS2675.53.S74 2007
227'.207—dc22   2007035627

Printed in the United States of America
07 08 09 10 / BPI / 10 9 8 7 6 5 4 3 2 1

CONTENTS

꿍

PUBLISHER'S PREFACE

Ray Stedman (1917–1992) served as pastor of the Peninsula Bible Church from 1950 to 1990, where he was known and loved as a man of outstanding Bible knowledge, Christian integrity, warmth, and humility. Born in Temvik, North Dakota, Ray grew up on the rugged landscape of Montana. When he was a small child, his mother became ill, and his father, a railroad man, abandoned the family. Ray grew up on his aunt's Montana farm from the time he was six. He came to know the Lord at a Methodist revival meeting at age eleven.

As a young man he moved around and tried different jobs, working in Chicago, Denver, Hawaii, and elsewhere. He enlisted in the Navy during World War II, where he often led Bible studies for civilians and Navy personnel and even preached on local radio in Hawaii. At the close of the war, Ray was married in Honolulu (he and his wife, Elaine, had first met in Great Falls, Montana). They returned to the mainland in 1946, and Ray graduated from Dallas Theological Seminary in 1950. After two summers interning under Dr. J. Vernon McGee, Ray traveled for several months with Dr. H. A. Ironside, pastor of Moody Church in Chicago.

In 1950, Ray was called by the two-year-old Peninsula Bible Fellowship in Palo Alto, California, to serve as its first pastor. Peninsula Bible Fellowship later became Peninsula Bible Church, and Ray served a forty-year tenure, retiring on April 30, 1990. During those years, Ray Stedman authored a number of life-changing Christian books, including the classic work on the meaning and mission of the church, *Body Life*. He went into the presence of his Lord on October 7, 1992.

This book, *Letters to a Troubled Church*, has been edited from two sermon series that Ray Stedman preached on Paul's letters to the church in Corinth. In lively, everyday language, he offers solid biblical insight into such questions as:

How can I live a Christ-honoring life in a depraved and post-Christian culture? How do we answer atheists and agnostics who say that Christianity is just a myth? What happens to us after we die? What does God have to say about marriage? What does God say about divorce? What encouragement does God offer for single people? Is it always wrong to go to court to resolve a dispute?

What is Christlike love, and how does it differ from worldly love? What does God say about Christian freedom and the moral "gray areas" of life? What does God really say about the roles of men and women? How should we resolve disputes and divisions in the church? How should we deal with scandals and sin in the church? What is the role of the gift of tongues in the history and life of the church? Whose job is it to do the ministry of the church?

All of these questions, and many more, are answered thoughtfully and biblically by one of the wisest Bible teachers of our time. Even if you've studied these New Testament letters many times before, you'll discover new and profound insights in Ray Stedman's writing. So turn the page and prepare to be challenged, instructed, and inspired by the life-changing truths of *Letters to a Troubled Church.*

—DISCOVERY HOUSE PUBLISHERS

PART I

⌒⥾⥾⌒

Living as God's People in an Ungodly World

1 CORINTHIANS

1

THE CORINTHIAN CRISIS

1 Corinthians 1:1–17

One Sunday morning, I got up before the congregation of Peninsula Bible Church in Palo Alto, California, and I began preaching a sermon from 1 Corinthians 6. In the course of that sermon, I read these verses to the congregation:

> Do you not know that the wicked will not inherit the kingdom of God? Do not be deceived: Neither the sexually immoral nor idolaters nor adulterers nor male prostitutes nor homosexual offenders nor thieves nor the greedy nor drunkards nor slanderers nor swindlers will inherit the kingdom of God. And that is what some of you were....
> (1 CORINTHIANS 6:9–11a)

I stopped reading at that point. I was struck by those words: "And that is what some of you were." I looked around at the congregation and said, "Do you realize what Paul was saying? He was describing the make-up of the church at Corinth. The Corinthian Christians came from a checkered and sordid background! Some were sexually immoral, others were idolaters, others were thieves and crooks and addicts and liars! Many, I'm sure, were still struggling with sinful habits even as believers. Now, how many here today have one or more of these sins in your background? If God has saved you from the kind of life Paul describes here, would you stand?"

For a moment, I thought I had made a mistake. Seconds ticked by, and no one stood. It was a terribly awkward moment.

Then an elderly lady sitting next to the aisle hesitantly rose to her feet. Then a few others stood. Then people stood in droves. I looked around and saw that *at least two-thirds* of the congregation was standing!

I said, "That's what I thought! We're just like the church at Corinth! This letter could just as well be called 1 Californians as 1 Corinthians."

Later, a young man came up to me and said, "Pastor, today was the first time I've ever been to church. I gave my life to Jesus Christ at a Billy Graham crusade a few days ago, and I knew that God wanted me to start attending church—so I came here. To tell you the truth, I wasn't sure what I was getting into.

"Then, when you asked for people to stand up, I just about freaked out! I thought, 'Oh, no! Do I have to stand up in front of all these church people and admit the kind of life I've led?' But when I looked around and saw that *most* of the congregation was standing, I said to myself, 'These are my kind of people!'"

When Paul wrote 1 and 2 Corinthians, he spoke directly to your heart and mine. The centuries seem to disappear as we realize that the Corinthian believers lived in times and under conditions very much like our own.

True, the Christians of ancient Corinth didn't have cellular phones or the Internet or air travel. But the parallels between Corinth and our own world far outweigh the differences. The Corinthian believers lived in a moral climate much like our own.

A city of great wealth—and great depravity

Corinth was a city of wealth and culture, seated at the crossroads of the Roman Empire. The city was the hub of trade and commerce in the first-century world. It was a resort city, located in a lush and desirable region. It was also a city of moral depravity—a place where prostitution and other forms of sexual immorality were rampant. People chased money, success, and status. They worshiped Aphrodite, the Greek goddess of sex.

Imagine some of the great sin capitals of today's world—places where sexual depravity is practiced openly, cities like Amsterdam, Buenos Aires, Bangkok, Las Vegas, or San Francisco. That's the kind of reputation Corinth had in its own day. The Temple of Aphrodite was on a hill behind the city. Every evening the priests and priestesses—male and female prostitutes—would come down from the temple into the streets to ply their trade. History records that there were as many as a thousand temple prostitutes employed at the Temple of Aphrodite at one time.

The Christians of Corinth were surrounded by immorality and temptation, just as we are today. It was not easy to take a godly stand in first-century Corinth, and it is not easy to do so today. So the words Paul addresses to the Christians in Corinth are meant for you and me as well. Paul writes:

Paul, called to be an apostle of Christ Jesus by the will of God, and our brother Sosthenes, To the church of God in Corinth, to those sanctified in Christ Jesus and called to be holy, together with all those everywhere who call on the name of our Lord Jesus Christ—their Lord and ours: Grace and peace to you from God our Father and the Lord Jesus Christ. (1 CORINTHIANS 1:1–3)

Paul wrote this letter from Ephesus in A.D. 56 or 57. In his greeting, Paul mentions Sosthenes, who was introduced in Acts 18:12–17. He was the chief official of the synagogue at Corinth, and he was beaten by a mob for failing to prosecute Paul according to Jewish law. Sosthenes later converted to Christianity and became a companion to Paul.

The church in Corinth was founded by Paul about five years before this letter was written. Paul had originally come alone to Corinth after being driven out of Macedonia by persecution there. Leaving Timothy and Luke behind, he had traveled to Corinth by way of Athens. Paul had spent a year and a half to two years planting the Corinthian church; then he went on other journeys. While Paul was in Ephesus, word came of problems in the Corinthian church. So Paul wrote the first letter to the Corinthians to address those problems.

The letter we know as 1 Corinthians was the second of four letters (that we know of) that Paul wrote to the Christians in Corinth. The first letter, which Paul refers to in 1 Corinthians 5:9, has been lost to us. All we know of that lost letter is what the apostle Paul says—that he wrote a previous letter telling the Corinthians not to keep company with immoral people.

Sometime later, three men traveled from Corinth to Ephesus to visit Paul. Their names, given in 1 Corinthians 16:17, were Fortunatus, Stephanas, and Achaicus. They brought word of problems in the Corinthian church; they also brought a letter from the church. The letter we call 1 Corinthians is Paul's reply to the letter from Corinth and to the reports of problems in that church.

In terms of its structure and themes, this letter divides into four parts. Here is a thumbnail sketch of the structure of 1 Corinthians:

Part I: Introduction (1 Corinthians 1:1–9)

Paul lays out the overarching theme of the letter: We are called into fellowship with God's Son, Jesus the Lord.

Part II: Problems in the Church (1 Corinthians 1:10–11:34)

Paul deals with issues of carnal living, immorality, divisions, marriage, divorce, singleness, gender roles, authority, Communion, and so forth.

Part III: The Holy Spirit (1 Corinthians 12–15)

Paul turns from issues of carnality to issues of spirituality and deals in-depth with the role of the Holy Spirit in the life of the church and the believer.

Part IV: Final Requests (1 Corinthians 16)

Paul closes with some practical requests, such as taking up the collection for people in need, and so forth.

Paul's greeting

In structure, 1 Corinthians differs markedly from Paul's other letters. First, most of Paul's letters begin with a section of doctrinal truths, and then close with a section of practical application of those doctrinal truths. In 1 Corinthians, Paul plunges immediately into the problems of the church, then intersperses practical application of doctrine throughout the rest of the letter.

We see Paul's deep concern for this church and its problems in the opening lines. Paul starts by emphasizing his apostleship: "Paul, called to be an apostle of Christ Jesus by the will of God." Paul is about to speak to this church in an authoritative way, so he opens with his authority as an apostle.

Let's begin by making clear exactly what an apostle is. The word comes from the Greek word *apostolos*, meaning "someone sent forth to carry out a mission." The original twelve apostles were hand-picked by Jesus. The Scriptures list several qualifications of an apostle: An apostle must have seen the Lord and must be an eyewitness that He is risen (the original Twelve saw Him in His earthly flesh; Paul saw the resurrected Lord during his Damascus road conversion experience, and possibly in a series of later visions). An apostle must have been chosen by the Lord Jesus or by the Holy Spirit. An apostle must have spiritual gifts enabling him to perform signs, wonders, and miracles. The apostles were commissioned by Jesus to establish the church and take the gospel to the whole world. All of these weighty qualifications are implied in 1 Corinthians 1:1, where Paul establishes his authority as an apostle.

In verse 2, he writes, "To the church of God in Corinth, to those sanctified in Christ Jesus and called to be holy." He lays great emphasis on the fact that God has sanctified these believers and called them to be holy. The word *sanctified* means "set apart and purified for sacred use." *Holy* means "whole and spiritually pure." The problem in Corinth was that the believers there were not behaving as sanctified, holy people. So Paul began by reminding them of the kind of people God had called them to be.

Paul's greeting concludes in verses 4 through 8:

> I always thank God for you because of his grace given you in Christ Jesus. For in him you have been enriched in every way—in all your speaking and in all your knowledge—because our testimony about Christ was confirmed in you. Therefore you do not lack any spiritual gift as you eagerly wait for our Lord Jesus Christ to be revealed. He will keep you strong to the end, so that you will be blameless on the day of our Lord Jesus Christ. (1 CORINTHIANS 1:4–8)

In these verses, Paul makes a number of observations about the Christians in Corinth. First, they are saved by grace: "I always thank God for you because of his grace given you in Christ Jesus." These people had once been pagans, alienated from God; now they were born again through God's grace.

It's interesting to note that many of the problems Paul had to deal with in the early church involved legalism. In his letter to the Colossians, he confronted that church's obsession with legalistic rituals. In his letter to the Galatians, he confronted that church's obsession with the legalistic rite of circumcision. In his letter to the Philippians, he confronted that church's misplaced emphasis on legalistic works.

But in the Corinthian church, the problem was not legalism. It was license—the opposite of legalism. The Corinthians had accepted the grace of God but had taken grace to such an extreme that they didn't think it mattered to God how they lived their lives.

Paul goes on to say that they "have been enriched in every way." That is, they have been well equipped to know and speak God's Word, having been taught by Paul himself. It would be fair to say that the Corinthians were theologians, and like most Greeks of that time, they loved to discuss philosophy and doctrine.

13

More than that, Paul says, they were not lacking in any spiritual gift. The Scriptures list at least twenty-one different spiritual gifts: apostle, prophet, evangelist, pastor, teacher, service, exhortation, giving, leadership, mercy, helps, administration, wisdom, knowledge, discernment, prophecy, tongues, interpretation, faith, healing, and miracles. These gifts are listed in Romans 12:3–7, 1 Corinthians 12:1–12, 28, and Ephesians 4:11. According to Paul, the Christians in Corinth did not lack any spiritual gift—they manifested all of them.

Can you imagine the fascinating meetings they must have had when they all got together? No one wanted to miss church in Corinth! They never knew whether somebody would be healed or a miracle might take place!

More than that, their expectation was sound. They awaited the coming appearance of our Lord Jesus Christ, when He would set things right on earth. They had no naive delusions that they, by their own efforts, would cure the problems of the world. They understood that Christ would sustain them to the end, and He would present them blameless before the Father.

The key verse of 1 Corinthians

In verse 9, the apostle seems to change the subject. He introduces a description of the kind of fellowship the Corinthian Christians needed to experience:

> God, who has called you into fellowship with his Son Jesus Christ our Lord, is faithful. (1 CORINTHIANS 1:9)

This is the key verse of 1 Corinthians. The rest of the letter centers on this one statement. Paul wants the Corinthians to understand that God has called them to a special relationship. The failure to maintain this relationship is the reason for all of the problems in the Corinthian church. In failing to understand the relationship they had with Jesus, they had fallen prey to a list of problems that the apostle was about to deal with: divisions, scandals, lawsuits, immorality, drunkenness, quarreling, and more.

Despite the array of spiritual gifts they possessed, the Corinthian church was failing in its mission. Instead of making an impact on Corinth, the pagan city of Corinth was impacting the church. The sinful and corrosive activities of the surrounding culture were infiltrating the church—and the result was that the power of God was not being manifested at Corinth.

Dr. Peter Marshall (1902–1949), the Scottish-born pastor who was twice appointed chaplain of the United States Senate, once said, "Christians are like deep-sea divers encased in suits designed for many fathoms deep, marching bravely forth to pull plugs out of bathtubs!"

Two thousand years after Paul wrote this letter to the Corinthians, nothing has changed. Churches still struggle with this very issue: We have lost the sense that Jesus is among us. We no longer live in the awareness that we are partners with Christ in everything we do. When that awareness fades, all of the troubles that the Corinthians experienced begin to crowd in upon us. Paul wrote this letter to call the Corinthians—and us!—to a full recognition of what it means to live in fellowship with Christ.

Fellowship with Christ is the work of the Holy Spirit. It is His task to take the things of Christ and make them known unto us. We need the Spirit to open our eyes to what Jesus meant when He said, "For where two or three come together in my name, there am I with them" (Matthew 18:20). We tend to think that Jesus is speaking only of giving us His guidance or His answer to our prayers. But He is also speaking of giving us His power and His ability to open doors in unusual and unanticipated ways.

That's what was missing in Corinth. As we go through this letter, we'll see how the apostle calls the Corinthians back to a rediscovery of authentic fellowship with the Lord Jesus Christ. The Corinthian believers suffered divisions because they had lost sight of the lordship of Jesus. They were immoral because they had forgotten that the members of their bodies were the members of Christ. They filed lawsuits against one another because they failed to see that Jesus is judge of the believer's heart. They quarreled because they forgot that they were all members of the body of Christ.

The first problem: Division in the church

The first problem the apostle Paul deals with is the matter of divisions in the church at Corinth. He writes:

> I appeal to you, brothers, in the name of our Lord Jesus Christ, that all of you agree with one another so that there may be no divisions among you and that you may be perfectly united in mind and thought. (1 CORINTHIANS 1:10)

Church unity is a very important matter, and Paul addresses this issue in a number of letters. In this letter, he places it first in the list of issues

15

he must deal with. In fact, many of the other problems in the Corinthian church sprang from the division within the congregation.

A number of years ago, I received a call from a young pastor in another state. His church had been split into several factions. One of those factions urged him to take half the congregation, move to another part of town, and start a new church. He wanted my advice: Should he go and start the new church—or stay and try to unify the church?

I said, "Well, it all depends on your motive. If you want to plant a new church to further the Lord's work in a neglected part of town, and the leadership of the church agrees with that, then I'm sure the Lord would bless your efforts. But if you are just thinking of going someplace new to escape the pressures and problems in your current situation, then that just might be the worst thing you could do. In John 17, Jesus prayed that His followers would be unified so that the world would believe in Him. If we allow the church to be divided, we present a poor testimony about Jesus and His church."

In 1 Corinthians 1:10, Paul shows us that the true basis of our unity in the church is the name of our Lord Jesus Christ. He says, "I appeal to you, brothers, in the name of our Lord Jesus Christ . . . ." Our relationship to Christ is the unifying factor of the church. There is only one basis on which you can get any roomful of Christians to agree on anything: the person of Jesus Christ.

Paul describes Christian unity this way: "that all of you agree with one another so that there may be no divisions among you and that you may be perfectly united in mind and thought." At first glance, it may seem that Paul is asking the impossible! How can everyone in the church be perfectly united in mind and thought on every issue? It's impossible to find two people who think alike, much less a congregation of hundreds!

But Paul isn't saying that Christians should all think alike. We find the key to his meaning in his letter to the Philippians:

Your attitude should be the same as that of Christ Jesus:

Who, being in very nature God,
    did not consider equality with God something to be grasped,
but made himself nothing,
    taking the very nature of a servant,
    being made in human likeness.
And being found in appearance as a man,

he humbled himself
and became obedient to death—
even death on a cross! (PHILIPPIANS 2:5–8)

The King James Version renders verse 5 this way: "Let this mind be in you, which was also in Christ Jesus" (Philippians 2:5 KJV). Each and every believer in the church should have the same attitude, the same mindset, that was in Christ. The mind of Christ is an attitude of humility and obedience. Though Jesus was God, He didn't consider His godhood something to be grasped but something to be surrendered. He took the form of a servant and obediently died a criminal's death.

You and I don't have to think alike or behave alike. But God expects that we both have the humble, obedient mind of Christ. That is how we are to maintain our unity in the body of Christ.

When you and I decide to put the things of Christ first, then we will bring to our congregation the harmony Jesus prayed for, that Paul pleaded for, and that God desires. The unifying factor in any church is a relationship with Christ exemplified by an attitude of humility and obedience.

Whose church is it?

Years ago, I heard Dr. Oswald Hoffman speak at a family conference in St. Louis. Dr. Hoffman was a dynamic radio preacher and an admired conference speaker. Before Dr. Hoffman spoke, he was introduced to the audience as "the great preacher of *The Lutheran Hour*." Dr. Hoffman squirmed uncomfortably as the introduction went on. Finally, Dr. Hoffman rose and said, "I want you all to know that I'm not 'Dr. Oswald Hoffman, the great preacher of *The Lutheran Hour*.' I'm nobody, just like you!"

I never forgot that. Dr. Hoffman's response captured the very attitude Paul describes here. Who are we, that we should put our interests and reputations above the interests and reputation of our Lord?

Over the years, I've been called upon to help settle disputes at a number of different churches. I have seen one common denominator in every case: People on both sides of the dispute spoke of the church they attended as "my church." They didn't merely mean "the church I go to"; they meant "the church that belongs to me." In every church dispute, you encounter people who feel a sense of proprietorship toward the church—a sense that they have a right to call the shots. These people forget who truly owns the church. They forget who paid for the church in blood.

17

The church belongs to the Lord Jesus Christ. He is the only One with an absolute right to call the shots. When we think of the church as "my church" instead of "His church," we lose sight of what it means to have the mind of Christ. Paul continues:

> My brothers, some from Chloe's household have informed me that there are quarrels among you. What I mean is this: One of you says, "I follow Paul"; another, "I follow Apollos"; another, "I follow Cephas [that is, Peter]"; still another, "I follow Christ." (1 CORINTHIANS 1:11–12)

Paul describes four distinct cliques within the Corinthian church. The believers had not yet split into multiple congregations, but battle lines had been drawn and the factions were squared off in a cold war.

There were the pro-Paul loyalists. They said, "We are of Paul. He started this church and led us to Christ. We'll stick with his teaching."

Then there were those who were impressed by a grand oratorical style—the dynamic preaching of Apollos. The book of Acts tells us:

> Meanwhile a Jew named Apollos, a native of Alexandria, came to Ephesus. He was a learned man, with a thorough knowledge of the Scriptures. He had been instructed in the way of the Lord, and he spoke with great fervor and taught about Jesus accurately, though he knew only the baptism of John. He began to speak boldly in the synagogue. When Priscilla and Aquila heard him, they invited him to their home and explained to him the way of God more adequately. (ACTS 18:24–26)

Apollos, says Acts, "spoke with great fervor." He was a fiery Jewish orator in a Greek culture that valued oratory. He had undoubtedly preached at the Corinthian church. Some were so drawn to his preaching that they said, "I follow Apollos."

Then there were the traditionalists who said, "Well, I don't know about Paul or Apollos. Let's get back to the beginnings of the church in Jerusalem. We are of Peter." Dionysius, bishop of Corinth about a century after Paul's death, wrote that both Peter and Paul had planted the Corinthian church (though Paul was clearly the first to arrive and make converts there). So a faction of Corinthian Christians said, "Peter was one of the first apostles Jesus called. We are of Peter."

18

So there were three factions that argued over the relative merit and authority of these three teachers, Paul, Apollos, and Peter. But there was also a fourth group—and I suspect that this group was the most obnoxious of all! They said, "You people may be of Paul or Peter or Apollos, but we are of Christ! We go back to the Lord alone. We listen to Him—and no one else." So they smugly separated from the rest, adding yet another fracture to this poor divided church.

But here's the most amazing truth of all: These same four viewpoints still divide Christians and churches today.

There are those who are emotionally attached to some great Christian leader who has helped them, as Paul helped establish the Corinthians, and they will idolize that leader. They read only his books, they listen only to his tapes, and what he says is the first, last, and only word on biblical truth!

There are those who are drawn to dynamic preachers (like Apollos) who keep them emotionally engaged, who capture their attention with powerful words, delivered in a forceful style. These people are emotionally moved by oratory—and they mistake their heightened emotional state for a spiritual experience.

There are still others who follow some religious school of thought. Some say, "Back to the Reformation!" Others proudly proclaim themselves Calvinists, Arminians, dispensationalists, Anabaptists, fundamentalists, or Pentecostals. Some say they follow the teachings of C. S. Lewis, or Dietrich Bonhoeffer, or Billy Graham, or Francis Schaeffer, or Bill Bright, or D. James Kennedy, or Bill Hybels, or Rick Warren—and I can tell you this: Not one of those leaders would want to viewed as the icon of a church faction. (And I pray that the words never be uttered, "I follow Stedman!")

Is Christ divided?

The tendency to set a leader on a pedestal and become cult followers is all too common in church history—and it is a destructive tendency. Whenever a cult of personality arises in Christendom, nothing comes of it but trouble, division, and a dishonoring of Jesus Christ and His gospel. Paul answers this tendency with a strong admonition framed as a series of rhetorical questions:

> Is Christ divided? Was Paul crucified for you? Were you baptized into the name of Paul? (1 CORINTHIANS 1:13)

Paul says that cliquishness in the church serves to chop Christ up in pieces and parcel Him out. When we identify ourselves only with this piece or that portion of Jesus, we lose our perspective on the whole of Christian theology.

When you follow the teaching of only one teacher, you get only one facet of Christ. The depths of the riches of our Lord Jesus Christ are infinitely deep; why should any of us settle for only skimming the surface of those riches by confining ourselves to one teacher's viewpoint? Even the Holy Scriptures did not settle for one version of the life of Christ but provided four different viewpoints so we could see His life in four distinct dimensions.

Paul then asks, "Was Paul crucified for you?" When Christians overemphasize a human pastor, teacher, author, or leader, they are committing idolatry. They are placing a mere human being on a pedestal where Christ alone belongs. On a number of occasions, people have said to me, "Pastor Stedman, I hang on every word you say. Whenever you tell me something, I know it's true!" When I hear that, I tremble! I don't want anyone to believe me without question. I want everyone to check everything I say against the Scriptures and to believe only what the Holy Spirit instructs them to believe.

It's dangerous to blindly follow any mere human leader. Jesus alone was crucified for you—and He alone is worthy of your absolute trust.

Paul then highlights another danger of divisions within the church:

> Were you baptized into the name of Paul? I am thankful that I did not baptize any of you except Crispus and Gaius, so no one can say that you were baptized into my name. (Yes, I also baptized the household of Stephanas; beyond that, I don't remember if I baptized anyone else.) (1 CORINTHIANS 1:13b–16)

Here is another source of division in the Corinthian church that still occurs regularly in churches today: Division over the meaning of symbols. Certain people in the church will take a beautiful symbol like baptism, which is meant as an outward manifestation of faith in Christ, and turn it into an identification badge: "At *my* church, we practice the *correct* form of baptism! The way *you* baptize people is *wrong!*" My group goes to war against your group, and soon the church is torn apart. As we fight over this beautiful symbol of the Lord's death and resurrection, we disgrace the gospel and drive people away from Christ.

That's what the Corinthian Christians had done to the sacrament of baptism. They boasted over who had baptized them. Some said, "Paul baptized me!" Others said, "Apollos baptized me!" Some even said, "I was baptized by Peter—and Peter is a man who once walked on water!" Baptism, which should have been a unifying symbol in the church, was splitting the church and disgracing the gospel of Jesus Christ.

The cure for divisions

Paul then goes on to prescribe the cure for the divisions that have left the church in such a weakened and unhealthy state:

> For Christ did not send me to baptize, but to preach the gospel—not with words of human wisdom, lest the cross of Christ be emptied of its power. (1 CORINTHIANS 1:17)

Paul says, in effect, "Christ didn't send me to cut notches on my gun handle as to how many baptisms I've performed. He sent me to preach the gospel—not with human eloquence and wisdom but with the power of the cross of Jesus."

The cross of Christ heals fragmented Christians and divided churches. When believers rediscover afresh the meaning of the cross, divisions disappear. Human selfishness and pride are scorched by the light of the cross. Human ideologies and systems are swept away by the power of the cross.

We are so quick to exalt ourselves against our fellow believers in the church—and even to exalt ourselves against the wisdom of God. But the cross uncovers our nakedness and wretchedness. The very fact that we are so lost in sin that we require an instrument of torture and the death of God Himself to save us proves that our wisdom and righteousness are as filthy rags.

No human being would ever have planned the cross. If it were left up to us to plan a program of salvation, we would never have included a cross. The cross of Christ is shocking. It shatters our egos. The cross leaves no room for divisions and factions, because it leaves no room for pride. That is why Paul, in addressing the problem of division in the church, points us back to the cross.

How can we argue about our little doctrinal differences or the meaning of this or that symbol when we think of what our Lord went through to save us: His suffering in the deep shadows of the olive trees of Gethsemane; His loneliness and the abandonment by His disciples; His sweat, like drops of blood; the traitor's kiss; the binding and mocking, the spitting and hitting, the bloody scourging and the crown of thorns; the weight of the cross as He carried it on His shoulders; the exhaustion and collapse; being stripped of His clothes; the hammering of the nails; the impaling of the feet and wrist bones; the slow loss of blood; the struggle for every breath; the darkness; the moment when He was forsaken by God; the thirst; the final breath . . .

What issue is so important that we would willingly disgrace our Lord's suffering and death? Let us heal the wounds of the body of Christ, and let us truly love one another in the church, lest the cross of Christ be emptied of its power.

Let us live lives that are worthy of that cross.

2

GOD'S NONSENSE

1 Corinthians 1:18–31

The most recognizable symbol of Christianity is the cross. Churches are adorned with the cross. Ladies wear diamond-studded crosses on gold chains around their necks. The cross decorates Bibles, plaques, Christian Web sites, bumper stickers, and other items that are a daily part of our lives.

The symbol of the cross has become so familiar that we have largely forgotten what the cross meant to Christians in the first century. To them, the cross was a thing of horror. The sight of it made people shudder. It sickened the soul. Why? Because the cross was an instrument of torture, cruelty, and agonizing death.

We could better appreciate what the cross meant to first-century Christians if we imagined substituting an electric chair for the cross. Suppose you walked into church, and at the front of the church, between two beautiful stained glass windows, you saw an electric chair. Picture that contrivance of death, with its scorched electrodes and brutal leather straps. Imagine if church steeples were topped by electric chairs, and if women wore diamond-studded electric chairs around their necks on gold chains.

Now, perhaps, you are beginning to see how the Christians of the first century viewed the cross. The theme of the next section of 1 Corinthians 1 is the cross of Christ. The message of the cross was urgently needed in first-century Corinth, and it is urgently needed in American churches today.

Offensive foolishness!

Paul makes a profound statement about the message of the cross:

> For the message of the cross is foolishness to those who are perishing, but to us who are being saved it is the power of God. For it is written:

> "I will destroy the wisdom of the wise;
> the intelligence of the intelligent I will frustrate."
>
> (1 CORINTHIANS 1:18–19)

Here we see that the cross exposes the fundamental conflict of life. The world is divided into two kinds of people—those who view the cross as foolishness and those who view the cross as the power of God. The cross confronts us and forces us to make a choice: we are committed to either error or truth. If you reject the message of the cross, you choose error and death; if you accept the message of the cross, you choose truth and life. The message of the cross always provokes one of two reactions:

(1) "This message is foolishness!"
(2) "This message is the power of God!"

The message of the cross is viewed as silliness, absurdity, and sheer nonsense by those who are perishing without Christ. Thomas Paine was one of the leaders of the American Revolution. He believed in a remote and impersonal God, but he did not believe in Jesus Christ or the God of the Bible. In *The Age of Reason*, Paine wrote:

> The Christian mythologists, calling themselves the Christian Church, have erected their fable, which for absurdity and extravagance is not exceeded by anything that is to be found in the mythology of the ancients.... They represent this virtuous and amiable man, Jesus Christ, to be at once both God and man, and also the Son of God, celestially begotten, on purpose to be sacrificed, because they say that Eve in her longing had eaten an apple.

Robert G. Ingersoll was a nineteenth-century politician and agnostic. In his writings, he ridiculed the message of the cross this way:

> [God's mercy] comes in what is called "the plan of salvation." What is that plan? According to this great plan, the innocent suffer for the guilty to satisfy a law. What sort of a law must it be that would be satisfied with the suffering of innocence? ... It strikes me that what [Christians] call the atonement is a kind of moral bankruptcy.

Without question, the message of the cross is foolishness to those who are perishing! But for us who are being saved, the message of the cross is the power of God to transform us and move us from death unto life. What is the message of the cross?

24

First, it is the announcement of the crucifixion of Jesus. The cross is a fact of history. When you become a Christian, you don't merely accept a philosophy or a process of meditation. You start with the facts of history that cannot be ignored: Jesus was born as a man and lived among us, and He was crucified—nailed to a cross of wood. This event occurred at a specific place and time. I have visited the hill outside of Jerusalem where this event happened.

One crucial element of the message is this: An innocent man, Jesus of Nazareth, died a death He did not deserve for a crime He did not commit—and He did so for the sake of every person who ever lived. That is part of the message of the cross—but not all of it.

Another element of this message is: The cross judges every human life. The cross tells us that we are sinners and that we are incapable of saving ourselves. We can be saved only by the death of Another. Paul speaks of this element of the cross as "the offense of the cross." Try telling a stranger, "Jesus died in your place on the cross because you deserve death and punishment for your sins." How will that person react? He will probably be offended. "I'm a good person! I haven't done anything to deserve death!" That's the offense of the cross, the offense of the gospel.

The cross imposes judgment on us all. That's why people dislike our message. The cross condemns our "righteousness" and says that our attempts to be "good" are worthless. That is extremely offensive to those who are perishing without Christ. The problem is that the perishing don't even know they are perishing! They haven't perished yet; they are on the way to perishing. Their spiritual death is so gradual that they think everything's fine.

To those of us who are being saved, the cross is the key to deliverance from the power of sin. It's the entryway to wholeness, peace, and joy.

Paul goes on to quote from the book of Isaiah:

"The wisdom of the wise will perish,
the intelligence of the intelligent will vanish." (ISAIAH 29:14b)

This statement occurs at a time when the kingdom of Judah was being confronted with an Assyrian invasion from the north. The leaders of the kingdom, including King Hezekiah, were trying to find a way out of this crisis through human ingenuity and political maneuvering. The leaders even considered making a mutual defense treaty with Egypt in an attempt to give the Assyrians another enemy to worry about. But God spoke through the prophet Isaiah and announced that He would deliver His people without any help from the intelligent politicians of the kingdom of Judah.

As we read in Isaiah 37, that's exactly what God did. The Assyrian army came right up to the gates of Jerusalem and surrounded the city. King Hezekiah saw the hordes of Assyrians surrounding the city. Their leader, Sennacherib, sent a letter to the king ordering him to surrender. The king spread the letter before the Lord and prayed. God answered, sending an angel who killed 185,000 Assyrian soldiers in one night. God destroyed the wisdom of the wise and the intelligence of the intelligent.

Knowledge versus wisdom

Next, Paul asks a series of rhetorical questions to draw a contrast between the wisdom of this world and the wisdom of God:

> Where is the wise man? Where is the scholar? Where is the philosopher of this age? Has not God made foolish the wisdom of the world?
> (1 CORINTHIANS 1:20)

Notice that these questions are really one question, which could be stated: "What standing does human wisdom give to you?" The self-evident answer: None.

Paul is not saying that education is worthless. He was a learned man who employed sound reasoning. When Paul says that God has made foolish the wisdom of the wise, he is referring to two general approaches to knowledge and wisdom.

The first approach is the wisdom of the scribes. That's the Jewish approach to wisdom. It involved the study of the wisdom and writings of the past. The Jewish scribes studied the ancient Scriptures and applied them to everyday life.

The second approach is the wisdom of the philosophers. That's the Greek approach to wisdom. The Greek philosophers sought wisdom by debating new ideas. This is the dialectic approach—the process of arriving at truth through thesis, antithesis, and synthesis.

Paul looks at the approach of the scribes and the approach of the philosophers, and he asks, "Where does that get you?" The answer: Nowhere. "What is it worth?" Nothing. That's a harsh judgment, isn't it?

At this point, we need to distinguish between human knowledge and human wisdom. Knowledge is the discovery of truth, and God always encourages us to seek truth. He created our minds. There's nothing anti-intellectual about the Scriptures. God is pleased when we search out the deep mysteries of biology, medicine, chemistry, astronomy, and physics.

But wisdom is not the same thing as knowledge. Wisdom is the use of truth. This is where Scripture always throws down the gauntlet. The Bible tells us that there is something faulty about human wisdom; it does not know how to use truth.

Human scientists have discovered the truth of the structure of the atom and how the atom can be split to produce energy. It is wisdom that decides whether to use that energy to light our homes, power our industry, and improve our lives—or to destroy cities and immolate millions. God's wisdom is creative and productive; human wisdom is frequently destructive and tragic.

Paul asks, in effect, "What is the true nature of human wisdom?" And his answer is, "Foolishness." Human wisdom may sound impressive and seem to work in limited ways, but in the end it comes to nothing. That is why, despite the relentless expansion of human knowledge, we never seem to grow any wiser. The German philosopher Hegel put it this way: "History teaches us that history teaches us nothing."

Paul goes on to say:

> For since in the wisdom of God the world through its wisdom did not know him, God was pleased through the foolishness of what was preached to save those who believe. (1 CORINTHIANS 1:21)

Despite man's pretentious claims to have penetrated the secrets of life, he has failed to acknowledge the greatest fact of all: God Himself. The great Cause behind all that exists is God; to leave Him out of our thinking is sheer foolishness. And this foolishness is spreading like an epidemic.

That is why in our public school systems, in our halls of government, and in our courtrooms, there is a conspiracy of silence where God is concerned. No one dares to mention His name. Teachers must be careful not to allow students to hear that the universe has been intelligently designed.

Yet, even though the world in its human wisdom does not know God or acknowledge His works, God still chose to work through the "foolishness" of the cross to save those who believe. Paul goes on to say:

> Jews demand miraculous signs and Greeks look for wisdom, but we preach Christ crucified: a stumbling block to Jews and foolishness to Gentiles, but to those whom God has called, both Jews and Greeks, Christ the power of God and the wisdom of God. For the foolishness of God is wiser than man's wisdom, and the weakness of God is stronger than man's strength. (1 CORINTHIANS 1:22–25)

Some people demand miracles as proof—or they will not believe in the crucified Messiah. Others demand philosophical wisdom as proof—or they will not believe that a crucified Man can save them. People still make these same demands today.

For years, people have been fascinated with the Shroud of Turin—a piece of ancient cloth that some believe to have been the burial shroud of Jesus. Others, of course, believe this cloth to be an elaborate medieval hoax. There is something within us that wants to see miraculous proof before we'll believe.

Intellectuals insist on having every aspect of Jesus' life explained before they will believe. They demand to know how God could become a man, how a baby could be born of a virgin, or how a dead man could live again. Unless you explain it all in scientific terms, they will not believe.

Yet God does not offer miraculous proof or scientific explanations. He simply offers us the story of a crucified Messiah, and He says, "This is your only hope for deliverance." This story is a well-attested fact of history. It may be too simple for the learned and wise, but you and I can understand it—and we can share the story with others. The message of the cross is the power of God to demolish foolish human wisdom.

In the National Gallery of Art in Washington, there is a drypoint drawing by the Dutch master Rembrandt van Rijn. The drawing is called *The Three Crosses* (1653), and it movingly depicts the scene of the crucifixion. We can see the indifference of the Roman soldiers, the cruel arrogance of the religious leaders, the inconsolable grief of the women, the agony of the two crucified thieves, and at the center of it all, we see the lonely suffering of the crucified Savior.

But there is a detail at the edge of the drawing that many people miss—a figure almost hidden in the shadows. Art historians believe that this figure represents the artist Rembrandt himself. He knew that his sins nailed Jesus to the cross and that the cross of Jesus was his only hope for meaning and salvation.

God's fools, God's tools

God not only works through the "foolishness" of the gospel, but He uses "fools" like us to transform the world. God's fools are God's tools! Paul writes:

> Brothers, think of what you were when you were called. Not many
> of you were wise by human standards; not many were influential; not

many were of noble birth. But God chose the foolish things of the world to shame the wise; God chose the weak things of the world to shame the strong. He chose the lowly things of this world and the despised things—and the things that are not—to nullify the things that are. (1 CORINTHIANS 1:26–28)

Here, the apostle contrasts the foolish wisdom of the world against the marvelous wisdom of God, which the world mistakes for foolishness. The people of Corinth, being Greeks, had a high regard for debate, philosophy, and new ideas. As a result, the church in Corinth was divided into factions. Each group followed a different teacher or leader, and they quarreled, boasted, and gloried in human insight and wisdom.

Paul answered this problem by telling the Corinthians to look at themselves and notice what God had done in their lives. He wrote, "Brothers, think of what you were when you were called. Not many of you were wise by human standards; not many were influential; not many were of noble birth." He pointed out two obvious facts that the Corinthian believers had lost sight of.

First, not many of the Corinthians were wise by human standards. Oh, there were a few who were regarded as learned or prominent people. Sosthenes, mentioned earlier as an official of the synagogue, was one. Another was Crispus, who had also been a ruler of the synagogue. In the letter to the Romans, which Paul wrote from Corinth, he mentioned a man named Erastus, the city treasurer of Corinth. Also, Paul mentioned a man named Gaius, who was evidently a wealthy businessman in Corinth. But Scripture records no other people of great reputation in the Corinthian congregation. The rest were common, ordinary, working-class people or even slaves—those the world regarded as fools.

This is not to say that God never uses people of reputation and influence. He does—but He rarely uses such people until after they have learned that their usefulness to God has nothing to do with their position or abilities. It derives solely from His presence in their lives.

Jesus once said, "That which is highly esteemed among men is abomination in the sight of God" (Luke 16:15 KJV). We have fallen prey to the idea that it takes money and organization to accomplish anything for God. "If only we could get so much money," we say, "then we could begin a great ministry!" That is a complete reversal of the message of Scripture, for God's Word tells us that you do not begin with money, you begin with ministry. Anyone can be a minister of God. That's the glory of the church, because

God has put us all in ministry. If you begin where you are and do what God calls you to do, money doesn't matter.

We have drifted so far from this simple truth—yet God delights in every generation to prove this great principle that Paul declares. God chooses the weak and the obscure, and He uses them in great power to remind us that it is not status, prestige, or money that makes ministry for God effective. It is the power of God, working through weak and foolish tools like you and me.

Hidden from the wise, revealed to children

When we realize that God works through our weakness, smallness, and inadequacy, we discover what it means to live the adventure of faith. You may have read the Newbery Award-winning children's fantasy, *A Wrinkle in Time,* by Madeleine L'Engle. It's an adventure story in which a group of children, led by thirteen-year-old Meg Murry, set off on a fantastic journey through time and space to rescue their missing scientist-father. Along the way, they encounter three mysterious women—Mrs. Whatsit, Mrs. Who, and Mrs. Which, who are akin to angels. In one scene, which takes place on the perilous world called Camazotz, Mrs. Who encourages Meg by quoting (in the King James Version) the very words we have been studying:

> Because the foolishness of God is wiser than men; and the weakness of God is stronger than men. For ye see your calling, brethren, how that not many wise men after the flesh, not many mighty, not many noble, are called: But God hath chosen the foolish things of the world to confound the wise; and God hath chosen the weak things of the world to confound the things which are mighty; And base things of the world, and things which are despised, hath God chosen, yea, and things which are not, to bring to nought things that are. (1 CORIN-THIANS 1:25–28 KJV)

After quoting these words, Mrs. Who adds, "May the right prevail!" And she sends Meg and the other children off to face the terrifying enemy known only as IT. There is a great truth embedded in this fantasy tale: God chooses to use weak and foolish and even childlike people in the war against Satan and his armies.

Remember how Jesus once put it: "I praise you, Father, Lord of heaven and earth, because you have hidden these things from the wise and learned, and revealed them to little children" (Matthew 11:25). You and I don't claim to be wise or learned. We are just children, simple and foolish and weak—yet as His children, we are His chosen tools for taking the battle to the very gates of hell. God opens the mouths of children and uses their simple words to confound the counsels of the wise and the mighty.

One of the greatest awakenings of the nineteenth century began at Cambridge University in England when the preacher Dwight L. Moody and the singer Ira B. Sankey came to share the gospel of Jesus Christ. In 1950, when I was traveling with Dr. H. A. Ironside, I met an Episcopal rector in Virginia who was present at Cambridge when Moody preached there. This man remembered that the entire university was in an uproar because this backwoods preacher from America would dare to preach at Cambridge, the cultural center of the English world.

A chief complaint was that Moody murdered the King's English. (Someone once said that Moody was probably the only man on earth who could pronounce "Jerusalem" in one syllable!) The rector told me that he and his classmates were determined to jeer Moody off the Cambridge chapel stage.

The day of the service came, and Moody opened by asking Ira Sankey to sing. After Sankey's song had quieted the audience, Moody stepped up, looked the students in the eye, and said, "Young gentlemen, don't ever think that God don't love you, for He do!"

The rector recalled, "We were so dumbfounded by those words that we didn't know how to respond—and we forgot to jeer him!"

Moody went on with his sermon. Every few minutes, he repeated his opening statement: "Don't ever think that God don't love you, for He do!" It was an atrociously ungrammatical sentence—but something about those words captured these young men. Moody's earnestness spoke to their hearts.

The rector told me, "That very day, I sought out Mr. Moody for a private interview, and he sat down with me, prayed with me, and led me to Christ. My life has never been the same." A great awakening came to Cambridge University because a humble servant of God dared to step onto the grounds of that place of higher learning and be a fool for Christ.

God created the human mind, and He encourages us to use it to seek knowledge. But our knowledge must be subject to His wisdom, as contained in the Scriptures.

Why does God seem opposed to the wisdom of the world? Is He jealous of human beings? Paul says that God deliberately seeks to shame the wise and the strong and to bring to nothing the things that are great. It almost seems as if God is vindictive toward humanity—but is He? Look at the next verse:

So that no one may boast before him. (1 CORINTHIANS 1:29)

Why does God oppose human boasting? The Creator of the universe surely finds nothing to envy in weak, frail human beings. No, the answer is that human boasting is always based on an illusion. God is a realist, and He is determined to eradicate untruth. Those who arrogantly boast about themselves think that they have no need of God, and God knows that such boastfulness is a lie.

So the kindest thing God can do is to puncture sinful human pride and shatter the illusion of human self-sufficiency. He does that by using the obscure, weak, and foolish things to confound the strong and the wise.

Boasting in the Lord

Next, Paul contrasts human foolishness with true wisdom. What is the secret of wisdom? It's the recognition that even if you are a fool or a failure in the eyes of the world, through Jesus you can achieve true success. The purpose of Scripture is to teach us to walk a different way, to live by a different power, and to look at reality from a different perspective. God calls us to do everything—even the simplest tasks—in the power of Christ. Paul writes:

It is because of him that you are in Christ Jesus, who has become for us wisdom from God—that is, our righteousness, holiness and redemption. Therefore, as it is written: "Let him who boasts boast in the Lord." (1 CORINTHIANS 1:30–31)

Jesus has become the wisdom of God for us—and contained in that one word *wisdom* are three concepts: righteousness, holiness, and redemption. Remember, there is a difference between knowledge and wisdom. Knowledge is the discovery of truth; wisdom is the right use of truth. It takes three elements to be wise.

First, we must understand the true nature of reality. We must be able to distinguish truth from error.

Second, we must be able to accurately evaluate the value of things. We must know the difference between what is trivial and what is important.

In marriage and in many other arenas of life, we tend to get embroiled in conflicts over trivial matters: a perceived insult in a tone of voice or an argument about taking out the garbage. We can get into irrational arguments over the silliest matters. Wisdom is the ability to focus on what's important and let go of what's trivial.

Third, we must be able to blend and balance the two essential ingredients of life: truth and love. We must speak the truth in love. We must love one another in truth.

We see that wonderful harmonious balance in the life of Jesus. He was always candid, frank, honest, and truthful—yet He was also loving, patient, gracious, and forgiving. He never spoke the truth without love, and He never showed love without speaking the truth. That is why Jesus is our model of perfect wisdom; He kept these two ingredients in perfect balance.

Jesus came to teach us how to live wisely—that is, how to exemplify God's righteousness, holiness, and redemption through our lives. So the mark of someone who is growing in Christ is that he or she is exhibiting more and more of this godly kind of wisdom.

We see the evidence of this wisdom in a lifestyle of righteousness, because Jesus Christ is our righteousness. We see the evidence of this wisdom in a lifestyle of holiness—the holiness of Christ that shines in our lives. We become more loving, truthful, patient, understanding, insightful, bold, and courageous—just as Jesus typified all of these qualities. Finally, we more completely exemplify redemption. To be redeemed is to be purchased and restored to usefulness.

A human life is much like a piece of valuable property that has been hocked at the pawnshop. While it is in the pawnshop, a diamond ring is useless. It sits in a display case gathering dust. But if the owner pays the price to redeem that ring and takes it out of the pawnshop, then we say that the ring has been redeemed. Human beings are like precious jewels consigned to a case in a pawnshop—useless. But Jesus has paid the price of our redemption. He has restored us to usefulness. Now it's up to us to live in a manner consistent with our redeemed state.

God does not expect us to be perfect. We are in a process of becoming more and more like Christ. We haven't gone all the way to Christlikeness yet, but we are on the way to Christlikeness. The world uses people up then throws them away. God, in His love and wisdom, keeps restoring and refashioning us for His use. When we fail, He gives us another chance. He never throws us away.

That's why Paul concludes 1 Corinthians 1 with the words, "Let him who boasts boast in the Lord." It is the Lord who saves us, redeems us, and transforms us. We cannot do it ourselves. We are God's fools, God's tools, God's instruments to demolish the false wisdom of this world and demonstrate the true wisdom of His grace. With the apostle Paul, we bow in wonder at the wisdom of our amazing God.

3

GOD'S HIDDEN WISDOM

1 Corinthians 2

A family gathered by the fireside for evening devotions. The father opened the Bible to Genesis 22 and read the story of Abraham leading his son Isaac up the mountain so that he could sacrifice the boy upon the altar. As the father read, his daughter interrupted. "Daddy!" she said. "I don't like that story! I don't believe it! No father would sacrifice his son that way!"

The father looked at his daughter and replied, "God did."

We recoil from the thought of what Abraham was about to do when he placed Isaac upon the altar and raised the knife—yet God carried out that same kind of sacrifice in sending His Son to die on the cross for your sins and mine. That is the message Paul now proclaims in the opening lines of 1 Corinthians 2:

> When I came to you, brothers, I did not come with eloquence or
> superior wisdom as I proclaimed to you the testimony about God. For
> I resolved to know nothing while I was with you except Jesus Christ
> and him crucified. (1 CORINTHIANS 2:1–2)

When the apostle Paul first went to Corinth to evangelize the city and plant the Corinthian church, he made a deliberate decision not to speak out of human wisdom. He would not use flowery phrases and high-sounding words. He would not try to impress people with his brilliant oratory. Instead, he began on a dark and gloomy note: the crucifixion of Christ.

Isn't that amazing? According to the wisdom of the world, we should use positive, uplifting words and surround those words with attractive images and beautiful background music. We should eliminate anything negative from our message, such as torture, death, blood, or suffering.

Yet when Paul came to Corinth, he came to preach the crucified Christ. Why? Because the cross of Christ pronounces judgment on the wisdom of man. What do the elite, sophisticated, learned, powerful people of this world do with Jesus of Nazareth? They crucify Him, reject Him, deny Him, mock Him, and put Him to death. That's what they did in the first century, and they still do so today.

They don't reject Jesus because they think He was wrong. They don't reject Him because they think He was crazy. They reject Him because they're afraid He's right. The elite, sophisticated, learned people of this world feel threatened by the carpenter from Nazareth because He speaks the truth about their lives. A truth teller is always a dangerous person, and people always try to silence a truth teller.

Dorothy Sayers, an insightful Christian essayist and novelist who was a friend to J. R. R. Tolkien and C. S. Lewis, said this about Jesus:

> The people who hanged Christ never, to do them justice, accused Him of being a bore—on the contrary; they thought Him too dynamic to be safe. It has been left for later generations to muffle up that shattering personality and surround Him with an atmosphere of tedium. We have very efficiently pared the claws of the Lion of Judah, certified Him "meek and mild" and recommended Him as a fitting household pet for pale curates and pious old ladies.

It's tragic but true: The church has portrayed Jesus as a meek and somewhat effeminate milquetoast. The real Jesus was a man who walked the dusty roads of the Holy Land and proclaimed the kingdom of heaven, confronted the respected and feared religious leaders as "hypocrites," and challenged the Roman governor to his face. With his own strong hands, he fashioned a whip and drove the merchants out of the temple. He commanded demons, and they obeyed. He asked tough, searching questions of his friends, and he tied his opponents in knots with his unassailable logic.

Jesus was a dangerous man. He disturbed the status quo. He exposed the evil secrets that men try to hide. He shone the light of truth on liars and frauds. So his enemies had to crucify Him.

When Paul came to Corinth, he preached this dangerous, crucified Man named Jesus. Paul didn't start with positive thinking or eloquent words. He started with Christ and the cross.

The crisis of our humanity

The message of the cross is a judgmental message. It makes a statement about everyone who hears it. The message of the cross says, "You're a sinner. You need a Savior. You cannot save yourself, so Jesus had to die in order for you to be saved." Paul writes in his letter to the Romans:

As it is written:

"There is no one righteous, not even one;
  there is no one who understands,
  no one who seeks God.
All have turned away,
  they have together become worthless;
  there is no one who does good,
  not even one." (ROMANS 3:10–12)

That is the crisis of our humanity—and there is only one solution to this crisis: We must by faith lay hold of what God has done on our behalf when He sacrificed His Son Jesus on the cross.

That's where Paul started. But Paul did not stop there. Though he begins with the message of the cross, Paul goes on to speak of all the various facets of the Christian faith and the Christian life. He writes:

I came to you in weakness and fear, and with much trembling. My message and my preaching were not with wise and persuasive words, but with a demonstration of the Spirit's power, so that your faith might not rest on men's wisdom, but on God's power. (1 CORINTHIANS 2:3–5)

To me, this is one of the most encouraging passages in Scripture. It isn't easy to go out into the non-Christian world and talk about the things of God to the worldlings, the people who are perishing. But it's liberating to realize that we don't have to take the message of the cross to the world in our own wisdom. All we need is the power of the Holy Spirit.

We may stumble and lose our train of thought, but that doesn't matter, because it is the Spirit who communicates the message and persuades the heart of our listeners. God doesn't want your eloquence; He only desires your obedience.

Paul tries a different evangelistic approach

The book of Acts tells us how Paul first came to Corinth. Acts 16 and 17 tell of how he was driven out of city after city where he had come to preach—Thessalonica, Philippi, Berea, and Athens. Wherever Paul preached, riots broke out or he was arrested. He was mocked, ridiculed, and physically assaulted. His message was rejected.

Finally, in Acts 18, Paul arrived in Corinth. He was alone in this great, corrupt city of wealth and commerce—and there he began to witness for Christ. He didn't come with eloquence. After weeks of rejection and persecution, he had no confidence that anyone would listen. Despite his fear and weakness, he preached in Corinth about Christ crucified.

Acts tells us that after Paul had been in Corinth for a few months, the Lord Jesus appeared to him in a vision and strengthened him. "Do not be afraid; keep on speaking, do not be silent," the Lord told him. "For I am with you, and no one is going to attack and harm you, because I have many people in this city" (Acts 18:9–10).

And the message took hold in Corinth. Why? Because Paul spoke in the power of the Holy Spirit.

How did Paul evangelize the people of Corinth? The Scriptures don't describe exactly how he went about it. Perhaps he held some large outdoor evangelistic rallies—but I doubt it. He had gone to the synagogues, marketplaces, and public squares in those other cities, and the result was always a riot or an arrest. I suspect he tried a different approach in Corinth.

We know that Paul spent a year and a half to two years in Corinth—a very long time, compared with his stays in other cities. Perhaps he was trying a different evangelistic approach among the Corinthians. I suspect that he was building relationships, getting to know the shopkeepers, peddlers, craftspeople, artisans, and working people in the city. He was getting to know them and their families, their needs and hurts, their joys and sorrows—and he showed them how the key to victory in life was a relationship with the living Lord Jesus Christ.

Thousands of people have come to Christ through the mass-evangelism efforts of preachers like Billy Graham, Franklin Graham, Luis Palau, and T. D. Jakes. But these evangelists will tell you that their efforts are effective only when grass-roots believers have laid an evangelistic foundation through individual caring and witnessing with friends and neighbors. The most effective evangelism takes place in relationships, where ordinary people share what God has done in their lives.

I first came to Palo Alto in 1950 to serve as pastor of the two-year-old body of believers which then called itself Peninsula Bible Fellowship (later renamed Peninsula Bible Church). In those early days, we held home Bible studies. Christians would make their homes available as a relaxed setting for reaching out to unchurched neighbors and friends. God blessed that witness.

One group started with a handful of people and quickly grew to almost three hundred! Numerous other groups grew to forty or fifty people. Because the atmosphere was so open and free, people would get into wide-ranging discussions of faith, life, and the Bible—and those discussions would sometimes last well past midnight.

That was a wonderful time in my ministry—but there was one problem that we had to deal with all too often. What was that problem? Christians! The Christians in those groups would invite non-Christians to come and participate—and sometimes the non-Christians would speak up and share their thoughts about the Bible, and the Christians would say, "No! Wrong answer! That's heresy! That's falsehood!"

We had to take some of these Christians aside and tell them, "We want people to feel free to speak up. We want them to wrestle with God's Word at their own level. We don't want them to feel embarrassed or ashamed. Let's find ways to graciously affirm them for thinking and struggling to apply God's Word, then let's gently steer the conversation toward an understanding of the truth. Allow for different viewpoints—and whatever you do, don't brand anyone as a heretic or send them out feeling shamed or angry because of something that was said."

As Christians in these groups learned to witness about their faith in a gracious way, humbly sharing their own experience of life in Christ while patiently listening to what others had to say, hundreds came to Christ. I believe that is much like the approach Paul used to spread the gospel and build the church in Corinth.

In *Body Life*, I point out that we at Peninsula Bible Church have never held an evangelistic meeting in our church building. Over the years, many people have said that they were startled and even appalled by that statement in the book. "How can you witness to the community without an evangelistic service?" they ask.

I say, "We see hundreds of people coming to Christ and joining the church every year, because we don't have one evangelist who holds a big meeting at the church. We have hundreds of evangelists—our entire congregation—and they are witnessing and leading people to Christ every day in their neighborhoods, offices, gyms, and wherever they happen to be."

Some people respond by saying, "It won't work."

All I know is that it has been working for many years. And that approach worked in Corinth. Paul did not go to Corinth with eloquent preaching. He went with the Holy Spirit at his side, giving him the words to say when he was talking to the vegetable seller, the scholar, the cloth merchant, the beggar, the soldier, the fishmonger. As a result, lives were transformed—and a church was founded.

Does that encourage you? It certainly encourages me! You may sit down with somebody over a cup or coffee and hardly know how to say it. But as you stammer out some word about what Jesus Christ has meant to you, your earnestness will show on your face. The compassion in your heart will come through. The Holy Spirit will bless those halting words so that they will have more power and impact than the loftiest speech ever spoken.

The simple truth

I would hasten to add that while Paul preached the cross of Christ, he did not come at people with heavy-handed, threatening, condemning language. He was not a fire-and-brimstone preacher. He described his own approach this way:

> We do not use deception, nor do we distort the word of God. On the contrary, by setting forth the truth plainly we commend ourselves to every man's conscience in the sight of God. (2 CORINTHIANS 4:2b)

Paul didn't need to buttonhole anyone and say, "You're a sinner! You're going to hell!" He knew that such an approach wouldn't do anything but anger people or scare them away. His approach was something like this: "Look, you only have to look at your own lives. How do you feel? Are you happy? Do you feel guilty and unfulfilled? Well, God has made it possible for you to have a new life in Him—a life filled with joy, peace, forgiveness, healing, and wholeness." People responded to that message by the hundreds.

Paul knew that no church could flourish in Corinth that did not recognize the weakness of human wisdom versus the infinite power of God. So, in the next few verses, Paul goes on to describe God's immense wisdom and power:

> We do, however, speak a message of wisdom among the mature, but not the wisdom of this age or of the rulers of this age, who are coming to nothing. No, we speak of God's secret wisdom, a wisdom that has been hidden and that God destined for our glory before time began. None of the rulers of this age understood it, for if they had, they would not have crucified the Lord of glory. However, as it is written:

> "No eye has seen,
> no ear has heard,
> no mind has conceived
> what God has prepared for those who love him"—

but God has revealed it to us by his Spirit. The Spirit searches all things, even the deep things of God. (1 CORINTHIANS 2:6–10)

Here, Paul makes several references to the hidden mysteries of God. He writes of "God's secret wisdom" (verse 7), "the deep things of God" (verse 10), "the thoughts of God" (verse 11), "what God has freely given us" (verse 12), and "spiritual truths" (verse 13). Finally, at the end of the chapter, he says it is "the mind of Christ" (verse 16).

What is Paul talking about? Understand, Paul is not saying that the deep things of God are "religious ideas" that only "religious people" would be interested in. The secret wisdom of God is the truth every human being needs in order to live a fulfilled life. This is the secret to true joy that everyone is searching for—though most people search in the wrong places. We don't have to hard-sell this truth; it sells itself.

The deep things of God are all about how to find meaning in life, how to live an effective and satisfying life, how to be set free from guilt and shame, how to overcome bitterness and resentment, how to find love, acceptance, belonging, and forgiveness. When people realize that this secret is to be found within the walls of your church, they will break down the doors to get in.

These are the fundamental realities of God, human life, and the universe. These are the lost secrets of our humanity, the permanent truths that will never pass away. As Paul says, our message is "a message of wisdom among the mature, but not the wisdom of this age or of the rulers of this age, who are coming to nothing." The rulers of this age are doomed to pass away; God's hidden wisdom endures forever. The apostle John put it this way:

The world and its desires pass away, but the man who does the will of God lives forever. (1 JOHN 2:17)

The wisdom of God, Paul tells us, is intended "for our glory before time began." God's wisdom was intended to fulfill all of our latent possibilities and potentials. It was given so that you might be able to discover the "real you," the "you" that God created you to be. If we want to reach our full potential as children of the living God, we need to seek out His wisdom for our lives.

God's wisdom can't be discovered by natural processes. The rulers of this age know nothing about it. Who are these rulers Paul speaks of? They are not just the government leaders of our age. They are also the secular opinion leaders, the mind benders, the thought shapers, the philosophers, scholars, educators, sociologists, media personalities, radio and TV commentators, entertainers, and others who constantly tell us how to think, what to think, and when to think it. These people do not know the secret wisdom of God. Their wisdom is worldly and false.

You cannot learn the hidden wisdom of God in school, for the schools have banned God from the campus. You will not learn it by watching TV news or reading the newspapers; media content is controlled and filtered by people who are perishing. You will not learn it by studying the history of the past, which is nothing more than yesterday's news. You will not gain God's wisdom by sitting in a lotus position and contemplating the lint in your navel.

The hidden wisdom of God is revealed only by His Spirit and by understanding His Word. The Holy Spirit is the greatest resource ever given to humankind, and the Word of God is the greatest body of knowledge ever set before humankind. The deep things of God aren't found in the world system, this vast latter-day tower of Babel that humanity has erected. The deep things of God can only be revealed by God Himself.

Without an understanding of the hidden wisdom of God, men and women stumble in moral darkness, homes break up, children are abused or neglected, violence breaks out in society, and all of the evils that surround us flood into our lives. But thank God, He has not left us to wander in darkness. He has not left us to struggle in futility against the emptiness of our lives. No eye has seen, nor ear heard, nor mind conceived what God has prepared for those who love Him—but God has revealed all of these things to us in His Word and by His Spirit.

The Teacher sent by God

Paul shows us that the Spirit of God is, in fact, a mighty Teacher who comes from God to lead us into God's truth. Paul writes:

> For who among men knows the thoughts of a man except the man's spirit within him? In the same way no one knows the thoughts of God except the Spirit of God. (1 CORINTHIANS 2:11)

Notice how the apostle underscores the Spirit's knowledge: "For who among men knows the thoughts of a man except the man's spirit within him? In the same way no one knows the thoughts of God except the Spirit of God." You can sit next to a person and not know his thoughts or feelings. The only one who knows is the spirit within that person.

In the same way, we know that the universe was created by God, a Being of infinite wisdom and power. But how can we know what God is thinking? Paul's answer: We can't—unless the Spirit of God discloses the thoughts of God to us. You cannot learn the innermost thoughts and secrets of God by searching for them. God Himself must disclose them to us by means of His Spirit. The Spirit is our Teacher.

You might say, "Well, I know what God is like and what He is thinking because God is like Jesus." That's true—but the work of the Spirit is to reveal to us what Jesus is like. As Jesus Himself said, "He [the Holy Spirit] will bring glory to me by taking from what is mine and making it known to you" (John 16:14). You can read the four Gospels and find there the historical record of Jesus of Nazareth—but you cannot experience the Lord as a living person in your heart and mind simply by reading the Gospels. The Spirit must illuminate those pages and make the person of Christ vivid and real to you. That's the work of the Spirit that Paul speaks of. He continues:

> We have not received the spirit of the world but the Spirit who is from God, that we may understand what God has freely given us. This is what we speak, not in words taught us by human wisdom but in words taught by the Spirit, expressing spiritual truths in spiritual words. (1 CORINTHIANS 2:12–13)

Here we find the reason non-Christians often find the Bible dull and irrelevant, while Christians find the Bible to be powerful and exciting. Christians have the Holy Spirit living within them, teaching them, bringing the truths of God's Word to life. Non-Christians do not have this advantage, so they find God's Word puzzling and even boring. The Spirit is the exciting difference; He illuminates us so that we can receive the wisdom and power of God's Word.

There's an unusual phrase at the end of verse 13 that has confounded translators for centuries. The New International Version renders this phrase "expressing spiritual truths in spiritual words." Several other versions have translated this phrase in much the same sense: "combining spiritual thoughts with spiritual words" (New American Standard Bible); "adapting spiritual words to spiritual truths" (Weymouth); "combining spiritual things with spiritual words" (American Standard Version); "comparing spiritual things with spiritual" (King James Version). In these translations, Paul seems to be talking about spiritual meaning.

But other versions give this phrase a very different sense: "interpreting spiritual truths to those who possess the Spirit" (Revised Standard Version); "because we are interpreting spiritual truths to those who have the Spirit" (New English Bible); "as we explain spiritual truths to those who have the Spirit" (Today's English Version). In these translations, Paul seems to be talking about people who have the Holy Spirit.

The problem here is a Greek word, *pneumatikoi*, which comes from the Greek word for "spirit," *pneuma*. The most literal translation of *pneumatikoi* would be "spiritual ones." It is not clear whether the term "spiritual ones" refers to "spiritual people" or "spiritual things." I am personally inclined to believe that Paul is speaking here of Christians as *pneumatikoi*, spiritual people, those who are indwelt by the Spirit.

You may be aware that there is disagreement in some parts of the church over what it means to be indwelt by the Holy Spirit. Some people teach that you receive the Holy Spirit only as a result of demonstrating a "sign gift," such as speaking in tongues, but I do not see that this view is supported by a sound understanding of Scripture. In the book of Romans, Paul says that if anyone does not have the Spirit of Christ, that person does not belong to Christ (see Romans 8:9). Such a person is not a Christian. But those who are led by the Spirit of God are the children of God (see Romans 8:14). All genuine Christians have the Spirit living in them and the power of the Spirit available to them.

A young woman once said to me, "The evidence of receiving the Spirit is speaking in tongues." I said, "Do you mean that everybody who has not spoken in tongues does not have the Spirit?" She looked surprised, as if she had never thought of it that way. "Well, no," she said, "I didn't mean that." "But you said that the evidence for receiving the Spirit is speaking in tongues," I replied. "Well," she said, "maybe there's something else there that I don't understand." I assured her that there was.

According to the Scriptures, you receive the Holy Spirit when you believe in Jesus. That is what Jesus said. On the day of the feast of Tabernacles in John 7, He said, "If anyone is thirsty, let him come to me and drink. Whoever believes in me, as the Scripture has said, streams of living water will flow from within him" (John 7:37–38). The Gospel writer, John, added this commentary: "By this he meant the Spirit, whom those who believed in him were later to receive. Up to that time the Spirit had not been given, since Jesus had not yet been glorified" (John 7:39). The Scriptures teach that the moment you believe in Jesus, you receive the Spirit.

The truth of Scripture is a treasure that is hidden from the great, the arrogant, and the wise. By the indwelling of the Spirit, that truth is revealed to "children"—to simple believers like you and me.

The natural man

In the last three verses of 1 Corinthians 2, Paul concludes his discussion on the wisdom of this dying world versus that secret and hidden wisdom of God:

> The man without the Spirit does not accept the things that come from the Spirit of God, for they are foolishness to him, and he cannot understand them, because they are spiritually discerned. (1 CORINTHIANS 1:14)

Paul uses a descriptive word in verse 14, which the New International Version translates as "the man without the Spirit." The Greek word Paul uses is *psychikos*, which derives from the root word *psyche*, which means "the soul." The Scriptures make a clear distinction between the life of the soul (our natural humanity) and the life of the spirit (our new spiritual humanity in Christ). God created us as threefold beings: body, soul, and spirit—and the spirit is the highest center of our humanity. Paul says that the natural man, the *psychikos*, lives on the basis of the soul and not the spirit. He cannot receive the wisdom that the Spirit brings.

The natural man, Paul says, "does not accept the things that come from the Spirit of God, for they are foolishness to him." The whole realm of the secret and hidden wisdom of God is not merely a mystery to him—he doesn't even know it exists! He isn't aware of anything but the realm of the senses, the emotions, and human reason. He is ignorant of the truth about God and reality that comes only from the Spirit of God.

This is why the natural man misunderstands the power and purpose of such God-given gifts as wealth and prosperity, human sexuality, love and marriage, children, and life itself. This is why greed, poverty, ignorance, selfishness, crime, the physical and sexual abuse of children, pornography, sexually transmitted disease, abortion, and other social ills are rampant in our society. The natural man does not understand any of these things; he doesn't understand himself, nor does he understand the things of God.

To the natural mind, for example, euthanasia makes good sense. When people become so old that they don't function as well as they once did, it seems sensible to the natural mind to put them out of their misery. The Bible tells us that euthanasia is murder. But the natural mind thinks it makes good sense to kill those who (in our opinion) no longer exhibit "quality of life." The idea of euthanasia does not begin to horrify the natural mind until it is practiced on a scale like that of Nazi Germany, where unwanted people were murdered by the millions and incinerated or buried in mass graves.

The reason many people do not value human life as sacred is that the sanctity of life is a spiritually discerned truth. The natural mind cannot grasp this truth because the natural man or woman does not have the indwelling of the Spirit of God, the mighty Teacher. Those who do not have faith in Jesus Christ do not have the Spirit in them, so their minds are darkened.

Without the indwelling Spirit, a human being lacks the basis for understanding and accepting many of the things that Christians say. The Christian faith makes no sense to them. The Bible makes no sense to them. That's why it is often fruitless to argue with worldlings beyond a certain point. They cannot understand what you are saying.

The mind of Christ

Next, in contrast to the natural man, Paul describes what the spiritual man—the human being indwelt by the Holy Spirit—is like:

> The spiritual man makes judgments about all things, but he himself is not subject to any man's judgment:
>
> > "For who has known the mind of the Lord
> > that he may instruct him?"
>
> But we have the mind of Christ. (1 CORINTHIANS 2:15–16)

Paul says that the spiritual man "makes judgments about all things, but he himself is not subject to any man's judgment." That is a remarkable statement! When Paul says "all things," he means *all* things. He means that spiritual Christians—those who understand the revelation of God in the Scriptures by means of the Spirit—are capable of pronouncing a moral or ethical judgment in any area of life.

Does that mean that we, as Christians, know everything? Of course not! There are many fields of knowledge in which I, as a Christian with the Holy Spirit living in me, am ignorant. I wouldn't know how to start a computer, much less operate one. I could certainly never tell a physicist or rocket scientist how to do his job.

Paul is saying that there are ethical and moral dimension to every arena in life. Everything can be used rightly or wrongly, and it is the task of the Christian to point out to himself and to the world around what is the right and the wrong way to live in these arenas of living. The Christian, then, is the judge of all things in that realm.

It's important to understand that you don't automatically have the right to go around pronouncing judgment on people because you are a Christian! There are many Christians who are not fit to judge ethics or morality because they do not obey the Spirit. They do not study their Bibles, and they do not grasp the secret and hidden wisdom of God. So their judgment is not sound and it is not Spirit-led.

There are also Christians who think they are fit to judge others based on quoting a verse or two of Scripture (frequently out of context) to prove that their judgment is right. This practice is called proof texting—taking a text of Scripture and using it as proof that you are right and another person is wrong. This is a terrible practice, and it gives rise to the widespread notion that you can prove anything you want to with Scripture. Proof texting is an abuse of Scripture.

The spiritual man has thoroughly studied the thoughts of God as they are revealed in the Old and the New Testaments and has been taught by the Spirit through prayer. He seeks to thoroughly understand the issues before him, and only then does he make a pronouncement that could be called a judgment from the Lord.

It is our ability to judge all things in an ethical dimension that makes it possible for Christians to go against the grain of society and speak God's grace and truth. The world says that every woman has a right to an abortion; we who have studied the mind of the Lord say that abortion is a sin and a crime against life; at the same time, we say that God loves the woman who faces a crisis pregnancy, and we reach out to her with the love of Christ. The world says that homosexuality is merely an alternate lifestyle; we who have studied the mind of the Lord say that homosexual activity is sin; at the same time, we say that God loves homosexual people, and we reach out to them in the love of Christ.

The second thing Paul says about the spiritual man is that he is not subject to judgment. This means that there are times when the spiritual man or woman must take action against human law and human judgment. This raises the question of civil disobedience. Christians have been at the forefront in opposing slave ownership and the slave trade. It was

Christians who led the civil rights marches against racial segregation. The Confessing Church in Germany took a bold stand against Nazism in the 1930s and 1940s.

Government is ordained by God to maintain an orderly and peaceful society. But when the laws of the land become oppressive and unjust, spiritual Christians take a bold and often costly stand. The Spirit does not lead us to protest in a destructive way, but He calls us to a gentle but firm insistence that the government listen to the conscience of Christians and be guided by the moral precepts of God's Word.

That is the spirit we see in Martin Luther when he stood before the religious authorities of Europe and the emperor of the Holy Roman Empire in April 1521. The church authorities had the power to imprison, excommunicate, or even execute Luther—and they demanded that he recant his teaching that salvation is by grace through faith in Jesus Christ alone. Luther replied, "Unless I am convicted by Scripture and plain reason—I do not accept the authority of popes and councils, for they have contradicted each other—my conscience is captive to the Word of God. I cannot and will not recant anything, for to go against conscience is neither right nor safe. Here I stand. I can do no other. God help me. Amen."

Paul supports this kind of bold action, rooted in a searching and conscientious study of the thoughts of the Lord. Wisdom from this source is beyond challenge, for the mind of the Lord is reality itself. God alone sees life as it truly is. When we have studied the mind of God, we open our eyes, our souls, and our spirits to a clear and accurate vision of reality. We make accurate judgments and are beyond the reach of human judgment.

This doesn't mean that Christians will always be on the same side of every social, political, or moral issue. For example, during the Vietnam war, there were Christians who opposed the war and called for peace, while other Christians supported the government's effort to defeat communism in Southeast Asia. Christians on both sides of that war had similar core values, rooted in the mind of Christ. Both sides wanted to see justice, liberation, and peace for the Vietnamese people, because that is what God wants for all people. But these believers disagreed on the means to achieve those goals. Some wanted the American military to leave Southeast Asia immediately while others wanted the American military to win the war in Southeast Asia.

In the end, America pulled out, South Vietnam fell to the communists, and the people have lived without war ever since—yet they live under an oppressive and godless government. To this day, Christians argue over what should have been the right and moral course of action in Vietnam—but all Christians who know the mind of the Lord will tell you that God wants people to be treated justly and to experience freedom and peace.

Paul concludes 1 Corinthians 2 with these words: "But we have the mind of Christ." We have the very way of thinking about life that Jesus had. We have that keen ability to observe what was going on around Him, to evaluate the changing standards of men, and to come right to the heart of a matter. That is the mind of Christ—the ability to know what was in man and to prescribe the solution. Jesus needed no one to tell Him because He understood human beings, their sins and their problems. That is the mind of Christ.

I submit to you there has never been a more radical proposal to change the world than this brief statement: "But we have the mind of Christ." If we would live our lives according to the mind of Christ, we would radically affect the world. We would change human history.

Let's face it: There are few Christians who manifest the mind of Christ on a consistent basis. That is one of the tragedies of the church. But we are all learning how to live according to the mind of Christ. We are learning to fashion our lives according to the revelation of the hidden wisdom of God. As we unleash godly thinking and godly judgment in our lives, we will have a history-making impact on the world.

4

HOW TO DESTROY A CHURCH

1 Corinthians 3

I'm told that when a herd of wild horses is attacked by wolves, they form a circle with each horse facing inward—then they kick with their hind legs, attacking the enemy. But when a herd of wild donkeys is attacked, those donkeys behave in the opposite fashion. They form a circle looking outward, their faces toward the attackers—and then they kick each other!

The response of those donkeys, I'm afraid, is all too often the response Christians show when the church is attacked by Satan. They attack and wound each other. No wonder Satan often seems to win!

Few things are more damaging to the witness and effectiveness of a church than strife and division. Over the years, I've been amazed at some of the trivial issues that have destroyed churches. I've seen division over the style of music, over whether a sanctuary should be furnished with wooden pews or folding chairs, and even over the color of the carpet in the fellowship hall.

A story is told of one long, loud, contentious church meeting that went on for hours because the people in the church couldn't agree on whether or not to buy a chandelier. Finally, one of the church elders stood up and said, "I'm opposed to buying a chandelier for two reasons: First, we don't have enough money in the budget for a chandelier. Second, no one in this church knows how to play one!"

The church at Corinth was split by factions and divisions because the people in that church loved human wisdom. They were proud of their ability to debate, proud of their point of view, and proud of their favorite teacher or leader. So Paul contrasted their human wisdom with the hidden wisdom of God, which is revealed to us by the Spirit. You cannot mix God's wisdom and human wisdom; they are mutually exclusive.

The natural man can only engage in natural thinking. It is worldly and confused in its judgment. The spiritual man has the mind of Christ. His thinking is comprehensive, authoritative, and reality-based. The spiritual man makes judgments about all things, but he himself is not subject to anyone's judgment.

Are you not worldly?

What is the problem with the church in Corinth? The apostle Paul says that the Corinthian Christians should be governed by spiritual thinking. Instead, they are governed by the natural philosophy of the world around them. They should be impacting the world for Christ; instead, the church is infected with worldly thinking. Paul writes:

> Brothers, I could not address you as spiritual but as worldly—mere infants in Christ. I gave you milk, not solid food, for you were not yet ready for it. Indeed, you are still not ready. You are still worldly. For since there is jealousy and quarreling among you, are you not worldly? Are you not acting like mere men? For when one says, "I follow Paul," and another, "I follow Apollos," are you not mere men? (1 CORIN-THIANS 3:1–4)

Notice that three times Paul uses the word *worldly* in referring to the Corinthian Christians. That word represents the problem at Corinth. Paul is saying, "I couldn't speak to you as spiritual people because you are worldly. Even though you have come to Christ and received salvation through faith in Him, you have not advanced very far beyond a natural, worldly outlook."

Though the Christians in Corinth are worldly, they are genuine Christians. Paul calls them "brothers" and "infants in Christ." Yes, they are just babies, in the spiritual sense, but they are "in Christ." And that's the problem! Paul was in Corinth for almost two years, teaching, preaching, mentoring—yet they never advanced beyond spiritual babyhood. They were still governed by worldly thinking.

Now there's nothing wrong with babies. They're delightful little creatures—up to a point. They're cute, they suck their toes, and they gurgle. I love babies—but they require a lot of care. They're messy, they spit up, and they spill things. Someone has described a baby as an alimentary canal with a mouth at one end and no sense of responsibility at the other!

No one minds the fact that a baby acts like a baby. That's normal. But when a child turns five or ten or more and still needs to be burped and bathed and have his or her diapers changed, something's wrong! It's disgusting! It's a case of arrested development! That's what Paul talks about

51

here. Spiritual babyhood is fine for babies but terrible for Christians who should be spiritually mature.

From milk to meat

What is the "milk" Paul speaks of? It is elementary teaching that doesn't progress beyond the basics of the Christian faith. For example, evangelistic preaching—telling people how to receive Jesus Christ as Lord and Savior—is an elementary teaching. It's milk, not meat. Unfortunately, there are thousands of churches where the only teaching people ever hear is how to become a Christian. That's all right for spiritual babies, if it helps establish them in their faith; but it's milk, not meat. Other churches major on rituals, such as baptism, or place a focus every week on healings or end-times prophecy or witnessing; again, that's all milk, not meat. As the writer to the Hebrews observes,

> Therefore let us leave the elementary teachings about Christ and go on to maturity, not laying again the foundation of repentance from acts that lead to death, and of faith in God, instruction about baptisms, the laying on of hands, the resurrection of the dead, and eternal judgment. And God permitting, we will do so. (HEBREWS 6:1–3)

God doesn't want us to remain babies forever. He wants us to acquire a taste for meat. What is meat? It's preaching that unfolds the riches of the gospel, so that we can stop being children and start growing into maturity. As Paul wrote to the Ephesians,

> Then we will no longer be infants, tossed back and forth by the waves, and blown here and there by every wind of teaching and by the cunning and craftiness of men in their deceitful scheming. (EPHESIANS 4:14)

Here's an example of milk versus meat: "Jesus died for my sins." That's milk. It's such a simple truth that children as young as five can understand it. "I have died with Christ and I am raised with Christ, so I am dead to sin." That's meat. It's a more difficult and demanding concept. It requires a response from us in our daily lives.

Spiritual milk flows into us and simply has to be swallowed in order to be digested. But spiritual meat is more substantial. It needs to be chewed. It doesn't go down as easily as milk. It requires more work on our part to ingest it and digest it.

One of the signs that you are growing up and maturing as a Christian is that you are learning to ingest the meat of God's Word, including those passages on loving one another and forgiving one another in the body of Christ. When Christians are able to be agents of peace and mutual acceptance, they demonstrate spiritual maturity.

When a church is torn by jealousy and strife, however, that church is demonstrating widespread immaturity. Wherever you have baby Christians who do not grow more mature, you can count on it: There will be division and strife. Immature Christians like to get their own way, and they like to gossip. They have not learned to love one another with Christlike love. So Paul writes, "For since there is jealousy and quarreling among you, are you not worldly? Are you not acting like mere men? For when one says, 'I follow Paul,' and another, 'I follow Apollos,' are you not mere men?"

God gave us His Spirit to change our thinking, so that we would stop competing against each other and begin loving one another. That is spiritual maturity; that is spiritual meat.

No bosses, just servants

In this next passage Paul brings out beautifully what the spiritual view of relationships is. We Christians are not competitors against each other. We are partners with each other—and each of us has a unique role to play. Paul writes:

> What, after all, is Apollos? And what is Paul? Only servants, through whom you came to believe—as the Lord has assigned to each his task. I planted the seed, Apollos watered it, but God made it grow. So neither he who plants nor he who waters is anything, but only God, who makes things grow. The man who plants and the man who waters have one purpose, and each will be rewarded according to his own labor. For we are God's fellow workers; you are God's field, God's building. (1 CORINTHIANS 3:5–9)

Here Paul describes God's view of Christian ministers and Christian ministry. Paul doesn't make the same distinction between ministers and laypeople that we do today. The separation of clergy as a special class of "professional Christians" is a false distinction. Pastors have no special pipeline to God. Such an idea is never found in Scripture. In God's view, all Christians are ministers, without exception. All are given gifts by the

Spirit. All are expected to use those gifts to serve God and build up the church.

The essence of ministry in the church, Paul says, is servanthood. "What, after all, is Apollos?" he says. "And what is Paul? Only servants." But go around to most churches in America and you get a very different picture. You usually see churches with a hierarchical structure. At the top of the organizational pyramid is a pastor who is treated as the CEO of the church. In some churches, you may also find hidden centers of power—church bosses who may or may not hold an official position in the church but who, because they wield money and influence, are treated as power brokers.

God never intended that there be a privileged class of high-ranking Christians in the church—neither official pastors nor unofficial bosses. God's plan was for His church to be made up of servants. In a biblical church structure, the highest rank anyone can achieve in the church is servant, and everyone has the same rank. When a church follows that model, there is no need for competition.

Jesus told us what our attitude should be when he said to His disciples, "You know that the rulers of the Gentiles lord it over them, and their high officials exercise authority over them. Not so with you. Instead, whoever wants to become great among you must be your servant, and whoever wants to be first must be your slave—just as the Son of Man did not come to be served, but to serve, and to give his life as a ransom for many" (see Matthew 20:25–28).

Who is more important, Paul or Apollos? That's like asking which blade of a pair of scissors is more important. You need both blades or the scissor won't cut. Don't ever think that anyone else could take your place in the body of Christ. You are irreplaceable.

Paul goes on to say, "We are God's fellow workers." What a high privilege it is to be in partnership with the Creator of the universe! What greater honor could we receive than that? Think of it: When your life is over and you stand before the King of creation, He will acknowledge you as one He used as an instrument of grace and salvation in the lives of the people around you.

As Paul goes on to say, "You are God's field, God's building." A field a piece of ground that is planted and tended so that it will yield a harvest. A building is something that is constructed, brick by brick, timber by timber, on a sturdy foundation. You are God's field, and He is bringing in a great harvest through your life. You are God's building, and He is raising you up as an edifice, a holy temple in which to house His glory. As Paul wrote to the Ephesians:

> In him the whole building is joined together and rises to become a holy temple in the Lord. And in him you too are being built together to become a dwelling in which God lives by his Spirit. (EPHESIANS 2:21–22)

The church is not a building made of wood and stones—but a building is an apt symbol for the church. We are the church; we are God's building. We are being changed, brick by brick. We are being shaped and fashioned and chiseled here and there. As we manifest the character and love of God, the world takes notice and sees that God truly dwells among His people.

The only foundation

Paul goes on to describe how we should build this building called the church—and what our foundation should be:

> By the grace God has given me, I laid a foundation as an expert builder, and someone else is building on it. But each one should be careful how he builds. For no one can lay any foundation other than the one already laid, which is Jesus Christ. (1 CORINTHIANS 3:10–11)

When you build a building, there is nothing more important than laying a strong foundation. A building is no good if the foundation is no good. And what is the only foundation upon which we are to build the church? Jesus Christ. What does that mean in practical terms? It means that we must know everything we can know about His life, His teachings, His doctrines, His death and resurrection, and His eventual return. Any church that departs from teaching about Christ is doomed to fail. Without the firm foundation of Jesus Christ, the building becomes weak and wobbly, the walls crack, and the whole structure collapses.

Paul says, "I laid a foundation as an expert builder." The original Greek word he uses for "expert builder" is *architectron*—the word from which we get our English word *architect*. Paul is not saying here that he is the architect of the church; God is the architect of the church, not Paul. When Paul says he laid the foundation of the church as an expert builder, he is comparing himself with a building contractor. God drew up the plans, and

Paul built the church following the designs and plans God gave him. By preaching and teaching the doctrines of Jesus Christ, Paul followed God's blueprint and laid the foundation.

Paul says, "I laid a foundation . . . and someone else is building on it." Who is building on the foundation Paul has laid? He obviously has in mind those Christian workers and teachers who had also gone to Corinth to build and strengthen the church—people like Apollos and Peter and probably other teachers and missionaries whose names are not mentioned in this letter.

Next, Paul notes the eternal implications of building on the foundation of Jesus Christ. He writes:

> If any man builds on this foundation using gold, silver, costly stones, wood, hay or straw, his work will be shown for what it is, because the Day will bring it to light. It will be revealed with fire, and the fire will test the quality of each man's work. (1 CORINTHIANS 3:12–13)

As you build upon the foundation that has been laid in your life, what are you building with? Paul lists three expensive yet permanent materials: gold, silver, and costly stones. When Paul says "costly stones," I don't think he means gemstones like rubies or diamonds. I think he is referring to the kind of stones that were commonly used in the construction of buildings—stones of granite or marble. These stones were quarried, cut, shaped, and fitted—and they were very expensive building materials. Gold and silver were often overlaid on stone to add to the beauty and durability of a structure.

But Paul also mentions three other materials that were used to construct buildings. These were cheap, combustible materials that were used in temporary construction: wood, hay, and straw. Hay and straw were sometimes used as roofing materials; wood was used for the framework. A single spark could turn a house of wood, hay, and straw into a pile of ashes.

Paul's point is clear: Not only must you and I build upon a strong foundation—Jesus Christ alone—but also we must build our lives out of materials that will stand up to the ravages of time and testing. We must build our lives out of the eternal wisdom of God, not the false and perishable wisdom of the world. We must build our lives by pleasing God, not pleasing others or pleasing ourselves. We must build our lives by serving God and others, not by chasing after money, fame, success, and pleasure. The accomplishments and achievements we accumulate to glorify ourselves will crumble to dust; the works we do to glorify God are stored up for eternity.

If you are building your life to gratify the self—that is, if you indulge all your impulses for pleasure, for acquiring material things, for seeking fame and status, and for yielding to anger and bitterness toward others—then you are building with wood, hay, and straw. If you are building your life to serve Christ and others, demonstrating compassion and forgiveness, living in a state of contentment, then you are building with gold, silver, and precious building stones. Paul goes on to say:

> If what he has built survives, he will receive his reward. If it is burned up, he will suffer loss; he himself will be saved, but only as one escaping through the flames. (1 CORINTHIANS 3:14–15)

As we shall see when we reach 2 Corinthians, Paul writes, "For we must all appear before the judgment seat of Christ, that each one may receive what is due him for the things done while in the body, whether good or bad" (2 Corinthians 5:10). And in the book of Revelation, John describes the Lord with these words: "His eyes were like blazing fire" (see Revelation 1:14). Those flaming, searching eyes will one day examine the lives we've led in Christ. He will see what our lives are made of and what kinds of materials we've been building with—and we shall receive what is due us for the things we've done in the body, whether they have been worldly acts (wood, hay, and straw) or spiritual service (gold, silver, and precious stones).

What are we building with? If we are building for eternity, our building will endure. If we are building for momentary self-gratification and self-glorification, then our building will be burned up as by fire—and we will escape this life as one who escapes from a burning building. As the apostle John says, "And now, dear children, continue in him, so that when he appears we may be confident and unashamed before him at his coming" (1 John 2:28).

God's temple is sacred

One of the most popular hymns of all time is "Onward, Christian Soldiers." The second verse is a great description of what God intended His church to be:

> Like a mighty army moves the church of God.
> Brothers, we are treading where the saints have trod.

We are not divided; all one body we,
One in hope and doctrine, one in charity.

That's what the church is supposed to be—but as we can see in Paul's letter to the church at Corinth, there is often a gap between what a church is supposed to be and what it is. Someone has written a parody of "Onward, Christian Soldiers," and this version is (unfortunately) much closer to the reality of all too many churches:

Like a plodding turtle moves the church of God.
Brothers, we are treading where we've always trod.
We are much divided, many factions we,
Strong in faith and doctrine, weak in charity.

Those words surely describe the church at Corinth. The potential of this church lay unrealized because of divisions, jealousies, and worldly ambitions. Paul saw behind all of these surface symptoms and identified the root problem of all of these conflicts: A prideful love of human wisdom. This, I believe, is still a huge problem in the church today. We want our church to appear successful as the world judges success. So we adopt the attitudes and methods of the world and import them into our churches.

To counteract our tendency to infect the church with worldliness, Paul calls us back to a true view of the church. He calls us to remember that the only foundation upon which the church can be built is Jesus Christ—His life, His message, His ministry, His power, His death, His resurrection, and His return. Once we have laid a strong foundation, we must build upon it. We build our own lives on that foundation—and we build into each other's lives. The things we do, think, and say affect everyone else in the church, so we have an obligation to build with gold, silver, and precious stones, not combustible wood, hay, and straw.

How are you building up the lives of the others around you? What materials are you using? Is it the wood, hay, and straw of human wisdom, the love of status, the lust for ambition and prestige and getting your own way? Or are you building with the precious metals and stones of Christlike truth, love, forgiveness, humility, and acceptance?

Next, Paul warns of a danger:

Don't you know that you yourselves are God's temple and that God's Spirit lives in you? If anyone destroys God's temple, God will destroy

him; for God's temple is sacred, and you are that temple. (1 CORIN-
THIANS 3:16–17)

Paul tells the Corinthian Christians, "you are God's temple."This truth
applies to the church as a whole and to every individual believer. As we
will later see, Paul also tells the Corinthians, "Do you not know that your
body is a temple of the Holy Spirit, who is in you, whom you have received
from God? You are not your own" (1 Corinthians 6:19). This is a great
truth—one that Paul underscores throughout this letter.

Our bodies are temples, and the Spirit indwells us. When we gather
with other Christians, who are also indwelt by the Spirit, the whole congregation becomes a great temple of the Holy Spirit. As Jesus said, "For
where two or three come together in my name, there am I with them"
(Matthew 18:20).

And here is the danger Paul warns of: It's possible to bring great harm
to God's temple. Paul writes, "If anyone destroys God's temple, God will
destroy him; for God's temple is sacred, and you are that temple."The original Greek word which the New International Version translates "destroys"
is probably better understood to mean "causes harm to." In other words,
that statement should read, "If anyone harms, corrupts, or defiles God's
temple, God will destroy him; for God's temple is sacred, and you are that
temple." Clearly, this is a serious warning.

We have a dramatic example of this principle in Acts 5 where Ananias
and Sapphira indulge in hypocrisy. They pretend to have a level of dedication and commitment that they did not fulfill. When they came before
Peter, the Holy Spirit gave Peter insight into their sin and he pronounced
them guilty. They both fell dead at Peter's feet. This is not to say that God
will strike us dead if we commit a sin of hypocrisy, but God wants us to
know that He takes it very seriously whenever anyone corrupts God's temple—either the temple of His congregation or the temple of an individual
believer. Whenever we defile ourselves or God's church, something within
us dies. This is a principle we need to take seriously.

I once met a woman at the Fellowship of Christian Airline Personnel
Conference in Chattanooga. This woman was a flight attendant, and she
told me of an incident that had taken place on a flight. She was serving
coffee while the plane was in the air. As she came down the aisle, a man
stopped her and did something of an obscene sexual nature, either as a
clumsy pass or simply as a rude joke.

The flight attendant at first tried to ignore the passenger, but what he had done was upsetting. She went to the back of the plane and prayed, asking God to show her what she should do. A few minutes later, she went back to the man, crouched in the aisle so that she was at eye level with the man, and she said, "What you did a few moments ago was offensive and unacceptable. There's something you should know. I'm a Christian. My life belongs to Jesus Christ, and my body is the temple of the Holy Spirit. The Scriptures say that God will destroy anyone who damages His temple."

The man stammered an apology. "Please don't say any more," he said. "It'll never happen again."

As the woman walked away from the passenger, she thanked God for reminding her of 1 Corinthians 3:17. That verse delivered her from an embarrassing situation and placed the shame on the offender where it belonged.

All things are yours

How does a person bring damage or corruption to God's temple? The answer is clear if we look at this warning in the context of everything Paul has already said: We corrupt the church whenever we introduce the so-called wisdom of the world into our lives or into the church. If we individually live according to the false wisdom of the world, we corrupt ourselves—and bring corruption into the church. Anyone who suggests that we should compromise with the spirit of this age is spiritually endangering himself and the church.

We damage the temple of God when we mistreat each other in the church, or seek our own way, or grab power in the church. We damage His temple whenever we show favoritism or disfavor based on race or politics or economic class. We harm His temple whenever we allow sin to go unjudged in our own lives or within the congregation.

We damage God's temple whenever we allow the church to be infected by formalism (reliance upon ceremonies and rituals), or by emotionalism or mysticism (seeking religious ecstasy instead of righteousness and relationship), or by asceticism (taking smug pride in observing legalistic rules or trying to prove ourselves more spiritual than others). God takes these sins against His temple very seriously—so seriously, Paul warns, that anyone who corrupts God's temple will himself be corrupted.

Next, Paul deals with the question, "Since God wants us to reject worldly wisdom, what would God have us be?" The answer: God wants us to become fools for Him! Paul writes:

Do not deceive yourselves. If any one of you thinks he is wise by the standards of this age, he should become a "fool" so that he may become wise. For the wisdom of this world is foolishness in God's sight. As it is written: "He catches the wise in their craftiness"; and again, "The Lord knows that the thoughts of the wise are futile." So then, no more boasting about men! (1 CORINTHIANS 3:18–21a)

We so often think we are serving God, witnessing for Him, spreading His good news when, deep down in our hearts, we are ambitious for prominence, praise, and attention. We are self-centered and self-seeking—yet we are self-deluded into thinking we only wish to serve God! So, in this passage, Paul says two things.

First, he says, "Stop kidding yourself! Don't be deceived! You may impress other people, but you don't impress God. You may think you are a great success, but God shakes His head at what He sees. God can't be fooled. He knows your heart. The world may applaud you, but God sees through your pitiful attempts to glorify yourself. It's foolishness in His sight. Anything that does not come from dependence on the wisdom and power of God is wasted effort."

Second, Paul says, in effect, "You should deliberately seek what the world says is foolish. If you think you are wise by worldly standards, that you are successful and sitting on top of the world—then think again! Let those who think themselves 'wise' become fools, so they can be *truly* wise! The wisdom of the world is foolishness to God. So if you really want to be wise, become a fool for God!"

I once met a pastor from another state—we'll call him Pastor Brown. He had read *Body Life* and was incorporating some of the Body Life principles into his church. He told me that another pastor in his town asked him, "What are you doing over there at your church?"

Pastor Brown replied, "We're sharing one another's burdens and meeting one another's needs. We have a service where we talk openly and honestly about some of our problems and failures as Christians, and we pray for each other."

"No other church in town behaves that way! Why do you do that?"

"Because," Pastor Brown said, "'the New Testament tells us to.'"

"Well, you won't get anywhere with that approach."

Pastor Brown said, "The Bible doesn't tell us we're supposed to 'get anywhere.' It just tells us how we're supposed to live, and that's all we're trying to do."

The other pastor was following the world's wisdom and telling Pastor Brown, in effect, "You're a fool to run your church according to the biblical model." Pastor Brown's reply was simple: "Okay, then we're a bunch of fools—but we're God's fools, following God's commands, obeying God's Word. And we're going to keep right on practicing this foolishness. We choose the foolishness of God over the wisdom of the world."

There is a song that George Beverly Shea has sung countless times—a song that speaks volumes to my heart. Penned by Rhea F. Miller, it's called "I'd Rather Have Jesus":

I'd rather have Jesus than silver or gold;
I'd rather be His than have riches untold:
I'd rather have Jesus than houses or lands.
I'd rather be led by His nail-pierced hand

Than to be the king of a vast domain
Or be held in sin's dread sway.
I'd rather have Jesus than anything
This world affords today.

It is amazing to me that so many Christians are obsessed with keeping up with the world and its status symbols, styles, films, televisions shows, music, philosophies, and ideologies. We say we want to follow Christ—yet we continually ape the fashions and fads of this hell-bound culture we live in. How foolish are the ways of the world!

That's why Paul tells us, "The wisdom of this world is foolishness in God's sight." Then, quoting Job 5:13, he says, "He catches the wise in their craftiness." And quoting Psalm 94:11, he says, "The Lord knows that the thoughts of the wise are futile." That word *futile* in the original language means a breath or puff of air. The ideas, goals, philosophies, and arguments of the so-called wise of this world are like a puff of air—here one moment, gone the next. When you choose the wisdom of the world, you align your life with futility and oblivion. When you choose the wisdom of God, you align your life with meaning and eternal purpose. That is why Paul goes on to write:

All things are yours, whether Paul or Apollos or Cephas or the world or life or death or the present or the future—all are yours, and you are of Christ, and Christ is of God. (1 CORINTHIANS 3:21b-23)

Choose the wisdom of God—and you gain the world! That is what Jesus told us: "Blessed are the meek, for they will inherit the earth" (Matthew 5:5). Blessed are the meek, the humble servants of God, the ones who are not too proud to be called God's fools by rejecting the false wisdom of this world—for they will inherit the earth, and all things shall be theirs.

Jesus also said, "For whoever wants to save his life will lose it, but whoever loses his life for me and for the gospel will save it" (Mark 8:35). Paul says, "Whoever seeks God's wisdom and disregards human wisdom will end up with everything. Why try to pit Paul against Apollos or Apollos against Cephas [that is, the apostle Peter]? Why divide up the church between them or form factions around them? You can have them all! Paul planted the church in Corinth—and his whole ministry is yours. Apollos watered what Paul planted—and his whole ministry is yours. Cephas shared with you his firsthand account of walking with the Lord—and his whole ministry is yours. Led by the Spirit of God, you can go anywhere, and God will give you experiences and adventures that money can't buy!"

The world is yours. Life with all its possibilities is open before you. Even death, which we all fear, has been mastered and defeated by God. When death comes to you, there is nothing for you to fear. It will not rob you of life; it will minister to you and lead you into a new life of unimaginable glory.

All things are yours because you are Christ's, and Christ is God's. All things belong to you because you belong to Him.

5

THOSE WHO MINISTER

1 Corinthians 4

Some anonymous writer has suggested a new approach to finding a replacement for your old, worn-out minister: a chain letter. The letter would read something like this:

> Are you tired of your minister? Is his preaching long-winded, repetitive, or just plain boring? Here's the solution to your church's problems! Just send a copy of this letter to seven other churches who are also tired of their pastors. Then place your current minister in a cardboard box and ship him to the church at the top of the list below (don't forget to poke air holes in the box!). Within one week, you'll receive 16,807 ministers from other churches—and one of them should be perfect for your church. This letter is guaranteed to work! But beware that you DON'T break the chain! One church broke the chain—and they were stuck with their old minister for the next twenty years.

How do you view your minister? Many people see a minister as "a mild-mannered man standing before a mild-mannered congregation, exhorting them to be even more mild-mannered." What a depressing definition of a Christian leader! I have also heard this definition of a minister: "A holy groan in a black suit." I hope that's not me!

In 1 Corinthians 4, we find Paul's definition of a minister of the gospel. By this time, stereotypes had already arisen in the church of what a minister should be: They saw ministers as traveling preachers, known for their knowledge and eloquence, who developed followings in every church they visited.

As we have seen, the church in Corinth was divided among those who said, "I am of Paul" or "I am of Apollos" or "I am of Peter." As a result, the church was breaking into quarreling factions that placed certain men, including Paul himself, on a pedestal. As we come to chapter 4, Paul corrects these false and divisive views:

So then, men ought to regard us as servants of Christ and as those entrusted with the secret things of God. Now it is required that those who have been given a trust must prove faithful. (1 Corinthians 4:1–2)

Here, Paul describes ministers as "servants of Christ" who have been entrusted with a message from God and who are to be faithful to God and His message. This is different from the concept most of us have of ministers or pastors.

Bosses—or "under-rowers"?

We tend to think of a minister as a full-time church employee whose job description includes (but is not limited to) preaching, teaching, counseling, performing weddings and funerals, conducting church meetings, managing the church staff, mentoring staff members and interns, visiting the sick and shut-ins, refereeing disputes, writing a column in the church newsletter, and unjamming the Xerox machine in the church office. This concept of the minister as a professional Christian was unknown in the New Testament. This idea arose in the church during the past three centuries.

A minister of Christ in the New Testament church was anyone—and I mean literally *anyone*—who, by virtue of a gift of the Spirit, was a preacher or teacher of the Word of God. That is the view Paul speaks of in this passage. There is a sense in which we are all ministers of Christ. God expects every believer to be a servant and a witness, ready at all times to minister to others in the name of our Lord.

But Paul is writing here in a special sense, speaking of all those who have the spiritual gift of teaching or preaching (called prophesying in Scripture). Even today, most churches have dozens or even hundreds of people with teaching or preaching gifts, and they may use these gifts as Sunday school teachers, Bible study leaders, and so forth. These are the people Paul is talking about in 1 Corinthians 4.

How are we to look upon such people in the church? Paul says we are to view them as servants of Christ. The original Greek word for "servant" that Paul uses in this passage is *huperetes*, which literally means "an under-rower."

Everyone in Corinth understood what that word meant. Corinth was a major port city where the war galleys of the Roman Empire often docked. The Corinthians knew that the lowest deck of a Roman war galley was comprised of rows of benches. The rowers sat on these benches and powered the ship. The captain stood on a raised platform in the bow so that all the rowers could see him and hear his orders. The rowers were required to instantly obey the captain's orders. These rowers were the *huperetes*, the under-rowers. They were servants of their master, the captain; they lived and died at his bidding.

That's the image Paul uses to describe those who are teachers, preachers and ministers of the Word of God. They are the under-rowers of Christ.

Jesus used this same image to describe His disciples. Standing before Pontius Pilate, He told the Roman governor, "My kingdom is not of this world. If it were, my servants [*huperetes*] would fight to prevent my arrest" (see John 18:36). An under-rower is not a boss; he's an errand boy who carries out orders without question. Paul says, "I don't want you to look at me and other ministers as little tin gods. We're just galley slaves, doing whatever God tells us."

A young pastor once said to me, "I'd like you to tell me what you would do if you were in my shoes. The board of elders at our church called me in and said, 'There are some things you need to understand. First, you are employed as pastor, but this is our church, not yours. We were here before you came, and we'll be here after you leave. So we expect you to take orders from us. If you don't, your days as pastor of this church are numbered.' How would you respond to an ultimatum like that?"

I said, "I'd call the elders of the church together and say, 'Brothers, I've thought about what you said, and I see two serious theological errors in your position. First, this is not your church. This is the Lord's church. In Matthew 16:18, Jesus said, "On this rock I will build my church, and the gates of Hades will not overcome it." No one in this room—not me, not you—is the proprietor of this church. We are all servants under the authority of the Lord. He is the only one with the right to say what the church ought to be and what it ought to do.

"'Second, you think you hired me as an employee of this church, but I didn't come here on that basis. I'm not an employee. I'm a servant. I appreciate the fact that this congregation has seen fit to give me financial support so that I can devote full time to the ministry of teaching and preaching—but I don't agree with your view that I am your employee. I'm your partner in ministry, according to the New Testament. If you don't accept those terms, I'll have to look elsewhere.'"

This young pastor went back to his church, said exactly what I suggested to him—and the church board promptly fired him. But this pastor kept in touch with me, and within a few months he was ministering at another church that shared his view of the ministry. There he served as an under-rower among many under-rowers. His ministry there has been very fruitful for God.

Under-rowers are servants, not bosses, not lords and masters. They have no special status. They live and die at Christ's bidding.

The secret things of God

What is the work God expects his servant ministers to do? To answer this question, Paul uses another term. In the New International Version, this term is translated "those entrusted with the secret things of God." The New American Standard Bible uses the phrase "stewards of the mysteries of God." A steward is someone who keeps something in trust on behalf of someone else.

A minister of Christ is to be a trusted steward of "the mysteries of God," the secret and hidden wisdom of God, the truths that are revealed only in the Word of God and nowhere else. "The mysteries of God" are the basis upon which all of God's purposes in our lives are worked out. What are these mysteries Paul speaks about?

We find one of them in Mark 4:11, "the mystery of the kingdom of God." This mystery refers to an understanding of how God is at work in history, carrying out His purposes through the great and small events of our day.

There is "the mystery of lawlessness" (2 Thessalonians 2:7). This mystery involves an understanding of why we are never able to make any progress in solving human dilemmas and why every generation without exception repeats the problems and failures of the previous generation. While we make continual advances in science, medicine, and technology, we cannot solve problems of crime, ignorance, and immorality. Why? Because of the mystery of lawlessness—the fallenness of our flesh, the influence of the world system, and the spiritual forces that distort our thinking.

Then there is "the mystery of godliness" that Paul speaks of in 1 Timothy 3:16. This is the amazing secret that God has disclosed to us whereby we can live righteous lives amid all the pressures, perils, and temptations of this corrupt world. We don't have to run away from life, and we don't have to conform to it. We can overcome our circumstances through the secret of "the glorious riches of this mystery, which is Christ in you, the hope of glory" (see Colossians 1:27). Christ is in each of us, available to us—His life, wisdom, strength, and power to act are available to us.

Then there is the "mystery of the church" that Paul unveils in Ephesians 3:1–6. The church is the new society God designed to demonstrate a new way of living. Though the church has no worldly power or armies, the gates of Hades cannot prevail against it. Though powerless, the church is on the march, transforming the world. That is a mystery.

These are some of the secret things of God that have been entrusted to the servant ministers of God. Paul writes, "Now it is required that those who have been given a trust must prove faithful." Faithful in what? In dispensing the mysteries so that the people understand them. As teachers and preachers in the church, we must continually set forth and explain the mysteries of God to His people.

That is the basis on which we will be judged by our Lord and Master; if we have been good stewards of His secrets, we will hear Him say, "Well done, good and faithful servant! . . . Come and share your master's happiness!" (see Matthew 25:21).

To judge or not to judge

Next, Paul talks about how to evaluate a minister. He writes:

> I care very little if I am judged by you or by any human court; indeed, I do not even judge myself. My conscience is clear, but that does not make me innocent. It is the Lord who judges me. Therefore judge nothing before the appointed time; wait till the Lord comes. He will bring to light what is hidden in darkness and will expose the motives of men's hearts. At that time each will receive his praise from God.
> (1 CORINTHIANS 4:3–5)

Paul speaks here of being evaluated by the congregation—and says that he places very little value on what others think of him. In fact, it's not important what anyone thinks of him or even what he thinks of himself! The only evaluation that matters, he says, is the evaluation of his Lord.

Stuart Briscoe says there are three kinds of congregational pressure: adulation, which swells the head; manipulation, which ties the hands; and antagonism, which breaks the heart. I have experienced all three—and so has every other person who has preached the Word of God.

There are those well-meaning people in the church who heap praise on your head until your hat no longer fits. Many a young pastor has been ruined by adulation. When I first came to Peninsula Bible Fellowship, there was a dear lady who was my number one encourager. She would say,

"Oh! Mr. Stedman, when you say something I really understand it, and I know I can believe everything you say!" I learned that, if you're not careful, you start preaching to please the people who praise you, hoping to hear still more praise—and you fail to preach the unpleasant and unpopular truths of Scripture.

Then there is manipulation. Every church has its unofficial power structure, those people who seek to manipulate and bend the church to their own will. Sometimes they manipulate by the force of personality, sometimes by loosening or tightening their purse strings, and sometimes by pressuring you until you give in to their demands. Though they claim to follow Christ, these control-obsessed manipulators use blackmail-like tactics to get their way in the church. A minister who succumbs to manipulation will avoid issues, doctrines, or Scripture passages that might stir up controversy or confrontation. Instead of boldly blazing a trail through the Word of God, he'll sit astride the safest hobbyhorse he can find, rocking and marking time.

Then there is antagonism and opposition. A young pastor once told me about a hostile encounter he had while on staff in a large Bay Area church. One Sunday after church, an elder took him aside. The man's face was dark with rage, and his voice was raised somewhere between a snarl and a shout. "Where are you getting all these wild ideas?" the elder demanded. "Have you been down to Stedman's church?" The young man answered truthfully, "No, I haven't. I don't know what you're talking about." The elder grabbed him by the front of his shirt—laid angry hands on him!—and said, "If I ever hear that you're going down to Stedman's church and coming back with those radical ideas, you're out!" That's antagonism—a display of naked threats and aggression.

If you are a minister and you are facing one of these forms of pressure, Paul says, "Don't be intimidated by it." Your answer should be, "I care very little if I am judged by you or by any human court. My conscience is clear. The Lord is my Judge—not you." It may cost you your position in the church and your livelihood to take that stand. But if you allow yourself to be intimidated or swayed, you cease to be a servant and a faithful steward of the mysteries of God.

Notice that Paul says, "I do not even judge myself." Paul realizes that human judgment is incomplete. Yes, he examines himself to make sure that he is being faithful to his calling—but he leaves the final evaluation to God. He doesn't glory in his successes, nor does he bemoan his failures. He keeps moving forward, doing God's will—and leaving the final judgment in God's hands.

I have discovered, as Paul must have discovered, that I cannot accept my own judgment of myself. I don't have the wise perspective to see myself clearly. Sometimes when I feel like I have been a complete failure, I learn that God has used me in a special way. At other times, when I feel like I have had amazing success, I learn that I let God down.

On April 18, 1942, Lt. Col. Jimmy Doolittle served as the lead pilot of a force of sixteen B-25 bombers that launched from the pitching deck of the aircraft carrier *Hornet*. After Japan's surprise attack on U.S. forces at Pearl Harbor, Doolittle conceived and planned the one-way mission to hit military targets in and around Tokyo.

The bombers flew low over the sea, hit their targets in Japan, and continued on toward China. Bad weather prevented the planes from finding their landing fields, so Doolittle and the other airmen bailed out in total darkness. Some were captured by Japanese occupation forces. Others were rescued by Chinese patriots.

Doolittle landed in a Chinese rice paddy, separated from his men. Alone, freezing, and convinced that his men and planes were lost, Doolittle wept. He believed that his mission was a failure and that if he ever made it back to the States, he would be court-martialed for losing his entire command.

A group of Chinese guerillas found him, helped him rejoin his men, and got him safely back into American hands. On the flight home, Doolittle was depressed, thinking he had failed his country. Only after arriving in the States was he told that his mission was a huge success. His raiders had damaged Japan's war-making industries and sent American morale soaring. Doolittle was rushed to the White House, where President Franklin Roosevelt presented him with his nation's highest commendation, the Congressional Medal of Honor.

Jimmy Doolittle learned the lesson stated here by the apostle Paul: We do not have the perspective to adequately judge ourselves. Lost in the darkness of his circumstances, Doolittle thought himself a failure, but when he returned home to his commander-in-chief, he was crowned with honor and success.

We do not minister in order to be judged or approved by people. We seek only the commendation of our Commander-in-Chief, Jesus the Lord.

The only evaluation that matters is the eternal evaluation we will one day receive from our Lord.

Paul concludes, "Therefore judge nothing before the appointed time; wait till the Lord comes. He will bring to light what is hidden in darkness and will expose the motives of men's hearts. At that time each will receive his praise from God." I try to continually live in the awareness that my whole life will one day be examined by my Lord. He will walk with me through the record of those years. There are some things in my past that I don't want Him to see—but I have already faced them and repented of them, so I'm not afraid; He has seen them and dealt with them.

At the same time, there are parts of my life that I'm eager for the Lord to see. I hope He will commend me for those actions—but I may be disappointed! Jesus may say, "You thought you were serving me, Ray, but your motives were tainted. You were really serving yourself."

There may also be parts of my life that I have forgotten, that meant little to me at the time, but that the Lord will point to and say, "Ray, when you did that little act of Christian love, it didn't seem like much to you, but your heart was right before me. You weren't looking for glory. You just wanted to do the right thing. I want you to know how pleased I am that you had such a sincere attitude at that moment. Well done, Ray! Well done."

Glory to the Giver of gifts

Next, Paul sets forth the freedom that a minister experiences when the congregation thinks rightly about him:

> Now, brothers, I have applied these things to myself and Apollos for your benefit, so that you may learn from us the meaning of the saying, "Do not go beyond what is written." Then you will not take pride in one man over against another. For who makes you different from anyone else? What do you have that you did not receive? And if you did receive it, why do you boast as though you did not? (1 CORINTHIANS 4:6–7)

When a congregation thinks rightly about its ministers, rivalries and jealousies are sharply reduced. I have seen many churches split because a rivalry has developed between two leaders in the church. Half the church lines up behind one person and half behind the other—and the church

71

comes apart like a cracked walnut. If the congregation would not take pride in one person against another, these splits couldn't happen.

And when the minister thinks rightly of himself, rivalries and jealousies are reduced even further. Conflict often arises because a minister thinks too highly of himself. I'm speaking here not merely of so-called clergy but also of so-called laypeople with ministry gifts. Paul asks, "For who makes you different from anyone else? What do you have that you did not receive? And if you did receive it, why do you boast as though you did not?"

In other words, Paul says, "What right do you have to brag or boast? If you are able to preach or teach or fulfill a leadership role, just where do you think you got that ability? You didn't manufacture it on your own—it's a spiritual gift, imparted by the Holy Spirit. Stop taking credit for God's handiwork. Stop glorifying yourself and stealing the glory that God alone deserves."

A young minister preached to his congregation, and God richly blessed his sermon. Many people came forward to commit or rededicate their lives to the Lord. Later, the young minister swaggered through the front door, gave his wife a big hug, and said, "Honey, I wonder how many really great preachers there are in the world!" Her tart reply: "One less than you think!"

As the apostle Peter warns us, "God opposes the proud but gives grace to the humble" (1 Peter 5:5). When we become proud and arrogant because of the gifts we have received from God, we set the stage for conflict in the church. We are tempted to disdain others in the church whose gifts are (in our eyes) not as many or as great or as important as our own. When God gives us ministry gifts, let's use them wisely and humbly and remember that all the glory belongs to the Giver, not to us.

Condemned to die

In the book of Revelation, Jesus says to the church in Laodicea, "You are neither cold nor hot. . . . So, because you are lukewarm—neither hot nor cold—I am about to spit you out of my mouth" (see Revelation 3:15–16). I think we would be horrified to know how many people have been turned away from faith in Christ because of the poor witness of lukewarm Christians. They are not fully alive or fully dead. They are neither a sizzling hot steak nor a delicious cold cut. They are like meat that has been sitting for hours at room temperature covered with waxy, congealed grease—yuck!

The same message Jesus delivered to the church in Laodicea is the warning Paul now delivers to the Christians at Corinth:

Already you have all you want! Already you have become rich! You have become kings—and that without us! How I wish that you really had become kings so that we might be kings with you! (1 CORINTHIANS 4:8)

Here Paul lists two marks of a church or an individual Christian who has become dangerously complacent. The first mark of a complacent church is a sense of "I have arrived, I have a corner on the truth, I'm rich and comfortable!" Unfortunately, many North American churches demonstrate this kind of smug, self-satisfied attitude. In terms of material wealth or doctrinal purity or good works or weekly attendance or by some other measure, these churches have become rich and complacent.

Why was the church in Corinth feeling this way? Because of spiritual gifts! The Corinthian church possessed them all. As we have earlier seen, the Scriptures list at least twenty-one specific gifts of the Spirit—and the Corinthian congregation manifested all of them. Many churches claim that the key to spiritual power is the knowledge and practice of spiritual gifts. The Corinthians could have put up a sign that read, "Come and Visit the Church That Has It All!"

Yet, over the course of this letter, Paul describes this church as being spiritually immature, divided, worldly, and scandal-ridden! Clearly, it takes more to build a complete, mature church than spiritual gifts alone. The Corinthian church was in danger, and Paul wrote to warn them and pull them back from the brink of destruction.

The second mark of a complacent church, Paul says, is an exclusive attitude. The Corinthian church demonstrated an attitude that said, "We don't need anyone else!" Paul writes, "You have become kings—and that without us!" The Corinthians felt they had no need of other Christians because they were so far ahead of everyone else—so Paul pictured them as having the arrogance of kings.

I remember a fellowship of believers who met together in the Palo Alto area. For a while, they joined with our church in various ministry and community efforts. They seemed vital and excited about the Christian faith and fellowship with other believers. But in time they pulled away from us and became very ingrown and exclusive. They were so in love with their own teaching that they began to tell people that they were the only true church and that other churches, including ours, were counterfeits. They described their own ministry as the only apostolic ministry in the Bay Area, and they said they had no need of any contact with other churches.

Exclusivism is a sign of human pride and spiritual smugness—and it's an offense to the Spirit of God. That's the kind of exclusive attitude that Paul (with heavy sarcasm) condemns in this passage. The problem is that the Corinthian believers were ensnared by the illusions of this fallen world. They were living in a dream world, thinking they were materially and spiritually rich, needing nothing.

So Paul jolted them back to reality, saying, "How I wish that you really had become kings so that we might be kings with you!" In other words, "I wish circumstances out here in the real world were as nice as that dream world you live in! You may be rich and living like kings—but I'm not. I'm always on the menu in this dog-eat-dog world!"

Paul goes on to say:

> For it seems to me that God has put us apostles on display at the end of the procession, like men condemned to die in the arena. We have been made a spectacle to the whole universe, to angels as well as to men. We are fools for Christ, but you are so wise in Christ! We are weak, but you are strong! You are honored, we are dishonored! To this very hour we go hungry and thirsty, we are in rags, we are brutally treated, we are homeless. We work hard with our own hands. When we are cursed, we bless; when we are persecuted, we endure it; when we are slandered, we answer kindly. Up to this moment we have become the scum of the earth, the refuse of the world. (1 CORINTHIANS 4:9–13)

What a stark contrast between life in the Corinthian dream world and life in the real world of the apostle Paul! He's saying, "You Corinthians are kidding yourselves. The Christian life is not a playground! It's a battleground! This is war—spiritual warfare! And some of us on this battlefield are being tortured, mistreated, starved, humiliated, cursed, persecuted, and even killed." So Paul calls the Corinthians back to reality.

He tells the Corinthians, in effect, "We apostles are what you might call 'pattern Christians.' God has put us on display so that we might demonstrate certain spiritual truths. He has exhibited us as last of all, as if we were condemned prisoners, a spectacle for all to see. God is using us to show you what the world is really like: a cruel arena of torture and death."

Here we see why the apostles are so important in the New Testament and why they have been so significant in the church ever since. The apostles are pattern Christians. They are the examples for us to follow. They were not super saints, as we often suppose. They loved life and feared suffering and death just as we do. Yet God sent them out amid the brutal realities of life, in order to show us how to handle life's battles.

Notice that Paul says the apostles are like "men condemned to die in the arena." Paul was thinking of the gladiators who fought in the great Coliseum at Rome. In those contests, two gladiators, both condemned to death, would engage in mortal combat. They would stand before the great assemblage and salute the emperor, saying, "*Ave, Imperator! Morituri te salutamus!*" ("Hail, Caesar! We who are about to die salute you!").

People who are sentenced to death never deal with trivialities; they are focused on what's important in life. They settle their business affairs, dispose of their property, and make sure their relationships are in order. Paul says that is how the apostles lived—as condemned men who are spending their remaining days on the things that truly count.

The apostles, Paul says, are persecuted Christians: "We are fools for Christ, but you are so wise in Christ! We are weak, but you are strong! You are honored, we are dishonored! To this very hour we go hungry and thirsty, we are in rags, we are brutally treated, we are homeless." Paul wants the Corinthians to understand that there is something about the gospel that will always make us unpopular in the world. And that's a huge problem, isn't it? Nobody likes to be unpopular. We all want to be accepted. Being rejected and ridiculed is one of the great tests of the Christian life: Are we willing to bear reproach for Christ's sake?

As we will later see, the Corinthians avoided reproach by accommodating themselves to the world. They put up with anything in the church, and they never judged any behavior as wrong. By compromising with the world, they escaped the world's reproach.

Paul goes on to say that apostles are peculiar people: "When we are cursed, we bless; when we are persecuted, we endure it; when we are slandered, we answer kindly." Clearly, apostles do not act like normal people. How do people of the world normally behave? When you curse them, they curse you back. Persecute them, and they get even. Lie about them, and they try to destroy you.

"Up to this moment," Paul adds, "we have become the scum of the earth, the refuse of the world." If you were treated like garbage, how would you respond? The apostles, these pattern Christians, respond with love and forgiveness, just as Jesus did. That is authentic Christianity.

Four final principles

The Corinthian church, says Paul, has become smug and arrogantly complacent, thinking itself rich and in need of nothing. Now, in the final verses of chapter 4, he calls the Corinthian believers back to reality and shows them how to cure themselves of their spiritual complacency:

> I am not writing this to shame you, but to warn you, as my dear children. Even though you have ten thousand guardians in Christ, you do not have many fathers, for in Christ Jesus I became your father through the gospel. Therefore I urge you to imitate me. For this reason I am sending to you Timothy, my son whom I love, who is faithful in the Lord. He will remind you of my way of life in Christ Jesus, which agrees with what I teach everywhere in every church.
>
> Some of you have become arrogant, as if I were not coming to you. But I will come to you very soon, if the Lord is willing, and then I will find out not only how these arrogant people are talking, but what power they have. For the kingdom of God is not a matter of talk but of power. What do you prefer? Shall I come to you with a whip, or in love and with a gentle spirit? (1 CORINTHIANS 4:14–21)

In this passage, we find four principles for dealing with problems in relationships in the church.

The first principle: *Always lead with love.* Paul writes, "I am not writing this to shame you, but to warn you, as my dear children. . . . For in Christ Jesus I became your father through the gospel." Paul speaks to the Corinthians with a fatherly love and affection. He makes it clear that he writes to them in love, not anger. He is not trying to hurt them but to heal them.

The second principle: *Always set a good example.* Paul writes, "Therefore I urge you to imitate me. For this reason I am sending to you Timothy. . . . He will remind you of my way of life in Christ Jesus, which agrees with what I teach everywhere in every church." Some people feel that Paul is conceited when he writes those words—but he's not. Paul recognizes that, as an apostle, he is a role model whether he likes it or not. People will imitate him whether he wants them to or not—so he has made a decision to live his life as an example to others.

The third principle: *Preserve liberty*. Never box people in. Give them a choice as to what they will or will not do. "What do you prefer?" Paul asks. "Shall I come to you with a whip, or in love and with a gentle spirit?" Paul is saying here, in effect, "I am not ordering you around. I'm appealing to you and urging you. I'm giving you the liberty to choose how you will respond to this appeal." Whenever you must confront problems, always preserve liberty.

The fourth principle: *Confront realistically*. Clear away falsehoods, illusions, and denial; make the real issues of the matter unmistakably clear. That is why Paul says, "I will come to you very soon, if the Lord is willing, and then I will find out not only how these arrogant people are talking, but what power they have. For the kingdom of God is not a matter of talk but of power." Paul is saying, in effect, "Talk is cheap, but change requires power. I'm interested in what people do, not just the words they say. When I come, I want to know what people are doing and how God's power is demonstrated through their lives."

Paul has given us a pattern for building a congregation that is vital and effective for the Lord. He challenges us to live the adventure of this life as it was meant to be lived: humbly, boldly, and with a willingness to risk all for the joy of serving our Lord Jesus Christ.

6

A SCANDAL IN THE CHURCH

1 Corinthians 5

I t's one of the oldest problems in the church—and it's a tragedy that continues to destroy churches to this day. It is the problem of sexual immorality among Christians.

Hardly a week goes by that I don't hear a report of a church rocked by scandal: A Christian leader who has left his wife and run off with the church secretary. A sexual predator who has abused children in the church. A prominent church member arrested for possession of child pornography. In 1 Corinthians 5, Paul deals with a scandal in the church at Corinth, showing that in two thousand years of church history, little has changed.

The Corinthian church of Paul's day was surrounded by a culture much like our own—drenched in lust, casually accepting perverted sexual practices, with the most obscene and degrading temptations available wherever you turned. We talk about how our North American culture worships sex—but the ancient Greeks literally worshiped sex in the form of the goddess Aphrodite. The two great temples of Aphrodite were located in Athens and Corinth, so Corinth was truly one of the centers of sexual promiscuity in the ancient world. Sexual intercourse with the priestesses of Aphrodite was considered an act of worship by the pagans of Corinth.

If you find it hard to deal with the temptations on your TV screen, your computer screen, your magazines and billboards, then you have something in common with the Corinthian believers. God expected the Christians in Corinth to meet the same standards of moral purity that we are measured by today. God hasn't changed, the world hasn't changed, and human nature hasn't changed.

Even the pagans were shocked

Paul opens chapter 5 by describing the problem in the Corinthian church:

> It is actually reported that there is sexual immorality among you, and of a kind that does not occur even among pagans: A man has his father's wife. And you are proud! Shouldn't you rather have been filled with grief and have put out of your fellowship the man who did this? (1 Corinthians 5:1–2)

The woman mentioned here was not the biological mother of the man; had she been the man's mother, Paul would have plainly said so. The phrase "his father's wife" tells us that this woman was the man's stepmother. The offender was cohabitating with his father's wife—a clear case of adultery made even worse by the fact that he was related to this woman. The fact that he was related by marriage and not by blood makes no difference. This was an incestuous relationship.

The pagans of Corinth would not be shocked by adultery. After all, adultery was commonplace and accepted in Corinth. But even the pagans drew the line at incest. They considered sex between relatives to be disgraceful and degrading.

So Paul writes, "It is actually reported that there is sexual immorality among you, and of a kind that does not occur even among pagans: A man has his father's wife." It's interesting that even in our own day the most degrading insult imaginable is the suggestion that one sleeps with his own mother. From the first century to the twenty-first, incest is regarded as degrading, even among pagans.

Amazingly, the only people not shocked by this practice were the Christians in the Corinthian church. This is what troubles Paul the most. He writes, "And you are proud! Shouldn't you rather have been filled with grief and have put out of your fellowship the man who did this?" These Christians were boastful of their tolerance toward sin!

Paul decided that if the Corinthians wouldn't judge sin, he would. He writes:

> Even though I am not physically present, I am with you in spirit. And I have already passed judgment on the one who did this, just as if I were present. When you are assembled in the name of our Lord Jesus and I am with you in spirit, and the power of our Lord Jesus is present, hand this man over to Satan, so that the sinful nature may be destroyed and his spirit saved on the day of the Lord. (1 Corinthians 5:3–5)

The Corinthian believers thought they were showing Christian love by their tolerant attitude toward sexual sin. Many Christians take the same attitude today. I remember one church where I worked for a brief time. The young pastor was caught in a sexual sin. Instead of disciplining the pastor, the church board looked the other way. I stood up in the board meeting and reminded the board of this very passage. The chairman was unfazed by my appeal to God's Word. "Well," he said, "he's a young man—and boys will be boys."

May the Lord save us from such a misplaced tolerance toward sin!

How to handle a scandal—a four-step process

Many Christians are so anxious to avoid being labeled judgmental or narrow-minded that they accept the most offensive and destructive behavior imaginable in the name of tolerance. Sin must never be tolerated in the church, because it destroys the purity of the Lord's Bride and brings dishonor upon the gospel of Jesus Christ. Few churches, it seems, are able to strike the biblical balance of loving the sinner while hating the sin. Paul, in this passage, shows us a practical four-step process for responding whenever a scandal is uncovered in the church.

Step 1: *Demonstrate a biblical attitude toward sin.* This attitude begins with a sense of grief and sorrow. Paul writes, "Shouldn't you rather have been filled with grief?" When a sin is uncovered and the stench of immorality fills the air, the church should react with shock, sorrow, and dismay. The church should mourn the loss of purity of one of its members. Sin damages lives and has a corrosive effect on the cause of Christ.

It is totally inappropriate, however, to point fingers of condemnation at those who are caught in sin. When we condemn another person, we place ourselves on a higher moral and spiritual plane than the sinner—and we forget that we are sinners, too! Whatever that person has done, we could do—and may have even done. That's why Paul, in his letter to the Galatians, writes:

> Brothers, if someone is caught in a sin, you who are spiritual should restore him gently. But watch yourself, or you also may be tempted. (GALATIANS 6:1)

When someone is caught in sin, our goal should be restoration, not condemnation. We, too, could fall if we faced certain circumstances. Though we understand and feel compassion for the sinner, the sin cannot be permitted to continue. We cannot allow the church to be destroyed by a lax attitude toward sin.

Step 2: *Follow the biblical steps of confrontation and restoration.* All too many churches, when confronted with a scandal, have no idea how to proceed—so they do whatever they feel like at the moment. If there is an uproar in the church over the sin, then the elders get caught up in the moment and punish the offender harshly. If the offender is a leader of a church faction or a major donor to the church budget, he may get a slap on the wrist. There will be favoritism shown to some, censure shown to others. When we operate on feelings and favoritism instead of biblical principles, we make a travesty of church discipline.

Paul tells us that God expects us to obey the absolute standard set by Jesus. He says, "When you are assembled in the name of our Lord Jesus and I am with you in spirit, and the power of our Lord Jesus is present . . ." Paul is saying that divine authority has spoken in these areas, so follow the guidance the Lord Jesus has given you.

Jesus said, "If your brother sins against you, go and show him his fault, just between the two of you. If he listens to you, you have won your brother over" (Matthew 18:15). Don't spread gossip about the sin, don't ask people to pray about it (often a Christianized form of gossip!), and don't talk about it to anyone. Go to the offender and deal with it one to one. If the offender hears you and repents, you have won your brother over—and the matter is closed.

What if the offender does not repent? Jesus says, "But if he will not listen, take one or two others along, so that 'every matter may be established by the testimony of two or three witnesses'" (Matthew 18:16). The additional witnesses establish the truth of what is said. While I was pastor of Peninsula Bible Church, literally hundreds of problems were dealt with at this level by Christians who practiced the Lord's teaching. People were gently held accountable by other Christians; they repented, the matter was closed, and most people in the church were never aware of the problem.

And if the offender still does not repent? Jesus says, "If he refuses to listen to them, tell it to the church" (Matthew 18:17a). At this point, when the offender demonstrates hardness of heart and a refusal to repent, the offender must be publicly censured, so that the church will know that sin is unacceptable and will not be tolerated. This is not done in a smug, judgmental, or self-righteous spirit but humbly and with sorrow—and with the hope that the offender still might have a change of heart. The matter is told to the church, and everyone in the church becomes responsible for trying to help that offender find his way back to repentance and restoration.

There is one more step to the process: "And if he refuses to listen even to the church, treat him as you would a pagan or a tax collector" (Matthew 18:17b). Treat the offender as if he is not a Christian. He has, in fact, declared himself not to be a Christian by his actions, even though he may still call himself a Christian. This does not mean we are to treat the offender with scorn, hatred, judgment, or retribution. It means that we recognize that he has deceived himself, he is not really born again, and he does not wish to live according to Christian principles.

That is what Paul refers to when he tells us that divine authority has spoken in this matter, and we are to assemble in the name and power of the Lord Jesus. Note that Paul also says, "When you are assembled in the name of our Lord Jesus and I am with you in spirit . . ." Paul is saying that not only has divine authority spoken in this area, but apostolic authority also requires that sin and scandal be dealt with in the church.

Delivered to Satan

Many people struggle with the necessity of judging sin in the church. They cite the words of Jesus elsewhere in Matthew: "Do not judge, or you too will be judged" (Matthew 7:1). When Jesus says, "Do not judge," he means, "Don't condemn, don't pass judgment on another person's heart or motives."

But that's not what we're talking about with regard to judging sin in the church. The church has a duty and an obligation to deal with immoral behavior. When we tell another person, "You have sinned and need to repent," we are not condemning that person or judging his motives or passing judgment on his soul. We are saying that his behavior must change; he needs to repent in order to be restored to full fellowship.

Next, Paul makes a statement that seems cruel and shocking but is loving and restorative toward the offender:

> When you are assembled in the name of our Lord Jesus and I am with you in spirit, and the power of our Lord Jesus is present, hand this man over to Satan, so that the sinful nature may be destroyed and his spirit saved on the day of the Lord. (1 CORINTHIANS 5:4–5)

Three times, Paul alludes to this course of action. In verse 2 he says the Corinthians should have "have put out of your fellowship the man who did this." Here he says, "Hand this man over to Satan." Finally, in verse 13, he says, "Expel the wicked man from among you." What does Paul mean when he says "hand this man over to Satan"?

The Scriptures always regard the world as Satan's dominion. There are two kingdoms at war in our lives: the kingdom of Satan and the kingdom of God. Though these two kingdoms are worlds apart in their philosophy and goals, there are no clearly marked boundary lines between them. Both kingdoms are at work on planet earth. Paul is telling the Corinthian Christians that they need to remove this man from their midst and send him back to the realm that is under Satan's control—the world outside of the church. As Jesus said, they are to treat this man as a Gentile or a tax collector.

This doesn't mean we have to physically eject a person or bar the church door. Some people, even after being disciplined, insist on making their presence felt. Very well, the individual may continue to attend—but he is to be regarded in a different light. Usually, however, the censured person withdraws—and the church allows him to go. No public announcement or ceremony of excommunication is called for by God's Word.

The reason for confronting sin in the church is indicated in verse 5: "so that the sinful nature may be destroyed and his spirit saved on the day of the Lord." God does not want to see the offender destroyed. He wants to see the offender restored. The goal of church discipline is not merely to remove a troublemaker but to save people from the effects of sin—both the offender and the congregation. When the offender sincerely repents, he is restored. All discipline ceases when repentance occurs.

The problem with yeast

Next, Paul gives three excellent reasons why the church must take action whenever sin and scandal arise:

> Your boasting is not good. Don't you know that a little yeast works through the whole batch of dough? Get rid of the old yeast that you may be a new batch without yeast—as you really are. For Christ, our Passover lamb, has been sacrificed. Therefore let us keep the Festival, not with the old yeast, the yeast of malice and wickedness, but with bread without yeast, the bread of sincerity and truth. (1 CORINTHIANS 5:6–8)

Paul's imagery is borrowed from the Feast of the Passover, when the Jews commemorated their deliverance from Egypt in the days of Moses.

On that first Passover, the Jews sprinkled the blood of a sacrificial lamb over their doorposts so the angel of death would pass over their home. Then they gathered and ate the roasted meat of the lamb.

Before this ceremonial meal, they would first go throughout the house with a candle and search out all the yeast that was in the house, for the Lord said they must never eat the Passover meal with any yeast (for example, in the form of raised bread). Even today, when the Jews celebrate the Passover, they first search out and remove all yeast from their houses. Why? Because, in the Scriptures, yeast is a symbol of sin. Paul says, "Don't you know that a little yeast works through the whole batch of dough? Get rid of the old yeast that you may be a new batch without yeast." Sin infects a congregation just as yeast spreads through a batch of bread dough.

It's important to recognize that even though this passage deals with a case of adultery and incest, sexual sins are not the only class of sins that the church must deal with. They are probably the most common and recognizable of sins, but we should also deal firmly with those who are habitually quarrelsome, who abuse alcohol or drugs, who cheat and steal, who engage in idolatry or the occult, or who spread gossip or dissension in the church. These are all yeast-like sins that can infect the congregation.

A church that judges sin in its midst is a church that celebrates Christian deliverance and liberty. As Paul writes, "Therefore let us keep the Festival, not with the old yeast, the yeast of malice and wickedness, but with bread without yeast, the bread of sincerity and truth." Yes, let's celebrate! Let's worship in joy! This kind of celebration is possible only in a church that has been cleansed by the Lord.

Paul concludes this section by setting limits on church discipline. In the closing verses of chapter 5 he writes:

> I have written you in my letter not to associate with sexually immoral people—not at all meaning the people of this world who are immoral, or the greedy and swindlers, or idolaters. In that case you would have to leave this world. But now I am writing you that you must not associate with anyone who calls himself a brother but is sexually immoral or greedy, an idolater or a slanderer, a drunkard or a swindler. With such a man do not even eat.
>
> What business is it of mine to judge those outside the church? Are you not to judge those inside? God will judge those outside. "Expel the wicked man from among you." (1 CORINTHIANS 5:9–13)

Here Paul refers to a lost letter that he had previously written to Corinth: "I have written you in my letter not to associate with sexually immoral people." The Corinthians had apparently mistaken Paul's meaning. They thought Paul was telling them to shun non-Christians who lived sinful lives. (Many Christians make the same mistake today.) Paul corrects that misimpression by making it clear that God expects us to go out into the world and to have an evangelistic impact on sinners. We are to reach out in friendship and love to the worldlings around us who are lost in sin. After all, they don't know any better.

But we are to judge sin that takes place in the body of Christ. We are to remove the yeast that threatens the entire batch. We are to cleanse ourselves and the Lord's church. Paul has written 1 Corinthians 5 to call us back to a recognition of the unique position the church holds in the world today—and our responsibility to demonstrate the purity of Christ to a watching world.

7

RIGHTS AND WRONGS

1 Corinthians 6

During the Cold War, I read a magazine report about two Christian organizations that smuggled Bibles behind the Iron Curtain. These two organizations, which should have been working hand in hand, were suing each other in court. As I read the article, I couldn't help wondering if they had read the Bibles they were smuggling. If they had, they would have seen that in 1 Corinthians 6, Paul makes it clear that believers are not to sue each other in civil courts.

There's an abrupt change of theme as we move from chapter 5 to chapter 6. Paul goes from talking about problems of sexual immorality to problems of lawsuits between brothers in Christ. This may seem like a jarring transition, but there's a logical flow to Paul's argument.

In 1 Corinthians 5, Paul is writing about one form of lust—sexual lust. In chapter 6, he writes about another form of lust—the lust we know as greed. Lawsuits usually arise out of greed and selfishness, a disproportionate desire for material possessions. When we sue our Christian brother, we behave as if things are more important than people.

Theme 1: Lawsuits are foolish

The first eleven verses of 1 Corinthians 6 divide into three sections. The theme of the first section: Lawsuits are foolish. The theme of the second section: Lawsuits are shameful. The theme of the third section: Lawsuits raise doubts about the spiritual state of the litigants. Paul writes:

> If any of you has a dispute with another, dare he take it before the ungodly for judgment instead of before the saints? Do you not know that the saints will judge the world? And if you are to judge the world, are you not competent to judge trivial cases? Do you not know that we will judge angels? How much more the things of this life! (1 Corinthians 6:1–3)

The apostle Paul suggests that those believers who sue other believers are foolish for doing so. They are dragging their fellow Christians before the secular Roman courts and airing their quarrels in public. Don't these believers know that the church is destined to judge the world and judge the angels? Isn't the church competent to judge petty legal cases?

Six times in this chapter Paul asks, "Do you not know?" He is quizzing the Corinthian believers on their theological knowledge—and he is pointing out that our behavior should align with our theology. If we believe that Christians will judge the angels and the world, then we had better learn now how to judge such minor matters as who owes what to whom.

Paul is not condemning the Roman judicial system; he admired Roman law and called upon it for his own defense. But he wants the Corinthians to know that they have become focused on flyspecks—and they are foolishly making a spectacle of themselves in the secular courts instead of demonstrating Christlike love.

Paul unveils a stunning truth when he says that we shall judge the world—and we shall judge angels. Think of it—we shall pass judgment on these amazing and mysterious beings of the unseen realm. Who are the angels we shall judge? They are the fallen angels who once served God but fell away by following Satan in his rebellion.

There are two other New Testament references to the judgment of angels. Peter reminds us that "God did not spare angels when they sinned, but sent them to hell, putting them into gloomy dungeons to be held for judgment" (see 2 Peter 2:4). And the book of Jude tells us, "And the angels who did not keep their positions of authority but abandoned their own home—these he has kept in darkness, bound with everlasting chains for judgment on the great Day" (Jude 1:6).

Theme 2: Lawsuits are shameful

Next, Paul wants us to know that lawsuits among Christians are shameful. He writes:

> But instead, one brother goes to law against another—and this in front of unbelievers! The very fact that you have lawsuits among you means you have been completely defeated already. Why not rather be wronged? Why not rather be cheated? Instead, you yourselves cheat and do wrong, and you do this to your brothers. (1 CORINTHIANS 6:6–8)

87

You can hear Paul's shocked tone of voice. He can scarcely believe that Christians would do this. No matter who wins the lawsuit, the gospel loses. If Christians need the secular courts to settle disputes, what good is Christian love? The gospel is a message of peace and reconciliation—but if believers in Christ are at war with one another, the gospel looks like a lie. When Christians fight each other in court, they give the world the right to reject the gospel.

So Paul suggests a Christlike alternative to going to court: "Why not rather be wronged? Why not rather be cheated?" Suppose we have to lose a hundred dollars—or a hundred thousand. Wouldn't that be a small price to pay to preserve the reputation of the gospel?

Many years ago, while I was traveling with Dr. H. A. Ironside, he told me of an incident from his Christian experience. When he was only eight years old, his mother took him to a church meeting where two brothers were arguing. One had apparently wronged the other. Young Harry Ironside didn't know what the trouble was, but it was clear that the people in the meeting were upset. One stood up and shook his fist, shouting, "I don't care what the rest of you do. I want my rights! That's all! I just want my rights!"

An elderly Scottish brother, who was hard of hearing, sat in the front row. He cupped his hand to his ear and asked, "Brother, what's that ye say?"

The angry man repeated, "I said I want my rights, that's all!"

The old man said, "Your rights, brother? Is that what you want? Why, the Lord Jesus didn't come to get His rights! He came to get His wrongs! And He got 'em!"

Dr. Ironside said, "I'll always remember how that fellow stood transfixed for a moment. Then he dropped his head and said, 'You're right, brother. Settle it any way you like.'" And in a few moments, the matter was settled.

As believers, we are called to a different lifestyle before the world—one in which we willingly surrender personal rights for the sake of Jesus. After all, He surrendered so much more for us.

Theme 3: Lawsuits raise doubts about the litigants

And Paul is still not through. Lawsuits call into question the spiritual state of the litigants. He writes:

> Do you not know that the wicked will not inherit the kingdom of God? Do not be deceived: Neither the sexually immoral nor idolaters nor adulterers nor male prostitutes nor homosexual offenders nor

thieves nor the greedy nor drunkards nor slanderers nor swindlers will inherit the kingdom of God. And that is what some of you were. But you were washed, you were sanctified, you were justified in the name of the Lord Jesus Christ and by the Spirit of our God. (1 Corinthians 6:9–11)

We could paraphrase Paul's words this way: "When you defend your rights before a secular court, you wrong your brother. Even though your cause is just, you are wrong in the way you treat your brother. Your actions make people wonder if you were ever justified before God. The unjustified, the unrighteous, the unregenerate cannot inherit the kingdom of God; so if you do evil by dragging a brother into court, can you claim to be an heir of the kingdom?"

Paul is not saying that if you sue another believer, you cannot be saved. Rather, he is saying that if you have experienced Christian conversion, it should make a marked difference in the way you live your life. If it doesn't, then people have a right to question whether your conversion is genuine or not.

How are our lives different from the lives of the worldlings around us? That's the question Paul puts to us as he writes, "Do not be deceived: Neither the sexually immoral nor idolaters nor adulterers nor male prostitutes nor homosexual offenders nor thieves nor the greedy nor drunkards nor slanderers nor swindlers will inherit the kingdom of God."

Then he concludes with this positive note: "And that is what some of you were. But you were washed, you were sanctified, you were justified in the name of the Lord Jesus Christ and by the Spirit of our God." He's saying, in effect, "I know there must be some among you who have committed some grievous sins—and by taking your brothers to court, you give testimony that you really haven't changed. That's what some of you were. But the rest of you were washed, sanctified, and justified in the name of the Lord Jesus. Because your conversion is real, I know you are going to change your way of life."

Notice the threefold process of conversion Paul writes of here: "you were washed, you were sanctified, you were justified." To be washed is to be cleansed and purified; all the dirtiness of sin is removed. To be sanctified is to be set apart for a special purpose; when we were converted, God gave our lives a purpose, a role to play in His kingdom. When we were justified, our sins were wiped off the ledger; we no longer have to earn our salvation because Jesus paid for our sins in full.

That's what conversion is all about. That's what Christianity is all about. It means our old selfish spirit has been shattered, so we no longer demand our rights. Instead, we follow in the footsteps of Jesus and become willing to suffer loss so that His gospel may be advanced. When we stop insisting on our rights, the world takes notice.

What are bodies for?

With verse 12, Paul returns to the problem of sexual sin, which he had previously addressed in chapter 5. As we have seen, Corinth was given over to the worship of sex. When Paul founded a Christian church in that city, he directly challenged the sexual depravity of that city. He writes:

> "Everything is permissible for me"—but not everything is beneficial. "Everything is permissible for me"—but I will not be mastered by anything. (1 CORINTHIANS 6:12)

Three phrases in this passage are enclosed in quotations marks, not only in the New International Version but also in the Revised Standard Version, the New English Bible, and several other modern English versions. This is the editors' way of showing that it appears that Paul was quoting statements that had been made to him, probably by the Corinthian Christians.

It's likely that the Corinthians had misapplied Paul's teaching on grace and Christian liberty. So they had written him, saying, "Paul, didn't you tell us, 'Everything is permissible for me' and 'Food for the stomach and the stomach for food'? We're just practicing our Christian freedom. Why do you say we're wrong?" So Paul quotes these phrases, then offers his commentary and explanation: "'Everything is permissible for me'—but not everything is beneficial. 'Everything is permissible for me'—but I will not be mastered by anything."

Here's the difference between legalism and true Christianity. The legalist looks at life and says, "Everything is wrong unless you can prove from Scripture that it's right." Legalism is negative and restrictive. It says that most things in life are illegal, immoral, or fattening—and therefore, to be avoided.

But New Testament Christianity comes at life differently. It is a positive approach that sees life's pleasures as permissible unless the Bible tells us otherwise. It says, in effect, "God made the earth and everything in it. Everything in the world is good and right except what the Word of God labels as wrong."

The Corinthians were saying, "Paul himself said, 'Everything is permissible for me.' The law of Moses tells us it's wrong to have sex outside of marriage. But Paul tells us that when Christ comes into our lives, we are no longer under the Law. So, by Paul's own words, we're free to indulge in some of the sexual practices that are accepted in Corinth."

How does Paul respond? He says, "Yes, in a broad sense, you have a point. We are under grace, not under law, so all things are permissible for us as believers. But truth must always be balanced." Then he says that while all things are permissible, some things are destructive and can ruin our lives.

Balancing spiritual truth is like walking along the top of a fence. When I was a boy I enjoyed walking along the back fences in Denver. I could go for blocks on the back alleys just by walking on top of the fence. It was a fun way to travel—but it was a very narrow path! Jesus said that this is what the Christian life is like. In Matthew 7:14, he refers to the Christian life as a straight and narrow way.

The problem with walking the top of a fence is that it's easy to fall off—and you can fall on either side. Both sides are equally dangerous. When you walk the pathway of Christian liberty, always remember that there is error on either side. On one side is the Law. The Law is an extreme; it makes rigid demands that no one can live up to. On the other side is license, which is also an extreme. The moment we declare ourselves free of the Law, we fall into license—and we *still* lose our liberty! The extreme of license makes us slaves.

The things that hurt us tend to be habit-forming: sex, drugs, alcohol, tobacco, gambling—all give some form of pleasure for a while. Eventually, even if we grow to hate these habits, we find we can't break them. We keep doing what we hate doing—and it destroys our happiness, our relationships, and our lives.

There is a famous photo that appeared in anti-smoking campaigns. It showed a man holding a cigarette to a tube protruding from his throat. This man lost his larynx to cancer and could no longer breathe through his nose or mouth. Instead, he breathed through a tracheotomy tube implanted in his throat. He also used that tube for smoking cigarettes.

Perhaps he started smoking because he liked the taste or thought that a cigarette hanging from his mouth made him look cool. Eventually, he smoked because nicotine had become his master. He couldn't taste the smoke, and that cigarette stuck in his breathing tube certainly didn't look cool, but he couldn't help himself. The cigarettes were killing him, yet he had to have them.

Paul says, "'Everything is permissible for me'—but I will not be mastered by anything." Some things that are permissible will master us if we give them a toehold in our lives. We may start out demanding our liberty to do these things, but we will end up as slaves of the things we think will set us free. Paul says, in effect, "The only way to truly be free is to stay balanced on the fence—don't fall to the left, don't fall to the right. Stay on the narrow path."

Our bodies are temples

Next, Paul addresses another argument among the Corinthians. He writes:

> "Food for the stomach and the stomach for food"—but God will destroy them both. The body is not meant for sexual immorality, but for the Lord, and the Lord for the body. By his power God raised the Lord from the dead, and he will raise us also. (1 CORINTHIANS 6:13–14)

When Paul writes, "Food for the stomach and the stomach for food," he is quoting what the Corinthians had said to him. Their point was that the sexual organs were made for sex in the same way that the stomach was designed for food. What is food for? It meets our nutritional needs and satisfies our hunger. No one would think it sinful or immoral to go to the refrigerator and grab a snack.

But the Corinthians made an argument by analogy that many people still make today. Their point was this: "The sex organs were made for sex, so it's natural and right that we should satisfy our sexual urges whenever they arise." Paul replies that there's a big difference between our appetite for food and our appetite for sex. Here we enter an area of biblical revelation where God's Word sees more clearly than human wisdom. The world has a shallow and superficial view of sex. The Bible reveals deep truths about the nature of our sexuality.

Paul tells us that the food-stomach arrangement is temporary. It is intended to last for this lifetime only; God has no eternal plans for the stomach. But God does have eternal plans for the body. Our sexuality is linked to the soul and spirit in ways that the stomach is not. Sexuality, according to the Scriptures, pervades our whole humanity—and it pervades our relationships with others.

Did you realize that the Bible teaches that worship is a form of sexual expression? Worship is a hunger to be possessed by God and to possess all there is of God. The worshiping spirit cries out and says, "O Lord, be with me, take me, use me, possess me." These same words are often used to express sexual passion.

God gives us a beautiful promise that He makes Himself available to us to be owned by us and to relate to us. Jesus put it in the most precise way when he said that the deepest relationship possible between a human being and God is, "You are in me, and I am in you" (John 14:20b). That is what Paul talks about in this passage.

The world wants us to believe that sex is merely a physical and biological drive. The world wants us to think that sex is for the sex organs, and the sex organs are for sex—that's all there is to it, nothing more. But God tells us that sex is a deep and spiritually significant experience. That's why Paul writes, "The body is not meant for sexual immorality, but for the Lord, and the Lord for the body." This is one of the most elevating and revolutionary teachings in the Word of God: We were made to be indwelt by God Himself!

And, as Paul further explains, God has a purpose for the body: "By his power God raised the Lord from the dead, and he will raise us also." Sexuality that penetrates our whole being will not be expressed on the physical level in the resurrected body, but it will have its expression on the soulish and the spiritual levels. God has a purpose for it in the life to come. That is why He has given us the physical act of sex. The sex act is not merely a form of recreation or an urge that must periodically be satisfied. Sex was designed to teach us what we are truly like—eternal beings who are created to know the rapturous experience of possessing another, being possessed by another, and of merging with another person in a holy and mystical way.

Next, Paul attacks the problem of prostitution that was rampant in Corinth:

> Do you not know that your bodies are members of Christ himself? Shall I then take the members of Christ and unite them with a prostitute? Never! Do you not know that he who unites himself with a prostitute is one with her in body? For it is said, "The two will become one flesh." But he who unites himself with the Lord is one with him in spirit. (1 CORINTHIANS 6:15–17)

Paul speaks here of temple prostitution, which was socially accepted in Corinth. He says that fornication is a grievous sin that involves taking the human body, the personal property of Jesus, and using it in a relationship with a godless woman and paying her to allow this to take place. This is equivalent to making Christ commit sexual sin with a prostitute!

The awfulness of this thought prompts Paul to express his own horror at the idea: "Shall I then take the members of Christ and unite them with a prostitute? Never!" He goes on to say that a Christian's union with the Lord transcends the depths of sexual union, and he quotes Genesis 2:24 when he writes, "The two will become one flesh." Sexual union, he says, is part of the mystery that God designed for humanity in the Garden of Eden. This is a profound insight that we must take seriously.

I have counseled men who lived sexually promiscuous lives, and they have told me of having a seemingly casual liaison with a woman one night, then encountering her again days or weeks later and experiencing a sense of having shared a deep mystery together. They might try to convince themselves that they only had recreational sex, but the reality is that an intimacy remains and can never be forgotten.

The Lord is a Spirit, and we are human spirits. When the mystery of conversion and regeneration occurs, there is a fusing of identity between ourselves and God. The apostle Peter says that we "participate in the divine nature" (2 Peter 1:4). We fuse with the person of God. He becomes the true you, your ultimate identity. This truth underscores the terrible effects of sexual sin. Paul continues:

> Flee from sexual immorality. All other sins a man commits are outside his body, but he who sins sexually sins against his own body. Do you not know that your body is a temple of the Holy Spirit, who is in you, whom you have received from God? You are not your own; you were bought at a price. Therefore honor God with your body. (1 CORINTHIANS 6:18–20)

This is Paul's apostolic advice on how to handle the arousal of sexual desire outside of marriage: "When tempted, get out of there! Don't flirt with temptation. Flee!" If you find yourself attracted to someone you cannot have, or if you struggle with the temptation of the Internet or cable TV, or if you're away from home and considering a visit to a prostitute or a place of indecent entertainment—*flee temptation!* Don't try to fight it or suppress it—*get away from it!*

Because our bodies are temples of the Holy Spirit, sexual sin is different from other sins. Sex within marriage exalts the body, God's temple; sex outside of marriage defiles that temple, so that it's not a fit dwelling place for God. Sexual sin damages us in ways we don't fully appreciate. Sex within marriage makes us fully and wonderfully human; sex outside of marriage dehumanizes us, reducing us to rutting animals. Those who indulge in sexual sin become coarse and insensitive. To be sex-centered is to be self-centered, desiring only to have one's own sexual needs met and not caring about the souls and spirituality of others.

A young Christian couple once came to me for counseling. They were engaged and looking forward to marriage—then something happened. They found themselves experiencing more and more conflict, and they came to me for help. We talked about the issues they fought about but could find no solution.

Finally, I asked, "Have you been having sex?" They were shocked by the question—but then they answered, "Yes." I said, "This conflict you're experiencing is the result. Sexual sin is destroying your relationship." These two young people didn't believe me, so they continued to have sexual relations—and their relationship continued to deteriorate. They married—but the marriage didn't last. Their witness for Christ was severely damaged.

Sexual sin violates our relationship with God. So Paul writes, "You are not your own; you were bought at a price. Therefore honor God with your body." Your body is not really your body; it belongs to God. We have no right to ourselves. God bought us, He owns us, and we are His by right of creation and redemption. When we honor God with our bodies, we demonstrate to the world what God seeks to do in the human race—and we show the world what a God-indwelt man or woman is like.

This is the wondrous lost secret of our humanity.

8

MARRIAGE AND DIVORCE

1 Corinthians 7:1–24

A mother received a call from her distraught daughter, who had just been married for a month. The mom took the portable phone into the bedroom and closed the door, leaving the father in the hallway, wondering what his wife and daughter were discussing. The call was brief—two or three minutes at most. The mother came out and found her husband pacing anxiously in the hallway.

"Well?" the father said. "What was that all about?"

"They had a fight," the mother replied. "She said she wants to come home."

"What did you say?"

"I told her she *was* home."

Whether a husband and wife are newlyweds or golden-agers, marriage is hard work. As American humorist Helen Rowland once said, "Marriage is like twirling a baton, turning handsprings, or eating with chopsticks. It looks easy until you try it." As we come to 1 Corinthians 7, Paul plunges into one of the most difficult aspects of marriage as he deals candidly with the issue of sex in marriage.

Paul's view of sex and singleness

You'll recall that this letter was written in response to a report delivered to Paul in Ephesus by three men, Stephanas, Fortunatus, and Achaicus. These men also brought a letter from the church in Corinth, asking the apostle certain questions. In the first six chapters, Paul has laid the groundwork for his reply to these questions. He has dealt with the subject of sex, the human body as the temple of God, and related themes. At this point, he begins to answer the questions that the Corinthians have posed to him:

> Now for the matters you wrote about: It is good for a man not to marry. But since there is so much immorality, each man should have

his own wife, and each woman her own husband. (1 CORINTHIANS 7:1–2)

The Corinthians' first question was apparently, "In view of the sexual temptations we face in Corinth, is it best to avoid contact with the opposite sex and renounce marriage for life?" Paul's reply is surprising: "It is good for a man not to marry."

The Corinthian Christians were constantly bombarded by sexually explicit messages from the culture. So they were considering giving up on sex and even removing themselves from society. (Centuries later, the monks and ascetics of the Middle Ages moved to the desert or into a cloistered monastery for this very reason, believing that celibacy would produce a deeper level of godliness.)

The problem is that the attempt to wall ourselves off from temptation has never worked. God didn't create two sexes so that they could live separate from each other; He created man and woman to be together as companions and partners in all areas of life, including their sex life. Your sex drive is built into your innermost being; you cannot run from what is inside you.

Why, then, does Paul say, "It is good for a man not to marry"? We must be careful not to pull this verse out of context. This is only the beginning of his answer, not his ultimate conclusion. Paul stresses that there is nothing wrong with celibacy; it is all right to be single if that is what a person chooses. But, because of the temptations around us and the urges within us, he goes on to say that marriage would be the preferable state for a believer living in a moral climate like that of Corinth: "But since there is so much immorality, each man should have his own wife, and each woman her own husband."

Some people read this statement and conclude that Paul had a low view of marriage. They take this statement to mean that celibacy is God's best and that marriage is second best in Paul's view. I would suggest that those who have this view of Paul's teaching have missed the context of Paul's message.

True, Paul was unmarried, at least at that time. Some scholars believe he must have been married at one time in his life, because he was once a member of the Sanhedrin, and membership in that religious body was open only to married men. What happened to Paul's wife? No one knows. This is one of the unsolved mysteries of Scripture and Christian tradition. She may have died, or she may have divorced Paul after his conversion. We simply don't know.

Several times in this chapter Paul says it is an advantage to be single, and he offers reasons for this view. But he also says that marriage is honorable and ordained by God. The major theme of this section, however, is not whether or not Christians should marry but how they should conduct themselves in the sexual aspect of the marriage relationship. He makes three important statements about sex in marriage.

First, sex within marriage permits a husband and wife to release sexual urges and relieve sexual pressures. Paul is not saying that a Christian should marry simply for sex. He is saying that when you are married, this is a benefit you derive from the married state. If you live in a sex-oriented society, it's easier to live as a married person.

This statement answers a false claim made by various religious groups that sex is only for making babies and growing families. God clearly intended sex as a means of showing love and giving pleasure within marriage.

When I was a young Christian in my early twenties, someone gave me a book called *The Way of a Man with a Maid* by Oscar Lowry. The book, which takes its title from Proverbs 30:19, was intended to teach me the Bible's perspective on sex. The book contains some helpful moral and spiritual insights, but it also contains considerable error. It teaches, for example, that a couple should have sex only when they want to have children. I didn't realize it at the time, but I now know that this is an utter distortion of what the Bible says about sexuality.

Paul makes it clear: Sex in marriage is God's gift for the mutual pleasure of the married couple. It's the highest form of physical ecstasy; nothing compares with it, and God designed it that way. He gave us our erogenous zones, and He intended human beings to experience the exquisite pleasure of orgasm. But it is equally clear that He designed sex to be experienced only within the secure confines of marriage.

Paul goes on to say that married sex teaches us something about ourselves:

> The husband should fulfill his marital duty to his wife, and likewise the wife to her husband. The wife's body does not belong to her alone but also to her husband. In the same way, the husband's body does not belong to him alone but also to his wife. Do not deprive each other except by mutual consent and for a time, so that you may devote yourselves to prayer. Then come together again so that Satan will not tempt you because of your lack of self-control. (1 CORINTHIANS 7:3–5)

Again, Paul makes the point that sex in marriage is designed for the fulfillment of each partner. This is what the Song of Solomon so beautifully captures. In that Old Testament book, the act of sexual intercourse is referred to by poetic images, including the metaphor of a garden:

Awake, north wind,
　　and come, south wind!
Blow on my garden,
　　that its fragrance may spread abroad.
Let my lover come into his garden
　　and taste its choice fruits. (SONG OF SOLOMON 4:16)

Unfortunately, Victorian squeamishness has so prevailed in the church that most people don't know what that passage means. They think it is merely an allegory about Christ and the church. While it is legitimate to view Song of Solomon as an allegory, the book was not written for that purpose. It was written to describe the God-given joys of married sex. To deny the most obvious meaning of the book is to rob God's Word of its power and truth.

Married sex should never be based on demands. Instead, Paul tells us, sex should be mutually offered to one another as a gift. A Christian's sex life should not be self-centered but centered on the desires of one's partner. Sex is designed so that we have no control over it ourselves; we need each other to minister to our sexual wants and needs. If you demand to have your own needs met, you lose the true joy of sex. If you meet each other's needs, you reach the heights of sexual joy and satisfaction.

So there is a beautiful reciprocity in sex: "The wife's body does not belong to her alone but also to her husband. In the same way, the husband's body does not belong to him alone but also to his wife." This is why sex with oneself—the solitary act of masturbation—is so unsatisfying. Solo sex is self-centered; there is no reciprocity, no partner to please and satisfy.

Reciprocity—the act of unselfishly giving pleasure to each other in sex—is so important to the overall health of a marriage that Paul says it takes precedence over everything else except an occasional spiritual retreat for prayer. "Do not deprive each other," he writes, "except by mutual consent and for a time, so that you may devote yourselves to prayer. Then come together again so that Satan will not tempt you because of your lack of self-control."

Next, Paul says that both sex in marriage and the ability to live celibate and unmarried are gifts from God:

> I say this as a concession, not as a command. I wish that all men were as I am. But each man has his own gift from God; one has this gift, another has that. (1 CORINTHIANS 7:6–7)

Marriage is a gift from God. Singleness is a gift from God. Neither marriage nor singleness is the superior state. God has given the gift of marriage to some and the gift of singleness to others, and neither state is for all. God treats us as unique individuals, and He gives us the gift that is best suited for us as individuals.

Sex within marriage is a beautiful experience. But singleness without sex reflects the beauty of God in a different way; the single Christian is able to dedicate his or her life to God in a way that married people cannot. No one should ever feel that his or her status (whether married or single) is a superior or inferior status. God will work through your marital state to produce His beauty in your life.

Advice for the unmarried and for widows

Next, Paul turns to the question of those people who were once married but are now single. What are they to do with their sexuality?

> Now to the unmarried and the widows I say: It is good for them to stay unmarried, as I am. But if they cannot control themselves, they should marry, for it is better to marry than to burn with passion. (1 CORINTHIANS 7:8–9)

If you have been married and are no longer, your sexual life has been fully awakened in marriage. You are used to having these drives satisfied, and now you are deprived of that satisfaction by divorce or widowhood. This can create a problem for even the most spiritually mature believer.

You may have read Catherine Marshall's book *A Man Called Peter*, the story of her husband, the Reverend Dr. Peter Marshall, who served as chaplain of the United States Senate in the late 1940s. Mrs. Marshall wrote candidly that after her husband died suddenly when he was only forty-seven, she struggled with what to do about her awakened desires for sexual love that she had experienced with her husband. This was a real problem in her life, and it's a problem in the lives of many people who are no longer married.

The apostle Paul's counsel is, "It is good for them to stay unmarried, as I am." In other words, "As a single person, having learned a great deal from your life experiences, you can now give yourself more fully to the work of the Lord. If possible, look upon your new status as an opportunity to serve God in new ways."

But Paul's advice is not inflexible. He recognizes that the single life is not for everyone. "But if they cannot control themselves," he continues, "they should marry, for it is better to marry than to burn with passion." This is in line with the advice he gives in his letter to Timothy:

> So I counsel younger widows to marry, to have children, to manage their homes and to give the enemy no opportunity for slander. (1 TIMOTHY 5:14)

In Paul's day, just as in our own day, a young, unmarried widow was sometimes the subject of gossip. But a widow who remarried and managed her household well would give Satan ("the enemy") nothing to work with in spreading baseless rumors about her character. So Paul's best advice was that younger widows should not hesitate to remarry, if a godly and loving man could be found. Of course, Paul's counsel here should not be taken as a command for younger widows. He is making a generalization, and God deals with every person as a unique individual.

From Paul's teaching on sex in 1 Corinthians 6 and 7, we can see that the essence of sexual satisfaction in marriage consists of three ingredients.

1. *Love for God.* The body is made for the Lord, as we see in 1 Corinthians 6:19–20. God's eternal plan for the body should govern our sexual behavior and thinking.

2. *Unselfish love for our mate.* We should be willing to put the needs of our partner ahead of our own sexual wants and needs. Sex is a gift we bring to our marriage partner, not a demand we make. In a healthy marriage, the husband and wife give gifts of love to one another on a continual basis. In our sex lives and our daily lives, we should continually find ways to say, "You're important to me. I appreciate you. I love you."

3. *Mutual respect.* The wife's body does not belong to her alone; the husband's body does not belong to him alone. They mutually belong to one another, and they respect and honor one another.

When two distinct individuals, husband and wife, unite in the Lord, their union is one of the most beautiful of all of God's earthly creations. There is only one thing more beautiful than the sweet and ecstatic love of two newlyweds, and that is the sweet and joyous love of a husband and wife who have grown old together in the Lord. Such a union is a blessing to all who see it. It is the ultimate demonstration of God's beautiful plan for marriage.

God hates divorce

I once saw a newspaper cartoon depicting a father talking to his daughter just before the wedding. She's in her bridal gown, he's in his tuxedo, ready to give the bride away—and he leans over to her and says, "Try to make the marriage last, dear, at least until the wedding is paid for."

Many people have such an attitude toward marriage. In wedding ceremonies, the vow to remain faithfully wedded "as long as we both shall live" has been replaced with a vow to stay together "as long as we both shall love." These couples anticipate a day when they fall out of love—and on that day, they will end the marriage.

Some say, "A marriage license is just a scrap of paper." Well, that's true. But when we place a commitment behind it, a scrap of paper can be very important. The paycheck you receive from your employer is just a scrap of paper—but you can use it to pay your mortgage and buy groceries. The deed to your home is just a scrap of paper—but it's also an iron-clad guarantee of your little piece of the American dream. The United States Constitution is just a scrap of paper, but it sets forth our rights and our form of government. A scrap of paper is what we make of it—and so is a marriage.

Paul now addresses the problem of divorce in Corinth. Though divorce was rare in the Jewish culture at that time, it was commonplace among the Greeks and Romans. Women could divorce their husbands as easily as men could divorce their wives. Divorce was accepted in the pagan culture of Corinth, and this attitude had infected the Corinthian church. So Paul writes:

> To the married I give this command (not I, but the Lord): A wife must not separate from her husband. But if she does, she must remain unmarried or else be reconciled to her husband. And a husband must not divorce his wife. (1 CORINTHIANS 7:10–11)

Paul begins with the fundamental position of Scripture: marriage is for life. People will say, "But what if a couple is hopelessly incompatible?" Well, I have a news flash: *All* couples are incompatible! There are personality conflicts and background differences and philosophical incompatibilities in every relationship. But God still says that marriage is for life. After all, that's what Christlike love is for: It's the industrial-strength lubricant that enables two incompatible personalities to mesh without grinding each other to pieces.

Paul's statements on divorce are clear and strong. He says, "To the married I give this command (not I, but the Lord)." He goes back to the Lord's own recorded words and quotes the teaching of Jesus on divorce. These words are found in the Gospels in Matthew 5 and 19 and in Mark 10.

God makes it clear in both the Old and New Testaments what He thinks of divorce. For example, we read, "'I hate divorce,' says the LORD God of Israel" (Malachi 2:16a). God hates divorce. Why? Because divorce hurts people; it is especially hurtful to children. God hates divorce because He loves people.

Having said that, we must recognize that God permits divorce to take place. God permits what He hates. This seems paradoxical, yet God permits many things He hates. God hates sin, but He allows it to continue in our race, and He allows people to make wrong decisions even though He hates the decisions they make.

Throughout the Scriptures, we see the permissive will of God at work. The Bible tells us that God is "not willing that any should perish, but that all should come to repentance" (2 Peter 3:9 KJV). It is God's will that no one perish, that no one go into eternity apart from Him—yet all who reject faith in Jesus Christ will perish and are already perishing.

This is how Jesus explained God's view of divorce to the Pharisees when they attempted to trap Him:

> "Why then," they [the Pharisees] asked, "did Moses command that a man give his wife a certificate of divorce and send her away?"
>
> Jesus replied, "Moses permitted you to divorce your wives because your hearts were hard. But it was not this way from the beginning." (MATTHEW 19:7–8)

It's important to understand that it was not Moses who permitted divorce in Israel; it was God speaking through Moses—and God, who hates divorce, permitted divorce to take place in response to the hardness of some of the Israelites' hearts. Moses was a prophet who spoke for God with prophetic authority, much as the apostle Paul spoke for God with apostolic authority. Any realistic discussion of marriage and divorce must face the fact that God allows divorce, and under some circumstances He permits remarriage after divorce.

The Lord Jesus acknowledges this truth. He says it is hardness of heart that creates the conditions that lead to divorce. What is hardness of heart? This phrase refers to a stubborn and willful refusal to listen to what God has to say and a determination to go your own way. A soft heart is open to instruction and to the Word and Spirit of God. A hardened heart is rigid, unteachable, and unwilling to hear and obey God's Word and Spirit.

You see it in the case of the pharaoh of Egypt. Every time Moses went to Pharaoh, demanding the liberation of his people, Pharaoh hardened his heart. He became willful and stubborn and refused the word of God that came to him through God's servant, Moses.

A hardened heart can turn a marriage into a living hell. A marriage partner may harden his or her heart by refusing to change a pattern of abusive behavior, or by refusing to end an adulterous relationship, or by refusing to give up alcohol or addictive drugs. A marriage partner with a hardened heart may endanger the spouse and children in many ways—through overt violence, or through gambling away the family's paycheck, or through driving while intoxicated (just to name a few examples).

When a hard-hearted partner becomes a threat to the innocent spouse and other family members, it may well be time to end the marriage. Paul states God's ideal will for every marriage—then follows with a recognition of God's permissive will regarding divorce. He writes, "A wife must not separate from her husband. But if she does . . ." This is Paul's recognition that some marriages become emotionally unbearable and even physically dangerous. Such marriages must be ended.

I have counseled abused spouses (overwhelmingly wives, but sometimes husbands are victims of abuse). I have seen women who have been beaten by their husbands so that their bodies are a mass of bruises and their eyes are so swollen they cannot see. God does not intend for His children to subject themselves to that kind of life-threatening abuse. When there is violence in the relationship, it is perfectly proper and wise for her to leave that marriage—at least for a while and possibly forever. Sometimes when a wife leaves, the husband comes to his senses and gets into counseling, and God is finally able to soften his heart.

The apostle Paul seems to acknowledge this reality—but he also adds some strict controls to the situation. He says, "But if she does [separate], she must remain unmarried or else be reconciled to her husband." She may leave temporarily (a separation), or she may even divorce her husband—yet in God's sight, Paul says, the marriage is not broken. In other words, she is not to remarry because even though she would be divorced in the eyes of the court, she would remain married in God's eyes—and remarriage would be a form of adultery.

While her mate lives and remains unmarried, she is not to remarry, because this allows for the possibility that God's grace can still work to restore the marriage (this principle applies to husbands who separate or divorce as well as wives). I have seen instances where wives or husbands separated and waited patiently for years with little hope of reconciliation—then God performed a miracle and restored the marriage.

What about adultery?

You might say, "What about sexual infidelity? Didn't Jesus say that adultery breaks a marriage?" Yes, Matthew's gospel records that Jesus said,

> "But I tell you that anyone who divorces his wife, except for marital unfaithfulness, causes her to become an adulteress, and anyone who marries the divorced woman commits adultery." (MATTHEW 5:32)

These words of Jesus underscore how important sex is in a marriage. When a person expresses his or her sexuality outside of marriage, it breaks the marriage. So Jesus, in His teaching on divorce, makes an exception in the case of adultery.

Why doesn't Paul mention this exception in his teaching on divorce? I believe it's because he has just dealt at length with the subject of sex in marriage. He has pointed out how central the sexual union is to marriage. He has even warned couples not to deny sex to each other, because sex is central to the working out of God's purposes in marriage. Because Paul has already referred to our Lord's teaching on marriage and divorce, he feels no need to do so again here. The exception that the Lord granted in Matthew 5:32 was undoubtedly known in the early church, so Paul does not mention it here.

The sin of adultery can be repented of and forgiven. A marriage broken by adultery can be restored. I have seen it happen in many marriages. But if there is no repentance, then the marriage is broken. A divorce granted on this basis frees an individual to remarry because the previous marriage was ended by the infidelity of the sinning partner. Remarriage is not permitted on any other grounds, and God expects Christians to obey His commands.

God designed marriage as a kind of a locked room into which he thrusts a couple who think they know each other very well. He locks the door and says, "Now you're going to *really* get to know each other!" Marriage is meant to provide an unbreakable bond for working out your differences and difficulties so that you can both grow to be more loving, forgiving, accepting, mature, and Christlike.

Spiritually mixed marriages

Paul has answered questions of marriage, singleness, and divorce. Now he takes up the issue of people who are in spiritually mixed marriages in which one partner is a believer and the other an unbeliever. This was a major issue in the Corinthian church, since many people had been converted from a pagan belief system; frequently, one marriage partner would become a Christian while the other would remain an idol worshiper. So Paul writes:

> To the rest I say this (I, not the Lord): If any brother has a wife who is not a believer and she is willing to live with him, he must not divorce her. And if a woman has a husband who is not a believer and he is willing to live with her, she must not divorce him. For the unbelieving husband has been sanctified through his wife, and the unbelieving wife has been sanctified through her believing husband. Otherwise your children would be unclean, but as it is, they are holy. But if the unbeliever leaves, let him do so. A believing man or woman is not bound in such circumstances; God has called us to live in peace. How do you know, wife, whether you will save your husband? Or, how do you know, husband, whether you will save your wife? (1 CORINTHIANS 7:12–16)

When Paul says he is speaking, not the Lord, he is not saying that his apostolic word represents an inferior level of authority. He is saying that Jesus did not speak directly to this issue in the Gospels; Paul's word, which is based on his authority as an apostle, is still God's word on the subject, because an apostle speaks for God.

What does Paul say to a believer married to a nonbeliever? He says that the marriage is just as sacred and binding as if both partners were Christians.

Christians have come to me and said, "We got married when we were both non-Christians. Now I'm a Christian and he (or she) is not, and the relationship is difficult. Since our marriage was not 'in the Lord,' I think I should be free to get a divorce." But God didn't give marriage to believers only; He gave marriage to the human race. Regardless of whether a husband and wife were believers when they were married, God recognizes their marriage as valid and binding.

Paul goes on to say that there is a positive value in remaining married to an unbelieving spouse: "For the unbelieving husband has been sanctified through his wife, and the unbelieving wife has been sanctified through her believing husband." Paul says that the unbelieving mate is sanctified—that is, set apart for special treatment by the Lord. Understand, Paul is not saying that unbelievers can be saved by the faith of a believing spouse. Every individual must make a choice to accept Christ; no one makes that choice for anyone else.

But a believing marriage partner can bring God's blessing and intervention into the life of a nonbelieving partner. That nonbelieving partner will receive the benefit of prayer, a loving witness, and the blessing of being ministered to by a believer who is indwelt by the Holy Spirit. Over time, it may be difficult for that nonbeliever to resist the witness of a believing spouse.

Paul goes on to say that the believing spouse is able to sanctify his or her children, even if the children's other parent is a nonbeliever. They will be exposed to a Christian witness and Christian ministry, and they will be prayed for by a Christian parent. Divorce is extremely destructive to children; it tears their world in half and often forces them to choose between Mom and Dad. If you, as a believing spouse, are able to maintain an intact marriage in spite of all difficulties (as long as neither you nor your children are threatened or endangered), then you'll enable your children to receive many blessings from God in the form of prayer, witness, and ministry to their needs.

In some cases, however, the unbelieving spouse will not accept being married to a Christian. The newfound faith of the Christian marriage partner often becomes a source of division, anger, and conflict in the marriage. The unbeliever says, "I don't want to be married to a Christian! I'm divorcing you!" In such cases, Paul says, "But if the unbeliever leaves, let him do so. A believing man or woman is not bound in such circumstances; God has called us to live in peace."

When Paul says, "God has called us to peace," he acknowledges that the continual antagonism and chafing between two people of different faiths can be damaging to a marriage. If the unbeliever takes the initiative and wants to leave, let him leave. This will dissolve the marriage, but at least it will allow both parties to live in peace. But if the two partners can live together in spite of their differing faiths, then there is at least the possibility that God can bless and convert the unbeliever: "How do you know, wife, whether you will save your husband? Or, how do you know, husband, whether you will save your wife?"

Don't be a slave to men

Next, Paul tells us how to handle difficult situations that arise in marriage and in other realms of life:

> Nevertheless, each one should retain the place in life that the Lord assigned to him and to which God has called him. This is the rule I lay down in all the churches. Was a man already circumcised when he was called? He should not become uncircumcised. Was a man uncircumcised when he was called? He should not be circumcised. Circumcision is nothing and uncircumcision is nothing. Keeping God's commands is what counts. Each one should remain in the situation which he was in when God called him. Were you a slave when you were called? Don't let it trouble you—although if you can gain your freedom, do so. For he who was a slave when he was called by the Lord is the Lord's freedman; similarly, he who was a free man when he was called is Christ's slave. You were bought at a price; do not become slaves of men. Brothers, each man, as responsible to God, should remain in the situation God called him to. (1 CORINTHIANS 7:17–24)

God has assigned each of us a place in life—and, if we are honest, we have to acknowledge that we have made choices that have put us where we are. God works through the choices we make, not to hurt us or control us but to allow us free will. There is a paradox at work in our lives: Even though we have free will, God is sovereign, and He is able to work out His eternal plan even through the choices we make. Nothing we do, not even our sin, is able to thwart His sovereign plan for human history.

You may not be where you want to be, but you are where you are because of your choices and because God oversees your life. So, Paul says, don't fight God's will for your life. Remain in the place He has assigned. Remember Paul's words at the beginning of this letter: "God, who has called you into fellowship with his Son Jesus Christ our Lord, is faithful" (1 Corinthians 1:9). That is our calling! God has placed us wherever we are so that we can experience fellowship with His Son.

Obviously, Paul is not saying that if you were in a sinful occupation before your conversion, you should continue in that occupation as a believer. If you were a drug dealer, a prostitute, an exotic dancer, a pornographer, or a thief, then God has clearly called you out of your life of sin and into a new profession. When Paul says that you should remain in the place God has assigned to you, he is speaking of your situation in life, not your occupation.

Were you circumcised before you became a Christian? Uncircumcised? Tattooed? These are mere marks in the flesh. The only thing that matters is your obedience to God.

Slavery was a major feature of the ancient Greek and Roman cultures. Paul says that the question of whether you are slave or free is not the overriding consideration of life. It's what you are inside that counts. If God makes it possible for a slave to gain his or her freedom, the slave should take it as a gift of God.

But whether you are a slave or free, your circumstances are external. Jesus lives within you. He will enable you to bear the unbearable and endure the unendurable. Regardless of the state in which you were called, remain in that state and endure it in God's strength. "You were bought at a price," Paul says. "Do not become slaves of men."

You might be in a difficult marriage; as long as your life or your children's lives are not in danger, don't seek to leave that marriage. What about a difficult job? Or a troubled church? Or a secular culture that is hostile to your Christian faith? Don't seek to leave that situation. Seek to become God's minister of grace in that situation.

When you focus on your circumstances, you give people power over you—and you become a slave of men. But when you focus on Jesus and His power within you, then you become a slave of Christ. He purchased your life at the cost of His own blood. Make sure that you are a slave to Him alone.

9

SINGLE BUT NOT ALONE

1 Corinthians 7:25–40

Gladys Aylward dedicated her life to God at a revival service in London in 1930. Soon afterward, with less than ten dollars in her handbag, she set out for China to help an aging missionary woman with her work. Traveling alone, a woman in her mid-twenties, Gladys made the perilous journey by train, bus, ship, and mule. She arrived in the city of Yangchen, where she helped the elderly missionary woman turn an old building into an inn. Whenever travelers came to the inn, the two Christian women provided food and lodging—and they told the weary lodgers about Jesus Christ.

Though Gladys didn't know a word of Chinese when she arrived, she quickly learned the language. Together, Gladys and the missionary woman saw many people come to Christ. Before long, the older woman died, but Gladys continued running the inn with the help of a Chinese Christian man who served as the chef.

Through her work at the inn, Gladys Aylward became acquainted with the mandarin (high government official) of Yangchen. The mandarin called upon Gladys to resolve the problem of repeated riots at the local prison. She told him to improve conditions and give the prisoners meaningful work to do, and the riots would end. The mandarin implemented her plan—and the riots stopped. From then on, the mandarin referred to Gladys Aylward by a Chinese name, Ai-weh-deh, which meant "The Virtuous One."

Gladys became a Chinese citizen in 1936. She lived a simple life and dressed in the Chinese style. She became acquainted with a Welsh missionary couple in the nearby town of Tsechow—and when she saw how happy this husband-and-wife missionary team was, she realized for the first time that she was lonely. So Gladys Aylward began to pray for a husband. She asked God to call an Englishman to come out to China, meet her, fall in love, and propose marriage—but no Englishman ever came. After a couple of years of praying without result, she confided to a friend, "I know that God answers prayer, so I believe God has told my Englishman to come to China—but he must not have obeyed God's call!"

In 1938, Imperial Japan invaded China. Japanese airplanes bombed the city of Yangchen, causing many deaths and forcing the townspeople to flee to the mountains. Gladys Aylward gathered ninety-four orphans and led them on a harrowing twelve-day trek over the mountains, eventually bringing the children to safety on the far side of the Yellow River. In 1947, she returned to England for health reasons but soon returned to China, eventually settling in the island province of Taiwan. Her story was made into a movie, *The Inn of the Sixth Happiness*, starring Ingrid Bergman. Gladys died a single woman in 1970, having never found her Englishman to marry.

Though single all her life, Gladys Aylward once remarked that she was sometimes lonely but never alone. Her life is a witness to the truth that the apostle Paul now brings us.

The blessings of singleness

In the closing paragraphs of 1 Corinthians 7, Paul writes of two advantages of the single life (verses 26–35), while also acknowledging the difficulties and pressures of being single (verses 36–40). He writes:

> Now about virgins [i.e., the unmarried]: I have no command from the Lord, but I give a judgment as one who by the Lord's mercy is trustworthy. Because of the present crisis, I think that it is good for you to remain as you are. Are you married? Do not seek a divorce. Are you unmarried? Do not look for a wife. But if you do marry, you have not sinned; and if a virgin marries, she has not sinned. But those who marry will face many troubles in this life, and I want to spare you this.
> (1 Corinthians 7:25–28)

Here Paul says that he does not have a command from the Lord; in other words, there is no moral issue connected with being single. He has already talked about the morality of dealing with sexual temptation, both for married and unmarried people, so here he is speaking merely about the practical aspects of being single. Even though Paul says he does not speak with a command from the Lord, the fact that he addresses the matter indicates that he has been asked for guidance by the Corinthian church.

Paul states that there are practical advantages in being unmarried. Note this key phrase: "Because of the present crisis . . ." In view of the crisis of persecution against Christians that was taking place across the Roman world, the unmarried state offered certain benefits. In truth, the church has always been living through times of crisis and persecution, and the church lives in dangerous times today.

The World Evangelical Alliance reports that two hundred million Christians worldwide suffer discrimination and persecution in Africa, the Arab world, and Asia. In many nations, national governments sponsor torture, murder, and even human slavery against Christians. Some governments have labeled Christian groups as evil sects and have sent pastors and other believers to labor camps.

So the advice Paul gives to the Corinthian believers is still timely today, in our own troubled world, in our own present crisis. During times of trouble, Paul says, the single life offers three distinct advantages. In these verses, he presents the first of those three practical blessings of the single life:

> What I mean, brothers, is that the time is short. From now on those who have wives should live as if they had none; those who mourn, as if they did not; those who are happy, as if they were not; those who buy something, as if it were not theirs to keep; those who use the things of the world, as if not engrossed in them. For this world in its present form is passing away. (1 CORINTHIANS 7:29–31)

The first advantage of singleness is this: *The single person is flexible and can respond quickly to God's call.* Time is short, and the world is passing away. Married people, who have acquired possessions and responsibilities—"the things of this world"—can easily become engrossed and entangled by them, so that they cannot respond to rapidly changing events. But the single person can hold the things of this world loosely and respond to change quickly. If God says, "Go!" a single person can go to another part of the world without the problems and expenses that come with a spouse, a house, children, pets, furniture, dishes, and the like.

Next, Paul describes for us a second advantage of singleness:

> I would like you to be free from concern. An unmarried man is concerned about the Lord's affairs—how he can please the Lord. But a married man is concerned about the affairs of this world—how he can please his wife—and his interests are divided. An unmarried

woman or virgin is concerned about the Lord's affairs: Her aim is to be devoted to the Lord in both body and spirit. But a married woman is concerned about the affairs of this world—how she can please her husband. I am saying this for your own good, not to restrict you, but that you may live in a right way in undivided devotion to the Lord. (1 CORINTHIANS 7:32–35)

The second blessing of the single life is this: *The single person can focus on devotion to God and to godly spiritual priorities.* A single person is not weighed down with concerns and responsibilities for a spouse and children and can be completely devoted to the Lord. This can be a great advantage for a person who feels called to a life of full-time ministry for God.

Does this mean that married people don't have to be devoted Christians? Certainly not! The spiritual priorities we find in the Bible—such as the Great Commandment to love God and love others, and the Great Commission to take the good news of Jesus Christ throughout the world—are binding on us all as believers, married or single. Paul's point is that it is easier to be focused on these priorities if we are single.

"The time is short," Paul says. He may be referring to the believer's expectation that the Lord could return at any moment, or he may refer to the fact that human beings have only seven or eight decades, on average, to live their lives in service to God—then it's over. Clearly, the Christian's approach to life should be, "I will use the brief span of my life for eternal purposes. The aim and center of my life shall not merely be to make a living but to make a life—a life that counts for Jesus Christ."

Paul wants us to arrange our priorities around the kingdom of heaven, and that is why he says there are practical advantages to being single. He's not encouraging husbands or wives to neglect their responsibilities to children and home. Rather, he's saying that we need to keep all the aspects of our life in proper focus, with our spiritual priorities first. Don't spend all your time pleasing your spouse, or maintaining your home, or enjoying this present life. Make sure you are living for eternity.

What the world owes to single people

The world owes an incalculable debt to Christian men and women who have chosen to remain single for the Lord's sake. John R. W. Stott is a great English preacher and a godly, saintly, single man. He is the author of more than forty books, including *Basic Christianity* and *The Cross of Christ*, and he served as chaplain to Queen Elizabeth II from 1959 to 1991. God's gift of singleness may be the principal reason he spends two or three hours every morning in Bible study, prayer, and worship and the reason he's had such a powerful impact for Christ in our time. As a married man and father, I can't spend two or three hours a day on devotional pursuits, but I'm grateful for men like John Stott who do.

The world owes a debt to Henrietta Mears, an energetic woman who dreamed big and accomplished the impossible many times over. She chose never to be married so that she might have time to study and teach God's Word. She spearheaded an effort to acquire a privately owned resort in the San Bernardino Mountains and transform it into a Christian retreat center, Forest Home. She founded the first Christian education publishing house, Gospel Light Publications. She founded the Hollywood Christian Group, a Bible study and fellowship group for people in the entertainment industry. Through that group she led many Hollywood entertainers to Christ. She also served on the staff of Hollywood Presbyterian Church for many years.

God used Henrietta Mears in a profound way when she mentored a young man from North Carolina who came to Forest Home with a soul full of doubts and struggles. Through Miss Mears's prayers and encouragement, this young man solidified a decision to serve God for the rest of his life. That young man, whose name was Billy Graham, later said, "I doubt if any other woman, besides my wife and my mother, ever had such a marked influence on my life. Henrietta Mears is certainly one of the greatest Christians I've ever known." Her greatness is undoubtedly due to her intense devotion to God, made possible by God's gift of singleness in her life.

The world owes a debt to so many others who exercised God's gift of singleness in their lives. C. S. Lewis didn't marry until he reached his sixties; he gave the world a rich array of books that probe the depths of Christian truth, from *Mere Christianity* to *The Screwtape Letters*. He also gave the world the gift of imaginative, inspirational fantasy in *The Chronicles of Narnia* and *Out of the Silent Planet*.

Then there is Robert Murray McChayne of Scotland, the saintly young preacher of the nineteenth century who converted and transformed thousands of lives throughout the British Isles by his godliness. He chose not to marry so that he could devote himself fully to his study of the Word and his preaching ministry. Though he died at age thirty, his influence continues to reverberate down through the ages.

And there is the prolific Canadian-born hymn writer Edith Margaret Clarkson, who remained single throughout her life. She was afflicted with juvenile arthritis and migraine headaches but was an attractive young woman, blessed with an amazingly creative and retentive mind. She authored many beloved hymns, including one of my favorites, "We Come O Christ to Thee."

Singleness was a struggle for Miss Clarkson in her early years. Like most girls, she had a glowing mental image of her wedding day from an early age. In time she realized that God had called her to a single life. Though reluctant at first, she ultimately embraced her singleness as a gift from God. In an article entitled "Single But Not Alone," she observed, "To know God, to know beyond the shadow of a doubt that He is sovereign and that my life is in His care: this is the unshakable foundation on which I stay my soul. Such knowledge has deep significance for the single Christian."

Paul himself exemplified what God can do through a life that is single-mindedly devoted to Him. As a single man, unencumbered by responsibilities to a wife and family, Paul was able to travel the length and breadth of the Roman Empire, preaching the gospel and planting churches. Out of that intense dedication of spirit and devotion of heart, he lived a life of moral purity, using his time and energy to write the remarkable letters that have changed the history of the world.

Those who choose the single life are not second-class citizens of the kingdom of God. In fact, they are free to serve God in ways that married people cannot. As Paul has previously noted, "Those who marry will face many troubles in this life, and I want to spare you this." If you choose not to marry in order to devote yourself fully to God, then you have made a noble choice that God will surely honor.

When I was a new Christian, I was inspired by the story of evangelist Dwight L. Moody. In his biography, I read that one of his favorite Scripture passages was this one:

> Do not love the world or anything in the world. If anyone loves the world, the love of the Father is not in him. For everything in the world—the cravings of sinful man, the lust of his eyes and the boasting of what he has and does—comes not from the Father but from the world. The world and its desires pass away, but the man who does the will of God lives forever. (1 JOHN 2:15-17)

Here the apostle John makes the same point Paul has been making: Don't live for the things of this world, which will pass away. Live to do the eternal will of God. Whatever you do in His name and according to His purpose will never pass away.

The pressures of singleness

Paul is a realist. He knows it's not easy to be single. He concludes his discussion of singleness by addressing one of the most difficult problems of the single life, the pressure of sexual temptation:

> If anyone thinks he is acting improperly toward the virgin he is engaged to, and if she is getting along in years and he feels he ought to marry, he should do as he wants. He is not sinning. They should get married. But the man who has settled the matter in his own mind, who is under no compulsion but has control over his own will, and who has made up his mind not to marry the virgin—this man also does the right thing. So then, he who marries the virgin does right, but he who does not marry her does even better. (1 CORINTHIANS 7:36–38)

This passage addresses the quandary that some Corinthian believers no doubt faced: Here is an engaged couple, planning for marriage—but now Paul says to them, "Because of the present crisis, I think that it is good for you to remain as you are.... Are you unmarried? Do not look for a wife." So they ask themselves, "Should we go forward and be married—or, in view of the present crisis, should we remain single?"

Paul's answer: If they find it difficult to keep their passions under control, then it is better for them to marry. It is not a sin to get married. But if these two people have the gift of self-control and can master their passions and resist temptation, then there will be spiritual advantages for them to remain single. Those who marry do right, Paul says—but those who can remain single do even better.

Finally, Paul writes:

> A woman is bound to her husband as long as he lives. But if her husband dies, she is free to marry anyone she wishes, but he must belong to the Lord. In my judgment, she is happier if she stays as she is—and I think that I too have the Spirit of God. (1 CORINTHIANS 7:39–40)

Paul writes here of an older woman, a widow whose husband has died. Now she is alone and facing the declining years of her life. She misses the companionship and fellowship she experienced with her husband. Paul

116

says she is free to marry—but she must be careful to marry a believer, someone with whom she can share her faith and devotion to God.

Though Paul permits such a woman to remarry, he also observes that in his judgment, such a woman is likely to be happier if she remains unmarried. Why? Because she is a mature woman who has learned the secret of living for God. Now that she is single, she has more time and fewer responsibilities, and she can devote herself fully to the Lord. This is a golden opportunity for her to find a renewed sense of adventure and excitement in her Christian faith. Paul backs up his opinion with apostolic authority: "And I think that I too have the Spirit of God," he says.

Marriage is a good and honorable status—but so is the single life. Neither state is intrinsically more spiritual or godly than the other. We are all unique individuals, and God deals with each of us in an individual way. He calls some to marriage, others to singleness. Some (like C. S. Lewis) he calls into marriage very late in life. Others may spend most of their lives in a married state, only to discover the advantages of singleness after being widowed in their golden years.

The most important factor in life is not whether or not we are married but whether or not we have aligned our lives with God's priorities. Whether single or married, God calls us to live not for this passing world but for the world to come. Because we belong to Christ, we know that, whether single or married, we are never lonely, because in Him we are never alone.

10

YOUR LIBERTY AND YOUR INFLUENCE

1 Corinthians 8:1–9:23

In Fyodor Dostoevsky's novel, *The Brothers Karamazov*, there is a famous parable told by Ivan, an atheist, to his brother Alyosha, a Christian monk. The parable is called "The Grand Inquisitor."

It is the time of the Spanish Inquisition. Every day, throughout the city of Seville, the Inquisition lights great bonfires to execute heretics—people who break the strict laws of the oppressive institutional church. So many heretics are burned in these fires that the pavement is still hot the following day.

Then a Man comes into the city. The blind call out to Him and receive their sight. The sick touch the hem of His garment and are healed. He raises a dead girl from her coffin. All the people recognize Him and are drawn to Him, because infinite compassion radiates from Him. There is no doubt about it: This Man is Jesus.

Before long, Jesus is arrested and thrown into prison. The Grand Inquisitor, an aging cardinal of the church, goes to visit Jesus in His prison cell. He tells Jesus that the church no longer needs Him. Why? Because Jesus came to set people free—and people can't handle the freedom Jesus brings them. Liberty, the Grand Inquisitor says, is a burden that only makes people unhappy. The people can be happy only by surrendering their liberty to the Inquisition.

Jesus remains silent while the Grand Inquisitor defends his long career of imprisoning, torturing, and executing heretics. Finally, without a word, Jesus kisses the Inquisitor—a symbol that Jesus wants even this murderous man to experience the freedom of forgiveness.

But the Grand Inquisitor's heart remains unchanged. He sends Jesus away, telling Him never to return. Jesus goes out into the dark alleys of the city while the Grand Inquisitor continues his reign of torture, terror, and death, feverishly trying to stamp out every last vestige of the Christian liberty that Jesus freely gives.

Throughout the letters of Paul, and particularly in Romans, Galatians, and 1 Corinthians, the apostle makes it clear that the essence of the Christian life can be characterized by one word: liberty. Once we were captives to the Law and to sin. Then Jesus died to set us free. The Christian is called to liberty in Jesus Christ. While the Grand Inquisitor of legalism seeks to keep us in bondage to rules and laws, Jesus has broken our chains and given us our liberty.

In 1 Corinthians 8, we come to another question the Corinthians put to Paul. The exact wording of their question is lost to history, but from Paul's answer, we can tell that their question must have been something like: "If Christ has set me free from the Law, what should I do when other people impose their legalistic views on me? Must I limit my liberty to accommodate the narrow-mindedness of legalistic Christians?"

The gray areas of life

Paul now tackles a problem every Christian in every era has had to face. People in the church differ widely over gray areas in life. In 1 Corinthians 8, the gray area concerns meat that has been sacrificed to idols: Is it a sin for a Christian to eat sacrificial meat or not? In other times, the gray areas have been different: Is social dancing an innocent pastime or a sin? What about playing card games? Going to the movies? Listening to rock music? Watching football on Sunday? Women wearing makeup and jewelry? Tattoos and piercings? Drums and guitars in the worship service?

Here's a big issue of contention: Drinking alcohol. The Bible condemns drunkenness but says nothing against drinking in moderation. In fact, Jesus drank wine and even made wine at the wedding in Cana. Yet many Christians are utterly convinced that even moderate drinking is a sin. I have known Christians who claimed that the Lord and His disciples drank grape juice, not fermented wine. Where is the scriptural evidence to support this view? There is none! In fact, in a warm country like Palestine, it is impossible to keep grape juice from fermenting.

Two of the most famous preachers in nineteenth-century England were Charles Haddon Spurgeon and Joseph Parker. They were close friends who sometimes held evangelistic meetings together. But they also had disagreements. On one occasion, Spurgeon learned that Parker had attended the theater in London. Spurgeon confronted his friend and said, "A truly spiritual Christian knows that it's worldly to attend the theater."

119

Parker chuckled. "Tell me, Charles—what's that hanging out of your mouth?"

Spurgeon puffed on his cigar. "Surely, you don't suggest there's anything wrong with having a smoke?"

Parker said, "Many Christians would say that a truly spiritual Christian should know that it's worldly to go around smoking like a chimney!"

Both men eventually agreed that there was not a word in the Bible against either the theater or a good cigar and that they would have to tolerate each other's Christian liberty in these gray areas of life.

Reasonable, godly Christians can and do disagree on many issues. The question is, "How much should I adjust my actions to suit my neighbor?" Paul answers this question regarding meat sacrificed to idols, but the principle that underlies his answer still applies to all the gray areas we face today.

Divided over meat

Paul begins by laying out the problem:

> Now about food sacrificed to idols: We know that we all possess knowledge. Knowledge puffs up, but love builds up. The man who thinks he knows something does not yet know as he ought to know. But the man who loves God is known by God. So then, about eating food sacrificed to idols: We know that an idol is nothing at all in the world and that there is no God but one. For even if there are so-called gods, whether in heaven or on earth (as indeed there are many "gods" and many "lords"), yet for us there is but one God, the Father, from whom all things came and for whom we live; and there is but one Lord, Jesus Christ, through whom all things came and through whom we live. (1 CORINTHIANS 8:1–6)

The best place to buy a good roast or steak in Corinth was right next to the pagan temple. There the pagans sacrificed animals, much as the Jews did in the Old Testament. The pagans reserved some of the meat for the priests and some for public sale. Everyone in town knew that if you ate meat, it was almost certainly meat that had been offered to an idol. So the question arose: "If a Christian eats meat offered to an idol, is he participating in idol worship?"

Some in the Corinthian church said, "Yes. If you enjoy a steak from the pagan butcher shop, you might as well be worshiping a pagan god! What's more, you're causing weak Christians to stumble in their faith, because they'll think there's nothing wrong with what you're doing! You'll cause them to sin, just as you're sinning."

Others said, "No. Meat is meat, and an idol is just a dead statue. You're not worshiping a pagan god—you're just having a steak! It's perfectly good meat, so enjoy!" Because of these contrasting views, there was a division in the church.

Does this conflict sound familiar to you? You may have encountered Christians who look upon some time-honored and widely accepted Christian practices as pagan. For example, I've know Christians who refused to have a Christmas tree in their house. They have concluded that the custom of decorating evergreen trees at Christmastime originated with some Germanic pagans who decorated trees at the winter solstice in honor of the Norse gods. (Many historians dispute this claim and believe that Christmas trees originated as a Christian symbol in sixteenth-century Switzerland.)

Other Christians refuse to allow Easter eggs in their Resurrection Day celebration, because they believe decorated eggs were involved in pagan festivals of springtime. They claim the egg, a symbol of fertility, was offered to a pagan goddess.

But where do we draw the line? Should we stop using the names of the days of the week? After all, the days were named for pagan gods. Sunday and Monday were originally dedicated to worship of the sun and the moon. Tuesday was named for the Norse god Tyr or Tiw. Wednesday was Woden's Day. Thursday was Thor's Day. Friday was the Day of Frige, the Norse goddess of beauty. While the other six days are named for Norse gods, Saturday managed to retain its association with Saturn, the Roman god of time. There are similar pagan associations with the names of many of the months—January is the month of the Roman god Janus, March is the month of the Roman god Mars, May is the month of the Greek goddess Maia, and so forth.

These ancient pagan associations are no longer a problem for us today—but you can see how this issue might be a difficult one to settle in a church that is surrounded by pagan idol worship. That's what the believers in Corinth wrestled with.

Freedom versus legalism

Paul recognized that the Corinthian church was divided into two groups, which we could call the Liberty Party and the Legalism Party. We could also call them the Strong Party and the Weak Party, respectively. Which group was right? To a degree, both were right—and both were wrong. Let's take a closer look.

First, there was the Liberty Party, the strong-faith group. These Christians boasted of their knowledge. Paul's response to them was, "We know that we all possess knowledge. Knowledge puffs up, but love builds up. The man who thinks he knows something does not yet know as he ought to know." What is the knowledge the Liberty Party boasted of? Paul states the attitude of this group in verse 4: "We know that an idol is nothing at all in the world and that there is no God but one."

The attitude of the Liberty Party was proud and boastful and could be stated this way: "We know there are no gods but God. We are not superstitious pagans, so there's no reason we shouldn't eat meat that was sacrificed to lifeless idols. Christians who have a problem with meat sacrificed to idols are just ignorant legalists with a weak faith. We believe in Christian liberty, and our faith is strong. Because of our knowledge, we don't need to live by a lot of senseless, silly rules."

Paul says, in effect, "What you say is true. There are no other gods. There is only one true God." He doesn't delve into the doctrine of the Trinity here, the great mystery that God is one God in three persons; he is not trying to teach doctrine in this passage. His goal is to resolve the issue of meat sacrificed to idols.

"For us there is but one God, the Father," Paul writes, "from whom all things came and for whom we live; and there is but one Lord, Jesus Christ, through whom all things came and through whom we live." In the Roman Empire, the deities were called gods, but Caesar was called Lord. Caesar was a man, yet the pagan Romans called him Lord. Much of the persecution of the early church involved the Christians' refusal to call Caesar Lord, a title they reserved for Jesus alone. So Paul affirms that there is one God, not many gods, and there is only one Lord.

So Paul says, in effect, "The knowledge you have is right—but there are two problems with knowledge. First, knowledge puffs up. It leads to pride and a sense of being superior to others. You in the Liberty Party look down your noses at those in the Legalism Party who lack your 'superior knowledge.' You knowledge has made you arrogant and condescending. Second, knowledge is incomplete. You think you understand all the relevant viewpoints and facts, but your knowledge is incomplete. You should not judge other people because you don't have all the facts."

Knowledge versus love

Paul is building up to an important principle: Knowledge cannot settle divisions in the church. In fact, knowledge tends to create divisions by puffing up human pride. So what can heal divisions and settle problems in the church? Love.

"Knowledge puffs up," Paul writes, "but love builds up." Love involves a willingness to get inside another person's skin, another person's viewpoint, and see the world through that person's eyes. Knowledge is self-centered: "I know such-and-such is true." Love is focused on others: "Because of my love for you, I want to know what you are thinking, what you are feeling, what you know to be true, what you need and want and desire." Love builds others up.

Moreover, love opens up a sense of intimacy with God. As Paul writes, "But the man who loves God is known by God." In other words, if you love God, then you are responding to the love God has for you—and you are known by Him as one of His own. Paul's appeal is this: Think about what God has done for you. Think of the thousands of times a day He manifests His love and faithfulness to you. As you think of His love for you, a feeling of humble gratitude will spring up within you. As you experience gratitude to God for all He has done in your life, you will realize that the people around you need to be treated with love and patience, just as God has treated you.

Since God has been so patient with you, how can you be critical and impatient toward others? God has patiently led you to a deeper understanding of His truth. He has waited for your lagging understanding and faltering faith to catch up.

Now other people are in the same position you were in. They don't have your knowledge, your understanding, your strong faith. You may be free, but they are struggling. How will you respond to your Christian brother or sister whose knowledge and faith lag a bit behind yours?

Free indeed!

In the first six verses of 1 Corinthians 8, Paul has set forth principles concerning liberty versus legalism and knowledge versus love. Now, in the last seven verses of the chapter, he shows us specifically how love should be lived out amid the problems and divisions in Corinth:

> But not everyone knows this. Some people are still so accustomed to idols that when they eat such food they think of it as having been

123

sacrificed to an idol, and since their conscience is weak, it is defiled. But food does not bring us near to God; we are no worse if we do not eat, and no better if we do. Be careful, however, that the exercise of your freedom does not become a stumbling block to the weak. For if anyone with a weak conscience sees you who have this knowledge eating in an idol's temple, won't he be emboldened to eat what has been sacrificed to idols? So this weak brother, for whom Christ died, is destroyed by your knowledge. When you sin against your brothers in this way and wound their weak conscience, you sin against Christ. Therefore, if what I eat causes my brother to fall into sin, I will never eat meat again, so that I will not cause him to fall. (1 CORINTHIANS 8:7–13)

Here Paul describes three distinct advantages of love over knowledge.

First, *love compensates for human weakness*. Paul acknowledges that the legalistic position is a position of weakness. Those whose conscience forbids them to eat meat sacrificed to idols, he says, have a weak conscience, and "since their conscience is weak, it is defiled." Their weak conscience needs instruction, training, and development. Those who lack liberty in Christ are weak.

The next question we have to ask ourselves is: How should I respond to my fellow Christian with the weak conscience? Before you answer, consider this: How do you respond whenever you encounter weakness? A baby is weak. A puppy is weak. A person who is sick or wounded is weak. Do you kick the weak in the face? Do you trample the weak? Do you show off your strength and make the weak feel ashamed of their weakness? Of course not. The Christian response toward the weak is one of compassion, not contempt.

Second, *love evaluates clearly*. Love enables us to separate the important from the trivial. When we love one another, we realize that the issues we thought were so important are meaningless compared with our love for our Christian brothers and sisters. Paul writes, "But food does not bring us near to God; we are no worse if we do not eat, and no better if we do." Ultimately, it matters little whether we eat meat or not, drink wine or not, smoke, dance, and wear jewelry or not. The things we indulge in are momentary and trivial; it's our love for God and love for others that lasts.

Third, *love for others equals love for Christ*. If we choose to flaunt our freedom at the expense of a weaker Christian, we are sinning against Christ. If we choose to act lovingly and considerately toward a weaker Christian, we are showing love for Christ. Paul writes, "Be careful, however, that the exercise of your freedom does not become a stumbling block to the weak. For if anyone with a weak conscience sees you who have this knowledge eating in an idol's temple, won't he be emboldened to eat what has been sacrificed to idols? So this weak brother, for whom Christ died, is destroyed by your knowledge. When you sin against your brothers in this way and wound their weak conscience, you sin against Christ."

Should the strong Christian always yield to the weak in order to keep the peace? No. It's healthy and edifying for Christians who are strong to gently and courteously voice their views. If the strong Christian never speaks up to talk about his Christian liberty, then every question in the church will be decided by those who are weak in the faith—the most narrow-minded and legalistic people in the church. That is unhealthy and would cause the gospel to become identified with legalism.

Arguments sometimes arise in the church not because a person's conscience is weak but because his prejudices have been inflamed. Such people are not in any danger of being led astray or having their faith damaged. They just want to have their own way, and they want to show others in the church who's the boss. That's a different matter. If we always yield to the bossiest and most intolerant people in the church, we are showing cowardice, not love. We should be careful not to always accommodate ourselves to the prejudices of the weakest brother in the church. Sometimes the most loving thing we can do for our fellow Christians is to respectfully challenge them to grow and embrace their Christian liberty.

Whatever we do should be done in love. If we live out our liberty, we should do so in Christian love. If we limit our liberty, we should do so in Christian love. If we have a glass of wine, we should do so only if we know that no one else at the table will be offended or harmed. If we abstain from wine, then we should do so out of a genuinely Christlike concern for others.

Jesus is the source of our liberty and the source of our love. Love limits liberty. As Paul writes in the conclusion of this section, "Therefore, if what I eat causes my brother to fall into sin, I will never eat meat again, so that I will not cause him to fall." Authentic Christlike love will sacrifice freedom, rights, and entitlements to meet the needs of others.

Rights—or wrongs?

As we move into 1 Corinthians 9, we find that Paul is still answering the question, "Is it right to eat meat that has been sacrificed to an idol?"

Another way to phrase this question: "How far should I go to accommodate the conscience of other people?" Or, "How far should I go to insist on my liberty and my rights?" As Paul continues:

> Am I not free? Am I not an apostle? Have I not seen Jesus our Lord? Are you not the result of my work in the Lord? Even though I may not be an apostle to others, surely I am to you! For you are the seal of my apostleship in the Lord. (1 CORINTHIANS 9:1–2)

Some Bible commentators think that Paul is defending his apostleship here. I don't he's defending his apostleship—he's asserting it! He knows that the Corinthian believers, whose church Paul founded, already accept and respect his apostleship. That's why they've come to him with these questions. They know he's the Lord's chosen spokesman, and they trust his apostolic authority.

He's saying, "Look at my example. I'm an apostle. I have seen the Lord Jesus with my own eyes on the road to Damascus. I founded the Corinthian church. And even though I have all the rights and prerogatives of an apostle, I do not insist on my rights. Why do you object to giving up a few of your rights when I have given up so many rights for your sakes?" Then he goes on to describe his rights as an apostle:

> This is my defense to those who sit in judgment on me. Don't we have the right to food and drink? Don't we have the right to take a believing wife along with us, as do the other apostles and the Lord's brothers and Cephas [Peter]? Or is it only I and Barnabas who must work for a living? (1 CORINTHIANS 9:3–6)

Here's Paul's answer to many questions people raise about those who labor in fulltime Christian ministry: "Should ministers be supported by a congregation?" There are many people who view ministers as parasites who make their living off of the collection plate instead of doing honest work. But Paul argues that one of the rights of a minister of the gospel is the right to earn a living in ministry. He has a right to the basic requirements of life—food and drink. He has a right to marry and take his wife with him on his journeys, just as other apostles do. And he has a right not to have to work at a secular job in order to make a living.

People have come to me and said, "Pastor Stedman, you have such an easy life. You're paid a fulltime salary, but you only work one day a week—Sunday. You have Monday through Saturday off! I wish I'd been a pastor so I wouldn't have to work so hard!" People are often unaware that many pastors work sixty, seventy, or more hours a week, and often sacrifice time with their families because of meetings, sermon preparation, counseling, visiting the sick, dealing with people in crisis, and so forth.

Paul says, "We have the right to be supported financially so that we can give our full time to Scripture study, prayer, meeting human needs, and preaching the Word." He then shows us the basis of that right:

> Who serves as a soldier at his own expense? Who plants a vineyard and does not eat of its grapes? Who tends a flock and does not drink of the milk? Do I say this merely from a human point of view? Doesn't the Law say the same thing? For it is written in the Law of Moses: "Do not muzzle an ox while it is treading out the grain." Is it about oxen that God is concerned? Surely he says this for us, doesn't he? Yes, this was written for us, because when the plowman plows and the thresher threshes, they ought to do so in the hope of sharing in the harvest. If we have sown spiritual seed among you, is it too much if we reap a material harvest from you? If others have this right of support from you, shouldn't we have it all the more? (1 CORINTHIANS 9:7–12a)

In a series of rhetorical questions, Paul makes his point clear: No one is expected to labor without reaping the rewards of his labor. Soldiers are not expected to pay for their own support. Those who work in a vineyard are allowed to enjoy a share of the fruit. A shepherd is entitled to a share of the milk, and a plowman is entitled to a share of the harvest. Why should a minister be treated differently from those professions?

Paul then cites a passage from the law of Moses (Deuteronomy 25:4): "Do not muzzle an ox while it is treading out the grain." This passage was a literal command of God concerning the humane treatment of animals. Paul quoted this passage, using it as a metaphor to describe the humane treatment of people, specifically ministers of the gospel.

This is a principle that runs throughout Scripture: If a minister labors among the people for their benefit, he has a right to be supported by the people. This is why finances are an important part of the life of a church: Money makes ministry possible.

The right to give up my rights

Just when it seems Paul is demanding his rights as a minister, he abruptly changes his tune:

127

But we did not use this right. On the contrary, we put up with anything rather than hinder the gospel of Christ. Don't you know that those who work in the temple get their food from the temple, and those who serve at the altar share in what is offered on the altar? In the same way, the Lord has commanded that those who preach the gospel should receive their living from the gospel. (1 CORINTHIANS 9:12b-14)

He says, "But we did not use this right." After hammering home the point that Paul, as a minister and an apostle, has a number of rights, he says he has relinquished those rights. These rights have belonged to full-time ministers ever since the Levites made temple sacrifices on behalf the people in Old Testament times. God commanded that those who worked in the temple should eat of the meat, meal, wine, and oil that were brought to the temple. Even so, Paul says he has willingly relinquished this right in order to prevent the gospel of Jesus Christ from being hindered.

This is the point Paul has been building up to throughout the first fourteen verses of 1 Corinthians 9. "I have a right to be supported as a minister but I did not exercise that right." Then he explains why:

But I have not used any of these rights. And I am not writing this in the hope that you will do such things for me. I would rather die than have anyone deprive me of this boast. Yet when I preach the gospel, I cannot boast, for I am compelled to preach. Woe to me if I do not preach the gospel! If I preach voluntarily, I have a reward; if not voluntarily, I am simply discharging the trust committed to me. What then is my reward? Just this: that in preaching the gospel I may offer it free of charge, and so not make use of my rights in preaching it. (1 CORINTHIANS 9:15–18)

There is a beautiful paradox in these words of the apostle Paul. He is telling the Corinthian Christians, "I would rather die than let you take away my right to give up my rights! The greatest right I have is the right to give up my rights!"

He goes on to say, "Yet when I preach the gospel, I cannot boast, for I am compelled to preach. Woe to me if I do not preach the gospel!" In other words, "I preach the gospel because I can't keep from preaching. If I don't preach, I'm miserable. So I can't boast for preaching the gospel—I can't help myself!"

I once heard of a missionary doctor who worked among leprosy patients in Africa. On a visit to England, he told friends about the appalling conditions he faced. Patients would arrive with foul, putrid, running sores. The stench was so bad he could barely stand it. Some of the patients he treated showed absolutely no gratitude.

One of the ladies listening to the doctor said, "I admire the love you have for these people to serve them as you do." He said, "Oh, no, it isn't love. To be candid, I don't feel an ounce of love toward these people." Surprised, the woman asked, "Then why do you do it?" His answer: "Duty."

There is nothing wrong with a sense of duty. There's nothing wrong with doing a job because we feel it must be done. That was Paul's motivation for preaching the gospel. "I am compelled to preach," he said. "Woe to me if I do not preach the gospel!"

But why preach without charge? You may recall that for much of his ministry, Paul earned his living as a tentmaker. During that time, he did not ask or receive support for his preaching ministry. Why? "If I preach voluntarily," he explained, "I have a reward; if not voluntarily, I am simply discharging the trust committed to me. What then is my reward? Just this: that in preaching the gospel I may offer it free of charge, and so not make use of my rights in preaching it." Paul preached for free to experience the joy of giving.

I was once invited by missionaries to speak at a Bible conference in the south of France. When they called, they said, "We can't afford to give you an honorarium." I said, "That's all right. I'll come anyway. Can you meet my travel expenses?" They said, "We'll certainly try."

So I went to France and spoke at a four-day conference at a convent south of Lyon. It was a great time of spiritual refreshment from the Word of God. At the close of the conference, my hosts said, "We have a check for you. We don't know if it will cover your expenses, but it's all the money we could raise." I looked at the check; it scarcely covered half of my expenses.

I turned the check over and endorsed it—then handed it back, saying, "Cash this and use the money to establish a fund to bring other speakers to minister in the future." The look of surprise and joy on their faces was all the reward I needed. That's the reward Paul talks about here.

Next, he goes on to speak of the glorious paradox of his life: Paul is free to voluntarily make himself a slave.

> Though I am free and belong to no man, I make myself a slave to everyone, to win as many as possible. To the Jews I became like a Jew, to win the Jews. To those under the law I became like one under the law (though I myself am not under the law), so as to win those under

the law. To those not having the law I became like one not having the law (though I am not free from God's law but am under Christ's law), so as to win those not having the law. To the weak I became weak, to win the weak. I have become all things to all men so that by all possible means I might save some. I do all this for the sake of the gospel, that I may share in its blessings. (1 CORINTHIANS 9:19–23)

"I'm an apostle, I'm free," he says in effect, "but I don't hold on to my rights as an apostle. Instead, I surrender my freedom and make myself a slave in order to win as many people as possible for Christ. If that means I must be Jewish to reach the Jews, then I'll observe all the Jewish rituals and ceremonies. If that means I have to live like a legalist in order to reach those who are under the law of Moses, I'll do so. I'll do whatever I must to save as many as I can." Paul selflessly accommodated himself to others, and that is how we all should live.

A young Christian once said to me, "I don't like to be told that I can't drink or dance just because it might offend someone else's conscience. That sounds like legalism to me."

I said, "I can identify with that. Like you, I don't like to be told what I can and cannot do, just because it might offend someone else. But the Bible calls that rebellious part of me 'the flesh.' It's the enemy within each of us that seeks to destroy our effectiveness for God. If we want God to use us to reach others, we need to love Him enough to deny the flesh and limit our liberty."

My mentor, Dr. H. A. Ironside, once told me about an incident at a picnic. Everyone at the picnic was a Christian, including one young man who had been converted to Christ from Islam. A young lady was passing out sandwiches to people in the group, and she went to the former Muslim and said, "Would you like a ham sandwich or pork?"

"Don't you have any beef sandwiches left?" the young man asked.

"I'm sorry, they're all gone."

"Then I won't have a sandwich—thanks, anyway."

The young woman said, "I know you couldn't eat pork as a Muslim, but now that you're a Christian, you're free to eat any food you like."

"I know I'm free to eat pork," he said, "but I'm also free not to eat it. I'm trying to be a witness to my family. They're all Muslims living in the Middle East. I visit them once a year, and I know that when I arrive, the first question my father will ask me is, 'Have those infidels taught you to eat that filthy hog meat yet?' If I say, 'Yes, father,' I'll be banished and no longer be able to witness to my family. But if I say, 'No pork has ever passed my lips,' then I will continue to have a relationship with my family, and I can tell them of the joy I've found in Jesus Christ. So I choose not to eat because of my love for my family and my love for Jesus Christ."

We are free in Christ—free to exercise our liberty or to relinquish our liberty for the sake of love. You have a choice: Your liberty or your influence? Are you willing to surrender your rights in order to influence more people for Christ? When you authentically answer yes, you follow in the footsteps of Jesus.

11

THE FOCUSED LIFE

1 Corinthians 9:24–11:1

Corinth was the site of the Isthmian Games, sister events to the ancient Olympics. Held every three years in honor of Poseidon, the Greek god of the sea, the Isthmian Games were the centerpiece of Corinthian civic pride. Next to the olive branch that was awarded to Olympic champions, the Corinthian pine branch wreath was one of the most coveted of all athletic awards.

The main event of the Isthmian Games was a foot race. If you go to Corinth today, you can visit the ruins of the arena where the races were run. The starting blocks where the athletes began their races are still embedded in the stones.

Knowing how important the Isthmian Games were to the people of Corinth, Paul uses a foot race as a metaphor to describe how the Christian life should be lived. In 1 Corinthians 8 and 9, he has suggested that Christians should practice self-denial and self-control in order to have an influence for Christ on other people. Here, in the closing verses of chapter 9 and on into chapter 10, Paul suggests that another good reason for maintaining a disciplined, self-controlled life is to protect ourselves against being disqualified. He writes:

> Do you not know that in a race all the runners run, but only one gets the prize? Run in such a way as to get the prize. Everyone who competes in the games goes into strict training. They do it to get a crown that will not last; but we do it to get a crown that will last forever. Therefore I do not run like a man running aimlessly; I do not fight like a man beating the air. No, I beat my body and make it my slave so that after I have preached to others, I myself will not be disqualified for the prize. (1 CORINTHIANS 9:24–27)

The sports-minded Corinthians knew that every athlete who participated in the Isthmian Games took an oath to train hard for ten months.

During training, the athletes had to give up certain foods in order to build up strength and endurance. The athletes willingly underwent a harsh and rigorous discipline. Why? Paul says, "They do it to get a crown that will not last"—a wreath woven from a pine branch.

But we should discipline ourselves for a much higher purpose, Paul says—"to get a crown that will last forever." As Christians, we run the race of life in order to be useful and pleasing instruments of God. Our joy and honor is to be used by God wherever and whenever He wants to use us.

The tragedy of being disqualified

Sooner or later, we all ask ourselves, "Why am I here?" God's answer in the Bible: God made you for His purposes. He designed you with a unique set of abilities, talents, personality traits, desires, and spiritual gifts so that He might use you in a way that is pleasing to Him. In order to fulfill your purpose in life, you must run the race that God has set before you. Only then will you win the prize, the crown that lasts forever.

How do you prepare yourself to compete in the Christian life? You must go into training. You must be self-disciplined. There are temptations and lures all around you that will pull you off course and defeat you if you let them. That's what Paul warns against in this passage.

Corinth was a city of great wealth and many seductive temptations. So the people in the Corinthian church were in great spiritual danger. They were at risk of being seduced and lured away from the goal of the Christian life. So Paul used the metaphor of an athlete in training so they could see the realities of the Christian life more clearly.

He said, in effect, "You must look upon yourselves as athletes undergoing the rigors of training in order to win a prize. You must discipline yourself to run the race of the Christian life. You must focus your spirit, mind, and body on the goal. If you are not disciplined and focused, you may end up disqualified."

What does Paul mean when he warns of being disqualified? First, we should note that the King James Version uses a different term, "castaway." That term has troubled many people through the centuries:

> But I keep under my body, and bring it into subjection: lest that by any means, when I have preached to others, I myself should be a castaway. (1 Corinthians 9:27 KJV)

Many people have thought Paul was saying that we might lose our salvation. But Paul teaches elsewhere that when we receive the new birth through faith in Jesus Christ, we become citizens of the kingdom—and our citizenship will never be revoked. We cannot lose our salvation.

The New International Version gives us a more accurate translation: "disqualified." Paul's concern was that, if he fails to discipline himself and keep himself spiritually and morally fit for ministry, he could end up being disqualified for ministry. In other words, his ministry might be removed from him and he would lose his opportunity to serve God. He didn't want laziness or self-indulgence to get in the way of his usefulness to God, so he disciplined himself for the race.

I've observed three stages in the lives of Christians who allow themselves to be disqualified for service to God.

Stage 1: *God turns off the power of one's ministry.* Over the years, I've known Christian pastors, teachers, missionaries, and authors who were used greatly by God—but in time, the power seemed to drain out of their ministry. Once they ministered with power from God and the message God gave them touched many lives. Now, unfortunately, the power is absent. They are merely going through the motions of ministry. They say all the right words, but God doesn't seem to bless their work. What went wrong? They failed to discipline themselves and exercise godly self-control. As a result, they entered the first stage of being disqualified for service. But it's not too late to turn back to God, to get back into training, and begin competing once more for the crown. If they fail to do so, they progress to the next step of being disqualified:

Stage 2: *God stops the performance.* First the power departs, then the performance. God takes us out of action and puts us on the sidelines. There is a young man I know who was very well known in the evangelical world. His books were Christian bestsellers, and he was one of the most sought-after conference speakers in the country. But somewhere along the line he was tempted and became involved in adultery. When the scandal broke, everything stopped: the books, the speaking schedule, the conferences. The performance ended. I have great compassion for this young man, and I pray that he will turn back to God and get back into the race for the crown that lasts forever. This is not to say that he should necessarily have a speaking and writing ministry once more, but I believe God can restore him and use him in new and unexpected ways. Those who reach this stage and still refuse to discipline themselves risk going to the next step in being disqualified:

Stage 3: *God calls the individual home.* The first two stages are chastening stages in which God tries to get the individual's attention. But if a person continually ignores God's chastening, there may well come a time when God will say, "Come on home. You refuse to discipline yourself. I cannot trust you on earth any longer." When we reach stage 3, we do not lose our salvation, but we do lose our opportunity to serve God—and our lives are wasted.

May God keep you and me from the tragedy of disqualification from His service.

The example of the Israelites

Paul goes on to provide us with examples that serve as warnings to the believer:

> For I do not want you to be ignorant of the fact, brothers, that our forefathers were all under the cloud and that they all passed through the sea. They were all baptized into Moses in the cloud and in the sea. They all ate the same spiritual food and drank the same spiritual drink; for they drank from the spiritual rock that accompanied them, and that rock was Christ. Nevertheless, God was not pleased with most of them; their bodies were scattered over the desert. (1 CORINTHIANS 10:1–5)

Notice the repetition of the word *all*. They were all under the cloud—the cloud of God's guiding presence in the form of the Shekinah glory. They all passed through the Red Sea—they passed from bondage and the curse of Egypt. Paul is saying that when they came out of Egypt, the people of Israel received blessings from God—and we, as Christians, are in a parallel position. Like the Israelites, we have God's guiding presence in our lives. We have passed from the bondage and curse of sin into the kingdom of light.

Paul goes on to say that the Israelites were all baptized into Moses in the cloud and in the sea. That's a strange phrase, "baptized into Moses." But this statement is a parallel to the Christian life, for we as Christians were all baptized into Christ. We are identified with Christ, with His death and resurrection, by baptism. Just as Moses was the great mediator between God and man in the Old Testament, Jesus is our Great Mediator in the New. Just as Moses spoke for God then, Jesus speaks for God now. The people had access to God through Moses, and we have access to God through Christ.

Then Paul says that the Israelites all ate the same spiritual food and drank the same spiritual drink. The spiritual food they ate was manna, the bread-like food that came from heaven. The spiritual drink they drank was the water that flowed from the rock when Moses struck it. The rock that supplied their need, Paul said, was Christ. Jesus was their Rock of refuge; He was symbolized in the "Ebenezer," the "stone of help" that Samuel erected (see 1 Samuel 7:12).

Don't ever suppose that the Old Testament believers knew nothing of Christ! They were told of Christ through the prophecies of the Old Testament, through the symbols of the sacrifices, and through the rituals and laws they followed. The Israelites were related to Jesus by faith just as we are, and He fed and refreshed them just as He feeds and refreshes us today.

But what happened to them? Paul writes, "Nevertheless, God was not pleased with most of them; their bodies were scattered over the desert." Isn't that a sobering thought! How many Israelites left Egypt? According to the book of Numbers, more than six hundred thousand men. With women and children, the number had to approach two million. How many of the original number entered the Promised Land? Just two men: Joshua and Caleb. The rest died in the wilderness. They were disqualified and no longer able to serve God.

Example and warnings

Paul goes on to apply the example of the Israelites to our own lives:

> Now these things occurred as examples to keep us from setting our hearts on evil things as they did. Do not be idolaters, as some of them were; as it is written: "The people sat down to eat and drink and got up to indulge in pagan revelry." We should not commit sexual immorality, as some of them did—and in one day twenty-three thousand of them died. We should not test the Lord, as some of them did—and were killed by snakes. And do not grumble, as some of them did—and were killed by the destroying angel. (1 CORINTHIANS 10:6–10)

Many Christians ignore Paul's warning.

A young Christian man told me of a problem he had with his Christian girlfriend. He wanted to remain sexually pure, but she kept tempting him to indulge in sexual immorality. He challenged her, saying, "But you're a Christian! You can't just sin as if morality doesn't matter!" She said, "We can do anything we want! Afterwards, we can just ask God to forgive us, and He will!"

That's a subtle lie that many Christians fall for. If they live as if their Christian faith doesn't matter, if they refuse to discipline their lives and run the race, they will be disqualified! That's what Paul feared for himself, for the Corinthians, and for all believers. In this passage, Paul cites four danger signs to watch for.

First, we must beware of falling into idolatry. Paul writes, "Do not be idolaters, as some of them were; as it is written: 'The people sat down to eat and drink and got up to indulge in pagan revelry.'" When Moses went up on Mount Sinai to receive the Law from God, he was gone for forty days and nights. The people who waited at the foot of the mountain grew impatient, so they held a big feast. There's nothing wrong with feasting. Then someone suggested they dance. There's nothing wrong with dancing, either.

But in their dancing and indulgence, they got carried away. The innocent feasting and dancing turned lascivious and lewd. Before long, the Israelites were worshiping a golden calf that Aaron claimed had come out of the fire when he threw in some gold (a likely story!). The Israelites started with feasting and dancing, but they ended up in idolatry, forsaking the one true God.

Paul is warning us against the ease with which we can be lured away from faithfulness to God. We would never think of bowing down to idols, but the lure of idolatry is usually so subtle that we don't even realize we are being seduced. We may not worship a golden calf—but we may end up worshiping our careers, our homes, our cars, our possessions, or some other idol.

Another way we can be disqualified, Paul says, is through sexual immorality. He writes, "We should not commit sexual immorality, as some of them did—and in one day twenty-three thousand of them died." Paul refers to Numbers 25, where some of the Israelites objected to God's leading, and the women of Moab and Midian tempted them into fornication. A plague broke out in the camp that was not arrested until Phinehas, the grandson of Aaron, took a spear and killed a couple engaged in fornication.

We read these accounts and we say, "Why is God's punishment so brutal?" But this is God's way of saying, "The sins you commit are destroying you. Death is a kindness compared with the horrors you are committing against your own bodies through sexual sin."

We can also be disqualified by a presumptuous spirit. Paul writes, "We should not test the Lord, as some of them did—and were killed by snakes."

This refers to the story in Numbers 21 of how the Israelites presumed to charge God with unfaithfulness. They said, "You brought us out of Egypt, and we are going to die in this wilderness. It's your fault, God! Why did you bring us out of Egypt?"

Have you ever accused God of harming you and leading you into the wrong place? Have you ever asked God, "Why did you bring me to this place in my life? God, it's your fault I'm in this mess!" The Scriptures call this testing the Lord, and it's a dangerous thing to do. Ultimately, it can lead to disqualification. In the life of the Israelites, the people were set upon and killed by snakes—and the only way the snake attacks could be stopped was by the lifting up of a brass serpent (a symbol of the crucifixion) on a pole. Jesus said, "Just as Moses lifted up the snake in the desert, so the Son of Man must be lifted up" (John 3:14).

We can also be disqualified by complaining against God's authority. Paul wrote, "And do not grumble, as some of them did—and were killed by the destroying angel." This refers to the story of Korah, Dathan, and Abiram, three young men who complained against the authority that God had invested in Moses. They felt they had a right to exercise the same authority as Moses, so they spread unrest in the camp of Israel. So God called them to task. The ground opened up and swallowed up the rebels. They were killed by the destroying angel.

So Paul adds this word of warning:

These things happened to them as examples and were written down
as warnings for us, on whom the fulfillment of the ages has come.
So, if you think you are standing firm, be careful that you don't fall!
(1 CORINTHIANS 10:11–12)

The stories of the Old Testament symbolize our own spiritual struggles. The enemies the Israelites faced are the enemies we face—the principalities and powers of darkness that seek to destroy us and disqualify us. The same enemies that seduced ancient Israel still attack you and me.

Let's shed this satanic delusion that we live in a beautiful, pleasant world designed for our enjoyment. We are soldiers on a battlefield, facing a deadly barrage of temptation. We are athletes in a race, competing to win a prize. Our opponents are ruthless and clever, and their strategies are subtle. We are not guaranteed success. We can fall. We can be disqualified. We can lose the race and fail to win the prize.

Paul concludes this theme with a word of hope:

No temptation has seized you except what is common to man. And God is faithful; he will not let you be tempted beyond what you can bear. But when you are tempted, he will also provide a way out so that you can stand up under it. (1 CORINTHIANS 10:13)

Trials and testings are common to us all. When trials come, we think, "Why is this happening to me?" The reason is simple: It's our turn. Everybody goes through trials—but God is faithful; He will not allow you to be tempted beyond your ability to withstand. When you are tempted, He will provide a way for you to withstand the pressure and win the prize.

In the hour of testing, God strips away all human support in order that we may learn that He is sufficient. He is our refuge and our strength, a very present help in time of trouble. He is our way of escape when the temptation seems more than we can bear.

The lure of idolatry

Paul begins the next section of his theme with the word *therefore*. Now, there's an old saying among Bible teachers: "Whenever you see the word *therefore* in the Bible, stop and see what it is there for." Paul writes:

Therefore, my dear friends, flee from idolatry. (1 CORINTHIANS 10:14)

Remember the context in which Paul now writes. He has just told the Corinthians, "No temptation has seized you except what is common to man. And God is faithful; he will not let you be tempted beyond what you can bear. But when you are tempted, he will also provide a way out so that you can stand up under it." Then, after taking a breath, he says, "Therefore, my dear friends, flee from idolatry."

Now we see what form of temptation Paul had in mind: idolatry. Corinth was a major center for the worship of Aphrodite, the goddess of sexual love. It was the site of the Temple of Aphrodite, where a thousand male and female prostitutes plied their trade in the name of religious worship. The Christians in Corinth had once been idol worshipers, allowing their lives to be ruled by the pagan philosophy of life.

I don't think Paul was terribly concerned that the Corinthian Christians would return to bowing and sacrificing to idols. When he says, "Flee from idolatry," I think he is writing instead of the atmosphere that surrounded the pagan Temple of Aphrodite. The temple area was regarded as the most exciting place in town—the place where you could find the finest foods, served in open-air restaurants. Amid the atmosphere of sexual revelry that surrounded the temple, one could enjoy the seductive pleasures of wine, women, and song.

Paul was concerned that the Corinthians, like the ancient Israelites, might sit down to eat and drink—then get up to indulge in pagan revelry. He worried that the Corinthians might be lured back into pagan practices by degrees. He goes on to say:

> I speak to sensible people; judge for yourselves what I say. (1 CORIN-THIANS 10:15)

Some people think that when Paul writes, "I speak to sensible people," he is being sarcastic. I don't agree. He is affirming the Corinthians as sensible, thoughtful Christians who are seriously committed to obeying the Word of God. Paul believes in the Corinthian Christians and their ability to judge right from wrong, based on the revelation of the Scripture. He's warning that a Christian, even while not outwardly bowing to an idol, could get caught up in a worldly atmosphere. This would place him at risk for disqualification. So Paul says, in effect, "Avoid the temple and its atmosphere, which could tempt you into the sensuous sins associated with the worship of Aphrodite."

There are similar dangers that surround us today. Our favorite television shows, movies, literature, music, gourmet foods, travel, our homes, antique collecting, skiing, sailing, fishing—all of these things can begin as perfectly innocent, enjoyable pastimes, then turn into idols that destroy our usefulness to God. Before you know it, you have a new love, a new master, a new god controlling your life.

A holy jealousy

Paul goes on to suggest three reasons why idolatry is so subtle and dangerous. First, idolatry will displace your love for Christ. He writes:

> Is not the cup of thanksgiving for which we give thanks a participation in the blood of Christ? And is not the bread that we break a participation in the body of Christ? Because there is one loaf, we, who are many, are one body, for we all partake of the one loaf. Consider the people of Israel: Do not those who eat the sacrifices participate in the altar? Do I mean then that a sacrifice offered to an idol is anything, or that an idol is anything? No, but the sacrifices of pagans are offered to demons, not to God, and I do not want you to be participants with demons. You cannot drink the cup of the Lord and the cup of demons

too; you cannot have a part in both the Lord's table and the table of demons. (1 CORINTHIANS 10:16–21)

There are factors and forces in life that are mutually antagonistic—and this is especially true in the matter of what we choose to worship. As Jesus put it, "No servant can serve two masters. Either he will hate the one and love the other, or he will be devoted to the one and despise the other. You cannot serve both God and Money" (Luke 16:13). Christians partake of the bread and cup of Communion, which commemorate the broken body and shed blood of Christ. We violate the Lord's table if we partake of the table of demons by slipping into the practice of idolatry.

You cannot mix the worship of the Lord and the worship of idols—and the word *idols* does not refer merely to stone statues of pagan gods. An idol is anything that takes the rightful place of God in our hearts. If love for any aspect of the world takes the place where only love for God belongs, then we are practicing idolatry. The apostle John agrees with Paul when he writes, "If any man love the world, the love of the Father is not in him. For all that is in the world, the lust of the flesh, and the lust of the eyes, and the pride of life, is not of the Father, but is of the world" (1 John 2:15–16 KJV).

The apostle Paul chooses Communion as an example to make this point because it is the central act of Christian worship. What does it mean when we celebrate the Lord's table and pass the cup and break the bread? We remind ourselves of what Jesus did and who we are. We are saying, "We died with Christ. We relinquished our own lordship over our lives and enthroned Him as Lord." If we do not have this profound meaning in mind every time we partake of the Lord's table, then we have turned Communion into a meaningless ritual.

Paul notes that this same principle was at work in the Jewish system of sacrifices: "Consider the people of Israel: Do not those who eat the sacrifices participate in the altar?" The sacrifices they ate expressed who they are. The same is true when we eat of the Lord's table. We manifest who we are when we partake of the Lord's sacrifice—or when we, through participating in idolatry, partake of the sacrifices of demons.

It is crucial that we understand that "eating," "drinking," and "partaking" are metaphors that represent the actions of our lives. These metaphors speak of the food we take into our lives through the things we read, view, hear, do, acquire, and delight ourselves in. Paul is warning us of the danger of becoming fascinated, bewitched, and seduced by the lure of otherwise innocent activities. He's warning us of becoming lured by the exciting atmosphere around the temples of worldly activity.

The person who has been lured into the idolatry of worldliness will probably not be found bowing before a statue of Aphrodite or Poseidon. That person's idol worship will take a subtler form, such as spending inordinate amounts of time and money on a recreational activity or collecting possessions. It could take the form of sitting in rapt fascination before a computer screen or continually walking around with stereo headphones on. The subtle and deceptive thing about idolatry is that it doesn't look like our mental picture of idolatry.

Paul goes on to say, "Do I mean then that a sacrifice offered to an idol is anything, or that an idol is anything? No, but the sacrifices of pagans are offered to demons, not to God, and I do not want you to be participants with demons." The subtle idolatry of seeking pleasures, acquiring possessions, and immersing ourselves in worldly fascinations seems innocent enough. But what is behind the seductive lure of seemingly innocent things? Paul's answer: Demonic control. This is no metaphor; this is literal, realistic truth. Invisible spirits, under the command of the god of this world, seek to divide our loyalties and seduce us into idolatry—into satanic mind control. The ultimate goal of these demonic forces is death—the destruction of human lives and souls.

Jesus said that Satan is a liar and a murderer (see John 8:44). Whenever you see violence, murder, terrorism, war, or genocide, you see Satan at work. If he had his way, we would all be slaughtered before the next sunrise. We ought to give thanks to God for every new morning we wake to, and for every breath and heartbeat, because it is only by God's grace that we are not destroyed by the malevolent spirit who rules this fallen world.

But even though Satan is thwarted, he still succeeds in accomplishing his objectives from time to time. He even succeeds in seducing Christians into becoming disqualified from serving God. How does he accomplish his objectives? Through deception. Satan is a liar. He deceives people into thinking they are gaining something good and achieving fulfillment when they are actually being seduced into idolatry and forsaking their love for God.

Our worship of God, Paul says, must be absolute. We cannot serve two masters. Either we belong to Christ or we belong to the god of this world—Satan. We cannot partake of the table of the Lord and the table of demons.

Next, Paul tells us that idolatry awakens the jealousy of God. He writes:

> Are we trying to arouse the Lord's jealousy? Are we stronger than he? (1 CORINTHIANS 10:22)

In many places in the Old Testament we are told that God is "a jealous God" (see Exodus 20:5, 34:14; Deuteronomy 4:24; 5:9; 6:15; Joshua 24:19). What does the Bible mean by describing God as "jealous"? Is God subject to capricious anger and green-eyed envy? No, the jealousy of God is a holy and proper jealousy. It is a love so intense that He becomes angry if anything threatens that love. God loves you too much to let you drift into idolatry. He will strike at it. If your love for God is so alienated by worldly affections that your soul is at risk, then He will do what He must to drive you back to His loving arms. Paul continues:

> "Everything is permissible"—but not everything is beneficial. "Everything is permissible"—but not everything is constructive. Nobody should seek his own good, but the good of others. (1 CORINTHIANS 10:23–24)

We cannot be like Cain, who said to the Lord, "Am I my brother's keeper?" (see Genesis 4:9). Yes, we are our brothers' keepers. We have a responsibility not to harm the spiritual well-being of a Christian brother or sister. When we find ourselves wanting something so much that it interferes with our love for God and others, we awaken God's jealousy and expose ourselves to His discipline.

In the world, not of it

While we are to be aware of the spiritual dangers in the world, we are not to cut ourselves off from non-Christian people. As Jesus said, we are to be in the world without being of the world (see John 17:11, 16). Many Christians would like to build a cozy little Bible City with a wall around it to keep the pressures and temptations of the world outside. The problem with that idea is that the sinfulness of the world is within as well as without. As soon as Christians seal themselves off from the outside world, a different form of worldliness takes hold—the sin of smug religious pride and self-righteousness.

God wants us to have many non-Christian friends so that we can be a witness and an influence on their lives. How do we keep ourselves safe

143

from the lure of idolatry? We must keep our love for the Lord Jesus at such a white-hot pitch that we are safe even while we are in the world.

Paul now turns to practical guidelines that will enable us to live in the real world without being tempted into idolatry.

> Eat anything sold in the meat market without raising questions of conscience, for, "The earth is the Lord's, and everything in it." (1 COR-INTHIANS 10:25–26)

In other words, "Don't run away from life. Live in the midst of it. Don't try to avoid being normal people enjoying the normal benefits of life. God has given you good things to enjoy, so enjoy them. Just make sure that you don't let anything displace your love for God." He continues:

> If some unbeliever invites you to a meal and you want to go, eat whatever is put before you without raising questions of conscience. (1 CORINTHIANS 10:27)

I am so glad Paul wrote this! This is how we are to live our Christian lives. Not only should we not isolate ourselves from non-Christians, but Paul expects us to live in such a way that non-Christians will invite us into their homes to break bread with them. This is an opportunity to be God's witnesses! While our fellowship is with Christ, we can still show friendship to the worldlings around us.

Paul says, "If someone invites you over to eat, then go." If you are a self-righteous, legalistic stick-in-the-mud, don't worry—you won't be invited anywhere! You'll have no witness for Christ and no impact on the world. But if you're an outgoing Christian who accepts and cares for struggling, needy people, you'll have many dinner invitations. God will bless your ministry as you are in the world and not of it.

Paul then adds this word of advice:

> But if anyone says to you, "This has been offered in sacrifice," then do not eat it, both for the sake of the man who told you and for conscience' sake—the other man's conscience, I mean, not yours. For why should my freedom be judged by another's conscience? If I take part in the meal with thankfulness, why am I denounced because of something I thank God for? (1 CORINTHIANS 10:28–30)

If someone makes an issue over the matter of meat sacrificed to idols, don't let yourself get drawn into a controversy. After all, why would someone invite you over, put meat on your plate, then say, "By the way, this meat was sacrificed to an idol"? Obviously, this person is testing you—either to prove that Christians aren't willing to stand by their principles or to provoke an argument with you. Don't get drawn into a contrived conflict. Don't give non-Christians reason to judge your conscience.

Paul closes with a rule of thumb for all occasions.

> So whether you eat or drink or whatever you do, do it all for the glory of God. Do not cause anyone to stumble, whether Jews, Greeks or the church of God—even as I try to please everybody in every way. For I am not seeking my own good but the good of many, so that they may be saved. Follow my example, as I follow the example of Christ. (1 CORINTHIANS 10:31–11:1)

Paul's life and words continue to transform lives and change history after all of these centuries. Why? Because Paul lived a totally focused life. He had a goal in life that he wanted to accomplish, and he focused his energies on reaching that goal.

He had the highest of motives for everything he did, even eating and drinking. He lived his entire life for the glory of God. He refused to do anything that would deliberately offend anyone, because he wanted to win as many as he could to a relationship with Jesus Christ. Sometimes, it is impossible not to offend people, because the gospel itself is offensive to some. But if people are going to be offended, let them be offended only by the truth of the gospel, not by our smug condescension or legalistic spirit. As much as it is possible, let us make every effort not to offend the Jew, the Gentile, or our Christian brothers and sisters.

Sometimes, in order not to offend others, we have to swallow some pride. We have to give up some rights. We have to put up with some discomfort. But Paul tells us we should not mind sacrificing some of our rights and comforts if, in doing so, we'll have a greater influence among those who are without Christ. It's all a matter of keeping our eyes on the goal of the Christian life.

> Do you not know that in a race all the runners run, but only one gets the prize? Run in such a way as to get the prize. Everyone who competes in the games goes into strict training. They do it to get a crown that will not last; but we do it to get a crown that will last forever. Therefore I do not run like a man running aimlessly; I do not fight like a man beating the air. No, I beat my body and make it my slave so

145

that after I have preached to others, I myself will not be disqualified for the prize. (1 CORINTHIANS 9:24–27)

Paul was running to win a prize—a crown that never fades, but lasts forever. Every decision he made was filtered through the question, "Will this help me or hinder me in my quest to win the race and gain the prize?" If we put God and others ahead of our own desires, we will always make the right choice—and we will have an impact on the world and on generations to come.

12

THE ROLES OF MEN AND WOMEN

1 Corinthians 11:2–16

A movie producer once asked actor Spencer Tracy why he insisted on always having top billing over Katharine Hepburn. "After all," the producer said, "she's the woman and you're the man. Ladies first."

Tracy replied, "This is a movie, not a lifeboat."

The respective roles of men and women have long been debated, whether in movies or in lifeboats or in the church. Should women submit themselves under the authority of men? The suggestion sounds outrageous to our ears in this age of the liberated woman. What does Paul say? Does he speak with the authority of God on matters of gender roles in the church? Does the teaching of the Bible ever go out of date? These are the questions we confront in 1 Corinthians 11.

The tradition of headship

The first verse of chapter 11 serves equally well as either the concluding thought on the issue of living a focused Christian life—or the opening thought on the issue of gender roles and authority in the church. Paul writes:

> Follow my example, as I follow the example of Christ. I praise you for remembering me in everything and for holding to the teachings, just as I passed them on to you. (1 CORINTHIANS 11:1–2)

In 1 Corinthians 4:1, Paul told us that the Christian faith is shaped, in part, by revealed truth—what Paul calls "the secret things of God," the realities that cannot be discovered by the natural mind but are revealed only by direct revelation in the Word of God. Here, Paul tells us that the Christian faith is also shaped, in part, by traditions and teachings that are handed down from generation to generation.

Today, people tended to be skeptical or even hostile to traditions. But traditions have value in forming beliefs, attitudes, behavior, and unity in a church. In 1 Corinthians 11, Paul looks at two traditions that were part of the life of the early church. One of these traditions involved the respective roles of men and women in the church. The other involves the tradition of the Lord's Supper, which was instituted in the upper room on the night that Jesus was betrayed.

After commending the Corinthians for holding on to the traditions he has passed on to them, Paul launches into a discussion of one of those traditions: the tradition of headship as a principle of authority in God's plan of governance. He already passed this principle on to them when he founded the Corinthian church. Now he clarifies this principle with regard to the conditions and culture in first century Corinth. He writes:

> Now I want you to realize that the head of every man is Christ, and the head of the woman is man, and the head of Christ is God. Every man who prays or prophesies with his head covered dishonors his head. And every woman who prays or prophesies with her head uncovered dishonors her head—it is just as though her head were shaved. If a woman does not cover her head, she should have her hair cut off; and if it is a disgrace for a woman to have her hair cut or shaved off, she should cover her head. (1 CORINTHIANS 11:3–6)

When the apostle says "the head of every man is Christ, and the head of the woman is man," he uses a Greek word for "head" that refers to the part of the body that contains the brain and all the facial features. Paul understood that the head was the control center of the body. Some Bible commentators have argued that the people of Paul's time didn't know that the brain was the center of thought, but this is not true. The ancients had observed that severe head injuries frequently impaired the ability to think, and it was clear to the ancients that the head was the site of four of the five senses—taste, smell, hearing, and vision. So the importance of the head was clearly understood by the people of Paul's era.

When the head is used as a metaphor, as it is here, it refers to a priority in function. The head is in charge of the body. It sets the direction for everything the body does. So the head symbolizes leadership. That is how Paul uses the term in this passage.

Paul first makes a statement that is easily accepted by Christians: "the head of every man is Christ." No problem there. But then he goes on to make another statement that is quite controversial today: "and the head of the woman is man." This statement is followed by another statement of a doctrinal nature: "and the head of Christ is God." Notice that the two statements about Christ—His relationship to man and His relationship to God—serve to bracket the statement Paul makes about the relationship of woman to man. The reason for this placement is obvious: The first and third statements about headship and Christ are placed to show us what the second statement, "and the head of the woman is man," means.

The first statement, "the head of every man is Christ," is a declaration of Christ's right to lead the whole human race. He is the leader of the human race in the view of God. Scripture tells us that there will come a day when all of humanity, without exception, shall bow the knee and confess that Jesus Christ is Lord (see Romans 14:11; Philippians 2:11). Whether men know Him or not, Christ is their head, and they are responsible to worship and obey Him.

The third statement, "the head of Christ is God," is a manifestation of headship demonstrated for us in history. Jesus, the Son of God, is totally equal to the Father in His deity. But when the Son took on our humanity, He submitted Himself to the headship of the Father. Everywhere Jesus went He said, "I always do those things which please the Father." He said, "My food . . . is to do the will of him who sent me and to finish his work" (John 4:34). On another occasion He said, "I and the Father are one" (John 10:30). On yet another occasion, he said, "The Father is greater than I" (John 14:28).

Is Jesus saying that He, being God the Son, is not equal to God the Father? No. He is saying that He has voluntarily consented to take a lower position than the Father. It is in this sense that He says, "The Father is greater than I."

These two examples of headship—Christ the head of man and God the head of Christ—help us to understand what the middle example means, where Paul writes, "the head of the woman is man." Undoubtedly, some who read these words may be thinking, "The apostle Paul is just a chauvinist who advocates male domination of women!" So I want to clearly state that, properly understood, headship does not mean domination. Headship is a condition of voluntary commitment carried out in obedience to God's will. God the Father did not dominate Jesus. The Father did not coerce the Son. Nor does Jesus treat the human race in that fashion. Men who dominate or oppress women are not practicing biblical headship as Paul uses the term.

A leader and a servant

All Christian leadership, according to Jesus, is servanthood. The man is the head, not because he is superior to the woman, but because he has a responsibility before God to serve her as a leader and because she has voluntarily undertaken the role of working under his leadership. That is the biblical principle of headship that Paul here states as clearly and objectively as can be stated. This explanation is consistent with the use of the metaphor of headship elsewhere in Scripture. In Paul's letter to the Ephesians, he says that Christ is the head of the church, which is His body; in other words, He is the leader of the church and has the right to set the ultimate direction for that relationship.

In verses 4 through 6, Paul applies this principle to the specific customs and practices in the Corinthian church: "Every man who prays or prophesies with his head covered dishonors his head. And every woman who prays or prophesies with her head uncovered dishonors her head—it is just as though her head were shaved. If a woman does not cover her head, she should have her hair cut off; and if it is a disgrace for a woman to have her hair cut or shaved off, she should cover her head." There are two things that are important to notice in this passage.

First, the focus of Paul's concern is the public ministry of the Word of God. He is talking about the church, the public gathering of believers. Paul says that in order to function effectively in that setting, a woman should wear a veil, but a man should not.

Second, the veil symbolizes the woman's acceptance of the principle of headship, as Paul has described it. Where public ministry is involved, it is just as important that a man should not be covered as that a woman should be covered. That was the application of headship in the custom of that culture and historical era.

It's significant to note that both men and women were free to exercise ministry in the church. Both could pray and prophesy in a public worship service. What the Bible calls prophesying is what we call preaching today. It is expounding the Word of God and applying biblical truth to everyday life. This form of ministry could be carried out by both men and women in the church. Men were to prophesy in a way that was distinct for men and women in a way that was unique to women.

Paul makes a remarkable statement here: "Every man who prays or prophesies with his head covered dishonors his head." While this statement is not surprising in our culture, it was very surprising in the culture of Paul. The practice among the Jews was for men to wear a head covering when they ministered. To this day, orthodox Jewish men still wear the yarmulke (head covering), and no orthodox Jewish male would ever think of reading Scripture or ministering in public with his head uncovered. Yet Paul, who was raised in the Jewish faith, says here that a Christian man who ministers with his head covered dishonors his head.

Notice, too, what Paul is actually saying: "Every man who prays or prophesies with his head covered dishonors his head." What does he dishonor? Not the hairy knob that sits on his shoulders, which we normally think of as his head. Remember, as Paul has already told us, "the head of every man is Christ." So the man who ministers with his head covered dishonors Christ.

By contrast, if a woman does not have a covering (in this first-century Christian setting), she dishonors her head. Who or what is her head? In the case of a married woman, her husband. Paul's reasoning becomes clear when you recall what the culture of Corinth was like. Corinth was the most sexually licentious city of the first century. The only women in the city who did not wear a veil in public were the temple prostitutes. So an unveiled woman on the street was assumed to be an immoral woman, available for a price. It was disgraceful for a woman to appear in public, much less minister the Word in church, without visibly acknowledging the principle of headship in her life. The veil or head covering was the visible symbol of that headship.

The meaning of glory

Next, we come to the heart of this passage, where Paul explains the rationale for his teaching.

> A man ought not to cover his head, since he is the image and glory of God; but the woman is the glory of man. For man did not come from woman, but woman from man; neither was man created for woman, but woman for man. For this reason, and because of the angels, the woman ought to have a sign of authority on her head. (1 CORINTHIANS 11:7–10)

Notice, the apostle Paul does not base his reasons on local custom. He goes back to creation to establish the basis for his teaching. The principle of headship has been true since the beginning of humankind. Paul says that, in the beginning, man was made in the image and glory of God. Man was made in God's image in order that any creature, looking at a man, would see the likeness of God. That's the dignity of humanity.

Genesis tells us that man was made in the image of God even before the two sexes were separated. Adam was created first, then Eve was separated from him; after that separation, woman shared the image and glory of God equally with the man. Male and female are both included when it is said that man was made in the image and the glory of God. That is why in Genesis 5 we read:

> When God created man, he made him in the likeness of God. He created them male and female and blessed them. And when they were created, he called them "man." (GENESIS 5:1B-2)

The original Hebrew word translated "man" is Adam. God did not name Adam and Eve "the Adams." He named them Adam. The woman and the man equally bear the name of man, and they equally bear the image and glory of God. They are equal in status and importance before God. The male, however, is called upon to manifest a certain aspect of the glory of God that is different from that of the woman.

What do we mean by glory? As used here, the word refers to something in which one takes delight. As Paul wrote to the Christians in Thessalonica, "For what is our hope, our joy, or the crown in which we will glory in the presence of our Lord Jesus when he comes? Is it not you?" (1 Thessalonians 2:19). So when humanity was created, God made man and woman to reflect the nature of God, and God takes great delight in humanity.

The glory of God is to be publicly and openly manifested, and that is why the man must not wear a covering. He is not to hide the creative glory of God. We see this principle in the life of Jesus. Everywhere He went, Jesus demonstrated the love of God for humanity. This is what drew multitudes to Him. As John's gospel tells us, "The Word became flesh and made his dwelling among us. We have seen his glory, the glory of the One and Only, who came from the Father, full of grace and truth" (John 1:14). This is the glory that a man is called upon to manifest through the ministry of the Word.

But the woman is the glory and delight of the man. Paul now deals with the woman as having been separated from the man. The distinction that took place when God took Adam's rib and made a woman now comes into focus. This delight involves a private, intimate glory—the intimacy a man finds in his wife, the intimacy of a sexual relationship and shared love. It is hidden and private, which is why this glory is symbolized by a veil. The covering of a woman marks something that is protected and set aside for a relationship with a single individual. The veil is not a mark of slavery or subjection or inferiority; it is a mark of intimacy and privacy, voluntarily accepted by the woman. She is not the man's property but his intimate companion.

Paul takes us all the way back to creation in establishing his rationale. He writes, "For man did not come from woman, but woman from man; neither was man created for woman, but woman for man." Woman was taken from man in order that she might fully share his nature. Man and woman are not two different species. Despite their differences, they share a common origin and a common Creator. This is what Paul means when he points out that woman came from man and was created for man.

The creation story tells us, "Then the LORD God made a woman from the rib he had taken out of the man, and he brought her to the man" (Genesis 2:22). God brought the woman to the man so that she might be for the man. This, I believe, is key to the biblical concept of headship. The woman is for her husband. She supports him and she delights and glories in his success. Together they achieve what neither could achieve alone. They accomplish the goals that Christ, the head of the man, has set before them. That is God's ideal image of a marriage.

Paul adds, "For this reason, and because of the angels, the woman ought to have a sign of authority on her head." Why does he say that a woman should have a sign of authority on her head? The context tells us that Paul is speaking of authority to minister the Word of God in a public setting, such as a worship service. The authority for her to do so is her recognition of the principle of headship. She is to declare that she does not pray or preach apart from her husband, and thus she is to wear a covering for her head as a sign of her voluntary submission to the headship (authority) of her husband, who is under the headship (authority) of Christ.

She is to do so, Paul says, "because of the angels." In a culture where unveiled women were regarded as idolaters and prostitutes, it would be an offense to the angels present for a woman to openly defy custom and deny the principle of headship. Angels, we are told, are ministering spirits sent by God to watch over Christians, who are heirs of salvation (see Hebrews 1:14). Angels were present at creation, and they understand the principle of headship. The Old Testament indicates that they veil their faces when they worship before the throne of God (see Isaiah 6:2), and so they are concerned to maintain the purity of human worship toward God.

The equality of the sexes

Next, Paul balances his teaching on headship with a strong statement on the equality of men and women in marriage.

> In the Lord, however, woman is not independent of man, nor is man independent of woman. For as woman came from man, so also man is born of woman. But everything comes from God. (1 CORINTHIANS 11:11–12)

Though distinct as sexes, men and women are equal as persons. Neither sex is inferior or superior. Neither has lesser or greater status. Men and women cannot exist without each other. Each gender has a role to fulfill that has been divinely ordered and is to be freely accepted. Men must voluntarily fulfill the headship role, which includes leadership and servanthood responsibilities. Women must voluntarily accept the headship of the man in order to demonstrate the delight of God in His creation and redemption of mankind.

Next, Paul talks about a seemingly trivial matter: the problem of hair. He writes:

> Judge for yourselves: Is it proper for a woman to pray to God with her head uncovered? Does not the very nature of things teach you that if a man has long hair, it is a disgrace to him, but that if a woman has long hair, it is her glory? For long hair is given to her as a covering. (1 CORINTHIANS 11:13–15)

This is a second argument the apostle gives to support women wearing a veil. He argues from nature. Not only does God's intent in creation sustain the principle of headship, but nature also illustrates it.

Over the centuries, people have struggled over this passage. I have wrestled with it myself. What is there about nature that indicates that a man with long hair dishonors himself while a woman with long hair is honored? There is a principle that science recognizes as true—the principle of baldness.

Baldness is an issue that affects many men but rarely affects women. Tradition tells us that Paul was bald, so he may have had his own experience in mind. In most cases, nature has given women a permanent covering for their heads, while for a significant number of men, a full head of hair is a temporary proposition. A woman's hair is her glory; nature has given women more beautiful hair than men so that women might more clearly manifest the principle of headship.

Paul is saying that women's hair is not just something for women to wash, style, curl, color, and blow-dry. Women's hair is an object lesson to illustrate biblical truth. Paul did not write this passage merely for the first-century Corinthians but for all Christians at all times. In a culture like our own, where the wearing of veils is not the custom, a woman's long hair illustrates the principle of headship.

In the Roman world, the wearing of veils was still the custom, so Paul concludes his discussion of gender roles with these words:

> If anyone wants to be contentious about this, we have no other practice—nor do the churches of God. (1 CORINTHIANS 11:16)

The universal custom in the Roman world was for women to declare the principle of headship by wearing a veil, so there's no point in debating the issue. We, of course, do not live in the first-century Roman world, and women in our culture do not wear veils. What, then, is Paul saying to us in this passage?

First, Paul has a message for men: Take seriously your responsibility as spiritual leaders in the home. Your head is Christ, and you have a responsibility to your Head to know the Word of God and to see that it shapes and molds the lives of your family members. You're a leader—but that doesn't make you a boss. It makes you a servant. So serve your wife and children every day by being a Christlike servant-leader in the home.

Second, Paul has a message for women: Take seriously your calling to voluntarily place yourself under the headship of your husband. This teaching may not be in step with our culture, but it is in step with God's truth and with nature. A woman will never know true fulfillment as long as she is in rebellion against God's plan for gender roles.

The secular women's movement claims to give women freedom of choice. Yet many women today do not feel free to make the kind of choice Paul urges women to make in 1 Corinthians 11—the voluntary choice to place themselves under the headship of a man who is himself under the headship of Christ. Women fear being scorned by their feminist sisters if they make the wrong choice, the old-fashioned choice, the politically incorrect choice. Isn't it tragic that so many women, in the name of freedom of choice, are made to feel they have no choice in how to live their lives?

Third, Paul has a message for the church: When women minister in public worship, they are to do so with humility and respect for the true headship and authority of the church. May we, as men and women under the headship of God, live as true leaders and servants and bearers of God's truth.

13

THE LORD'S TABLE

1 Corinthians 11:17–34

In *The Body*, Charles Colson tells about a hospital chaplain in Boston who encountered a patient named John, a man in his sixties. The doctors could not diagnose John's illness. Medical tests showed no reason for his failing health, yet he was unable to swallow and seemed to be wasting away. The chaplain found John lying in bed, hollow-eyed and listless. They chatted a while, and the chaplain felt God prompting him to offer Communion to John.

"I can't take Communion," John said. "I've sinned and can't be forgiven."

The chaplain replied, "You're wise not to take Communion in an unworthy manner. In 1 Corinthians 11, Paul said, 'Whoever eats the bread or drinks the cup of the Lord in an unworthy manner will be guilty of sinning against the body and blood of the Lord. A man ought to examine himself before he eats of the bread and drinks of the cup.' John, if you confess your sin and repent of it, God will forgive you, and you can take Communion with a clean conscience. Would you like to do that?"

"Yes, I would," John said. Weeping openly, he confessed the sin to the chaplain and repented of it to God in prayer.

The chaplain hugged John and told him his sins were forgiven. "I'll be back," he said. He left John's room and returned sometime later with a Bible, a piece of bread wrapped in a paper napkin, and a cup of grape juice. He read to John from 1 Corinthians 11, then he offered the elements of Communion—the bread and the cup. It was the first time John had tasted solid food in weeks. Though he had been unable to swallow before, he had no trouble taking Communion.

Three days after the chaplain first visited, John walked out of the hospital. His recovery was amazing. His sin had robbed him of his health.

Confession, forgiveness, and the bread and cup of the Lord's table restored his vitality.

We come now to the passage the chaplain read from—Paul's discussion of the Lord's Supper in 1 Corinthians 11.

Differences of opinion

Paul now holds up a mirror to the Corinthian Christians and confronts them with their behavior at the table of the Lord:

> In the following directives I have no praise for you, for your meetings do more harm than good. In the first place, I hear that when you come together as a church, there are divisions among you, and to some extent I believe it. No doubt there have to be differences among you to show which of you have God's approval. (1 CORINTHIANS 11:17–19)

When Paul speaks of the church coming together, he is not talking primarily about a morning worship service. In the early church, as described in the book of Acts, the church commonly came together for a meal, an "*agape* feast" (*agape* being the Greek word for Christian love). These were wonderful first-century potluck dinners where all shared together in glorious Christian fellowship.

This practice was common in churches across the ancient Christian world—but in Corinth, it was spoiled by cliques and factions. These divisions prompted Paul to write, "your meetings do more harm than good." He felt that the contentious spirit of these *agape* feasts were destroying the fellowship and reputation of the Corinthian church.

Is it a sin for a church to have diverse points of view? Of course not. As Paul writes in verse 19, "No doubt there have to be differences among you to show which of you have God's approval." The King James Version translates verse 19 this way: "For there must be also heresies among you, that they which are approved may be made manifest among you." This is a good translation of the original Greek. Paul is saying that there ought to be differences—and yes, heresies!—in a healthy church so that it will be clear who are the spiritually mature members of the church.

People come from different backgrounds and experiences, have different kinds of upbringing and training, and will have differing points of view. That's healthy. Out of these differing points of view, the truth emerges, and it becomes clear who are approved by God as being spiritually mature.

I once spoke to a conference of youth leaders in the Midwest. We had an open question-and-answer session, and one of the participants asked me about our Body Life service at Peninsula Bible Church. I said, "At Body Life, we encourage people to share freely. Anyone can stand up and speak on any subject."

Some of the people at the conference were shocked by that. One asked, "Aren't you afraid someone will stand up and make an unbiblical statement? Aren't you concerned that heresies could be publicly spoken at your church?"

I said, "I don't see it that way. Remember, in 1 Corinthians 11:19, Paul writes, 'For there must be also heresies among you, that they which are approved may be made manifest among you.' At Peninsula Bible Church, we like heresies! We encourage heretical ideas to be expressed because they are great teaching opportunities. How are you going to know who in your congregation is able to handle heresies unless they have some heresies to work on?"

That's what the apostle Paul recognizes here. There is nothing wrong with differences of opinion—or even heretical opinions, as long as they can be freely aired and examined in the light of God's Word. When people feel free to express their opinions, the entire church is better able to answer questions and help people with their struggles.

Paul is not troubled by differing viewpoints in Corinth. He is troubled by the outrageous behavior in the church's *agape* feasts. He writes:

> When you come together, it is not the Lord's Supper you eat, for as you eat, each of you goes ahead without waiting for anybody else. One remains hungry, another gets drunk. Don't you have homes to eat and drink in? Or do you despise the church of God and humiliate those who have nothing? What shall I say to you? Shall I praise you for this? Certainly not! (1 CORINTHIANS 11:20–22)

In other words, "Your love feasts have become a sham and a mockery. The Lord's Supper is an expression of the unity of the church—but even though you observe the ritual of Communion during your feasts, you do not have a spirit of unity. You are acting selfishly toward one another."

Some of the Corinthian believers were bringing a lot of food to the feast, then gathering in their own little family groups to eat it. Others had little or nothing, and they went hungry amid all that feasting! Paul says, in effect, "You're so proud of your love feasts—but where is the love? You don't care for one another. Some go hungry while others get drunk! Shall I praise you for this? No! You should be ashamed!"

Paul asks, "Don't you have homes to eat and drink in?" He's not saying that church suppers are a bad idea. They're great opportunities for Christian fellowship. Rather, he is saying, "If all you do when you get together is eat and get drunk, do it at home. If you are going to come together for Christian fellowship, then get real! Share together! Love one another!"

The meaning of the Lord's table

Next, Paul instructs the Corinthian Christians in the origin and meaning of the Lord's table:

> For I received from the Lord what I also passed on to you: The Lord Jesus, on the night he was betrayed, took bread, and when he had given thanks, he broke it and said, "This is my body, which is for you; do this in remembrance of me." In the same way, after supper he took the cup, saying, "This cup is the new covenant in my blood; do this, whenever you drink it, in remembrance of me." For whenever you eat this bread and drink this cup, you proclaim the Lord's death until he comes. (1 CORINTHIANS 11:23–26)

Here, Paul makes an amazing apostolic claim: "I received from the Lord what I also passed on to you." Who told Paul what took place in the upper room the night Jesus was betrayed? Jesus Himself. In his letter to the Galatians, Paul writes,

> I want you to know, brothers, that the gospel I preached is not something that man made up. I did not receive it from any man, nor was I taught it; rather, I received it by revelation from Jesus Christ. (GALATIANS 1:11–12)

Paul didn't learn of Christ and Christianity from any man. No apostle taught him. He had never read the gospels of Matthew, Mark, Luke or John, because they hadn't been written yet. He received his instruction straight from the Lord. This passage in 1 Corinthians 11 is, in fact, the earliest written description of the Lord's table as it was originally instituted in the upper room—and this description came from Jesus.

Here, Paul passes on to the Corinthians—and to us—two remarkable symbols: the bread and the cup. After the Passover feast, Jesus took the bread and broke it so that all eleven faithful disciples could partake of it

(Judas had already gone out to betray Him). Jesus said to them, "This is my body."

Catholicism teaches that Jesus meant that the bread literally became His body, but I think He clearly meant these words in a symbolic sense. If the bread literally became His body, then there were two bodies of Christ present in the upper room, the body in which He lived and the body which He held in His hand, the bread. Clearly, our Lord meant this as a symbol.

Jesus told His disciples, "This is my body, which is for you; do this in remembrance of me." The King James Version uses the phrase "which is broken for you." That's not an accurate translation. The word *broken* does not appear, because the body of Jesus was later pierced but not broken. This was to fulfill Old Testament prophecies that Messiah's bones would not be broken (see Exodus 12:46; Numbers 9:12; Psalm 34:20).

When Jesus said, "This is my body, which is for you," He was telling us that His body was given for us to live on. That is the symbolism. So when we take the bread of the Lord's table, and we break it and pass it among ourselves, we are reminded that Jesus is the Bread of Life, and we are to feed on Him daily. As Jesus said, "Just as the living Father sent me and I live because of the Father, so the one who feeds on me will live because of me" (John 6:57).

The death of the old life

Paul also instructs the Corinthians in the origin and meaning of the cup. The wine of the cup symbolizes Jesus' blood, the blood of the new covenant, the new arrangement for living that God has made, by which the old life is ended. The shedding of blood means the end of a life—in this case, the old life in which we lived only for ourselves. When we drink of the cup, we publicly proclaim that we agree with the death sentence that God has pronounced on our old life.

The cup is a beautiful picture of what Jesus said of Himself, "I tell you the truth, unless a kernel of wheat falls to the ground and dies, it remains only a single seed. But if it dies, it produces many seeds" (John 12:24). The King James Version expresses this thought even more descriptively: "Except a corn of wheat fall into the ground and die, it abideth alone." The emptiness of the old life is poignantly captured in the image of a seed that abides alone—a lonely and miserable abiding. That is the life that is lived for one's own wants, needs, and rights.

The Christian life is a life freely surrendered. If the wheat kernel falls to the ground and dies, Jesus says, it will bring forth much fruit. When we partake of the cup, we declare this beautiful truth. Every time we celebrate the Lord's table, we symbolically tell and retell the essential truth of the Christian faith: the old life is dead; the new life has come.

Next, Paul explains the serious meaning and symbolism of the Lord's table:

> Therefore, whoever eats the bread or drinks the cup of the Lord in an unworthy manner will be guilty of sinning against the body and blood of the Lord. A man ought to examine himself before he eats of the bread and drinks of the cup. For anyone who eats and drinks without recognizing the body of the Lord eats and drinks judgment on himself. That is why many among you are weak and sick, and a number of you have fallen asleep. But if we judged ourselves, we would not come under judgment. When we are judged by the Lord, we are being disciplined so that we will not be condemned with the world. (1 CORINTHIANS 11:27–32)

God guards the table from being defiled by unworthy attitudes and behavior. The Corinthians have been approaching the Lord's table as an empty ritual. This, Paul says, is a dangerous practice, because the Corinthians are behaving as if the death and resurrection of Jesus mean nothing to them.

Moreover, we share the guilt of those who crucified the Lord when we partake of the Lord's table without a genuine and heartfelt sincerity. According to Paul, a proper participation in Communion demands that we carefully examine ourselves. No one should eat the bread or drink the cup without searching his heart and soul.

To examine ourselves is to deal honestly with our sins. We do not cover them over or pretend they don't exist. Authentic self-examination requires that we admit our sin, call it what God calls it, and repent of it—that is, change our minds and put those sins out of our lives. As David writes, "The sacrifices of God are a broken spirit; a broken and contrite heart, O God, you will not despise" (Psalm 51:17). When you take inventory of your sins, confess them to God, and repent of them, you are qualified to partake of the Lord's table.

Some Christians take the Lord's table seriously, as they should—but instead of examining themselves and repenting of sin, they refuse to eat.

They pass up Communion and cling to their sin. "If I don't partake," they reason, "then I'm not dishonoring the Lord's table—and I'm not incurring judgment."

But God is not impressed with our ruses and mental evasions. He reads the heart. He knows if we are lying to ourselves and pretending to live the Christian life while clutching our hidden sins. God seeks to create in us a heart that is honest, obedient, and willing to put away sin. You may think you can play games with God by passing up the bread and the cup, but God doesn't play games. He is our ultimate reality.

Let's be honest with God and with ourselves. Then we can partake of the bread and cup with grateful, joyful hearts.

Sobering warnings

Paul writes, "For anyone who eats and drinks without recognizing the body of the Lord eats and drinks judgment on himself." What does "recognizing the body of the Lord" mean? First, it means understanding the meaning of the symbols. "The body of the Lord" refers to His death on the cross for us, His life made available to us. Second, it means being concerned for the other members of the church, which is also "the body of the Lord." As Christians, we are members one of another, and we recognize those ties.

Next, Paul warns that God guards the Lord's table by means of a sobering physical judgment. He writes, "That is why many among you are weak and sick, and a number of you have fallen asleep. But if we judged ourselves, we would not come under judgment. When we are judged by the Lord, we are being disciplined so that we will not be condemned with the world."

God knows that pain often makes us stop and think. Sometimes, we realize that we have been drifting away from the Lord only when we go through a painful experience. That is what was happening at Corinth. Some believers were weak or sick. Some were even dying—a sign that they had rejected God's warnings and were persisting in their sin to the point where they had been disqualified from further service to God—a principle we examined when we looked at 1 Corinthians 9:27. God had to say to some, "I can't trust you any more on earth. Come home where I can keep an eye on you."

We may be tempted to think, "But God doesn't work that way anymore, does He?" Well, why not? Does God change? Did Paul write these

163

warnings to be valid only during the first century? If these warnings were valid then, they are valid today.

Of course, not all sickness comes as discipline from God. He allows sickness in our lives for many reasons. When we are dealing with other believers who are sick, we should never assume that their illness is the result of sin in their lives. In the gospel of John, we see this exchange between Jesus and His disciples:

> As [Jesus] went along, he saw a man blind from birth. His disciples asked him, "Rabbi, who sinned, this man or his parents, that he was born blind?"
>
> "Neither this man nor his parents sinned," said Jesus, "but this happened so that the work of God might be displayed in his life." (JOHN 9:1–2)

We should never assume that sickness comes only as a judgment from God. Still, when we are sick, it's wise to ask ourselves, "Is God trying to tell me something about the way I'm living my life?" A time of illness is a good time for self-examination. As Paul says, "But if we judged ourselves, we would not come under judgment. When we are judged by the Lord, we are being disciplined so that we will not be condemned with the world."

God doesn't discipline you to hurt you or to get even with you. His discipline is that of a loving Father. As Hebrews 12:6 tells us, "The Lord disciplines those he loves." If you can go month after month, engaging in sin without consequences, then perhaps you aren't a Christian. If you don't want to be judged along with the world, then judge yourself. Confess and repent of any sins that you find in your life.

Finally, Paul speaks of the proper way to celebrate the Lord's table. He writes:

> So then, my brothers, when you come together to eat, wait for each other. If anyone is hungry, he should eat at home, so that when you meet together it may not result in judgment.
>
> And when I come I will give further directions. (1 CORINTHIANS 11:33–34)

God wants His children to behave thoughtfully and courteously toward one another, especially toward their brothers and sisters in His family of faith. When Paul says "wait for one another," he does not necessarily mean at the Lord's table, though that is a good thing to do. He means, "Be aware of the needs and problems of others and do something to meet those needs and solve those problems. Then, when you come together, your meetings will be a blessing and delight, not a curse. There will be love, not chaos. You will demonstrate God's grace, not human selfishness."

This is what Paul has been aiming at all along. He wants the Corinthian believers to embody the central meaning of the Christian life. The old selfish ways are ended; the new life has come. The bread and the cup are symbols of what our lives are to exemplify every day of the week.

14

THE GIFTS OF THE SPIRIT

1 Corinthians 12

The famed polar explorer Roald Amundsen took a homing pigeon with him on a trip to the North Pole. Upon reaching the pole, he released the pigeon from its cage. A few days later, the pigeon arrived on the windowsill of Amundsen's home in Norway. When Mrs. Amundsen saw the pigeon, she was overjoyed. It was proof that her husband had achieved his mission—and he was alive.

The Holy Spirit serves the same purpose in our lives. Since Jesus ascended after His death and resurrection, we have not been able to see Him face to face. But He has sent the Holy Spirit as a messenger to prove to us that He has achieved His mission—and He is alive.

As we come to 1 Corinthians 12, we encounter a major new section of the letter. You may recall that the book of 1 Corinthians divides into four main parts. Here is a thumbnail sketch of the structure of this book:

Part I: Introduction (1 Corinthians 1:1–9)
Paul lays out the overarching theme of the letter: We are called into fellowship with God's Son, Jesus the Lord.

Part II: Problems in the Church (1 Corinthians 1:10–11:34)
Paul deals with issues of carnal living, immorality, divisions, marriage, divorce, singleness, gender roles, authority, Communion, and so forth.

Part III: The Holy Spirit (1 Corinthians 12–15)
Paul turns from issues of carnality to issues of spirituality and deals in-depth with the role of the Holy Spirit in the life of the church and the believer.

Part IV: Final Requests (1 Corinthians 16)
Paul closes with some practical requests, such as taking up the collection for people in need, and so forth.

As we begin part 3, The Holy Spirit (beginning with 1 Corinthians 12), we address the subject of spiritual gifts and how these gifts function in the body of Christ. We will especially look at an issue that is controversial in many parts of the church, the gift of tongues.

The mark of error, the mark of truth

Much of the controversy surrounding the gift of tongues could be resolved if Christians would heed the first three verses of 1 Corinthians 12. Paul writes:

> Now about spiritual gifts, brothers, I do not want you to be ignorant. You know that when you were pagans, somehow or other you were influenced and led astray to mute idols. Therefore I tell you that no one who is speaking by the Spirit of God says, "Jesus be cursed," and no one can say, "Jesus is Lord," except by the Holy Spirit. (1 CORINTHIANS 12:1–3)

Verse 2 shows us the unmistakable mark of religious error. Many false cults use words and ideas that seem Christian, yet the people in those cults end up in serious spiritual error—and sometimes, like the followers of Jim Jones in Guyana or David Koresh in Texas, they end up dead.

Paul says, "When you were pagans, somehow or other you were influenced and led astray to mute idols." In his day, the cultural norms involved worship of images. Idolatrous religion was widespread in the first-century world, and the worship of images was the normal path idolatry would take.

Today, the images are gone, but the idolatry remains. Idolatry is still the mark of religious error. As we have seen, idolatry is anything that possesses us, controls us, and consumes our time and thinking. We were made to be possessed by God, and that is a righteous possession. When anything replaces God in our affections, it becomes our idol.

Paul says that idolatry involves being led astray, which suggests an element of control over us. When we give ourselves over to idolatry, we invite the god of this world to exercise mind control over us. You may scoff at the idea that Satan and demonic forces could control your mind. You may not believe in a real personal devil. But if you do not recognize the reality of evil spirits, then your worldview is different from that of Jesus and the apostles. The Old and New Testaments tell us that the visible institutions of our world are controlled by invisible forces that Paul calls the rulers, authorities, powers, and spiritual forces of evil in the heavenly realms (see Ephesians 6:12).

Paul wants us to recognize the true mark of the Spirit of God at work, so he writes, "Therefore I tell you that no one who is speaking by the Spirit of God says, 'Jesus be cursed,' and no one can say, 'Jesus is Lord,' except by the Holy Spirit." The Spirit came into this world to exalt Jesus Christ. That's all He does—and He will never do anything else. Paul states it both negatively and positively: No one who speaks by the Spirit of God ever demeans or diminishes the lordship of Christ (in effect saying "Jesus be cursed"); and only those who speak by the Spirit of God affirm the centrality and lordship of Christ ("Jesus is Lord").

Anyone who says that Jesus Christ was nothing but a mere man is saying, in essence, "Jesus be cursed," because the Spirit of God has told us through the Scriptures that Jesus is God the Son. It may sound like an affirmation of Jesus to say, "Jesus was a great human teacher. I don't think Jesus was God, but I respect His teachings." In reality, however, that's like saying, "Jesus be cursed." The person who demeans the Lord's deity has rejected the very reason Jesus died: He came as a sinless sacrifice for our sins. To deny the significance of the Lord's death is to say, "Jesus be cursed."

The Bible says that the human race is cursed by Adam's sin. So if you say Jesus was nothing but a man, a great human teacher, then you are saying that He is part of the cursed human race. If you deny the virgin birth, you're saying that Jesus was not God's Son but was tainted by sin and cursed by Adam. If that is so, then He cannot be our Deliverer. Any teaching that denies the deity of Christ is like saying, "Jesus be cursed."

When the Spirit is at work He exalts Christ as Lord. "Jesus is Lord" was the creed of the early church. The Romans attacked the Christian creed; they tried to force the Christians to say, "Caesar is Lord." If the Christians said, "Caesar is Lord," they would be delivered from death; if they insisted on saying, "Jesus is Lord," they faced torture and death. Most early Christians gave up their lives rather than deny that Jesus is Lord.

Why are those three words so important? Because the one who is Lord is in charge of all human events. We tend to think of Jesus as the One who will one day reign in triumph. One day, every knee shall bow and every tongue confess that Jesus Christ is Lord. But the Scriptures tell us that Jesus is Lord now; He is in charge of human events now. That's the truth the Holy Spirit manifests.

The idolatry of our age is the spirit that proclaims that something other than Jesus is Lord. Some say, "Sex is Lord." Others say, "Money is Lord." Others say, "Success is Lord." Others say, "Science is Lord." The spirit of our age is a spirit of idolatry.

Where the Spirit is at work, Christ is glorified. Jesus said, "But when he, the Spirit of truth, comes, he will guide you into all truth. He will not speak on his own; he will speak only what he hears, and he will tell you what is yet to come. He will bring glory to me by taking from what is mine and making it known to you" (John 16:13–14). Therefore, any individual, church, or religious movement that places a central focus on the Spirit is not emphasizing Christian truth. The Spirit points us to Jesus.

Paul goes on to write:

> There are different kinds of gifts, but the same Spirit. There are different kinds of service, but the same Lord. There are different kinds of working, but the same God works all of them in all men. (1 Cor-
> inthians 12:4–6)

Notice those words: "different kinds" and "same." God is the ultimate example of diversity within unity. He is triune, and He is one. Wherever you find God at work, you find diversity balanced with unity. You find many spiritual gifts but one Spirit. You find many kinds of service but one Lord over them all.

"There are different kinds of gifts," Paul says, "but the same Spirit." It is the task of the Spirit to give gifts to every believer without exception. These gifts are special capacities for service in the body of Christ. Nobody is left out; everybody receives a gift. Many believers have not discovered their gifts, but they have gifts nonetheless.

As the Spirit gives gifts, the Lord Jesus assigns different kinds of service for us to do. "There are different kinds of service," Paul writes, "but the same Lord." The original Greek word translated "service" in this passage is *diakonia*, the word from which we get "deacon." This word refers to the opportunities the Lord gives you to use your spiritual gifts. The Spirit gives the gifts; the Lord Jesus opens the opportunities.

We should never assume that the only place we can use our gifts is within the walls of the church. Yes, these gifts were given to edify (build up) the church—but they were also given for us to use in our homes, neighborhoods, workplaces, military units, and every other place where we live our lives. Our gifts are within us and opportunities for service are all around us.

"There are different kinds of working," Paul writes, "but the same God works all of them in all men." God the Father is in charge of the workings, the energizings, the results. Our God is alive, electrifying, and innovative. He is moving in these days.

I truly pity the Christian who has not taken the time to discover the gifts of the Spirit, who has not seized the opportunities provided by the Son, and who has never achieved the energized potential that the Father brings. When we discover and use our gifts, the Christian life becomes the exciting adventure God intended it to be.

The manifestation of the Spirit

Next, Paul explains that the Spirit of God has come to dwell among us and to give to each of us a pattern of gifts that Paul calls "the manifestation of the Spirit." He writes:

> Now to each one the manifestation of the Spirit is given for the common good. To one there is given through the Spirit the message of wisdom, to another the message of knowledge by means of the same Spirit, to another faith by the same Spirit, to another gifts of healing by that one Spirit, to another miraculous powers, to another prophecy, to another distinguishing between spirits, to another speaking in different kinds of tongues, and to still another the interpretation of tongues. All these are the work of one and the same Spirit, and he gives them to each one, just as he determines. (1 CORINTHIANS 12:7–11)

These various gifts of the Spirit, which are collectively called "the manifestation of the Spirit," form the foundation by which the work of the church is done. God always starts by equipping His people with gifts. People like to start by forming a committee, but God begins with gifts. He wants us to ask ourselves, "What is my gift? What has the Spirit given to me as a capacity for service in the body of Christ?"

It's important to notice three things that Paul underscores for us in these verses.

First, Paul says that the manifestation of the Spirit is given "to each one." He makes this statement in verse 7 and repeats it in verse 11, so it's an important point. If you are a Christian, you can never say that you were behind the door when the gifts were given out. Every Christian is gifted for service.

God has an infinite variety of gifts to give, and He has chosen a unique combination to suit you and your personality. He has placed you in a unique place for exercising your gifts, and He is bringing you a series of unique opportunities for using them. The manifestation of the Spirit in our lives is as unique as our fingerprints; no two are alike.

Second, when Paul speaks of "manifestation of the Spirit," he makes it clear that spiritual gifts are not a matter of normal, natural talents and abilities. Spiritual gifts are a supernatural function. In some quarters of Christianity, when the phrase "gifts of the Spirit" is used, it seems to apply only to certain miraculous gifts such as tongues, healing, or miracles. But we need to understand that all of the gifts are supernatural. Every gift listed in Scripture is (in the original Greek) a *charisma*, a supernatural gift.

If you have a talent for singing or speaking or painting or athletics, that's wonderful. You can use those talents for God's glory—but they are natural abilities, not supernatural gifts. All people, Christians and non-Christians, have abilities and talents—but spiritual gifts are given only to Christians. Non-Christians do not have spiritual gifts because they do not have the Holy Spirit.

Third, Paul says that spiritual gifts are "given for the common good." They are not for our own enjoyment or blessing—though we will experience joy as we use them. The primary purpose of spiritual gifts is to bless and edify others and glorify God. The blessing we receive as we use our spiritual gifts is a byproduct, not the primary reason they were given. If you use your spiritual gifts to boost your own ego and to glorify yourself, God will turn off the faucet.

Does this mean spiritual gifts can be used for fleshly, selfish reasons? Yes, they can—and the result is the spread of dissension and division in the body of Christ. Spiritual gifts, rightly used, release the power of God; wrongly used, they disgrace the church and the gospel of Jesus Christ. So we must always use our gifts for the common good and the glory of God.

Speaking gifts and serving gifts

In 1 Corinthians 1:7, Paul told the Corinthians, "Therefore you do not lack any spiritual gift as you eagerly wait for our Lord Jesus Christ to be revealed." This is an amazing statement. The Scriptures list at least twenty-one different spiritual gifts—and Paul told the Corinthians that they didn't lack a single one of them.

The gifts of the Spirit are listed primarily in three New Testament passages: Romans 12:3–7, 1 Corinthians 12:1–12, 28, and Ephesians 4:11. As Paul listed them, they are apostle, prophet, evangelist, pastor, teacher, service, exhortation, giving, leadership, mercy, helps, administration, wisdom, knowledge, discernment, prophecy, tongues, interpretation, faith, healing, and miracles.

The apostle Peter also writes of spiritual gifts. He divides spiritual gifts into two major divisions: speaking gifts and serving gifts. Peter writes:

> Each one should use whatever gift he has received to serve others, faithfully administering God's grace in its various forms. If anyone speaks, he should do it as one speaking the very words of God. If anyone serves, he should do it with the strength God provides, so that in all things God may be praised through Jesus Christ. To him be the glory and the power for ever and ever. Amen. (1 PETER 4:10–11)

In 1 Corinthians 12, Paul lists nine gifts. He begins with two speaking gifts, wisdom and knowledge. He writes, "To one there is given through the Spirit the message of wisdom, to another the message of knowledge by means of the same Spirit." The Greek word translated "message" is *logos*, which literally means "word." The word of wisdom and the word of knowledge are supernatural abilities, given by the Spirit.

Wisdom is the application of God-given knowledge to specific problems. It is the ability to take God's Word and apply it to real-life issues in your home, your marriage, your church, your business, or wherever problems arise that can be solved by scriptural principles. You have probably seen this gift in operation many times—for example, in a church meeting where someone stands up and says, "Well, it seems that such-and-such passage of Scripture applies to this situation. If we would do this, as God's Word indicates, then the problem will be solved." And everyone says, "Of course! Why didn't we see that?"

Knowledge is the ability to search the Word of God, to see the truth that is there, and to make it understandable in a systematic way. Though all believers should study the Word and understand its truth, some believers have a supernatural ability to grasp God's truth and communicate it to others.

Next, Paul writes, "to another faith by the same Spirit." A gift of faith? Aren't all Christians supposed to have faith? Of course! You can't be a Christian without faith. But some people have the gift of an increased expression of faith—and this underscores a truth that characterizes all spiritual gifts: They are heightened expressions of qualities that all believers are expected to possess. We are all to have faith, but a few of us have a heightened and intensified gift of faith. We are all to help one another, but some have a heightened and intensified gift of helps. We are all expected to support God's church, but some of us have a heightened and intensified gift of giving.

Another name for the gift of faith is "vision." It's the ability to perceive the invisible God as if He were visible and to act on the basis of His infinite resources. People with the gift of faith often say, "I believe God wants us to do such-and-such." It's as if they can see God with eyes of faith and know His will for a given situation.

Then Paul writes, "to another gifts of healing by that one Spirit." The word translated "healing" is plural in the Greek and should read "healings." The American Standard Version of 1901 is one of the few translations that renders this phrase correctly: "and to another gifts of healings." The plural is important because there are three levels of life where we need healing—physical, psychological, and spiritual. Though we tend to focus on physical healing, the gift of healings can be exercised at any one of these three levels.

In the early church, the gift of healings was frequently exercised with regard to physical health. The apostles had the ability to lay hands on people and see them instantly made whole. Though I cannot say that I know anyone who has the gift of healings, I'm convinced that healings occur today. I've known people in my congregation who have been prayed for by the elders of the church, and they experienced a healing or remission that the doctors could not explain; in those instances, however, I believe God worked through prayer, not through a spiritual gift.

We should also remember that the spiritual gift of healings can be applied to the level of emotional and spiritual healing. I can think of a number of Christians who seem to have the gift of healings in the emotional and spiritual realm. God continually brings hurting people into their lives, and they reach out and have just the right thing to do or say to minister God's healing power to their painful memories, wounded emotions, and burdened spirits.

Next, Paul writes, "to another miraculous powers." In the Greek, this phrase means "the energizing of powers." This refers to the ability to release the power of God in a supernatural way, much as Jesus did when He turned water into wine and walked on water. Although there are claims of miracles taking place in our day, and those claims may be true, it seems that the release of miraculous power is rarely given today.

As you read the story of the early church in Acts, you see that many miraculous events take place in the early chapters. Those miraculous events become increasingly rare in the later chapters of Acts. It may be that in those early days, soon after the crucifixion, resurrection, and ascension of our Lord, the church needed the unleashing of miracles, healings, and other supernatural signs in order to establish the fledgling faith of the new believers. Remember, there were no mature, longtime Christians in the early church; everyone was a new Christian. But as the church became established and mature, the need for supernatural signs seemed to diminish. This may explain why we rarely, if ever, see the gift of miracles legitimately exercised today.

Next, Paul writes, "to another prophecy." This is a common gift—and a vitally important one. In fact, it may be the most important of all the gifts. I say this because Paul devotes a whole chapter to this gift—1 Corinthians 14. When we hear the word *prophecy* or *prophesying*, we tend to think of predicting the future. But that's not what the Bible means when it speaks of this gift.

In the Bible, the gift of prophesying is the ability to speak forth the mind of God. It may include an element of prediction, but usually the gift of prophesying involves speaking about what God is doing in the present world. It involves knowing what the Scriptures say, understanding God's activity in history, and setting it forth in such a clear way that people can relate His will and His workings to their everyday lives.

Next, Paul writes, "to another distinguishing between spirits." The ability to spot a phony and detect false doctrine is a much-needed spiritual gift. There are religious leaders, preachers, authors, and speakers who are charming and persuasive, who speak wonderful sounding words that seemed to fall from heaven itself—but they are deceivers. Many people follow them, support them financially, and hang upon their every word—yet these are false teachers. They enrich and empower themselves at the expense of the gullible. Every church needs a few people with the gift of discerning which spirits are of God and which are from Satan.

The most controversial gift

Then Paul writes, "to another speaking in different kinds of tongues, and to still another the interpretation of tongues." The gift of tongues is really two different gifts—the ability to speak in tongues and the ability to interpret tongues. The gift of tongues is the ability to speak—or interpret—a language you've never learned. It's not the ability to learn a language quickly. Many non-Christians can do that. The gift of tongues is a supernatural manifestation, not a natural ability.

This is the most controversial of all spiritual gifts. Many churches and individual Christians place a great deal of emphasis on this one gift. Despite its prominence in some Christian circles, we need to ask ourselves: Why, if it is such an important gift, does the New Testament not treat it more prominently?

After all, the foundational books of the New Testaments, the four Gospels, do not mention this gift—unless you count one brief reference in the closing verses of the gospel of Mark. There Jesus says, "And these signs will accompany those who believe: In my name they will drive out demons; they will speak in new tongues" (Mark 16:17). The earliest and best Greek manuscripts of Mark's gospel do not contain verses 9 through 20.

Bible scholars generally agree that those verses were not originally part of Mark's gospel. Now, I wouldn't say that Mark 16:9–20 is not inspired Scripture. But I would say that Mark 16:17 is not a firm biblical basis for the practice of tongues in our day.

The gift of tongues is mentioned only three times in the book of Acts—and each of these three instances involves a historic occasion in the church: when the Holy Spirit first came upon the church at Pentecost (Acts 2); when Peter first took the gospel to the Gentiles (Acts 10:46); and when Paul founded the church in Ephesus (Acts 19:6). Besides these three instances in Acts and one debatable instance in Mark, there is only one other place in the New Testament where tongues are mentioned: here in 1 Corinthians. None of the other epistles of Paul refer to this gift, nor do the epistles of Peter, John, or Jude. Clearly, the early church did not place a strong emphasis on this gift.

Why, then, are so many churches obsessed with this gift today? Some churches teach that every believer should exercise the gift of tongues. Christians are sometimes made to feel that if they do not exhibit the gift of tongues, they are second-class Christians—or possibly not even Christians at all. This, I would suggest, is evidence of an unhealthy and unbiblical emphasis on tongues.

The first occurrence of the gift of tongues was in Jerusalem on the day of Pentecost (Acts 2). The Holy Spirit came upon the apostles, and these men—all Jews from the region of Galilee—began speaking in a variety of languages. Sixteen different languages are specifically mentioned—languages the apostles had never learned.

On that day, the gift of tongues had a specific purpose: It was a sign to unbelievers of the power of God. As we look at the exercise of the gift of tongues in the New Testament, we have to ask ourselves: Is the manifestation of the gift today the same manifestation that we see in the Bible? I believe that much of the controversy in the church today is the result of the failure to ask these essential questions.

How can we know if a manifestation of tongues is legitimate or fraudulent? One test is to look for a specific trademark of God: diversity arising out of unity and unity out of diversity. Paul writes, "All these [gifts] are the work of one and the same Spirit, and he gives them to each one, just as he determines." Many gifts, one Spirit. Paul says, in effect, "No matter what gift you have, no matter how your gifts differ from the gifts of others, the same Spirit is behind all true spiritual gifts."

Can we go down the list of gifts, check off the ones we want, and ask God to give them to us? No. Paul writes that the Spirit of God "gives them to each one, just as he determines."

Many people ask, "Why don't we have miraculous gifts today as they did in the first-century church?" The answer: The Spirit has not determined that He should give those gifts. Some would say that the Holy Spirit withholds the miracle gifts today because the church is fleshly and infected with worldliness. Well, it's true the church today has become worldly in many ways—but remember, the church in Corinth was very infected with worldliness, yet the gifts of the Spirit abounded there. God chose to shower all the gifts of the Spirit on the church in Corinth despite its worldliness. God doesn't bestow spiritual gifts on us as a reward for being spiritual Christians; He determines where the gifts are needed, and He bestows them as He wills.

Baptized into one body

At some point in your Christian life, you've probably been asked, "Have you been baptized with the Holy Spirit?" This question is not easy to answer, because there are conflicting viewpoints as to what the baptism of the Holy Spirit consists of. In the closing section of 1 Corinthians 12, we see what the Scriptures say about the baptism of the Holy Spirit. Paul writes:

The body is a unit, though it is made up of many parts; and though all its parts are many, they form one body. So it is with Christ. For we were all baptized by one Spirit into one body—whether Jews or Greeks, slave or free—and we were all given the one Spirit to drink. (1 CORINTHIANS 12:12–13)

Here Paul introduces an analogy to help us understand how the church is designed to function: the human body. It is no mere figure of speech to say that the church is the body of Christ. This is a spiritual reality, and God takes it seriously. So this is where Paul begins: Just as the human body is a unit made up of many parts, he says, "so it is with Christ." Notice, he does not say "So it is with the church" but "so it is with Christ." This is vitally important to understand. The church is not like the body of Christ. It's not a metaphor of the body of Christ. It literally and mystically is the body of Christ.

Stand before a full-length mirror and look at your body. What do you see? One body that divides into two major sections: the head; the torso with its limbs. The head is not large, compared with the rest of the body, but it is the control center of the body. The torso and limbs comprise the largest part of the body, but every part of this section of the body is under the command and control of the head. That is how the church, the body of Christ, is intended to function.

The church is a body with many members, and yet it is only one body. We are tempted to think that the church is many bodies, because we see it divided up into many denominations. But the church is truly one body, a single shared life under the authority of one head, which is Christ.

How did we become members of that body? Paul writes, "For we were all baptized by one Spirit into one body." That is the "baptism with the Holy Spirit" that was predicted by John the Baptist and by Jesus, fulfilled for the first time on the day of Pentecost. When we receive Jesus as Lord and Savior, we are baptized by the Spirit into the body of Christ and we become part of the living Christ.

So, if someone asks you, "Have you been baptized with the Holy Spirit?" the biblical answer (if you are a Christian) is, "Yes." You cannot be a Christian without having been baptized by the Holy Spirit. Some people claim that the baptism of the Holy Spirit is accompanied by speaking in tongues or miraculous signs, but there's no biblical support for that idea. In fact, the baptism of the Spirit, which accompanies conversion, is often a quiet experience. The fact that it takes place quietly and without miraculous signs doesn't make it any less real.

Paul goes on to say, "We were all given the one Spirit to drink." It doesn't matter whether we are Jews or Greeks, slave or free, we are all made to drink of one Spirit and are all indwelt by one Spirit. When you drink water, you take water into yourself; when you drink of the Spirit, you take the Spirit into yourself. This passage establishes a truth that some believers seem to have missed: All believers are baptized by the Spirit and indwelt by the Spirit. There are no exceptions.

No insignificant members

When Paul tells us we were all baptized by one Spirit into one body and were all given one Spirit to drink, he is restating a truth that Jesus revealed to His disciples in the upper room the night He was betrayed. John's gospel records that Jesus told the disciples about the coming of the Holy Spirit. He said that the Spirit's role would be to strengthen, encourage, comfort, and guide the Lord's followers into all truth. Above all, Jesus said, the Holy Spirit "will bring glory to me by taking from what is mine and making it known to you" (John 16:14).

In other words, the Spirit will make Jesus real to every believer. He will make it possible for Christians who have never seen Jesus to know Him just as if He were a close and intimate friend—which, in fact, He is. The Spirit's work of making the personality of Jesus real to us is what keeps us grounded in our faith. If not for the work of the Spirit, we would fall away.

Non-Christians can't understand this. They think Christianity is a set of creeds, doctrines, rules, and intellectual convictions. In reality, Christianity is the reality of Christ in our lives. That's why Christians often say that Christianity isn't a religion; it's a relationship. Building and maintaining that relationship is the work of the Holy Spirit.

Jesus expressed this reality in a little formula: "You are in me, and I am in you" (John 14:20). When the Spirit baptizes us into the body of Christ, He puts us into Christ ("you are in me"). He merges our life into His. Then, when we are indwelt by the Spirit, when we all drink from one Spirit, then Christ enters into us ("I am in you"). That is the power by which we are to live.

Next, Paul explains how this understanding of the church as the body of Christ changes how we relate to each other as fellow believers. He writes:

Now the body is not made up of one part but of many. If the foot should say, "Because I am not a hand, I do not belong to the body," it would not for that reason cease to be part of the body. And if the ear should say, "Because I am not an eye, I do not belong to the body," it would not for that reason cease to be part of the body. If the whole body were an eye, where would the sense of hearing be? If the whole body were an ear, where would the sense of smell be? But in fact God has arranged the parts in the body, every one of them, just as he wanted them to be. If they were all one part, where would the body be? As it is, there are many parts, but one body. (1 CORINTHIANS 12:14–20)

It would be absurd for the different parts of the body to say, "If I can't be an eye or an ear, then I have no place in the body." Every part of the body is important, and each has its own unique function. Yet some Christians are tragically self-deceived about their importance to the body of Christ. They say to themselves, "I'm not equipped to be a preacher or a youth leader or a Sunday school teacher, so I'm going to sit in the back of the church and do nothing." You are a unique and irreplaceable part of the body; stop thinking and acting as if you've been amputated!

There are no insignificant members of the body. You have a vital role to play, and no one else can be who you are and do what you do. God may not have called you to lead a worship service—but He has given you spiritual gifts and opportunities for service. Can you visit shut-ins, prisoners, or hospital patients? Can you lend a sympathetic ear to people with hurts and problems? Can you serve meals at a homeless shelter or a battered women's shelter? Can you open your home and provide hospitality for a neighborhood Bible study? There is something you can do—something God is calling you to do—in the body of Christ. Ask God to show you your place and your function; then go where He sends you.

We belong to each other

Next, Paul addresses the problem of a cliquish attitude in the church:

The eye cannot say to the hand, "I don't need you!" And the head cannot say to the feet, "I don't need you!" On the contrary, those parts of the body that seem to be weaker are indispensable, and the parts that we think are less honorable we treat with special honor. And the parts that are unpresentable are treated with special modesty, while our presentable parts need no special treatment. But God has combined the members of the body and has given greater honor to the parts that lacked it, so that there should be no division in the body, but that its parts should have equal concern for each other. If one part suffers, every part suffers with it; if one part is honored, every part rejoices with it. (1 CORINTHIANS 12:21–26)

I never cease to be amazed at the unloving attitudes many Christians display toward fellow believers. All too many Christians seem to think they don't need the rest of the body. They have their own ministry, their own vision, their own gifts, their own priorities—and they don't want anything to do with anyone else. They look upon other ministries and individuals in the church as competitors, not partners.

As Paul observes, the eye can't say to the hand, "I don't need you!" The head can't say to the feet, "I don't need you!" The parts of the body of Christ that receive less honor should be singled out for special honor. One of the great tragedies of the church is that we do so little to honor the more modest members of the body.

Once, after I preached at a conference on the East Coast, a doctor came to me and said, "You may be interested to know that there's a part of your body that is absolutely essential to you as a preacher. You probably don't even think about it when you preach, yet you'd be lost without it."

"Is it my tongue?" I said. "My brain? What is it?"

"No, it's your big toe!"

"You're kidding me!" I said. "I don't use my big toe when I preach."

"Oh, yes you do," he said. "If you didn't have a big toe on each foot, you couldn't stand up to preach. Your big toe has the ability to sense when your body begins to lean too far and lose its balance. Without your big toe, you'd fall on your face every time you tried to stand up and speak."

I now guard my big toe with great care!

We need to lavish the same care on those in the body of Christ who serve humbly, quietly, and without fanfare. They are the people who set up chairs, brew coffee, clean restrooms, and serve food. They are always there when needed, but they never get the applause. Few people know their names. They are the big toes of the church—rarely honored but indispensable.

Paul observes, "If one part suffers, every part suffers with it; if one part is honored, every part rejoices with it." It's important to note that Paul does not say all should suffer; he says that when one suffers, all suffer. If one member of the body hurts, we all hurt—whether we know it or not. And if one member of the body falls into sin, scandal, and disgrace, the entire body suffers from it. We are all affected.

Unity and diversity

Paul has just been telling us that the body of Christ is an indivisible unit. Now he is going to show us that, along with the unity of the body, there is great diversity:

> Now you are the body of Christ, and each one of you is a part of it. And in the church God has appointed first of all apostles, second prophets, third teachers, then workers of miracles, also those having gifts of healing, those able to help others, those with gifts of administration, and those speaking in different kinds of tongues. Are all apostles? Are all prophets? Are all teachers? Do all work miracles? Do all have gifts of healing? Do all speak in tongues? Do all interpret? But eagerly desire the greater gifts.
>
> And now I will show you the most excellent way. (1 CORINTHIANS 12:27–31)

When Paul says that God has "appointed first of all apostles, second prophets, third teachers, then workers of miracles" and so forth, he is not listing these gifts in order of rank or importance. He is listing them in order of their chronological appearance in the church. The apostles were the first to arrive on the scene. These were followed by the prophets, then the teachers, and so forth. Why did God place so many different kinds of gifts in the church? Because diversity is necessary to the functioning of the church.

No one has all the gifts. No one can do everything. God has equipped some people to preach the Word, while equipping others to carry on different ministries. A church that was made up of nothing but preachers would be a strange and dysfunctional church, just as a human body that was nothing but an eye would be strange and dysfunctional. We must exercise our diverse gifts within the unity of the Spirit.

When it is exercised, a spiritual gift becomes an office. Instead of saying, "John has a gift of teaching," we say, "John is a teacher." That's his office. Instead of saying, "Mary has a gift of administration," we say, "Mary is an administrator." That's her office.

Finally, Paul says, "But eagerly desire the greater gifts." He's speaking to the entire congregation. This statement is in the plural form, addressed to many people at once, not an individual. We've already seen that we can't choose our gifts, because the Holy Spirit gives gifts to each individual as He determines. Our gifts are chosen for us by the Spirit. So what does Paul mean when he tells us to "eagerly desire the greater gifts"?

He's saying that the entire church (the collective, plural "you") should eagerly desire that the higher gifts be manifested in the congregation. The higher gifts, of course, are those that edify and help others.

The last thing Paul says in 1 Corinthians 12 is, "And now I will show you the most excellent way." This is Paul's introduction to the great Love Chapter, 1 Corinthians 13. While the gifts of the Spirit are the source of our diversity, love is the source of our unity. The body of Christ is continually beset by internal and external forces that seek to divide and destroy it. Love is the only force that can keep the body of Christ together in harmony and unity.

15

THE LOVE CHAPTER

1 Corinthians 13

Dr. George Crane was a psychologist and the author of a nationally syndicated newspaper column, "Worry Clinic," that appeared in newspapers for over four decades. He once wrote about a woman who came to his office for counseling. "I hate my husband!" she announced. "I don't just want to divorce him—I want to pay him back for all the pain and suffering he's caused me!"

"I think I have the perfect plan for getting even with your husband," Dr. Crane replied. "Here's what you should do: Go home and start pretending that you really love your husband. Build him up! Praise him for every little thing he does. Go out of your way to be considerate and loving. Then, when he's convinced of your undying love for him—drop the bomb! Tell him you want a divorce!"

"Perfect!" the woman said. "He'll be so shocked, he may never recover!"

The woman left and put the plan into action. A month later, she returned for a follow-up session.

"So," Dr. Crane said, "are you ready to divorce your husband?"

"Divorce him!" the woman said. "Absolutely not! I found out I really love him!"

This woman had made an amazing discovery: Love is not just a feeling. Love is a decision. When you do the actions of love, the feelings of love follow.

Agape love

We come now to the most beautiful chapter in the whole New Testament, 1 Corinthians 13. This chapter is justly famous not only for its majestic language but also for its practical teaching on how we can make a decision to love even the unlovely, the unloving, and the unlovable. After teaching

183

on the gifts of the Spirit, he makes this transitional statement: "And now I will show you the most excellent way." Then he begins chapter 13 with these words:

> If I speak in the tongues of men and of angels, but have not love, I am only a resounding gong or a clanging cymbal. If I have the gift of prophecy and can fathom all mysteries and all knowledge, and if I have a faith that can move mountains, but have not love, I am nothing. If I give all I possess to the poor and surrender my body to the flames, but have not love, I gain nothing. (1 CORINTHIANS 13:1–3)

It seems a shame to subject these words to the cold light of analysis. But some analysis is necessary in order to grasp what the apostle Paul is saying.

He explores three aspects of love in these verses: the preeminence of love over all else; the principles of love; and the permanence of love. Though chapter 13 is often read by itself at weddings and other occasions, it's helpful to remember its context, coming immediately after chapter 12, where Paul discusses matters pertaining to the Holy Spirit.

Here we come to what Paul calls "the most excellent way," the fruit of the Spirit. You may say, "I thought the 'fruit of the Spirit' was the subject of a completely different letter by Paul—the fifth chapter of Galatians." And you'd be right. There, Paul writes:

> But the fruit of the Spirit is love, joy, peace, patience, kindness, goodness, faithfulness, gentleness and self-control. Against such things there is no law. (GALATIANS 5:22–23)

It's no accident that Paul places love at the top of this list. Love is not only the first fruit of the spirit; it is the one fruit that contains all the rest. All the other qualities are really different forms of the first one, love. Joy is love enjoying itself. Peace is love at rest. Patience is love that's willing to wait. Kindness is love's reaction to other people. Goodness is love making righteous decisions. Faithfulness is love keeping its word. Gentleness is love empathizing with others. Self-control is love resisting temptation.

The fruit of the Spirit is expressed in many diverse ways, but love is the key to them all. So the Love Chapter, 1 Corinthians 13, sets forth the quality of love that the Holy Spirit generates in us as He reproduces the character of Christ in us. If you have Christlike love, all of the other fruit of the Spirit become possible to you.

One of the deadliest enemies of the Christian cause is phony love. That's why Paul says, "Let love be genuine" (Romans 12:9a). Disingenuous love is hypocrisy.

It's important to understand exactly what the apostle Paul meant by this word *love*. In the first-century Greek language, there were a number of distinct words that we would translate as "love." One Greek word Paul did not use in this chapter was *eros*—a word that referred to sexual love or romantic attraction, the kind of feeling you have when you fall in love with another person. Another Greek word Paul did not use was *philia*, which refers to affection, the love between brothers or friends. Instead, the word Paul used in 1 Corinthians 13 is *agape*, love that is a commitment to do good to others.

Because *agape* love is a decision, not a feeling, it's the only kind of love that enables us to love the unlovely, the unloving, and the unlovable. It is the only kind of love that can obey the command of Jesus, "Love your enemies." There is no one in the world more unlovable than your worst enemy—yet Jesus says you should love the person who hates you and hurts you. Obviously, you are not going to have warm, fuzzy feelings toward your enemy—but you can make a decision, in spite of your feelings, to seek the best for your enemy.

Agape love is only possible for those who love God. If you try to exercise *agape* love without having the love of God within you, the love you show will be a phony, fleshly love. The Scriptures tell us that there are two great commandments, and the first has priority over the second.

> One of the teachers of the law came and heard them debating. Noticing that Jesus had given them a good answer, he asked him, "Of all the commandments, which is the most important?"
>
> "The most important one," answered Jesus, "is this: 'Hear, O Israel, the Lord our God, the Lord is one. Love the Lord your God with all your heart and with all your soul and with all your mind and with all your strength.' The second is this: 'Love your neighbor as yourself.' There is no commandment greater than these." (MARK 12:28–31; *see also* MATTHEW 22:37–39, LUKE 10:27)

Many of us try to turn that around, loving our neighbor, whoever he may be, without first loving God. It's impossible to do that. The love of God enables us to love other people (see Romans 5:5). So it's pointless to try to authentically love others until we first love God.

We love God by recognizing His love for us. He created us, He supplies our needs, He gave His Son to die for us, He forgave us and redeemed us, He removed our guilt, He healed our inner hurts, He called us to Himself, He adopted us and gave us a place of belonging in His forever-family. To remember all of that is to be stirred with love for God.

Once God has awakened our capacity to love, it's much easier to love other people. While you were a sinner, rebelling against God and rejecting Him, He sacrificed His Son for you. The awareness of that fact makes it easier to love your enemies even while they hate you, reject you, and sin against you.

Love is preeminent

Paul's discussion of love in this chapter cannot be understood apart from its context. The Love Chapter comes immediately after Paul has said that all believers are baptized with the Holy Spirit and are made part of the body of Christ. We are filled with the Spirit, indwelt by the Spirit, and made to drink of one Spirit. That is the basis of our capacity to love others with *agape* love.

Here, in chapter 13, Paul builds on all that he has just said. His theme in this chapter is, "Now that you have the capacity to love others, do it! Here is what your love should look like." Then he shows us some of the qualities of Christlike *agape* love.

Paul begins by describing the preeminent value of love. What makes life worth living? Love! Paul contrasts love with things that were highly regarded in the culture of Corinth. First, there is the ability to speak eloquently and persuasively. The ancient Greeks admired oratory—the ability to hold an audience spellbound by the power of the spoken word. So Paul writes, "If I speak in the tongues of men and of angels, but have not love, I am only a resounding gong or a clanging cymbal." Without *agape* love, the greatest orator is nothing but a brassy noisemaker.

Some people suggest that Paul speaks here of glossolalia, the gift of speaking in tongues. Some claim that the gift of tongues enables a person to speak in the language of angels, but there is no passage of Scripture to support such a claim. The only reference in all the Scriptures to the tongues of angels is this poetic phrase in 1 Corinthians 13:1—hardly the kind of clear, strong statement on which to base sound doctrine. Paul is not making a statement about speaking in tongues, but about love. He is saying that love is infinitely more important than any supposed ability to speak in other languages, whether the languages of earth or of heaven.

Next, Paul compares love with two other qualities that were admired in the culture of Corinth and in our culture: knowledge and power. He writes, "If I have the gift of prophecy and can fathom all mysteries and all knowledge, and if I have a faith that can move mountains, but have not love, I am nothing."

Here Paul refers to theologians who have the intellectual ability to understand the riddles of the Scriptures. There are many mysteries that trouble the faithful: "Why doesn't God just kill the devil?" "Where did Cain get his wife?" "Why does God, who is all-loving and all-powerful, allow suffering and tragedy in the world?" Paul says, "If I could explain all the mysteries of God and the Scriptures, yet I did not demonstrate love, I would be nothing. Knowledge without love has no value."

He also speaks of power. If he had such great faith that it amounted to the power to move mountains, but he had no love, he would be nothing. Power without love has no value. Faith without love has no meaning.

Well, what about religious zeal? Paul writes, "If I give all I possess to the poor and surrender my body to the flames, but have not love, I gain nothing." There are many people who give sacrificially for the sake of the poor or for social justice or for some other great cause—but they don't give out of love. They give to make themselves look good, or so they can feel superior to other people, or as a means of advancing themselves socially or politically. If we display sacrificial zeal but we have no love, then all of our sacrifices are for nothing.

There have even been people who poured gasoline over their bodies and set fire to themselves to protest a war or make some other kind of statement. Those people make the supreme sacrifice for the sake of a cause they believe in, body and soul. Do they have love in their hearts as they give their bodies to be burned? I don't know. God alone knows. But as Paul says, a sacrifice not motivated by love is of no benefit to anyone.

Love that never lets go

Next, Paul shows us that love must be practical. He is not treating love as an ethereal ideal but as a pragmatic force for keeping human relationships functioning as God intended. So Paul gives us a series of benchmarks against which we should measure our own love. He writes:

Love is patient, love is kind. It does not envy, it does not boast, it is not proud. It is not rude, it is not self-seeking, it is not easily angered, it keeps no record of wrongs. Love does not delight in evil but rejoices with the truth. (1 CORINTHIANS 13:4–6)

Notice that Paul lists only three positives; the rest are negatives. In other words, love is three simple things: patience, kindness, and honesty (it rejoices with the truth). The rest of Paul's description of love is a list of all the things love is not. If our love is characterized by any of these negative qualities, then our love is tainted. These are the things that can pollute and poison our love: envy, boastfulness, pride, rudeness, selfishness, anger, grudge keeping, and taking delight in sin.

Many people admire the poetic language of 1 Corinthians 13, but they do not understand how to produce this kind of love. Part of the reason is that while we want to experience this kind of love, we also reserve the right to cling to these poisonous actions. "Yes, I want to be a loving person," we say, "but I want to continue to envy the possessions and achievements of others. I want to continue to puff myself up with pride. I want to continue to show rudeness and rage when I'm offended. I want to continue being selfish and holding on to resentment. And yes, I want to continue my secret life of sin. Can't I do those things and still be a person of love?"

"No, Paul says, we cannot."

The love he speaks of in 1 Corinthians 13 is not a human love that we can turn on and off like tap water. It is God's own love, expressed through our lives. In order to be channels of God's love, we have to renounce the false, destructive, sinful actions of the flesh. We have to be purified and cleansed of our all-too-human desire to get even, to blow of steam, to give people a piece of our minds!

We have to be cured of our impatience, our eagerness to interrupt, our need to push people out of our way. We have to give up the right to intimidate people, boss them around, and put them in their place. And as long as we hold on to our right to strike back, lose our temper, and indulge in sin, we cannot be channels for *agape* love.

What keeps us from showing kindness to those who are rude to us? Why do we insist on being sarcastic and insulting right back? Why do we envy the accomplishments of others and try to tear them down? Why do we gloat over the misfortunes of others instead of praying for them? The answer: We are full of ourselves. We cannot express God's *agape* love until we empty out the self.

Paul then shows us what love should look like when we put it into action:

It always protects, always trusts, always hopes, always perseveres. (1 CORINTHIANS 13:7)

When love learns an unpleasant secret about someone, it doesn't rush to spread the news around. Love protects. Love keeps the secret. Love does not gossip. As Christians, we know it's a sin to gossip—but many of us don't know what gossip is. We say, "Oh, I'm not gossiping. The story I'm spreading is true!" True or not, it's still gossip. Spreading a false story is slander. Spreading any hurtful story, true or not, is gossip—and gossip is a violation of love. *Agape* love protects.

Love trusts. This does not mean that love is gullible; it means that love is ready to believe anything that has a ground of reality to it. Love is always willing to forgive and start over. It does not say, "You've had your chance. I can never trust you again." If you or I were finished after failing God two or three times, where would we be?

And love always hopes. No person is ever pronounced hopeless where *agape* love is concerned. There is always a place for us to begin again.

Finally, Paul says that love always perseveres. It never quits, never gives up. It's like trying to bail water out of a boat with a big hole in the bottom: The water floods in faster than you can bail it out! Our Christlike love should flood into the lives around us in the same way. Even if people reject our love and try to toss it out of our lives, we keep loving them and loving them until they are neck-deep in Christian love!

Love that perseveres is the love that the hymn writer described in the song "O Love That Will Not Let Me Go." Persevering love goes on loving even when it has been disappointed, rejected, and abused. Persevering love never lets go.

And did you happen to notice that everything Paul says about *agape* love also applies to our Lord? Jesus always protects; Jesus always trusts; Jesus always hopes; Jesus always perseveres. What does this tell you? It tells you that the character of Jesus is love. So when we love, the character of Jesus shines through our lives. That's what the Holy Spirit seeks to reproduce in us: Christlikeness.

Another word for Christlikeness is maturity—spiritual maturity. There are Christians who never seem to grow and change and become more Christlike even after twenty or more years in the faith. You do not see love in their lives. Instead, they are querulous and cantankerous and difficult to get along with.

The goal of the Spirit is to produce Christlike maturity in our lives. He is teaching us to be loving, patient, kind, forgiving, understanding, protective, trusting, hopeful, and persevering. These are the qualities that make the Christian life worth living. These are the marks of true Christian spirituality.

The greatest of these is love

My friend, Dr. Stephen Olford, was born in Zambia, the son of English missionaries, Frederick and Bessie Olford. His father died when Stephen was a young boy, and his mother took him from Africa to England aboard a tramp steamer. Just a few days into the two-week voyage, one of the seamen was injured. His wound festered and smelled so terribly that the other seamen refused to go near him. There were no medicines to treat the man, so he was placed out on the deck to die. In his agony, the man cursed and screamed, but his shipmates refused to help other than to pass food to him at the end of a pole.

Bessie Olford, Stephen's mother, took pity on this man and went up on the deck. Braving the stench, she took a basin of warm water and washed the pus and dead flesh from the man's wound. As she ministered to him, the man cursed her, just as he had cursed everyone else on the ship. But Bessie cared for him throughout the voyage.

Finally, they docked in London, and the man hobbled off the ship. In response to Bessie Olford's patient, persistent *agape* love for him, the man gave his life to Christ—and he became Mrs. Olford's servant for the rest of his life.

That's the kind of love Paul writes about in 1 Corinthians 13—a love that is a decision of the will, not a feeling; a love that braves stenches and curses and wrath; a love that does not quit. As Paul writes:

> Love never fails. But where there are prophecies, they will cease; where there are tongues, they will be stilled; where there is knowledge, it will pass away. (1 CORINTHIANS 13:8)

Notice what Paul is saying here: The apostle is comparing love with spiritual gifts. Love never fails—but what about spiritual gifts? There will be an end to the gift of prophesying—the gift of unveiling the mysteries of God. There will be an end to the gift of tongues—the supernatural ability to speak in a language one has never learned. There will be an end to the gift of knowledge—the supernatural ability to understand and systematize biblical truth.

It's interesting to note that Paul uses a different Greek word to indicate the end of the gift of tongues. It's as if he is saying that prophesying and knowledge will fade away—but the gift of tongues will absolutely cease. This is because tongues is a sign gift, intended to arrest the attention of unbelievers in a dramatic way. Once that has been accomplished, there is no further need for the gift, so it ceases in the individual.

The prophesying and knowledge gifts will fade away, Paul says, because they are gradually being replaced by something else—something that Paul describes as "perfect." He writes:

> For we know in part and we prophesy in part, but when perfection comes, the imperfect disappears. (1 CORINTHIANS 13:9–10)

What is this perfect thing that gradually increases in our lives, replacing our concern about gifts? Some Bible commentators suggest that the perfect thing Paul speaks of here is the written Word of God. When Paul wrote these words, the New Testament as we have it today did not exist. The early Christians relied on the teaching of apostles, prophets, and evangelists who spoke the mind of God in bits and pieces. These Bible commentators interpret Paul's words as meaning that as the written New Testament came into being, the gifts began to fade, so that prophesying, tongues, and knowledge were no longer needed alongside the perfect written Word. There is a lot of truth in that, but I don't think that's what Paul had in mind in this passage.

Other Bible scholars suggest that Paul was talking about heaven. Life is imperfect, but when the perfection of heaven comes, prophesying, tongues, and knowledge will pass away. There is truth in that as well, but again, I don't think that's what Paul had in mind.

If we take this passage in its full context, in relationship to all that Paul has been saying, then it is clear that the word *perfect* refers to love. Christlike love is that perfect thing that replaces our need to be so concerned about the gifts of the Spirit. Once we have been perfected in love, the gifts, which are designed to point us to Christlike maturity and Christlike love, are no longer needed. The gifts are a means to an end. The end is love. That's why Paul goes on to say:

When I was a child, I talked like a child, I thought like a child, I reasoned like a child. When I became a man, I put childish ways behind me. (1 CORINTHIANS 13:11)

There is nothing wrong with a child who acts like a child. Children are supposed to be childlike. But when a child grows up into adulthood it's time to put away childishness. Paul is saying that the mark of spiritual maturity is love—the willing decision to love the unlovely, to love the ungrateful, to even love our enemies. As our capacity for *agape* love increases, it will replace our childish concern about the gifts of the Spirit.

Have you ever watched children playing on Christmas morning after they have opened their gifts? They play with one gift for a few minutes, then cast it aside and begin grabbing for the gifts of a brother or sister. Soon, these children who were so thrilled with their gifts a few minutes ago are now squabbling over each others' gifts.

The same thing happens in churches. We are thrilled with the ministry gifts the Spirit gives us—but soon we find ourselves envying or competing with our brothers and sisters over differences in our gifts. If we weren't so childishly focused on gifts, if we were more mature and filled with Christ-like love, our fascination with spiritual gifts would fade away—and so would our squabbling and division.

To focus on spiritual gifts and forget the end to which they are to lead us is the height of foolishness. It's like saying, "I just looked up the Grand Canyon on a roadmap, so there's no need to actually go and see it." The gifts are good, but they are passing away. Gifts are the roadmap; love is the destination.

Paul goes on to observe:

Now we see but a poor reflection as in a mirror; then we shall see face to face. Now I know in part; then I shall know fully, even as I am fully known. (1 CORINTHIANS 13:12)

Here, Paul anticipates the end of his life. He knows that a new day will dawn when he will see his Lord face to face. No longer will he see a dim, blurry reflection in a mirror, as he sees now. Paul knows that, on that day, he will understand spiritual reality with absolute crystal clarity.

We wonder why the world is the way it is. Why is there so much suffering in the world? Why do evil men seem to win while the good are oppressed? Why does God allow innocent little children to die of diseases such as leukemia? Why does He allow children to be abused, neglected, or exploited by child pornography? Why does God allow hundreds of thousands of people to die in natural disasters, such as earthquakes and tsunamis? Why does He allow wars?

Facing these questions, we realize that we have a blurry and incomplete grasp of what God is doing in the world. We can't understand His purposes. Many of our questions go unresolved year after year

At the close of this chapter, Paul gathers up all he has said with these words:

> And now these three remain: faith, hope and love. But the greatest of these is love. (1 CORINTHIANS 13:13)

Faith remains because faith is a human response to a divine provision—both in this life and in the life to come. Our faith relationship with God will continue throughout eternity. Hope remains because hope is the expectation that God will provide in the future as He has in the past.

Love remains because God is love. Paul says that love is the greatest of these. God is not faith and God is not hope, but God is love. Learning to love as He loves is the most important task a human being has in this entire universe. Learning to love is learning to become like God.

The lie of the devil in the Garden of Eden was, "If you disobey God, you will become like God." That lie has produced thousands of years of sin, terror, and torment in the world. The truth of the Scriptures is, "If you love like God, you will become like God." That is the promise of 1 John 3:2:

> Dear friends, now we are children of God, and what we will be has not yet been made known. But we know that when he appears, we shall be like him, for we shall see him as he is.

We shall be like Him! Our love will be like His. Our character will be like His. That is why love remains. And that is why "the greatest of these is love."

16

SPEAKING OF TONGUES

1 Corinthians 14:1–25

For almost nineteen centuries, the gift of tongues appeared to be a lost gift in the Christian church. The fourth-century church father, John Chrysostom, once wrote that the miracle gifts, including tongues, had ceased long before his own day and that no one could say for certain what a manifestation of those gifts looked like. The gift of tongues was not practiced in the era of Luther and Calvin and the other Reformers. It was not practiced in the evangelical awakening of the 1700s, the era when John and Charles Wesley founded the Methodist movement.

In fact, history records that the modern tongues movement did not begin until the dawning of the twentieth century. That movement was ushered in by Charles Fox Parham, a minister who was also a Freemason, a member of a fraternal order with secret mystical rites and signs. As a Methodist minister, Parham had many odd ideas about worship and was continually in conflict with the Methodist hierarchy. Finally, he broke away from the Methodists and founded an independent school, Bethel Bible School in Topeka, Kansas.

Convinced that the church in America lacked spiritual vitality, Charles Parham urged some of his students to search the book of Acts for the secret of the power of the early apostles. Parham and his students noticed that three times in Acts, the Holy Spirit came upon the church accompanied by an outpouring of tongues. They concluded that speaking in tongues was the key to spiritual power.

On New Year's Eve 1900, Parham and several students prayed from morning to evening, pleading for "the baptism of the Holy Spirit," which they believed would be accompanied by the gift of tongues. (As previously noted, 1 Corinthians 12:13 teaches that we were baptized by the Holy Spirit when we received Jesus as Lord and Savior.)

A little after midnight, a student named Agnes Ozman asked Parham to pray that she would be filled with the Holy Spirit through the laying on of hands. So Parham and several students placed hands on her head and prayed for her—and she began speaking in an unknown language. The language she spoke was said to be Chinese, though there was no language expert who could confirm it. Soon, Parham and many of the other students also began speaking in unknown languages. Within weeks, this tongues phenomenon spread to Texas, then to Los Angeles, where it became known as the Azusa Street revival, and eventually around the world.

For the first fifty years of the twentieth century, speaking in tongues took place only in certain denominations. Later, however, this practice, called glossolalia, spread into other Protestant denominations and segments of the Roman Catholic Church. Today, the subject of tongues is one of the most controversial and divisive issues in the church.

Make love your aim

The fourteenth chapter of 1 Corinthians is devoted to a comparison of two gifts: tongues and prophesying. Both gifts were being exercised in the church in Corinth. Here Paul gives us some helpful insights into these gifts and how they contrast one with another. The key to 1 Corinthians 14 is the opening verse:

> Follow the way of love and eagerly desire spiritual gifts, especially the gift of prophecy. (1 CORINTHIANS 14:1)

I like the way this verse begins in the Revised Standard Version: "Make love your aim." This verse ties chapter 14 to chapter 13, the Love Chapter. Paul reminds us that love is essential to the exercise of spiritual gifts. Love, in fact, is our reason for exercising spiritual gifts.

Love is the Christlikeness within us that motivates us to reach out to serve others. Love must control. Though the theme of this chapter is a discussion of tongues and prophesying, love is the foundation of everything Paul says. The purpose of the gifts is to build others up; the gifts are instruments of Christlike love. If we do not understand that the gifts are to be motivated and controlled by love, we do not understand spiritual gifts.

Then Paul says, "eagerly desire spiritual gifts." Paul does not mean that we should start planning what kinds of spiritual gifts we would individually like to have. Paul does not address these words to individual Christians but to the congregation. The Christians at Corinth should desire that these spiritual gifts be exercised among them to help them grow in their witness and their spiritual maturity.

The one spiritual gift that is most effective for this purpose is the gift of prophesying. We have already noted that the gift of prophesying is not the ability to predict the future. It's the ability to explain life issues in the light of God's Word. Today, we would call this expository preaching—delving into a particular passage of Scripture and applying it to the daily struggles of life.

Next, Paul compares and contrasts these gifts, tongues and prophesying:

> For anyone who speaks in a tongue does not speak to men but to God. Indeed, no one understands him; he utters mysteries with his spirit. But everyone who prophesies speaks to men for their strengthening, encouragement and comfort. (1 CORINTHIANS 14:2–3)

This is an important verse for helping us to clear away the controversy surrounding tongues. Note, first of all, that the word *tongue* in the original Greek refers to a language. Though this word can also refer to that fleshy, muscular organ attached to the floor of the mouth, it was commonly used to mean "language." There are many other instances in Scripture where the same Greek word is translated "language," and properly so. It is the normal word for language, and this gives us a hint that the gift of tongues is the gift of supernaturally speaking languages that have not been learned.

To God or to men?

Paul also tells us that the supernatural gift of tongues is not addressed to men. The person is not speaking to the other people in the room; he is speaking to God. No one else understands what the speaker is saying; his spirit is expressing mysteries to God.

This a key factor in discerning whether the gift we hear being expressed in our times is the true, biblical gift of tongues: Ask yourself, "Is this gift being addressed to men?" Sometimes, when tongues are spoken and interpretations given, the content makes it clear that the words spoken are a form of exhortation to the audience. If that is so, then what we are hearing is not the authentic gift of tongues, because God's Word tells us that the gift of tongues is never used for the preaching to men.

The same principle can be found in the book of Acts. On the day of Pentecost, when the gift of tongues was given, a group of Christians began to speak in tongues—foreign languages that they had never learned. Some claim that these Christians were preaching the gospel to the people who had gathered in the city on that day. But that is not what Acts 2 says. Look at the passage:

When the day of Pentecost came, they were all together in one place. Suddenly a sound like the blowing of a violent wind came from heaven and filled the whole house where they were sitting. They saw what seemed to be tongues of fire that separated and came to rest on each of them. All of them were filled with the Holy Spirit and began to speak in other tongues as the Spirit enabled them.

Now there were staying in Jerusalem God-fearing Jews from every nation under heaven. When they heard this sound, a crowd came together in bewilderment, because each one heard them speaking in his own language. Utterly amazed, they asked: "Are not all these men who are speaking Galileans? Then how is it that each of us hears them in his own native language? Parthians, Medes and Elamites; residents of Mesopotamia, Judea and Cappadocia, Pontus and Asia, Phrygia and Pamphylia, Egypt and the parts of Libya near Cyrene; visitors from Rome (both Jews and converts to Judaism); Cretans and Arabs—we hear them declaring the wonders of God in our own tongues!" Amazed and perplexed, they asked one another, "What does this mean?"

Some, however, made fun of them and said, "They have had too much wine." (Acts 2:1–13)

The Christians who were speaking in tongues were not preaching, they were praising. They were not addressing the people in their various languages; they were addressing God. They were "declaring the wonders of God." That's praise, not preaching. When people authentically speak in tongues, they speak to God, not to men. No one can understand them because they utter mysteries with their spirits.

That's why, in the next few verses of Acts 2, Peter gets up and interprets the event to the crowd. He says, "Let me explain this to you; listen carefully to what I say. These men are not drunk, as you suppose. It's only nine in the morning!" (see Acts 2:14–15). If these Christians had been preaching in various languages, no one would have thought them drunk; but because they were praising *God* in various languages, the people who heard them were baffled by their behavior.

So what did Peter do after interpreting this event? He began to preach the gospel. Why? Because the gospel hadn't yet been preached. So far, there had only been praise and worship in this open-air meeting in Jerusalem. Now it was time for the sermon! And Peter delivered a powerful sermon.

The praise and worship, expressed through the gift of tongues, was addressed to God. The preaching of Peter was addressed to men. In fact, he was prophesying. That is always the nature of these two gifts: the gift of tongues is expressed toward God and the gift of prophesying is expressed toward men. Paul makes this point even more strongly later in this chapter, where he writes:

> For if I pray in a tongue, my spirit prays, but my mind is unfruitful. So what shall I do? I will pray with my spirit, but I will also pray with my mind; I will sing with my spirit, but I will also sing with my mind. If you are praising God with your spirit, how can one who finds himself among those who do not understand say "Amen" to your thanksgiving, since he does not know what you are saying? You may be giving thanks well enough, but the other man is not edified. (1 CORINTHIANS 14:14–17)

Here Paul shows us that speaking in tongues consists of four elements: prayer, singing unto God, praise, and thanksgiving. He says, "I will pray with my spirit," that is, in tongues. Then he says, "I will sing with my spirit." Next he speaks of the importance of "praising God" with our spirit. Finally, he speaks of thanksgiving. So Paul describes four ingredients that should be part of any expression of the gift of tongues. Those four ingredients—prayer, singing, praise, and thanksgiving—are forms of worship expressed to God, not preaching directed to men.

Notice that Paul says that when his spirit prays in tongues, his mind is unfruitful. His mind and soul are not part of the process of worship that his spirit pours out in tongues. So though Paul prays through his spirit in tongues, he also prays through his soul with his mind. Though he sings with his spirit in tongues, he also sings through his soul using normal comprehensible words that his mind understands. Paul acknowledges that when he praises God and gives thanks to God through tongues, the people around him cannot agree with him in prayer (they can't say "Amen," may it be so), and the people around him can't understand what he's saying in tongues.

So the gift of tongues is a form of worship, prayer, singing, praise, and thanksgiving directed to God alone. It's a direct connection from the human spirit to God, bypassing the human mind. It does not build up (edify) other people; it was never intended to. The gift that builds others up is the gift of prophesying, not tongues.

Some critics claim that when Paul writes about tongues, he is describing a practice borrowed from the pagans. The famous oracle of Delphi was located at the sanctuary of Apollo, less than fifty miles from Corinth. There, a sibyl, a priestess of Apollo, would speak in strange, ecstatic utterances. Though her words sounded like nonsense syllables to the people around her, they were said to be the words of Apollo, the god of the sun and prophecy.

Because the oracle of Delphi is located near Corinth, some commentators believe that the gift of tongues, as practiced in Corinth, involved mimicking the ecstatic utterances of the Delphic sibyl. I strongly disagree with such a claim. Throughout this chapter, the apostle Paul makes reference to his own use of the gift of tongues. He makes no distinction between the way he spoke in tongues and the practice of the Corinthians. It is inconceivable that Paul would be writing here about a pagan practice that crept into the church. Paul wrote of a genuine gift, which was first manifested on the day of Pentecost.

The gift of prophesying

Paul continues:

> But everyone who prophesies speaks to men for their strengthening, encouragement and comfort. (1 CORINTHIANS 14:3)

Prophesying, as we have already said, is the act of explaining the realities of life in the light of God's Word. The great Reformer John Calvin called it "the peculiar gift of explaining revelation." Prophesying has a threefold function.

First, *prophesying strengthens people.* The word translated "strengthening" is *oikodomen* in the original Greek; *oiko* means "house" and *domen* means "to build." This Greek word suggests the image of building a house on a strong foundation. The goal of prophesying is to give people a strong and solid foundation for their lives, so that they will be built up in the faith.

Second, *prophesying encourages people.* The word for "encouraging" in the original Greek is *paraklesis*, which is a form of one of the titles of the Holy Spirit: *paraclete*. This word literally means "one called alongside," and it suggests that the Spirit is alongside us, supporting and steadying us, building up our courage to go on. Through the gift of prophesying, the Word of God is applied to the trials and sufferings we go through, so that we are encouraged to continue the good fight of the Christian life.

Third, *prophesying comforts people.* The Greek word for "comfort," *paramuthian*, means to empathize, to put yourself in the place of another person. Often, when the Scriptures are applied to our lives in a prophetic way, we feel as if God Himself is with us, feeling what we feel, comforting us from within, letting us know that we are not alone. That is one of the most powerful ways that prophesying ministers to our need.

Next, Paul compares the effect of tongues versus the effect of prophesying:

He who speaks in a tongue edifies himself, but he who prophesies edifies the church. (1 CORINTHIANS 14:4)

There is a benefit to the individual who praises God in a language he has never learned; he is blessed and refreshed by the very act of giving praise. But praising God in tongues does not benefit the church. What gift benefits the church? The gift of prophesying. "Make love your aim," Paul said at the beginning of this chapter—and love builds up, blesses, and strengthens those around you. So it follows that we should desire the gift that edifies (builds up) the entire church, not just one individual. Paul continues:

I would like every one of you to speak in tongues, but I would rather have you prophesy. He who prophesies is greater than one who speaks in tongues, unless he interprets, so that the church may be edified. (1 CORINTHIANS 14:5)

Paul says that speaking in tongues is a good gift—but prophesying is a great gift, because it edifies the entire church. That is Paul's theme throughout this chapter.

The interpreting of tongues

Paul seems to be responding to a situation in Corinth that we could describe this way: People were glorying in the supernatural manifestations of tongues. They were thrilled to be able to do what no natural man could do—speak a language they had never learned. The Corinthians thought this was marvelous, and it was—but they were encouraging the gift of tongues to the detriment of the gift of prophesying. So Paul wrote to correct the imbalance in the thinking of the Corinthian believers.

He continues this theme in the next few verses:

Now, brothers, if I come to you and speak in tongues, what good will I be to you, unless I bring you some revelation or knowledge or prophecy or word of instruction? Even in the case of lifeless things that make sounds, such as the flute or harp, how will anyone know what tune is being played unless there is a distinction in the notes? Again, if the trumpet does not sound a clear call, who will get ready for battle? So it is with you. Unless you speak intelligible words with your tongue, how will anyone know what you are saying? You will just be speaking into the air. (1 CORINTHIANS 14:6–9)

Paul offers a series of examples. He says that speaking in tongues may benefit the speaker, but to the hearer it is nothing but meaningless sound—just noise on the air. A flute or harp produces music, and a trumpet may signal a call to battle—but speaking in tongues doesn't benefit the hearers. They can't make any sense of it.

Next, Paul offers an illustration from the languages of the world:

Undoubtedly there are all sorts of languages in the world, yet none of them is without meaning. If then I do not grasp the meaning of what someone is saying, I am a foreigner to the speaker, and he is a foreigner to me. So it is with you. Since you are eager to have spiritual gifts, try to excel in gifts that build up the church. (1 CORINTHIANS 14:10–12)

Every language has meaning to those who speak and understand it, but if I don't know the language, then it is meaningless sound to me. This passage makes it clear that the gift of tongues is a gift of languages. If you don't know the language, then someone must interpret it for you or it will remain meaningless noise to you.

Next, Paul explains how to make it possible for the true, biblical gift of tongues to benefit the entire church, not just the speaker:

For this reason anyone who speaks in a tongue should pray that he may interpret what he says. For if I pray in a tongue, my spirit prays, but my mind is unfruitful. So what shall I do? I will pray with my spirit, but I will also pray with my mind; I will sing with my spirit, but I will also sing with my mind. If you are praising God with your spirit, how can one who finds himself among those who do not understand say "Amen" to your thanksgiving, since he does not know what you are saying? You may be giving thanks well enough, but the other man is not edified. (1 CORINTHIANS 14:13–17)

This passage suggests that when God gives the gift of tongues, He gives with it the gift of interpretation. Paul urges the Corinthians who exercise the gift of tongues to pray and expect to exercise the gift of interpretation as well.

Paul brings his own experience to bear on this subject. He tells us that his spirit cries out to God, but his emotions are not articulated with words. He doesn't intellectually understand his own prayer. He knows he is worshiping, but he doesn't know how. So Paul says, "If I pray in a tongue, my spirit prays, but my mind is unfruitful."

What, then, should he do? He should interpret. Paul makes it clear that the exercise of tongues in a public assembly is a self-centered act that doesn't allow others to even say "Amen" unless the speaker's words can be made intelligible to all. He then adds quite pointedly:

> I thank God that I speak in tongues more than all of you. But in the church I would rather speak five intelligible words to instruct others than ten thousand words in a tongue. (1 CORINTHIANS 14:18–19)

Paul's attitude toward tongues could not be any plainer. His statement that he speaks in tongues more than all of the Corinthians is fascinating. We naturally ask, "When did the apostle Paul speak in tongues?" Not in churches, certainly; he made it clear that he exercised the gift of prophesying there.

Some would say, "This shows that the gift of tongues is for private use; Paul must have used tongues in private as a prayer language." That sounds logical at first glance—but I don't think this is true. Nowhere in the Word of God is the exercise of the gift of tongues presented as a private matter. Every manifestation of tongues in the New Testament, without exception, is a public demonstration.

Tongues as a warning sign

When did Paul speak in tongues? I think the only situation that fulfills all the biblical requirements for the gift of tongues would be when he went into the Jewish synagogues. In those settings there was a provision made for public praise of God by visiting people. To praise God in a language never learned would be an impressive thing to the Jewish people present, especially if it was a Gentile tongue. That, I believe, is when Paul spoke in tongues, and he did so more than all the Corinthians. The use of this gift in the synagogue would fulfill every requirement of the biblical gift of tongues.

Next, Paul gives us a word of caution:

Brothers, stop thinking like children. In regard to evil be infants, but in your thinking be adults. (1 CORINTHIANS 14:20)

Why does Paul offer this exhortation? It's because there was more than one form of speaking in tongues practiced in Corinth. In the mystery religions, such as the oracle of Delphi, the priestess practiced a kind of ecstatic babbling that sounded like a strange language. To an uninitiated person, it would be hard to tell the difference.

So Paul warned, "Investigate this matter with care. Don't be naive like a child and assume that every strange tongue you hear is a gift of the Holy Spirit, because some are not. Don't be naive about evil. Grow up in your thinking! Search out the truth—and if you find evil at the base of a certain practice, stay away from it!"

Then Paul gives us the basis upon which to discern whether the tongues we hear are from God or not. He goes back to the book of Isaiah, to the only prediction of tongues in the Old Testament:

In the Law it is written:

> "Through men of strange tongues
>   and through the lips of foreigners
> I will speak to this people,
>   but even then they will not listen to me," says the Lord.
>
> (1 CORINTHIANS 14:21)

This quotation is from Isaiah 28:11 and 12b. In quoting this passage, Paul makes it clear that the gift of tongues is a sign. A sign to whom? Isaiah was speaking to the whole nation of Israel at a time when the Assyrians were about to attack Jerusalem. Through the prophet, God warned the nation that if they did not repent and turn from their idolatrous ways, they would hear Gentile tongues spoken freely in the Holy City. God, through Isaiah, urged Israel to restore its relationship with Him lest He turn away from Israel and toward the Gentile world.

If you examine the day of Pentecost in that light, you'll see how fully that event accords with Isaiah's prediction. On Pentecost, the streets of Jerusalem were filled with thousands of people, mostly Jews, who had come from all around, and they heard the disciples speaking in strange Gentile languages. It was a sign to unbelieving Jews that God was about to turn to the Gentile world.

On that day, Peter stood and warned the people that they were facing the judgment of God. Being convicted in their hearts, the people said, "Brothers, what must we do?" (see Acts 2:37), and three thousand people turned to God that day. The rest of the city, the greater mass of the population, remained in unbelief. Isn't that what Isaiah said would happen? "'But even then they will not listen to me,' says the Lord." Paul is telling us that the purpose of the gift of tongues is that it was to be a warning sign to unbelieving Jews that God was turning to the Gentiles.

Not for the church

Many people are confused by the next few verses. Paul writes:

> Tongues, then, are a sign, not for believers but for unbelievers; prophecy, however, is for believers, not for unbelievers. So if the whole church comes together and everyone speaks in tongues, and some who do not understand or some unbelievers come in, will they not say that you are out of your mind? But if an unbeliever or someone who does not understand comes in while everybody is prophesying, he will be convinced by all that he is a sinner and will be judged by all, and the secrets of his heart will be laid bare. So he will fall down and worship God, exclaiming, "God is really among you!" (1 CORINTHIANS 14:23–25)

People say, "That sounds like just the opposite of what Paul has been saying. He previously said that tongues are a sign for unbelievers, and yet he goes on to say that if people speak in tongues in the church and a nonbeliever comes in he will not be impressed with the sign. He will say, 'They are all mad; they are crazy; they all speak in languages I cannot understand.'"

But if they prophesy, Paul says, the unbeliever will hear the Word of God and be convicted. He will fall on his face and say, "God is among them."

What does Paul mean? He's going back to his essential theme throughout this passage: the gift of tongues is not intended for the church. It is not for believers; it is for unbelievers. If it is exercised in a church, and people speak in tongues and nobody interprets, the unbelievers who are there will not understand it as a sign gift because it is not addressed to them. They will see it as an attempt to minister to the people present—and since nobody will understand what's being said, the unbelievers will think everyone is crazy. I have seen this happen in meetings where people were speaking in tongues; unbelievers who were present walked away saying, "Those people are crazy!"

But if prophesying occurs, the unbelievers will hear the Spirit of God speaking the mind of God—and they may be convicted of the truth. In my preaching ministry at Peninsula Bible Church, I focused on prophesying—on applying the thoughts of God to the everyday issues faced by people in the congregation. Even though I was teaching to Christians, I saw hundreds of people come to Christ over the years. There were always some unbelievers in the congregation, and they would be convicted of their need for Christ. They heard the truth, the Holy Spirit caused the truth to take root in their lives, and they were converted. That is what Paul says will happen when the gift of prophesying is exercised in the church.

When the gift of tongues is properly exercised, it's addressed particularly to the unbelieving Jews. This means, of course, that it could be exercised today. There are many unbelieving Jews in the world today (that is, Jewish people who do not believe in Jesus as their Messiah, Lord, and Savior). God is still drawing all people to Himself, both Jews and Gentiles, and a biblical manifestation of the spiritual gift of tongues could certainly reappear in our day as a sign to the Jewish people. If the gift does reappear in our day, it will have all the marks of the biblical gift of tongues, as Paul has described them.

This raises a final question: Is the expression of tongues that we hear around us today the biblical gift of tongues? This expression of tongues was introduced to the world in the early hours of New Years Day 1901 by Charles Fox Parham and his Bible school student, Agnes Ozman. Did they discover a gift of the Spirit that had been lost for nineteen centuries—or, in their heightened emotional state, did they exhibit a purely human and psychological form of glossolalia?

Based on my study of Scripture, I have concluded that the expression of tongues that is so common in some churches today is not a biblical expression of the gift of tongues. I have heard hundreds of manifestations called tongues, and I'm alarmed by the fact that people rarely ask, "Does this manifestation agree with Scripture?"

Dr. William T. Samarin, professor of linguistics at the University of Toronto, made an intensive study of speaking in tongues. He concluded:

> Over a period of five years I have taken part in meetings in Italy, Holland, Jamaica, Canada and the United States. I have observed old-fashioned Pentecostals and neo-Pentecostals. I have been in

small meetings in private homes as well as in mammoth public meetings. I have seen such different cultural settings as are found among Puerto Ricans of the Bronx, the snake handlers of the Appalachians and the Russian Molakans of Los Angeles.... I have interviewed tongue speakers, and tape recorded and analyzed countless samples of tongues. In every case, glossolalia turns out to be linguistic nonsense. In spite of superficial similarities, glossolalia is fundamentally not language. It is not a language, and it is not often addressed to God. It is usually addressed to a crowd of people present, so it does not fit that qualification. And it is primarily exercised privately today, whereas there is no manifestation of the private use of tongues in the New Testament. Finally, it is not a sign to unbelievers, therefore, we have to judge that the phenomenon that we see and hear today is not the biblical gift of tongues.

What should we make of the expression of tongues in Christian circles today? I am convinced that people are experiencing a purely psychological phenomenon that results in a repetition of meaningless sounds and syllables. They are misinterpreting these sounds and syllables as language—as a spiritual gift of tongues. Ecstatic utterance, expressed in nonsense syllables, was a common phenomenon in the ancient world; Plato discusses this phenomenon in several of his discourses. It is often associated with religious ecstasy and excitement. This, I believe, is what is commonly practiced today as the gift of tongues.

At the end of 1 Corinthians 14, Paul writes:

> Therefore, my brothers, be eager to prophesy, and do not forbid speaking in tongues. But everything should be done in a fitting and orderly way. (1 CORINTHIANS 14: 39–40)

If the true spiritual gift of tongues is given by the Holy Spirit, Paul says we should not forbid it. But when we encounter expressions that are not the biblical gift but are mistakenly called a gift, then we have a duty to discourage its use because it has been such a divisive force in the church.

You may or may not be convinced by what you have just read on the matter of tongues. In any case, the subject is not yet exhausted, and we will explore one more aspect of the issue of tongues in the next chapter.

17

WHEN IS A CHURCH A CHURCH?

1 Corinthians 14:26–40

When is a church a church?

Is the church only a church when it is gathered together on Sunday mornings? Or is the church still the church when it is scattered around the community throughout the week, in homes and neighborhoods, in shops and office complexes, along roadsides and in airports, as the people of the church live their daily lives? When we put it that way, it becomes obvious that the Lord's concept of the word *church* was the latter one—an image of God's people in action, carrying out His will in the world.

Next question: How many people does it take to make a church?

A dozen? A hundred? A thousand? Jesus said, "For where two or three come together in my name, there am I with them" (Matthew 18:20). Jesus breaks the concept of church down to its fundamentals. If two or three Christians are gathered together in His name, at any time, in any place, for any reason having to do with the work of the kingdom of God—then you see the church in action.

It's hard to define a church, especially a local church, in the New Testament concept. It is almost like nailing gelatin to the wall! Every time you think you've grasped it, the concept slips through your fingers. But one thing is clear from the biblical accounts: The early church met together. From the earliest times, Christians felt the urge to meet together and share together, with brothers and sisters in the family of God.

What did they do when they met? They ministered to one another. They shared their spiritual gifts. They exercised what God had given them for each other's benefit.

For the strengthening of the church

Here is how Paul describes the moment when Christians come together to become a church:

> What then shall we say, brothers? When you come together, every-
> one has a hymn, or a word of instruction, a revelation, a tongue or an
> interpretation. All of these must be done for the strengthening of the
> church. (1 CORINTHIANS 14:26)

We don't know how large the church at Corinth was. By the time Paul
wrote this letter, several years after the founding of the church, it may have
reached a considerable size. Certainly the church numbered in the hundreds—and perhaps thousands. We know that shortly after Pentecost, the
early church in Jerusalem consisted of as many as ten thousand members,
so the church in Corinth could have been very large.

Obviously, in a large church, it's difficult, if not impossible, to allow
time for every person to present "a hymn, or a word of instruction, a revelation, a tongue or an interpretation." One such meeting could last for days.
It is likely that Paul was not speaking here of the large meeting where
the entire Christian community of Corinth gathered in one place but of
smaller house churches or home Bible study meetings. In small group settings, it's possible to have this kind of intimacy and participation.

The first-century churches seemed to hold two types of meetings: the
small, intimate home gathering where people shared together, often ate
together, and exercised their spiritual gifts, and large teaching and preaching meetings where a few people recognized as having the gift of prophesying would get up and speak to the whole body.

These large meetings are the kind described in Acts 20, where Paul
met with all of the Christians in the city of Troas. That famous meeting probably began around nine o'clock at night, but Paul, we are told,
"kept on talking until midnight" (see Acts 20:7). It was on this occasion
that a young man named Eutychus fell asleep "as Paul talked on and on."
The young man fell from a third-floor window and was dead. Paul rushed
down, threw himself on the young man, hugged him—and Eutychus was
alive again.

As a preacher, this story has always encouraged me over the years—
especially whenever I'd see a parishioner nod off in the pews. I have always
been grateful that Peninsula Bible Church was built on the ground level,
because I don't have the gift of healing as Paul did.

Whether first-century church meetings were large or small, one thing
was clear. There was one purpose for gathering: edification. "All of these
must be done," Paul wrote, "for the strengthening [edification, building
up] of the church." What builds us up? The ministry we experience when

we gather together: the worship, the praise, the prayer, the music, the fellowship, the sharing, the prophesying—all the actions that contribute to the uplifting of the spirit, the renewing of the mind, the strengthening of the heart.

When we gather together as a church, we are built up in our faith, our understanding, and our spiritual maturity. Through the preaching and application of the Word, we are challenged to expect God to work through us and empower us throughout the week.

In many ways, the church meeting is like the huddle in a football game. That's where the players gather together to find out what play has been called. After the players get their assignments, the huddle breaks up, and the players go to the line and play football. The huddle is important, but the huddle isn't the game. The game is played on the line of scrimmage.

All too many Christians mistake the huddle for the game. They think that the Christian life takes place in the huddle, in the church. The real game is out in the world, out on the line of scrimmage. That's where the yardage is won or lost. That's where the church truly becomes the church. That's what Paul is telling us: When Christians come together, they should do the things that build up, strengthen, and edify one another for the tough realities of this world.

Three problem areas in the church

In the next section, Paul deals with three problem areas in the church. These three problem areas involve the exercise of three spiritual gifts that have the potential to produce friction and disharmony in the church. You will readily see that the same three problem areas still exist in the church.

The first problem area is the exercise of the gift of tongues. As we have previously seen, the gift of tongues involves praising God in a language that was never learned. Since the tongues experience involves praise, rejoicing, and thanksgiving, it is essentially an ecstatic emotional experience. If a church meeting devotes a great deal of time to this kind of experience, then the meeting becomes emotionally charged. This was a problem in the first century; it is still a problem today.

If a church becomes too focused on emotionalism, the people in a church become spiritually shallow. They may not seek a true depth of understanding of the Scriptures, a deeper relationship with the Lord, and a more mature character that can withstand the pressure of life. Instead, they will only seek a series of emotional highs.

On a number of occasions, I have been in a meeting that was a riot of hand clapping, shouting, singing, raising hands, speaking in tongues, and even dancing in the aisles. These were wild, emotional experiences. Some people think this is the only kind of religious meeting that has any value. If church is not an emotional thrill ride, then for them it's not really church.

When people experience intense emotions, their pituitary glands and hypothalamus produce biochemical compounds called endorphins, which act like opiates in the brain, producing a sense of well-being. There are a number of activities that can stimulate the production of endorphins, including aerobic exercise, romantic feelings, listening to pleasurable music, and intense religious experiences. When people experience an endorphin rush, that biochemical sense of well-being, they want to feel that way again and again. That's one reason why religious emotionalism is so addictive. A spiritual high feels so good that people want to experience it again and again.

Unfortunately, some people feel close to God only when they are on an emotional high. When they go about their daily lives, they miss the excitement and the endorphin rush—and they don't feel God's presence. Their spiritual experience is a roller-coaster ride of alternating highs and lows, and they never seem to progress in a steady way toward maturity and stability in their Christian experience.

The second problem area is the matter of prophesying—the application of the mind of God and the Word of God to the specific problems of the day. The gift of prophesy, when exercised to an extreme, can result in an over-theologizing that turns a worship and fellowship meeting into a dull, dry classroom experience in which the truth of God's Word goes over people's heads. The gift of prophesying can be misused. This was Paul's second concern, and it remains a concern for the church today.

The third problem area is the matter of how much freedom women should have to minister in the church. For obvious reasons, this is a highly controversial passage. As Paul describes the problem, there is a tendency, when women minister in the church, for there to be a digression from the process of edifying (building up) the body. There is, Paul says, a greater tendency toward debate, division, and dissension.

So here are three problem areas of the church that can divert a church from its task of edifying believers. The first problem area, the exercise of tongues, can move a church too far toward mysticism and emotionalism. The second problem area, the exercise of the gift of prophesying, can move a church too far toward a reliance on theological knowledge. The third problem, involving women ministering in the church, can produce too much debating and division.

Paul's rules of order

Eager to avoid these problems, Paul suggests certain rules. You may say, "But I don't like rules. I don't like restrictions." The truth is I don't like rules either! I naturally resist restrictions on my freedom. We are all, as human beings, rebellious by nature, and rules and regulations have a way of provoking that rebelliousness within us.

But I learned years ago that people need rules in order to function together. You cannot play a game of football or chess without rules; the rules make the game possible. You cannot drive in traffic without rules, or you will soon injure yourself and others. And you cannot operate a church without rules and a sense of order. So the apostle Paul suggests a set of rules, beginning with rules about the gift of tongues:

> If anyone speaks in a tongue, two—or at the most three—should speak, one at a time, and someone must interpret. If there is no interpreter, the speaker should keep quiet in the church and speak to himself and God. (1 CORINTHIANS 14:27–28)

Three simple limits govern the exercise of the biblical gift of tongues. First, only one or two should speak; in exceptional cases, three at the most. Why? Because the exercise of tongues is an emotional experience, and too much emotion in a meeting is destructive. Too little emotion makes a meeting dull, of course, so Paul is trying to regulate the activity of the meetings so that there would not be too much—or too little—of a good thing.

Second, the tongues must be interpreted. The speakers should speak one at a time, not all at once. And someone must interpret, so that the tongues are a blessing to all, not just to the speaker.

Third, if no one is able to interpret, then no one is to speak in tongues. Paul makes it clear that tongues must be interpreted or they do not edify the church. That is why he seems to imply that one who speaks in a language ought to discover whether someone has the ability to interpret before he speaks. If there is no one to interpret, Paul says, then "let him speak to himself and God." In other words, let him praise God in his spirit, in his thoughts, but not in audible words.

Next, Paul turns to rules concerning prophesying:

Two or three prophets should speak, and the others should weigh carefully what is said. And if a revelation comes to someone who is sitting down, the first speaker should stop. For you can all prophesy in turn so that everyone may be instructed and encouraged. The spirits of prophets are subject to the control of prophets. For God is not a God of disorder but of peace. (1 CORINTHIANS 14:29–33a)

Once again, Paul offers three simple controls. The first involves controlling the number of people who may speak. Here, Paul is considering a small home meeting where there are probably ten to twenty people present. In this meeting, two or three people with the gift of prophesying may take turns speaking. As with tongues, Paul limits the number of speakers to two or three. This was in order to prevent meetings from getting out of control and running too long.

Prophesying takes time, because it involves explaining and expounding (which is why we preachers are notoriously long-winded!). Paul seems to be aware of the truth of the old preacher's dictum, "The mind can only absorb as much as the seat can endure." So Paul wisely limits the duration of the meeting.

The second control Paul lays down is a rule that prophesying should be examined: "The others should weigh carefully what is said." Prophesying is an attempt to explain the mind of God; not everything a prophet says is necessarily inspired or automatically true. As John Calvin has said, prophesying is the gift of explaining revelation; therefore, it is subject to the judgment and comment of others. In these small meetings in Corinth it was expected that someone who spoke as a prophet would be subject to the confirmation and correction of others.

The third control Paul lays down is that prophesying should be done in an orderly fashion: "And if a revelation comes to someone who is sitting down, the first speaker should stop. For you can all prophesy in turn so that everyone may be instructed and encouraged." In other words, nobody was to take over the meeting.

Paul says that the spirit of the prophet is subject to the prophet. Someone might have said, "I can't help what I say. The Spirit of God is in me, and He is speaking through me. Therefore, everything I say is of God." Paul says, "Rubbish! The spirit of the prophet is subject to the prophet. You can control what you say. Don't make the claim that you can't help what you say."

He also makes it clear that the Spirit of God never creates confusion or disorder. Therefore, no one is to dominate a meeting, because God doesn't work that way. A meeting should be orderly and should allow time for others to speak. If there is strife, confusion, argument, and division, that meeting is not being led by the Spirit of God.

The ministry of women

Paul then addresses the third major problem area in the church:

> As in all the congregations of the saints, women should remain silent in the churches. They are not allowed to speak, but must be in submission, as the Law says. If they want to inquire about something, they should ask their own husbands at home; for it is disgraceful for a woman to speak in the church. (1 CORINTHIANS 14:33b–35)

This passage has caused many people to reject the apostle Paul and regard him as a chauvinist or a misogynist, a man who feels threatened by gifted women. Such a view is unfair to Paul and does an injustice to Scripture. When we look at everything that is written and known about Paul, it becomes clear that Paul had a respect for women, including women in ministry. Of the roughly forty people Paul mentions in his letters as fellow workers in ministry, sixteen are women. He singles out several, including Priscilla, Phoebe, and Junia, as leaders in the early church.

To slander Paul as a woman-hater and disregard his words in this passage is to slander Scripture. We should also note that in 1 Corinthians 11, Paul strongly defends the right of women to pray and prophesy in church meetings.

So why do we seem to have a problem in this passage? It's because of a misunderstanding of Paul's point. He is saying that the church must recognize God's moral order of leadership—that is, the principle of headship. Paul dealt at length with the principle of headship in 1 Corinthians 11 (see chapter 12 of this book).

Paul is not saying that women shouldn't minister or speak in church. The problem Paul addresses is disorder and confusion—a problem that probably grew out of the very freedom that women did have to minister in the church at Corinth. Both the Jewish community and the Greek community tended to diminish the status of women. But in the Christian church, women were permitted to minister under the principle of headship.

But some women in ministry apparently went too far. They ran away with their freedom. They were asking questions and entering into debates, thereby turning an orderly meeting into a disorderly discussion group. Some, as Paul indicated earlier in this letter, had abandoned the head covering, which in the Corinthian culture signified the order of headship that God had instituted. The result was dissension.

The fact that this is Paul's concern is affirmed by his choice of words. He does not say that women are forbidden to minister in the church; he does not say women are forbidden to prophesy, pray, or teach. Women are forbidden, he says, to speak in a conversational way. They are not permitted to interrupt the proceedings with conversation or questions. The Greek word Paul uses is *laleo*, which is the most common word for simple conversation or even chatter. This is what Paul said must be silenced: women who would start talking and get carried away and turn a meeting into an unruly debating society. Theological debates do not edify the church; they get the church off track. This passage should not be viewed as a rule against women being engaged in legitimate ministry in the church.

If a more extensive discussion of these matters is needed, Paul says, the place for it is in the home. If you come to my house when my wife, Elaine, and I are involved in a theological discussion, you'll see exactly what the apostle Paul means. Our talks go on for hours, upstairs and downstairs. When it's time to eat, we pick up the discussion at the table. Elaine has a keen, theological mind, which I greatly appreciate. She has sharpened and refined my thinking in many areas. Paul says that the home is where these lengthy discussions and debates ought to take place, not in the church meeting.

Fitting and orderly

Paul knows that his teaching will not go down easily with some in the church, and he anticipates their arguments:

> Did the word of God originate with you? Or are you the only people it has reached? If anybody thinks he is a prophet or spiritually gifted, let him acknowledge that what I am writing to you is the Lord's command. If he ignores this, he himself will be ignored. (1 CORINTHIANS 14:36–38)

This is clearly satire. Paul recognizes that there was a tendency among some in Corinth to think they had unique revelation from God. So Paul takes a verbal swipe at this attitude, saying, "Did the word of God originate with you? Or are you the only people it has reached?"

My mentor in the ministry, Dr. H. A. Ironside, told me of an encounter he once had with a woman after a meeting. He had spoken on 1 Corinthians 6:11, where Paul says to the Corinthians, "But you were washed, you were sanctified, you were justified in the name of the Lord Jesus Christ and by the Spirit of our God." The woman said, "Dr. Ironside, you know you got those words in the wrong order. You put sanctification before justification. Everyone knows that we are justified before we are sanctified."

"Well," Dr. Ironside said, "I simply quoted the apostle Paul."

"Oh, that couldn't be," she said. "Paul would never say such a thing!"

"Just look," Dr. Ironside said, handing her an open Bible. "Here's the passage."

The woman read it—then she said, "Well, Paul couldn't have been very clear on the doctrine of holiness if he wrote that!" There are some people who are so sure of their own inspired understanding of Scripture that they will even set aside Scripture itself to sustain it. Of such people Paul asks, "Did the word of God originate with you?"

Next, Paul writes:

> If anybody thinks he is a prophet or spiritually gifted, let him acknowledge that what I am writing to you is the Lord's command. If he ignores this, he himself will be ignored. (1 CORINTHIANS 14:37–38)

In other words, truly spiritual people recognize the authority of the Scripture. Some will claim to have a private word from the Lord that violates the written Word of the Lord. Don't believe it! The Spirit of God never contradicts the written Word of God—never! Anyone who is Spirit-minded and Spirit-filled will recognize the authority of God's Word.

"If he ignores this," Paul says, "he himself will be ignored." In other words, do not pay attention to the one who contradicts God's command. Don't let him speak in the church. Don't engage him in debate. Don't listen to him. Ignore him.

Finally, Paul writes:

> Therefore, my brothers, be eager to prophesy, and do not forbid speaking in tongues. But everything should be done in a fitting and orderly way. (1 CORINTHIANS 14:39–40)

215

Here, Paul gathers up the theme of the whole passage: Be eager to have the gift of prophecy practiced in your church, for that gift builds up, comforts, and strengthens people. As for tongues, make sure the gift is exercised in a proper and orderly way. An unbeliever may come into church, and God will use that gift to reach that unbeliever.

God is sovereign, and He has the right to give gifts as He pleases, so do not forbid the exercise of this gift. But if it is the true biblical gift, it will have the effect that the Scriptures suggest it should—a sign to unbelievers. If it is not the true biblical gift but a psychological phenomenon, then we have every right to forbid it in the church as a divisive and destructive practice.

When is a church a church? When God's people come together to carry out His will in the world and manifest His true character to the world. That is why Paul tells us that everything in the church must be done decently and in order. We have a solemn responsibility not to misrepresent the beautiful and orderly character of God.

May the evidence of our lives always be that we serve a God of truth and love.

18

DEATH AND RESURRECTION

1 Corinthians 15:1–11

"How do you know Jesus rose from the dead?" the atheist asked.

"Because," the wise old believer softly replied, "I spent an hour with Him this morning."

Those who truly know the risen Lord need no other arguments than the evidence of their personal experience with Him every day.

The greatest news the world has ever heard was first reported from a graveyard outside of Jerusalem: The tomb is empty. Jesus is the victor over death and corruption. He has faced the ultimate enemy of mankind, and He has won.

The most frightening and troubling question we ever ask ourselves is "What happens to us after we die?" The resurrection of Jesus Christ means that this question has been convincingly, triumphantly answered.

Hundreds of books have attempted to answer this question apart from the fact of the resurrection. Some of those books involve philosophical and religious speculations. Others involve testimonies of near-death experiences, in which a person supposedly dies, then is resuscitated and experiences a few moments of an afterlife during the time that he or she is clinically but temporarily dead.

But the most authoritative answer we could ever have to that question is found here in 1 Corinthians 15. Paul shows us that the resurrection of the body is an essential and foundational part of our Christian faith. It is the essence of the gospel.

What does the word *gospel* mean? It comes from two Old English words, *god* (meaning "good") and *spel* (meaning "news"). The word *godspel* was a translation of the original Greek word for "good news," *euangelion*, from which we get such words as "evangelism" and "evangelical." The good news of the gospel is that death is not the end of the believer; it's the doorway to a new and better life in a world that has no end.

Paul writes:

> Now, brothers, I want to remind you of the gospel I preached to you, which you received and on which you have taken your stand. By this gospel you are saved, if you hold firmly to the word I preached to you. Otherwise, you have believed in vain. For what I received I passed on to you as of first importance: that Christ died for our sins according to the Scriptures, that he was buried, that he was raised on the third day according to the Scriptures. (1 CORINTHIANS 15:1–4)

Here, Paul sets forth the good news about Jesus. There are two divisions to this message. First, Paul tells us what the gospel does; second, he tells us what the gospel is.

Let's reverse that order and talk first about what the gospel is, because a lot of people do not understand it. If you ask people what the gospel is, they may tell you, "Jesus lived and died" or "Jesus died and rose again." But that's not the gospel. Paul tells us that the gospel actually consists of three elements:

1. "Christ died for our sins according to the Scriptures,"
2. "He was buried," and
3. "He was raised on the third day according to the Scriptures."

Notice the source of this gospel. Paul writes, "For what I received I passed on to you as of first importance." Paul doesn't say in these verses where he received this gospel, but he does tell us in his letter to the Galatians. There he writes, "I want you to know, brothers, that the gospel I preached is not something that man made up. I did not receive it from any man, nor was I taught it; rather, I received it by revelation from Jesus Christ" (Galatians 1:11–12).

The Lord Himself spoke this gospel to Paul, and Paul passed it on to the Christians in Corinth. Some Bible commentators mistakenly say that Paul was instructed by the other apostles in this gospel, but Paul says he received it directly from Jesus.

The three elements of the gospel

Let's look at each of those three elements of the gospel.

First, "Christ died for our sins according to the Scriptures." It's amazing that Paul does not mention a word about the entire life of Jesus. He doesn't mention the marvelous virgin birth in Bethlehem, or the silent years of His boyhood in Nazareth, or His teachings and miracles on the hillsides of Judea and Galilee, or His confrontations with the Pharisees in the streets and temple courts of Jerusalem. Paul focuses directly and immediately on the Lord's death. That, Paul says, is the first element of the gospel.

Notice that Paul does not merely say, "Christ died." There is nothing unusual about such a fact. Everyone eventually dies. What makes the death of Christ striking and special is that "Christ died for our sins according to the Scriptures." That is a startling statement. Most people believe that Jesus lived and died—even agnostics and atheists generally believe it. There is no good news in that.

But only a Christian believer can say, "Christ died for my sins according to the Scriptures." The death of Christ has accomplished something for that believer: it has changed him, delivered him, and set him free. As Peter puts it, "He himself bore our sins in his body on the tree" (see 1 Peter 2:24).

The phrase "according to the Scriptures" means that the death of Jesus fulfilled certain Old Testament prophecies concerning the Messiah. For example:

> But he was pierced for our transgressions,
>> he was crushed for our iniquities;
> the punishment that brought us peace was upon him,
>> and by his wounds we are healed.
> We all, like sheep, have gone astray,
>> each of us has turned to his own way;
> and the LORD has laid on him
>> the iniquity of us all.
> He was oppressed and afflicted,
>> yet he did not open his mouth;
> he was led like a lamb to the slaughter,
>> and as a sheep before her shearers is silent,
>> so he did not open his mouth.
> By oppression and judgment he was taken away.
>> And who can speak of his descendants?
> For he was cut off from the land of the living;
>> for the transgression of my people he was stricken.
>> (ISAIAH 53:5–8)

That's the good news. On the cross, Jesus canceled out our guilt and sin. Without His death upon the cross, we have no hope. Some people prefer to think that as long as they live a good life, in which their good deeds outweigh their bad deeds, then God will accept them into heaven. That commonly held idea is not only unbiblical but also illogical. How could a holy God accept any amount of evil in us? He is perfect, and he requires perfection. As the apostle James wrote, "For whoever keeps the whole law and yet stumbles at just one point is guilty of breaking all of it" (James 2:10).

On the cross of Jesus, God dealt with our sin and guilt. In our own power, it is impossible for us to be perfect, but by God's power, we can be forgiven.

Second, "He was buried." Why does Paul include the fact of the burial of Jesus as the second element of the gospel? Is it not enough that Jesus died and rose again? Would that not be good news enough? There is a reason why the burial of Jesus is so important to the gospel: It marked the disciples' acceptance of the fact that Jesus died.

Have you ever stopped to think of how hard it was for Jesus' followers to accept His death? They truly experienced an amazing degree of denial. They didn't want to believe Jesus when He predicted His own death. He told them repeatedly that He was going to be killed, but they refused to hear it. They shut their minds to it.

When Jesus was nailed to a cross, they went away stunned and dis-believing, unwilling to accept the notion that their hopes and dreams had just been crucified. All of the great words of Jesus, especially His promise of a coming kingdom, seemed to have crumbled to dust and ashes. Finally, Joseph of Arimathea came forward and offered his own tomb. With the help of Nicodemus, Joseph took the body of Jesus, embalmed the body in spices, bound it in linen, and placed it in the tomb. In the disciples' minds, there was at last no doubt: Jesus was dead—and buried.

Third, "He was raised on the third day according to the Scriptures." Once again, Jesus fulfilled the Old Testament prophecies: "Because you will not abandon me to the grave, nor will you let your Holy One see decay" (Psalm 16:10; see also Psalm 49:15; Hosea 6:2). On the third day, to the amazement of the disciples, Jesus fulfilled all the Old Testament predictions. He was not merely resuscitated—that is, restored to the same mortal life He had before. He was resurrected. He came back to life in a form of glorified immortality that the world had never seen before.

Jesus had a body that the disciples could touch and inspect—even the wounds of the cross were imprinted on His resurrected body. Yet it was a body that did not have the fragility and limitations of the former body.

That is the story of the gospel. Our faith does not rest upon a philosophy or a myth. It rests upon a historical event that occurred in time and space and cannot be taken away from us.

What the gospel does

We began by looking at what the gospel is. Now we will go back to the first few verses and see what the gospel does. You'll recall that Paul wrote:

> Now, brothers, I want to remind you of the gospel I preached to you, which you received and on which you have taken your stand. By this gospel you are saved, if you hold firmly to the word I preached to you. Otherwise, you have believed in vain. (1 Corinthians 15:1–2)

Notice the condition that Paul sets forth: We are saved by this gospel if we hold firmly to the word that Paul preached; otherwise, we have believed in vain. In other words, it is possible to believe in vain. It is possible to have a faith so superficial that we accept the words of the gospel as a fire escape against hell—but we don't allow this gospel to change our lives. If the gospel doesn't affect the way we live, Paul says, we have believed in vain.

Over the years, I have known a number of people who have believed in vain. They have fallen into a sinful lifestyle or have walked away from their faith. Jesus said that this would happen in the lives of some who outwardly seem to be well-grounded Christians: "Many will say to me on that day, 'Lord, Lord, did we not prophesy in your name, and in your name drive out demons and perform many miracles?' Then I will tell them plainly, 'I never knew you. Away from me, you evildoers!'" (Matthew 7:22–23).

The test of true faith is that it does not quit. It may be strained and stretched by doubting and trials and moral lapses, but a genuine believer always returns.

A young man once said to me, "I'm tired of being a Christian. I'm fed up with it. I've tried my best and nothing seems to work so I'm going to quit."

I said, "I think it's a good idea. Why don't you do that? Why don't you give it up?"

He seemed shocked. I think he had expected me to talk him out of his decision. "What do you mean?" he asked.

"Well," I replied, "you said you were going to quit, and I think it's a good idea. Why don't you stop trying to be a Christian and go ahead and live the way you like? Forget what the Bible says. Just have a good time doing whatever you like."

There was a look of horror on his face. "You know I can't do that!" he said.

"Yes, I know," I said. "I just wanted to make sure you knew it, too."

What does the gospel do for us? Two things, according to Paul.

First, it enables us to stand. He writes, "I want to remind you of the gospel . . . on which you have taken your stand." In other words, the gospel is your foundation. It is the strong basis upon which you can build your life so that it will withstand pressure, testing, trials, and temptation. When you believe that God has forgiven your sins and accepted you as His child, you have power to handle anything life can throw at you.

Second, the gospel continually saves us. Paul writes, "By this gospel you are saved," and he puts this statement in the present tense. He does not say, "By this gospel you were saved" or "you will be saved." He says that we are now being saved. It is a continuous and ongoing process.

If we believe in Jesus as our Lord and Savior, we have been saved in the past, we are being saved in the present, and we will be saved in the future. There are three tenses of salvation because there are three parts of our human nature. Your spirit is the essential you. We are all spirits, and when we came to Christ, our spirit was regenerated and made alive in Christ. That is salvation in the past tense.

Your body is the physical you. We all have bodies, and that is the theme of this great chapter on resurrection. God has a plan for your body; He will not grind it up and throw it away. He's going to redeem your body, restore it, and make it useful to you throughout all eternity. That is salvation in the future tense.

Your soul is the daily, present-tense you. It is the part of you that is being saved from day to day on a continual basis. The gospel gives us stability, steadiness, and an immovable foundation. It gives us a place of recovery, healing, and wholeness.

So Paul reminds us of the gospel on which we take our stand, the gospel by which we are continually saved. The foundation of our lives is the fact that Christ died for our sins, was buried, and rose again in fulfillment of the prophecies of Scripture. The goal of our lives is that we might learn to die to our sins, to bury them, and to rise again to the freshness and newness of life that is ours by faith in Jesus Christ.

The evidence of eyewitnesses

Did Jesus Christ literally and physically rise from the dead? Our entire faith hangs on the answer to that question. Paul now reviews the evidence:

> For what I received I passed on to you as of first importance: that Christ died for our sins according to the Scriptures, that he was buried, that he was raised on the third day according to the Scriptures, and that he appeared to Peter, and then to the Twelve. After that, he appeared to more than five hundred of the brothers at the same time, most of whom are still living, though some have fallen asleep. Then he appeared to James, then to all the apostles, and last of all he appeared to me also, as to one abnormally born. (1 CORINTHIANS 15:3–8)

According to the Gospel accounts, the risen Lord appeared first to Mary Magdalene, whom Paul does not mention here. Perhaps Paul does not list her because, according to the first-century mentality, a woman's testimony wasn't accepted as valid.

We don't know when and where our Lord first appeared to Peter. We do know that Peter was filled with shame and guilt after denying his Lord three times before the crucifixion. Paul, who received his revelation directly from the risen Lord, tells us that Jesus sought Peter out before He appeared to the other disciples. That's just like Jesus, isn't it? He found Peter wallowing in his brokenness and guilt, and He forgave Peter. At some later time, beside the Sea of Galilee, Jesus restored Peter to a role of ministry and leadership (see John 21:15–23).

Next, Paul says that Jesus appeared to all the apostles—to the Twelve. Paul probably groups several appearances together, such as the Lord's appearance to the two disciples on the Emmaus road, His later appearance to the disciples in Jerusalem, and His still later appearance to Thomas. The Scriptures indicate that Jesus appeared repeatedly to the disciples during the forty days between His resurrection and His ascension.

Paul also mentions an appearance before more than five hundred Christians at one time. Most of those who witnessed this appearance, Paul wrote, were still living at the time this letter was written. This evidence clearly refutes one of the explanations advanced by skeptics to dispute the resurrection—the claim that the postresurrection sightings of Jesus were mere hallucinations. One person might experience a hallucination—but five hundred at the same time? Unthinkable.

Paul does not say where this mass sighting occurred, but he mentions the event as if it were commonly known. I think this event probably occurred on a mountainside in Galilee. Even before His crucifixion, the Lord said He would meet His disciples in Galilee after the resurrection. The first message He sent by the women at the tomb was, "Go and tell my brothers to go to Galilee; there they will see me" (Matthew 28:10).

Then Paul refers to another appearance not reported in the Gospels: "Then he appeared to James." This is a reference to the half-brother of Jesus. Before the crucifixion and resurrection, the brothers of Jesus didn't believe that Jesus was the Messiah. Afterwards, however, James became convinced that Jesus was indeed the Son of God. He became one of the leaders of the early church and the author of the New Testament epistle of James.

Next, Paul mentions that Jesus appeared to all the apostles—a reference to the event in Acts 1 where Jesus, while teaching the apostles on the Mount of Olives, was taken up into the heavens, where a cloud hid Him from their sight. Then two angels appeared and said, "Men of Galilee, why do you stand here looking into the sky? This same Jesus, who has been taken from you into heaven, will come back in the same way you have seen him go into heaven" (Acts 1:11).

Finally, Paul says, Jesus "appeared to me also, as to one abnormally born." This is clearly a reference to the remarkable scene on the Damascus road, when young Saul of Tarsus, who burned with hatred against these Christian cultists, as he thought them, was struck blind and thrown to the ground. He heard a voice say to him, "Saul, Saul, why do you persecute me? I am Jesus, whom you are persecuting" (see Acts 9:4–5). Saul was converted to faith in Christ and changed his name to Paul.

What does that phrase mean, "as to one abnormally born"? Paul is telling us he did not come to spiritual birth in the usual way. The Greek word he employs means "miscarriage." Paul saw himself as a miscarriage, an abortion. To Paul's thinking, the other apostles were born again in a normal way: They heard the word of the Lord Jesus, the message took root in their hearts, they believed and were converted. Their spiritual birth followed a normal spiritual pregnancy.

Paul's spiritual birth was sudden and abnormal. Jesus had to blind him, throw him to the ground, and speak to him from the sky in order to get his attention. After his dramatic conversion, Paul spent three years in Damascus and Arabia and another seven years in his home town of Tarsus before he was ready to begin his ministry of teaching, preaching, and planting churches.

The least of the apostles

Next, Paul offers this self-evaluation:

> For I am the least of the apostles and do not even deserve to be called an apostle, because I persecuted the church of God. But by the grace of God I am what I am, and his grace to me was not without effect. No, I worked harder than all of them—yet not I, but the grace of God that was with me. Whether, then, it was I or they, this is what we preach, and this is what you believed. (1 CORINTHIANS 15:9–11)

People sometimes accuse the apostle Paul of being conceited. Those who make such a charge must not have read this passage, where Paul calls himself "the least of the apostles" and speaks of how undeserving he is for having persecuted the church.

By this time, Paul was a well-known apostle, a leader in the church, and the most remarkable missionary and evangelist who ever appeared on the earth. He took no credit for his accomplishments, but pointed to "the grace of God that was with me." God's grace overcomes all human folly and perversity, so that He is able to use even a great sinner and persecutor of the church to advance His cause.

Paul's words serve as an encouragement to us all. Many of us feel we have sinned and failed God so badly that we have given up the right to be used by God. Yet God chose Paul, an enemy of the faith, to become His ambassador, spreading His gospel and extending His church throughout the known world.

God wants to work the same way through you and me today. He wants us to be His witnesses, His ambassadors, in the troubled neighborhoods, offices, shops, and highways where we live our daily lives. He wants to use us as His channels for blessing and transforming power.

When I was a boy of eleven, I knelt in a Methodist camp meeting in North Dakota, and I prayed to receive Jesus as Lord of my life. I clearly remember the emotions I felt and the changes that occurred in my heart after I made that decision for Christ. My encounter with Jesus was real and powerful.

A few weeks passed, and my emotions faded. I began to drift back into some pre-Christian habits and behavior. Anyone seeing the things I did in those days would have thought my conversion was a lie. Yet, even though I wasn't living for the Lord at that time, I knew that something real had happened. My life would never be the same.

In my early twenties, I returned to God and began walking with Him again. I found that the risen Lord still lived in my life and was still making changes in my character. After decades of following Jesus, I can tell you with absolute certainty that Jesus is alive and He lives within me. My Lord does not watch disinterestedly from space as we poor mortals struggle and suffer on earth. He is intimately involved in our day-to-day realities. From the first century to the twenty-first, our Lord is still in the business of changing the world—

One life at a time.

19

IMMORTAL BEINGS

1 Corinthians 15:12–34

I once visited Poland while the country was still a Soviet-dominated communist nation. There I met Christians who had learned to live under constant persecution from an atheist government—a government that spied on them and indoctrinated their children with atheist propaganda. Under those conditions, doubt was a continual problem. The believers had to contend with such questions as, "What if the government is right? What if God doesn't exist and religious belief is only an illusion? Life would be so much easier if we would simply surrender to the pressure and deny our faith." Yet they stood firm.

Today, communism is a thing of the past in Eastern Europe—yet here in the Western world, our faith is under assault in new and subtle ways. Our government is not officially anti-Christian, but the culture is clearly post-Christian and growing increasingly intolerant of our faith. In our education establishment, our news and entertainment media, and other sectors of our society, attacks on Christianity are commonplace. Jesus is treated as a myth; Christians are caricatured as fools or bigots; Christian values are viewed as old-fashioned, unrealistic, and intolerant.

Sometimes we, as Christians, are tempted to wonder, "What if our faith is based on nothing but wishful thinking? What if the atheists are right? What if everything I believe about Jesus is wrong? What if He never rose from the grave? What if the Bible is nothing but a collection of legends?"

Many similar doubts had crept into the Corinthian church when Paul wrote this letter. Some in Corinth accepted the resurrection of Jesus but denied that there would be a bodily resurrection for Christians. Many were undoubtedly infected by Greek philosophy, which held that the body is evil; so they believed that, upon death, the spirit would be saved but disembodied. This kind of thinking about the spirit and the body is still with us—but it's not what the Bible teaches.

The truth of our resurrection bodies

In the Scriptures, the body is never presented as evil. Our bodies, after all, are temples of the Holy Spirit, the chosen dwelling places of God. In contrast to pagan teaching from the ancient Greeks to the New Age, the Bible takes an exalted view of the human body. This view is suggested by Paul in his teaching about the resurrection:

> But if it is preached that Christ has been raised from the dead, how can some of you say that there is no resurrection of the dead? If there is no resurrection of the dead, then not even Christ has been raised. And if Christ has not been raised, our preaching is useless and so is your faith. More than that, we are then found to be false witnesses about God, for we have testified about God that he raised Christ from the dead. But he did not raise him if in fact the dead are not raised. For if the dead are not raised, then Christ has not been raised either. And if Christ has not been raised, your faith is futile; you are still in your sins. Then those also who have fallen asleep in Christ are lost. If only for this life we have hope in Christ, we are to be pitied more than all men. (1 CORINTHIANS 15:12–19)

Paul's logic is unassailable: If human bodies cannot survive death, then Christ's body did not survive death. He was as human as we are, so it is irrational to argue, "Jesus rose from the dead, but the rest of us cannot." If Christ was not raised, there is no hope for our resurrection; but if Christ was raised, then we can be raised as well.

As we contemplate death, the question arises: "Do we lose all pleasurable sensations when we die? We enjoy eating, drinking, beautiful sights, sweet fragrances, the touch of a loved one's hand, the joys of sex—but will we ever experience these pleasures after we die? Or are these pleasures available to us in this life alone?"

The pagan answer is Enjoy life while you can. Eat, drink, and be merry, for tomorrow you die. You will never enjoy the pleasures of the senses again.

But the Christian answer is very different: As wonderful as these pleasures are in this life, there will be even richer and more intense pleasures in the life to come. In the resurrection, our bodies will be transformed, enhanced, and enriched. We will experience life more fully than we can imagine right now. God has a wonderful purpose and plan for our bodies, as well as our souls and spirits.

Some have asked me, "What about sexual pleasure? The Lord Jesus said, 'At the resurrection people will neither marry nor be given in marriage; they will be like the angels in heaven'" (Matthew 22:30). I reply that the joy of sex in marriage is given to teach us the exquisite ecstasy of an intimate relationship with another person. Though the Scriptures suggest that sexual desire will not be physically expressed in heaven, marital sex is a picture of a far greater delight we will discover in relating to people and to God. To simply sit and talk with other people will be a bliss beyond our imagining. To worship God in a resurrection body is to find your whole being suffused with a glory that far transcends sexual release.

C. S. Lewis wrote a short book called *The Weight of Glory* in which he described what we and our fellow human beings will become after the resurrection:

> It is a serious thing to live in a society of possible gods and goddesses, to remember that the dullest and most uninteresting person you talk to may one day be a creature which, if you saw it now, you would strongly be tempted to worship, or else a horror and a corruption such as you now meet, if at all, only in a nightmare. All day long we are, in some degree, helping each other to one or the other of these destinations. It is in the light of these overwhelming possibilities, it is with the awe and circumspection proper to them, that we should conduct all our dealings with one another, all friendships, all loves, all play, all politics. There are no ordinary people. You have never talked to a mere mortal.

An eternity of unimaginable glory awaits those who have placed their trust in the Lord Jesus Christ. That is the great truth of our resurrection bodies. The thought is so exciting, I can hardly wait for eternity to arrive!

What if . . . ?

In verses 14–19, Paul considers the question "What if . . . ?" What would the world be like if Jesus had not been raised? What if the women who went to the tomb on that resurrection morning had found the stone unmoved, the guards still in place at their posts? What if the body of Jesus still lay in the darkness of the tomb, cold and lifeless? What would life be like? Paul lists six history-changing consequences that would have followed if Jesus had not been raised.

First, "if Christ has not been raised, our preaching is useless." Without the resurrection, preaching is a waste of time. We might as well not bother going to church. Why write Christian books? Why produce Christian music? It's all a waste of effort—if Jesus is still in the grave.

But what about all of the teachings of Jesus? The Sermon on the Mount? The parables? The moral lessons? Even if Jesus was just a great moral teacher who died and never rose again, his teachings have value! Yes—but without the resurrection, His teachings are no use to us. His teachings would condemn us, because we cannot keep His teachings in our own strength. The death of Jesus would be nothing but an unfulfilled promise. Without the resurrection, we would still be dead in our sins.

Second, if Christ has not been raised, then all Christian faith is useless. In that case, Paul says, "Our preaching is useless, and so is your faith." What would be the point of attending church, reading the Bible, or praying? It would all be a meaningless religious exercise. Bertrand Russell, one of the twentieth century's most eloquent spokesmen for unbelief, wrote:

> The life of Man is a long march through the night, surrounded by invisible foes, tortured by weariness and pain, towards a goal that few can hope to reach and where none can tarry long. One by one, as they march, our comrades vanish from our sight, seized by the silent orders of omnipotent Death.
>
> Brief and powerless is Man's life; on him and all his race the slow, sure doom falls, pitiless and dark. Blind to good and evil, reckless of destruction, omnipotent matter rolls on its relentless way. For Man, condemned today to lose his dearest, tomorrow himself to pass through the gates of darkness, it remains only to cherish, ere yet the blow falls, the lofty thoughts that ennoble his little day.

What despair! What darkness! But that is all we have left when the resurrection of Jesus has been taken away.

Third, if Christ was not raised, Paul says, "we are then found to be false witnesses about God, for we have testified about God that he raised Christ from the dead." If the resurrection is untrue, the apostles are the world's greatest liars. The apostles have staked their lives and their reputations to the fact that Jesus rose from the dead.

Fourth, "and if Christ has not been raised, your faith is futile; you are still in your sins." If there was no resurrection, we would be unforgiven. We'd have to stand before God and account for our sins—and there would be no hiding place, no mercy, no Advocate for our cause, no Sacrifice for our transgressions.

Fifth, "then those also who have fallen asleep in Christ are lost." Not only are we lost in our sins if there is no resurrection, but also everyone we love is lost. When they die, they are gone. We will never see them in heaven. Parents, children, friends—everyone to whom we have bidden a weeping farewell will be lost to us forever.

Sixth, "if only for this life we have hope in Christ, we are to be pitied more than all men." If we are holding onto a mirage, what miserable fools we are! If there is no resurrection, then we aren't even living for the moment. We are foregoing even the few pleasures this brief life affords in order to chase fantasies. Meanwhile, the One we call Lord is lying in a cold, dark cave. So, we are to be pitied.

What if those six consequences characterized your life? Well, consider this: Millions of people live lives exactly like that today. They do not know about the reality of the risen Lord—so for them, it's as if Jesus was never resurrected. Everything they believe is futile. They have no hope for themselves or their loved ones. They are tragic figures, worthy of our pity and compassion.

The firstfruits of the resurrection harvest

Thank God, then, for Paul's next words:

> But Christ has indeed been raised from the dead, the firstfruits of those who have fallen asleep. For since death came through a man, the resurrection of the dead comes also through a man. For as in Adam all die, so in Christ all will be made alive. But each in his own turn: Christ, the firstfruits; then, when he comes, those who belong to him. (1 CORINTHIANS 15:20–23)

These verses transform our perspective. All of the hungers and desires of our lives can be satisfied because of this great truth: Jesus has risen from the dead! And because He is risen, we will rise, too. Paul's thoughts sweep across the centuries to declare the ultimate impact of the resurrection on our world and our lives.

First, the resurrection of Christ guarantees the physical resurrection of the bodies of all who believe in Him. Our resurrection is tied to His. The key to this passage is the twice-repeated word *firstfruits*. Paul refers here to the ritual that was given to Israel in Leviticus 23. On the Feast of Unleavened Bread after the Passover, on the morrow after the Sabbath, there was to be an offering of the first fruits of the barley harvest. The Jews were commanded to bring a sheaf of grain, the first of the harvest, to the priest, who would wave it before the Lord.

When did the resurrection of Jesus take place? On that very morning—on the Feast of Unleavened Bread, following the Passover, on the morrow after the Sabbath! The feasts of Old Testament Israel predicted that the resurrection of Jesus would represent the first fruits of a harvest. What sort of harvest? A resurrection harvest!

Paul's argument is that Jesus not only rose from the dead on the exact day predicted by the Old Testament ritual, but also His resurrection was literally the first fruit of a coming harvest of resurrected human beings—all those who believe in Him.

It's important to understand that Jesus was the first human being ever resurrected from the dead. You might say, "Well, what about Lazarus? And before Lazarus, what about the Old Testament stories of people who were raised from the dead?" Yes, it's true that people who died were returned to life—but they were not resurrected.

To be resurrected means more than merely coming back to life. When we are resurrected, we don't merely get our old lives back. True resurrection confers upon us a totally new quality and dimension of life that we have never known before. It is a marvelous dimension of existence such as we can scarcely imagine. Jesus was the first human being to experience this new dimension of life. He was the same Jesus—but He came back in a new resurrection body.

Paul goes on to say that our future resurrection is an absolute certainty. He writes, "For since death came through a man, the resurrection of the dead comes also through a man." Death passed upon our race because of the fall of Adam, so all who are part of the new creation, the new race in Christ, shall also participate in the resurrection of the dead. "For as in Adam all die," Paul writes, "so in Christ all will be made alive."

When Paul says that "all will be made alive," is he preaching universalism—the idea that all of humanity will be saved, both the believers and the unbelievers? No, Paul makes it clear that the resurrection will not be experienced by the entire human race, but only by believers. For he writes, "But each in his own turn: Christ, the firstfruits; then, when he comes, those who belong to him."

Understand, Scripture teaches that there will be a resurrection of both the just and the unjust. Jesus put it this way:

"Do not be amazed at this, for a time is coming when all who are in their graves will hear his voice and come out—those who have done good will rise to live, and those who have done evil will rise to be condemned." (JOHN 5:28–29)

Those who "rise to live" are the same ones that Paul calls "those who belong to Him," to Christ. Those who do not belong to Christ will be called back to an awareness, a terrible and fateful sort of resurrection—but in that resurrection, there will be no wonderful and glorious new dimension of life.

The moment of death, the moment of resurrection

It's sobering to realize that we are all dying. We begin to die the moment we are born, and the process goes on relentlessly. Though we can cover up the outward signs of aging and dying by coloring our hair and other cosmetic means, the inward advance of time cannot be arrested. We are all moving steadily toward the moment of our death.

There was an epitaph on a tombstone that read:

Remember, friend, as you pass by,
As you are now, so once was I.
As I am now, soon you will be,
Prepare for death, and follow me.

Some wag had written underneath it:

To follow you I'm not content,
Until I know which way you went.

Content or not, we will follow. As Paul says, "in Adam all die." This truth is dead certain. But there is good news that's equally certain: The resurrection is coming! Just as surely as death works in us because of Adam, new life works in us because of Christ.

When will this resurrection take place? Paul writes, "But each in his own turn: Christ, the firstfruits; then, when he comes, those who belong to him." When Jesus returns, the resurrection will take place. Paul writes elsewhere:

For the Lord himself will come down from heaven, with a loud command, with the voice of the archangel and with the trumpet call of

233

God, and the dead in Christ will rise first. After that, we who are still alive and are left will be caught up together with them in the clouds to meet the Lord in the air. And so we will be with the Lord forever. (1 THESSALONIANS 4:16–17)

There are some who will never die, even though death is at work in them. For two thousand years, every generation of believers has hoped to be the generation still living when Christ returned. That hope still blazes in hearts today, particularly as we look at world conditions, which seem like those predicted for the last days. Yet world events flow and rearrange, and what looks like a precursor to Armageddon one day turns out to be just another brushfire war. Every past generation has had to go through death in order to prepare for the resurrection.

What happens to the believer between the moment of death and the moment of resurrection? At death, the believer steps out of time and into eternity. In eternity, there is no past or future. So the first thing the believer becomes aware of is that great event at the culmination of history: The Lord is returning for His own! The moment a person dies, he instantly experiences the return of the Lord and the resurrection of the body. There is no waiting for those who go to be with the Lord.

The last enemy

Next, Paul moves on to that final scene when Christ has returned and has reigned throughout a millennium of peace and righteousness on earth. At that time, He will have completed His work, subdued His enemies, cast Satan and death and Hades into the lake of fire (as we read in Revelation), then delivered the kingdom back to the Father. This is what Paul now describes:

Then the end will come, when he hands over the kingdom to God the Father after he has destroyed all dominion, authority and power. For he must reign until he has put all his enemies under his feet. The last enemy to be destroyed is death. (1 CORINTHIANS 15:24–26)

Notice that the reign of Christ does not begin after He subdues his enemies. His enemies are still present during his reign—and He must reign until He has put all of His enemies under His feet. That is a powerful truth to remember in times of discouragement, defeat, and oppression: Jesus now reigns. He is the King even now.

Yes, there are enemies around us. There is persecution. There is violence. There are obstacles and opponents in our path. But Jesus reigns, and

He will reign until He has put all enemies under His feet. When He rose from the dead, He said, "All power is given unto me in heaven and in earth" (Matthew 28:18 KJV).

Then Paul says, "The last enemy to be destroyed is death." This enemy, death, will never disappear from the earth until that moment, described in Revelation, when a new heaven and a new earth shall come into existence. Death will be present even during the millennium. The prophet Isaiah, in describing the age of the millennium, wrote:

> Never again will there be in it
> an infant who lives but a few days,
> or an old man who does not live out his years;
> he who dies at a hundred
> will be thought a mere youth;
> he who fails to reach a hundred
> will be considered accursed. (ISAIAH 65:20)

In other words, there will be death in the millennium, but it will be rare—so rare that the one who merely lives to be a hundred will be thought to have died as a mere youth. But Jesus reigns, and this last enemy, death, shall be destroyed in the end. Once we pass through death to resurrection, we shall be like our Lord and shall never die again.

Paul goes on to describe this future time when death has been destroyed and the kingdom has been restored to God the Father:

> For he "has put everything under his feet." Now when it says that "everything" has been put under him, it is clear that this does not include God himself, who put everything under Christ. When he has done this, then the Son himself will be made subject to him who put everything under him, so that God may be all in all. (1 CORINTHIANS 15:27–28)

Here Paul describes the end of Christ's work as a mediator between God and man. During this present time, our Lord Jesus is singled out, as it were, from the persons of the Godhead as the supreme object of worship, and we are invited to worship Him and give honor to Him. In his letter to the Philippians, Paul tells us:

> Therefore God exalted him [Jesus] to the highest place
> and gave him the name that is above every name,

that at the name of Jesus every knee should bow,
  in heaven and on earth and under the earth,
and every tongue confess that Jesus Christ is Lord,
  to the glory of God the Father. (PHILIPPIANS 2:9–11)

Worshiping Christ honors God. But a time is coming, Paul says, when the work of the Son in subduing a lost creation will be finished. When the full results of the atonement of the cross have been completed and all the harvest of the earth is gathered, the Lord Jesus will return the kingdom to the Father in order that "God may be all in all."

At that time, we will finally understand the mystery of the Trinity. For now, we only know that the Bible teaches something that is impossible to comprehend—that there are three persons in the Godhead, that they are equal in glory and honor, and that they somehow coalesce as three persons but only one God. One day we will fully and finally grasp this great truth. It will make intellectual, intuitive, and emotional sense to us for the first time. God will be everything to every one; He will be all in all.

Fighting wild beasts

Next, Paul reveals another remarkable characteristic of the resurrection, beginning with this somewhat puzzling verse:

Now if there is no resurrection, what will those do who are baptized for the dead? If the dead are not raised at all, why are people baptized for them? (1 CORINTHIANS 15:29)

The Mormon church uses this verse to justify the practice of baptizing living church members on behalf of the dead. You might ask, "What good does it do to be baptized for the dead?" The Mormons believe you can go back through history and be baptized for all your ancestors. That's why the Mormon church puts a great deal of emphasis on tracing one's ancestry. I once met a Mormon woman who said that she had saved more people than Jesus Christ because she had been baptized for thousands of people. Some Mormons pick out famous people in history and are baptized on behalf of Julius Caesar, Alexander the Great, Napoleon, and others, all on the basis of this one verse.

There is no other reference in the Bible to being baptized on behalf of the dead. What, then, does this verse mean? To be absolutely candid, I don't know!

Paul is evidently speaking of a form of proxy baptism. But it is worth noting that he does not refer to proxy baptism as a practice carried on by the Christians in Corinth. He does not say that the Corinthians do this, nor does he say that he does it. He simply notes that proxy baptism is done somewhere by someone, but we don't know who or where or why.

Clearly, Paul is not advocating this practice. He is using this practice to make a point: People were being motivated to take this action. What moved them to go out of their way to be baptized on behalf of people who had died? The fact of the resurrection. Whether or not proxy baptism has any merit (and Paul does not say it does), the very fact that people carried out this action was evidence that people were motivated by the truth of the resurrection of Christ and the hope of the resurrection of the saints.

Belief in the resurrection has a great effect upon you. It changes your life. It makes you do things you would not otherwise do. It makes you concerned about the salvation of others.

Paul goes on to speak of how the truth of the resurrection motivates him to accept great risks and great suffering for the cause of Christ:

> And as for us, why do we endanger ourselves every hour? I die every day—I mean that, brothers—just as surely as I glory over you in Christ Jesus our Lord. If I fought wild beasts in Ephesus for merely human reasons, what have I gained? If the dead are not raised,
>
> "Let us eat and drink,
>> for tomorrow we die." (1 Corinthians 15:30–32)

Paul makes reference to an experience in his life we don't know much about—his experience of having "fought wild beasts in Ephesus." Later, in 2 Corinthians 1, Paul again makes reference to this experience:

> We do not want you to be uninformed, brothers, about the hardships we suffered in the province of Asia. We were under great pressure, far beyond our ability to endure, so that we despaired even of life. Indeed, in our hearts we felt the sentence of death. But this happened that we might not rely on ourselves but on God, who raises the dead. (2 Corinthians 1:8–9)

Ephesus was in Asia Minor, "the province of Asia," so these are probably both references to the same event. Paul says that his faith in the resurrection of the dead was the only motivation that could have carried him through the suffering and despair of that experience. Paul wants us to know that the resurrection is the ample recompense for any and all human suffering, no matter how bad it may get.

It's not clear whether he "fought wild beasts" in a literal or figurative sense. Paul was a Roman citizen, and no Roman citizen could be compelled to fight in the arena against wild beasts. Therefore, I suspect that Paul was using a metaphor to describe persecution from men who were wild and bestial in their attacks upon him.

Bad company corrupts good character

Paul closes this section with an appeal: Let the hope of resurrection determine your lifestyle. He writes, "If the dead are not raised, 'Let us eat and drink, for tomorrow we die.'" Paul was quoting the philosophy of Epicureanism, which was widespread in that day, as in our own time. It's a philosophy that says, "Live it up. Enjoy yourself! Life is short, so grab all the pleasure you can before you die!"

Then he adds:

> Do not be misled: "Bad company corrupts good character." Come back to your senses as you ought, and stop sinning; for there are some who are ignorant of God—I say this to your shame. (1 CORINTHIANS 15:33–34)

The Christians in Corinth were surrounded by a hedonistic, Epicurean, pagan society. The live-it-up philosophy was all around them. The Christians in Corinth undoubtedly had many pagan friends who followed this way of life. Paul is not saying, "Don't associate with pagans and hedonists." He's saying, "Don't keep company with people who will drag down your morals and your character. Don't do the things they do, and don't let their hedonistic, Epicurean philosophy infect your thinking."

Employing an oft-quoted proverb of the day, "Bad company corrupts good character," Paul says, in effect, "Come to your senses. Come to your right mind. Don't get caught up in the mindset of sinners who have nothing to live for. Be realistic about life. Live as a Christian, as one who has the hope of the resurrection. Yes, this life is short—but we have all of eternity ahead of us, so let's live worthy of that fact. Make good use of this life—use it for God's glory."

This section of Paul's letter closes on an elevating, uplifting truth: We are not creatures of time. We are immortal beings. When we gather at the throne of God, our greatest privilege will be the knowledge that we have used our mortal lifetime to bring glory to Him.

Life is short. Make the most of it for God.

20

RESURRECTION BODIES

1 Corinthians 15:35–58

Many people are under the mistaken impression that the resurrection was a new idea that was introduced during the first century. According to this notion, the Jews of the Old Testament had no conception of, or belief in, the resurrection but believed that when the body died, the individual was dead forever. A careful look at the Old Testament reveals that this notion is untrue.

In Job, probably the oldest book in the Bible, Job makes this statement:

> I know that my Redeemer lives,
>> and that in the end he will stand upon the earth.
>
> And after my skin has been destroyed,
>> yet in my flesh I will see God;
>
> I myself will see him
>> with my own eyes—I, and not another.
>
> How my heart yearns within me! (JOB 19:25–27)

Notice how specific Job was in describing not just an afterlife, such as the survival of a disembodied soul. Job is describing a bodily resurrection when he says, "And after my skin has been destroyed, yet in my flesh I will see God." Similarly, the prophet Daniel tells us:

> Multitudes who sleep in the dust of the earth will awake: some to everlasting life, others to shame and everlasting contempt. Those who are wise will shine like the brightness of the heavens, and those who lead many to righteousness, like the stars for ever and ever. (DANIEL 12:2–3)

The prophet Isaiah also wrote unmistakably of the hope of a physical, bodily resurrection:

But your dead will live;
> their bodies will rise.
You who dwell in the dust,
> wake up and shout for joy.
Your dew is like the dew of the morning;
> the earth will give birth to her dead. (ISAIAH 26:19)

The Jewish rabbis even had a tradition to explain how the physical process of the resurrection would take place. There is a legend told about a meeting between the Roman emperor Hadrian, who ruled more than fifty years following the death of Paul, and the great Jewish rabbinical scholar Joshua Ben Hananiah. They discussed Jewish beliefs, especially the Hebrew view of life after death. Hadrian asked, "How does a dead man come back to life in the world to come?"

"From the luz," Joshua Ben Hananiah replied. "It's an indestructible bone located in the spine." The Hebrew scholar then produced a small white bone from a pouch he carried. "This is a luz." According to this story, he then conducted tests on the luz for the emperor to witness. Water would not dissolve the luz, fire would not consume it, a mill could not grind it, and a hammer and anvil could not crush it. "The luz is the nucleus of the body and cannot be destroyed. On the day of resurrection, God will add bone and flesh to the luz, and the man will live again in the body."

Of course, medical science tells us that there is no such thing as a luz. God certainly does not need a luz in order to rebuild a complete human being. The entire blueprint of our lives, including our physical form, is etched in the mind of God. He will not require so much as a molecule around which to build our bodies.

How are the dead raised?

We now come to the key question of 1 Corinthians 15, the great resurrection chapter of the New Testament. Paul writes:

> But someone may ask, "How are the dead raised? With what kind of body will they come?" (1 CORINTHIANS 15:35)

Paul cites a question that oozes skepticism. Earlier, in verse 12, Paul wrote, "But if it is preached that Christ has been raised from the dead, how can some of you say that there is no resurrection of the dead?" Word has come to Paul that some in the Corinthian church denied the doctrine of the resurrection. These people said, "We don't understand how the resurrection could happen. We can't see any process that would enable a dead body to be restored to life—so we don't believe it could happen."

For twenty centuries, skeptics have continued to pose questions and objections that they think are unanswerable. For example, "If a body were embalmed and all of its constituent parts were there—the skeleton, the flesh, and so forth—then God might have a way to reanimate those dead tissues and resurrect the dead individual. But what about a person whose body has been destroyed? What about those whose bodies have been cremated? Or people who were lost at sea or died in the desert, and their bodies were eaten by animals or absorbed back into the ecosystem? How could God possibly sort out the recycled matter and return people to their bodies?" Such questions always arise when unbelief confronts the reality of the resurrection.

The Greeks of Paul's day taught that it was a good thing to be rid of the body. The material human body, they taught, was a prison that limited and restricted the spirit. The idea that the immaterial spirit was superior to the material body had infected the Corinthian church, causing some in the church to deny the resurrection. So Paul replies:

> How foolish! What you sow does not come to life unless it dies. When you sow, you do not plant the body that will be, but just a seed, perhaps of wheat or of something else. But God gives it a body as he has determined, and to each kind of seed he gives its own body. (1 CORINTHIANS 15:36–38)

First, Paul says that the question itself is foolish. Why? Because examples abound of everyday miracles that are instructive parallels to resurrection. When a farmer plants a crop, he doesn't plant wheat stalks or corn stalks—he plants seeds. The seeds are dry, hard, and dead-looking—yet from those seeds emerges the body of a plant.

I don't think it's an accident that Easter occurs in the spring, the season of new life and growth. We don't know what time of year Jesus was born (there's no historical proof that He was born in late December). But we do know when Jesus died, because His death has been dated precisely by the Jewish celebration of the Passover. We know beyond any doubt that Easter Sunday is the day our Lord rose from the dead.

Easter, therefore, always falls amid the awakening of the earth from the death of winter. Things that were once dead become green and alive. So Paul points out that we have ample evidence in the processes of nature to believe in the resurrection of the body. Nature teaches two lessons about death and resurrection.

First, death is a necessary part of the resurrection process. Far from being an obstacle to resurrection, death is essential to resurrection. Nothing can be resurrected unless first it dies. The fact that people die and the body decomposes should be no hindrance to believing in resurrection. The body must die just as the seed must die.

Second, the body that emerges from a dead seed is different from the body that was planted. Plant a seed in the earth and what springs up? Another seed? No! A green stem that doesn't look at all like the seed. It has a continuous identity with the seed, but it is different, it is new. The resurrection is like that. Plant a mortal, corruptible dead body in the earth, and what springs up? Another mortal, corruptible body? No! A new kind of body, immortal and incorruptible—a resurrection body.

On one occasion, Paul stood before the court of King Agrippa, the last of the Herods, and said, "Why should any of you consider it incredible that God raises the dead?" (Acts 26:8). And Paul is right: Why should it seem incredible, since we have the testimony of nature that death and resurrection take place all around us, all the time?

Scientists now know that it is possible to take a single cell from a human body and clone that cell to produce an exact copy of the original individual. Understand, I'm not suggesting that the resurrection involves a process of cloning; I'm only making an analogy. If a body can be restored from a single cell by means of human science, then surely God can restore not only the body but the spirit and soul from the exact blueprint that exists in His own mind!

Computer scientist Gerhard Dirks, who devised more than a hundred patented inventions for IBM, once told me that it's technically feasible to take the genetic structure of a human being, convert it to an electronic signal, bounce that signal off the moon and back to earth, then reconstruct that information into a human being again. If such a thing is technically possible for human science, then it is surely a practical possibility for God. Why, then, should anyone find it impossible to believe in the resurrection?

A soulish body versus a spiritual body

Next, Paul confronts the skeptics' second question: "With what kind of body will they come?" In other words, "Supposing the resurrection were true, what would the resurrection body be like? How would it differ from the bodies we have now?" Paul replies by returning to the lessons of nature:

> All flesh is not the same: Men have one kind of flesh, animals have another, birds another and fish another. There are also heavenly bodies and there are earthly bodies; but the splendor of the heavenly bodies is one kind, and the splendor of the earthly bodies is another. The sun has one kind of splendor, the moon another and the stars another; and star differs from star in splendor. (1 CORINTHIANS 15:39–41)

Here, again, Paul teaches from the world of nature, the realm of observable phenomena. Here is the first truth that he brings out: All bodies are not alike. Human bodies are different from bird bodies, and mammal bodies are different from fish bodies. Even the very nature of their flesh is different.

Similarly, all heavenly bodies are not alike. The sun, moon, and stars differ from each other, and heavenly bodies differ markedly from earthly bodies, such as men and animals. Heavenly bodies give a glorious light; earthly bodies do not shine but have a different function. Heavenly bodies move in limitless space, which we measure in light years; earthly bodies are limited to a single planet.

The differences between earthly bodies and heavenly bodies parallel the differences between the mortal human body and the imperishable resurrection body. If you would only read the lessons of nature you would see a panorama of theological truth spread before you. Paul continues:

> So will it be with the resurrection of the dead. The body that is sown is perishable, it is raised imperishable; it is sown in dishonor, it is raised in glory; it is sown in weakness, it is raised in power; it is sown a natural body, it is raised a spiritual body. If there is a natural body, there is also a spiritual body. (1 CORINTHIANS 15:42–44)

The human body is a perishing body. Over time, it loses its ability to function. It slows down, breaks down, and eventually dies. But just as a seed dies, is planted in the earth, and emerges as a beautiful plant, so a perishable body dies, is planted in the earth, and emerges as an imperishable body. It dies as an earthly body; it rises as a resurrection body, no longer subject to death and decay. It dies in dishonor and corruption; it rises in glory and power. The natural and earthly is exchanged for the spiritual and heavenly.

We like to think of ourselves as powerful beings. Yet this mortal, perishable human body that temporarily houses our spirits is so fragile that it can be sickened and killed by something as tiny as a microbe. The human body is weak and easily destroyed. But the resurrection body will truly be powerful and immortal.

Paul says that our mortal body "is sown a natural body" but "is raised a spiritual body." The word translated "natural" literally means "soulish" in the original Greek. The human body is a "soulish" body. It is designed to function by the control of the soul—the mind, emotions, and will. I like to think of my body as an earth suit designed for living in time and space. This earth suit is not me. I merely live in it. Someday, I'm going to shed my earth suit and put on an eternal suit—a heaven suit, a real body, a resurrection body that cannot wear out or die.

We get a glimpse of the heaven suit when we look at the resurrected body of Jesus. He rose from the dead, and the marks of the crucifixion were still on His body—but what a difference! It was functioning at a different level of existence. It was able to pass through doors, appear and disappear, eat or not to eat. It was able to function in fellowship with people in their earth suits, and yet it was able to disappear from the earthly scene and function on a heavenly plane. It was equally at home in time and space or in eternity. What a marvelous body we look forward to!

The first Adam and the last Adam

Next, Paul goes on to prove his case. He writes:

> So it is written: "The first man Adam became a living being"; the last Adam, a life-giving spirit. The spiritual did not come first, but the natural, and after that the spiritual. The first man was of the dust of the earth, the second man from heaven. As was the earthly man, so are those who are of the earth; and as is the man from heaven, so also are those who are of heaven. And just as we have borne the likeness of the earthly man, so shall we bear the likeness of the man from heaven.
> (1 CORINTHIANS 15:45–49)

Here Paul contrasts two men, two Adams. There is the first Adam and the last Adam. The first Adam was the head of the human race in the Garden of Eden. The last Adam, Jesus, is the only other human being to serve as head of the entire human race.

The first Adam, Paul says, was made a living soul. He had a body made from the dust, and God breathed a spirit into that body. The joining together of spirit and body produced another phenomenon called the soul, the personality. It is the presence of a spirit in a body that creates the soul and allows a person to function as a human being with mind, emotion, and will. That is what the first Adam was.

When Adam sinned and humanity fell, the Holy Spirit, who dwelled in the human spirit of Adam, was withdrawn, and the human spirit became dead. Man, therefore, was governed by his soul, the highest part of his being. The soul can feel and touch and taste and reason, but it has no contact with anything beyond and above.

As Paul tells us in Ephesians 2:1, we were all born dead in sin. Why? Because every human being is a son or daughter of the first Adam by nature.

But then came the last Adam, Jesus. Paul calls Him "a life-giving Spirit." The first Adam came from the dust, but the last Adam, Jesus, came from heaven. In our mortal bodies, we bear the likeness of the first Adam; but in our resurrection bodies, we will bear the likeness of Jesus, the man from heaven.

There are cults that teach that human beings were spirit beings first who came to earth and became human beings, who will one day return to a purely spiritual existence. That is a lie, according to Paul. He says that we came into existence on a physical level, according to God's design. In the resurrection, we will have spiritual bodies; they will be real bodies, not immaterial—but they will be glorified and transcendent. Death is the gateway from the physical to the spiritual, from the earthly to the heavenly. I love the way the apostle John expresses this truth:

> Dear friends, now we are children of God, and what we will be has not yet been made known. But we know that when he appears, we shall be like him, for we shall see him as he is. (1 JOHN 3:2)

What a reassuring hope! What a difference this truth makes to every aspect of our lives! It transforms the way we think and speak and act. It transforms our dreams, our aspirations, and how we use our time. Your entire life hinges on whether you see yourself as a person made of dust or a person made for heaven.

The mystery

Next, Paul pulls back the veil on an amazing and wonderful mystery. He writes:

> I declare to you, brothers, that flesh and blood cannot inherit the kingdom of God, nor does the perishable inherit the imperishable. Listen, I tell you a mystery— (1 CORINTHIANS 15:50–51a)

Flesh and blood cannot inherit the kingdom of God. Our fallen, mortal, perishable humanity can do nothing of value in the kingdom. It cannot even enter the kingdom. This is the truth that so startled and perplexed a man named Nicodemus who came to Jesus by night. Nicodemus was a respected leader in Israel, a man of great accomplishments and honors—yet Jesus told him that his position and status meant nothing in the kingdom. Nicodemus needed to exchange his perishable self for an imperishable self. Jesus explained it this way: "You must be born again" (John 3:7).

Just as Paul said that flesh and blood cannot inherit the kingdom of God, Jesus said, "I tell you the truth, no one can enter the kingdom of God unless he is born of water and the Spirit. Flesh gives birth to flesh, but the Spirit gives birth to spirit. You should not be surprised at my saying, 'You must be born again'" (see John 3:5–7). Perishable people cannot inherit an imperishable kingdom. We must be remade into imperishable people.

At this point, Paul says, "Listen, I tell you a mystery." A mystery! Everyone loves a mystery. Of course, this word *mystery*, when used in Scripture, doesn't refer to something that is hidden or hard to understand. It refers to a truth about reality that can be known only because it has been revealed by God. What is the mystery Paul unveils for us here? It is the mystery of the resurrection. He writes:

> We will not all sleep, but we will all be changed—in a flash, in the twinkling of an eye, at the last trumpet. For the trumpet will sound, the dead will be raised imperishable, and we will be changed. For the perishable must clothe itself with the imperishable, and the mortal with immortality. (1 CORINTHIANS 15:51b–53)

What is this mystery?

First, it is the fact that "we will not all sleep." Some of us will never die. Scripture constantly anticipates that a generation of believers will one day experience a transformation from perishable to imperishable without having to go through death. This change will occur "in a flash, in the twinkling of an eye."

Second, whether we are dead or alive when that moment comes, "we will all be changed." The dead in Christ will be changed. The living in Christ will be changed. All will be changed in the same flash of time, the same twinkling of an eye. Our earth suits will instantly become heaven suits. The perishable will become imperishable.

Third, this will take place at a specific moment in time. When is that moment? Paul says, "At the last trumpet. For the trumpet will sound, the dead will be raised imperishable, and we will be changed." When will that trumpet sound? Elsewhere, Paul tells us it will occur at the return of Jesus:

> For the Lord himself will come down from heaven, with a loud command, with the voice of the archangel and with the trumpet call of God, and the dead in Christ will rise first. After that, we who are still alive and are left will be caught up together with them in the clouds to meet the Lord in the air. And so we will be with the Lord forever. (1 THESSALONIANS 4:16–17)

That is the great event that is coming, when Jesus will step out of eternity and back into time—and we will step out of time and into eternity. At that moment, the perishable will clothe itself with the imperishable and the mortal with immortality. Death will be conquered by the victorious Lord Jesus:

> When the perishable has been clothed with the imperishable, and the mortal with immortality, then the saying that is written will come true: "Death has been swallowed up in victory."
>
> "Where, O death, is your victory?
> Where, O death, is your sting?" (1 CORINTHIANS 15:54–55)

When death is finally swallowed up in victory, the fear of death will be gone. As natural, perishable beings, we fear death. As spiritual, imperishable beings, we can know that we have nothing to fear from death.

The sting of death

Fyodor Dostoevsky is considered one of the greatest Russian writers. He was arrested in 1849 for plotting against Czar Nikolai I. He was sentenced to death, then blindfolded and taken out in freezing weather to be shot by a firing squad—and at the last moment, his sentence was commuted to exile at hard labor. After his release from prison in 1854, he abandoned his revolutionary ideals and became a Christian. Dostoevsky once observed, "The certainty of death fills us with dread. But the uncertainty of what follows death is the most dreadful anguish in the world." It is this uncertainty and fear of death that Paul has in mind when he writes about "the sting of death."

What is the sting of death? Paul explains:

> The sting of death is sin, and the power of sin is the law. (1 CORINTHIANS 15:56)

248

The sting of death is sin—the certainty of judgment, the realization that we owe a debt to God for the sins of a lifetime. Hebrews 2:15 tells us that Jesus came to "free those who all their lives were held in slavery by their fear of death." When He freed us from the curse of sin, He freed us from the sting of death.

The fear of death keeps us in bondage. It turns us into driven workaholics. It makes us feel that we must seize every opportunity, because life is so short. We dare not stop or rest but must be driven, driven, driven by the fear of death! This fear makes us anxious and obsessed with our health, with threats and dangers, with the aging process. It robs us of our joy and our sleep.

The fear of death haunts and oppresses us. Even during times of laughter and joy, the thought will sometimes pop up: "Someday, this will all be over. The laughter will end. I'll be stretched out in a casket. My whole life, which was once ahead of me, will be behind me." We fear death because it is an unknown. We can't control it, evade it, or avoid it. We put it off as long as we can, but it will surely overtake us in the end.

But there is good news! The resurrection of Jesus has broken the power of sin and death. We do not have to be driven by death, obsessed with death, or haunted by death. Sin's power has been broken and death has been swallowed up in victory.

Next, we come to the heart of the mystery Paul unveils in 1 Corinthians 15:

> But thanks be to God! He gives us the victory through our Lord Jesus Christ. (1 CORINTHIANS 15:57)

Notice that this triumphant statement is in the continuous present tense. Paul is not saying that God will give us the victory in the future or that He has given us the victory in the past. He is saying that God is continuously giving us the victory throughout all the todays of our life. Jesus Christ is dynamically, explosively alive in our lives, and we can draw upon His resurrection power from moment to moment.

Whenever I fail or falter, whenever I'm afraid, I go to Him for forgiveness, for strength, for courage, for a fresh taste of the resurrection life. Whenever I am tempted to sin, I'm reminded that sin is the sting of death, and Jesus gives me new resurrection power to say no to Satan's deadly trap. Death has lost its sting. Thanks be to God, Jesus has given me the victory! That is why Paul concludes:

Therefore, my dear brothers, stand firm. Let nothing move you. Always give yourselves fully to the work of the Lord, because you know that your labor in the Lord is not in vain. (1 CORINTHIANS 15:58)

We can stand firm and immovable upon the fact of the resurrection of Jesus Christ, and the certain hope of our coming resurrection. We will all be changed. Whether we are dead in Christ or alive in Him when He returns, we will be transformed in a flash, in the twinkling of an eye, at the last trumpet. On that day, as Paul says in Romans 8:19, the great suspense of history will be ended and the sons of God—you and I and all believers—will be radiantly revealed.

Thanks be to God, who gives us the victory through our Lord Jesus Christ!

21

GIVING, LIVING, AND LOVING ONE ANOTHER

1 Corinthians 16

One Sunday morning, a church took up an offering for overseas missionaries. The ushers started at the front of the sanctuary and worked their way down the aisles. One of the ushers noticed a man sitting on the center aisle near the back of the church. The man had surliest scowl he had ever seen on a churchgoer. The man sat with his arms folded and his chin jutted out, and he glared at the usher with undisguised hostility.

That fellow obviously doesn't want to be here, the usher thought. *The woman next to him is probably his wife—perhaps she forced him to come.*

Reaching the place where the frowning man sat, the usher held out the collection plate. The man in the pew refused to even take the plate to pass it along.

The usher leaned close to the man and whispered, "Sir, this is a collection for the missionaries."

The man in the pew snorted, "Missionaries! I don't believe in giving money to missionaries!"

"In that case," the usher replied, "feel free to take some money out. It's all going to benefit the heathen anyway."

We come now to 1 Corinthians 16, where Paul writes about taking up collections in the church. He makes an abrupt transition at this point. In chapter 15, he has been writing about the grand and lofty themes of the resurrection. Now, while the echo of the last trumpet still reverberates in our ears, Paul suddenly shifts gears and writes, "Now about the collection for God's people . . ."

Our English Bibles contain chapter divisions at this point, but in the original Greek, there was no division. Paul simply switched subjects—from resurrection bodies to the collection plate. I think the fact that Paul makes such an abrupt transition shows that the issue of finances should not be separated from the other great issues of the Christian faith.

The practicalities

This would be a good place to remember once again the overall structure of 1 Corinthians. Here is an overview of the entire letter:

Part I: Introduction (1 Corinthians 1:1–9)
Paul lays out the overarching theme of the letter: We are called into fellowship with God's Son, Jesus the Lord.

Part II: Problems in the Church (1 Corinthians 1:10–11:34)
Paul deals with issues of carnal living, immorality, divisions, marriage, divorce, singleness, gender roles, authority, Communion, and so forth.

Part III: The Holy Spirit (1 Corinthians 12–15)
Paul turns from issues of carnality to issues of spirituality and deals in-depth with the role of the Holy Spirit in the life of the church and the believer.

Part IV: Final Requests (1 Corinthians 16)
Paul closes with some practical requests, such as taking up the collection for people in need, and so forth.

As you see, part 3, consisting of chapters 12 through 15, dealt with what I call the spiritualities—issues involving the activity of the Holy Spirit in our lives. Now we come to part 4, the final division of the letter, consisting of chapter 16. I call this section the practicalities because it deals with practical issues of Christian giving, Christian living, and Christians loving one another as God intends.

We start with the issue of Christian generosity. Money is a major issue, not only in 1 Corinthians but throughout the New Testament. In the gospels of Matthew, Mark, and Luke, fully one out of every six verses deals with money. Jesus told twenty-nine parables in the Gospels, and sixteen of them have to do with people and their money.

This closing chapter grows out of the last verse of chapter 15, where Paul writes:

> Therefore, my dear brothers, stand firm. Let nothing move you. Always give yourselves fully to the work of the Lord, because you know that your labor in the Lord is not in vain. (1 CORINTHIANS 15:58)

I like the vivid wording of the King James Version even better:

Therefore, my beloved brethren, be ye stedfast, unmoveable, always abounding in the work of the Lord, forasmuch as ye know that your labor is not in vain in the Lord. (1 CORINTHIANS 15:58)

Note that phrase: "always abounding in the work of the Lord." I love the image suggested by those words—an image of a Christian who is constantly, abundantly, energetically engaged in the Lord's work. Throughout chapter 16, Paul writes about what it means to always abound in the work of the Lord. He begins with the matter of giving:

Now about the collection for God's people: Do what I told the Galatian churches to do. On the first day of every week, each one of you should set aside a sum of money in keeping with his income, saving it up, so that when I come no collections will have to be made. Then, when I arrive, I will give letters of introduction to the men you approve and send them with your gift to Jerusalem. If it seems advisable for me to go also, they will accompany me. (1 CORINTHIANS 16:1–4)

Paul speaks here of the collection being taken up in churches to help the afflicted church in Jerusalem. This need is close to Paul's heart, and he mentions it in several of his letters. He is eager to see the Gentile churches take part in the needs of persecuted saints in Jerusalem.

As you read the book of Acts, you see two reasons why the church in Jerusalem was experiencing troubles. The first reason was a circumstance beyond the control of the Jerusalem Christians: a series of famines caused by drought.

The second reason was a failure on the part of the Jerusalem Christians. They were suffering in part because they had failed to obey the Lord's command. Just before His ascension, Jesus said to the Christians in Jerusalem, "You will be my witnesses in Jerusalem, and in all Judea and Samaria, and to the ends of the earth" (Acts 1:8). As you read through Acts, you see that the Jerusalem Christians largely ignored those words.

There was great fellowship in Jerusalem. They had the teaching and miracles of the apostles and the manifestation of the gifts. Tremendous numbers of people were being converted. Nobody wanted to leave!

So the Lord, in His wisdom, sent a time of persecution. Acts tells us that the persecution began on the day that the deacon Stephen, the first Christian martyr, was stoned to death: "On that day a great persecution broke out against the church at Jerusalem, and all except the apostles were scattered throughout Judea and Samaria" (Acts 8:1b). Isn't it interesting that they were scattered to the very places Jesus had said they were to go next—to Judea and Samaria!

During the famine and persecution, the Jerusalem church was reduced to poverty. So it became the privilege of the Gentile churches, which had been blessed by the Jerusalem church in earlier times, to minister to the needs of the believers in Jerusalem. This is a beautiful picture of the oneness of the church throughout the world. When one congregation is in need, the entire church responds in love and generosity.

Seven principles for wise giving

There are seven principles about giving in the first four verses of chapter 16.

First, *all Christians are expected to give*. Paul writes, "Now about the collection for God's people: Do what I told the Galatian churches to do." Paul was not imposing some special obligation on the Corinthians. Everywhere he went, wherever he had planted a church, he taught Christians to give. Sharing is not an option; it's essential. Jesus said, "Freely you have received, freely give" (Matthew 10:8b). If you have not received anything from the Lord, then do not give anything. But if you have been blessed by Him, then give accordingly.

What should you give? Pocket change? Ten percent? Fifty percent? Ninety percent? That's a question only you can answer. But here's something to think about: God judges our generosity not by what we give but by what we hold back. Mother Teresa once said, "If you give what you do not need, it isn't giving." And C. S. Lewis put it this way: "I am afraid the only safe rule is to give *more* than we can spare." The apostles taught the early Christians to give even when they had hardly anything, because giving is the essence of Christianity.

Second, *giving is to take place on a weekly basis*. Paul writes, "On the first day of every week, each one of you should set aside a sum of money." This is one of the first indications in the New Testament epistles that Christians gathered regularly for worship and fellowship on Sunday, the first day of the week. The Jewish day of worship is the Sabbath, which starts Friday evening and continues into Saturday. But the Christians worshiped on Sunday, the first day of the week—the day of the resurrection. Paul says that giving should be a regular part of their weekly worship of the risen Lord.

Third, *giving is a personal act*. Paul writes, "Each one of you." He doesn't leave anyone out. Even children should learn to give of their pennies and dimes. The amount is not important; the habit of giving is what matters. You have freely received, so freely give.

Fourth, *giving should be set aside regularly*. Paul writes, "Each one of you should set aside a sum of money." In the first-century culture, people got paid for a day's work at the end of each day. So Paul said that they were to go home, put a portion of the day's wages in a cookie jar, then bring it to church on Sunday. By setting that money aside as soon as it was earned, the money was sure to be available for the collection on Sunday.

Fifth, *giving should be proportionate*. Paul writes that a Christian should give "in keeping with his income." This means that you should give according to the way God has given to you. Has he poured out abundant blessing? Then give abundantly. Are you just barely eking out an existence? Then your gift may be reduced proportionately.

When Jesus saw a poor widow donate two copper coins worth a fraction of a penny—all she had in the world—He told His disciples, "I tell you the truth, this poor widow has put more into the treasury than all the others" (see Mark 12:41–44). Like this widow, you ought to give something even if you are poor—but remember that God is not interested in the dollar amount. He's interested in the motive of your heart.

You may ask, "But didn't God decree that we should give a tithe?" The word *tithe* means 10 percent. In the Old Testament, the Israelites were told to give a tithe, and the percentage was the same whether you were rich or poor. A poor man's tithe might be difficult to give; a rich man's tithe might never be missed.

Many Christians have the mistaken notion that God expects 10 percent, so we can spend the other 90 percent on ourselves. That's not what the New Testament teaches. In fact, the Old Testament requirement of tithing isn't taught anywhere in the New Testament. What is the New Testament's teaching on giving? We should give more than the Old Testament tithe. If God has richly blessed you, then give 20, 30, 50 percent. In fact, I have known Christians who have given away 90 percent of their income while living on the 10 percent.

God does not set a legalistic standard of giving. Instead, He gives us a principle: Let your giving be proportionate to the blessing you have received. Freely you have received; freely give.

Sixth, *giving should be motivated by the giver's own faithfulness—not manipulation or emotional blackmail.* Paul writes, "so that when I come no collections will have to be made." Why would Paul say that? I believe it's because Paul knew that he had a forceful personality, and when he spoke, he had a tremendous impact on people. He wanted the Corinthian believers to give freely and generously, not because of emotional appeals or manipulation.

I think it's tragic and shameful that there is a so much manipulation in Christendom today. Churches employ professional fundraisers; religious broadcasters use slick psychological gimmicks to induce people to open their checkbooks. But Paul didn't want people to be psyched up to give. He wanted giving to flow freely from a heart that was moved by the grace of God. The purpose of giving, after all, is not to raise money for buildings and programs; the purpose is to focus the believer's heart on God's priorities. And God's first priority is that His people be filled with love, compassion, and gratitude for the blessings they have received from Him.

Seventh, *the receiving of gifts should be done responsibly by people who are trustworthy, accountable, and dependable.* Paul writes, "Then, when I arrive, I will give letters of introduction to the men you approve and send them with your gift to Jerusalem. If it seems advisable for me to go also, they will accompany me." Paul wants the people in Corinth to know that the gifts they collect will be in good hands. He will not handle the money. He is making sure no one can accuse him of enriching himself with these contributions. But he is willing to accompany those to whom the funds are entrusted, serving as a guarantor that these funds will be handled responsibly.

When we give, we should always know to whom we are giving our money. We shouldn't just write a check to the organization that makes the most heart-wrenching appeal. Instead, we should invest our giving in ministries that have shown they can be trusted to put God's resources to effective use.

Some years ago, I visited communist Poland. A Polish pastor told me that in several Eastern European countries there were huge warehouses filled with Russian-language Bibles. The Bibles had been bought with contributions from American Christians. The Christians were told that the Bibles would be sent into Russia and placed in the hands of persecuted Russian believers. Unfortunately, there was no way to get the Bible across the border into Russia—so they sat in warehouses.

This pastor told me, "The American organization gave me a shipment of Russian Bibles and told me I should try to get them into Russia. They didn't explain how I should do it. They just shipped cartons of Bibles to me, and that was that. I'm embarrassed to admit it, but I didn't know what else to do, so I buried the Bibles in my back yard."

When I returned to the States, I saw that this organization continued to appeal for funds to send Bibles to Russia. Most missionary organizations are responsible in the handling of the Lord's money. But we should be careful when we give. We have a responsibility to see that the money we give to the Lord's work is invested wisely for the kingdom, not squandered.

How to live your life

From the issue of giving, Paul turns to the issue of living. In the next few verses, he offers us keen insights into how a Christian should schedule his life. He writes:

> After I go through Macedonia, I will come to you—for I will be going through Macedonia. Perhaps I will stay with you awhile, or even spend the winter, so that you can help me on my journey, wherever I go. I do not want to see you now and make only a passing visit; I hope to spend some time with you, if the Lord permits. But I will stay on at Ephesus until Pentecost, because a great door for effective work has opened to me, and there are many who oppose me. (1 CORINTHIANS 16:5–9)

How gloriously indefinite Paul is! How unlike our overscheduled pastors, missionaries, and lay Christians Paul was! While I was pastor at Peninsula Bible Church, hardly a month went by that I wasn't asked, "What are your ten-year plans for the church?" My reply: "I have no idea. Our only plan is this: We are committed to consistently, year after year, carrying out the principles that God has taught us from the Word. We plan to keep doing that until the Lord returns."

I think that was the apostle Paul's program for the future. He didn't know where he was going or when he would get there. Yes, he had a strong desire to go to Rome, but he'd been planning to do that for years. His plans kept changing! So Paul remained flexible. From his example I have derived a number of principles for Christian living.

First, *set immediate, achievable, short-range goals.* Paul writes, "After I go through Macedonia, I will come to you." The time frame Paul had in mind here was probably less than a year. The apostle James suggests that we should not try to plan more than a year ahead (see James 4:13–15). It's all right to have dreams of the future—but limit your thinking to achievable, short-range projections. Accomplish today's work today, and be flexible about tomorrow, because God may have plans that you can't even imagine right now. Always leave room in your life for God's surprises.

Second, *make flexible commitments*. Don't make commitments you can't keep—or can't get out of. Paul writes, "Perhaps I will stay with you awhile, or even spend the winter. . . . I hope to spend some time with you, if the Lord permits." Paul didn't box himself in. It wasn't that Paul merely wanted to keep his options open. Rather, he wanted to be open to every new thing God might do in his life. All of his plans were subject to that little phrase, "if the Lord permits." Paul was always ready to set aside his own plans in order to answer the Master's call.

Third, *rely on God to make provision for you as you go along*. Paul writes, "so that you can help me on my journey, wherever I go." Paul didn't have an American Express card for his travel expenses. He relied on God, working through God's people, to provide for him along the way. And so should we.

Fourth, *live by faith, but don't be reckless; allow for problems, obstacles, and the storms of life*. Paul wrote, "But I will stay on at Ephesus until Pentecost." Why is Pentecost significant to Paul's travel plans? Historians tell us that Pentecost, which comes fifty days after the Passover, was the time when shipping resumed on the Aegean Sea. During the winter months, the frail boats of that time could not survive the great storms of the Mediterranean region.

Paul was planning to travel from Ephesus in western Asia Minor to Corinth, 250 miles across the Aegean Sea—but he prudently took the weather and other circumstances into account while making his plans. Paul set a good example for you and me. We should live by faith—but we should not take foolish chances and expect God to protect us from the consequences of our foolishness.

Fifth and finally, *always be alert to the opportunities for ministry that God brings your way*. Paul writes, "A great door for effective work has opened to me." Paul chose to stay in Ephesus because there is a great opportunity for ministry there. Acts 19 tells us about that "great door for effective work" in Ephesus.

After Paul was driven out of the Ephesian synagogue by his opponents, he rented a hall where he could preach. For five hours a day, six days a week, he taught the Word of God there. People came from all over the region to hear Paul's message, and the gospel exploded throughout the

Roman province of Asia. Churches were planted in cities throughout the Lychus Valley, in places like Colossae, Laodicea, Sardis, and Pergamum. So Paul chose to stay in Ephesus for a while so that he could take advantage of this amazing opportunity for the gospel.

Along with this significant opportunity, however, there were significant problems. Paul writes, "And there are many who oppose me." Who were Paul's opponents? Again, we find the answer in Acts 19.

Ephesus was the second greatest city in the Roman world. At the heart of the Ephesian culture was the Temple of Diana, a pagan temple where idols were worshiped in sexually degraded ways. The Christian church opposed the sexual practices in the city, yet the temple was the hub of city life. It was the banking center for the merchants and the gathering place for the culture.

Ephesus was also a center of Jewish worship. There were synagogues in the city, and the Jewish religious leaders were bitterly opposed to Paul's message.

Against these adversaries stood the fledgling Christian church. Despite its small size, the church spoke to the culture with power and authority. The little Ephesian church was having such a profound effect that it was affecting the economic system. The silversmiths of Ephesus were in an uproar because they made their living making pagan idols—and Paul and the other Christians were turning people away from idol worship. Paul and the gospel were bad for business!

So Paul had a wide-open door for ministry—yet he also had many adversaries. Here's a good thing to remember: Beware the wide door of opportunity where there are no adversaries. That could be the trick of the devil to lift you up in pride and make you overconfident. But where there is an open door and many adversaries, seize the opportunity and live the adventure! This may be one of the most exciting opportunities of your life.

The care and feeding of fellow workers

Next, Paul takes up the issue of caring for those who serve as fulltime ministers of the gospel. Paul begins by talking about Timothy:

> If Timothy comes, see to it that he has nothing to fear while he is with you, for he is carrying on the work of the Lord, just as I am. No one, then, should refuse to accept him. Send him on his way in peace so that he may return to me. I am expecting him along with the brothers. (1 CORINTHIANS 16:10–11)

Perhaps no other companion of Paul's is as well-known to us as Timothy. Two New Testament letters were written to him. He was a young man, perhaps as young as his late teens, when he first came to be mentored by Paul in ministry. They met in Timothy's home city of Lystra. On that occasion, Paul was stoned and left to die on the city rubbish heap, but God graciously intervened and restored him. This must have made a great impression on Timothy, who joined Paul and traveled with him.

Some commentators view Timothy as a timid young man because of Paul's exhortations to Timothy that he be more bold and aggressive. But I don't think he was timid; rather, I believe he had a temperament that was quiet, humble, and unassuming. Timothy was not comfortable forcing his way to the forefront. So Paul wrote to the Corinthians, "If Timothy comes, see to it that he has nothing to fear while he is with you." In other words, "Put him at ease. Make him feel welcome."

Why should they receive Timothy and make him feel welcome? Because, Paul said, "he is carrying on the work of the Lord, just as I am." In other words, Timothy's work was valuable, as Paul's was—so they should value Timothy and his ministry. He may seem young and quiet, but he's an effective minister of the gospel.

Paul says, "No one, then, should refuse to accept him." Why should anyone refuse to accept Timothy? Because he was young. Paul was concerned that people would judge Timothy by his youthful appearance, thinking him inexperienced and not worth listening to. Paul wanted the Corinthians to know that young Timothy was wise beyond his years and mature in the faith.

Then Paul says, "Send him on his way in peace so that he may return to me. I am expecting him along with the brothers." This doesn't mean that they were to pat him on the back and say, "Get going! Paul's waiting for you!" No, "send him on his way" means that they were to support Timothy financially and give him the funds and support he needed for the return trip. This is a biblical principle: If someone ministers to you spiritually, then you should support him materially.

Next, Paul tells the Corinthians how they should treat another of Paul's partners in ministry, Apollos:

> Now about our brother Apollos: I strongly urged him to go to you with the brothers. He was quite unwilling to go now, but he will go when he has the opportunity. (1 CORINTHIANS 16:12)

Some people are under the impression that the apostles were Christian generals who ordered the early Christians around. This verse shows that this is not the case. Paul clearly does not have authority over Apollos. He urged Apollos to go to Corinth, but Apollos chose not to go at that time.

Jesus told His disciples, "You know that those who are regarded as rulers of the Gentiles lord it over them, and their high officials exercise authority over them. Not so with you" (see Mark 10:42–43). And Paul once wrote, "Not that we lord it over your faith, but we work with you for your joy, because it is by faith you stand firm" (2 Corinthians 1:24). Though he had the authority of an apostle, Paul refused to lord it over anyone.

The problem of church bosses is one of the great curses of the church today. Sometimes church bosses are pastors; they believe the office of pastor gives them the right to order people around; the church board is nothing but a rubber stamp for the pastor's ambitions. In other churches, the bosses are unofficial power brokers—laypeople who are looked up to and admired by some and feared and loathed by others. They use their wealth or their seniority or the force of their personalities to lord it over the brothers and get their way in the church.

Paul was an apostle—but he was not a boss. He respected the personal freedom of Apollos to follow his own sense of God's leading. Paul urged Apollos strongly—but in the end, he allowed Apollos to make his own choice. Paul accepted the fact that Apollos was committed to the Lord and led by the Lord, just as he himself was. The apostle respected the principle stated by Jesus: "You have only one Master and you are all brothers" (see Matthew 23:8).

Why did Paul want Apollos to go to Corinth? We don't know for sure, but it may be that Paul wanted Apollos to go there to help heal the divisions in the Corinthian church. You may recall that at the beginning of this letter, Paul wrote:

> My brothers, some from Chloe's household have informed me that there are quarrels among you. What I mean is this: One of you says, "I follow Paul"; another, "I follow Apollos"; another, "I follow Cephas [that is, Peter]"; still another, "I follow Christ." (1 CORINTHIANS 1:11–12)

Perhaps Paul thought that Apollos could go and teach the Corinthians regarding the need to love and value one another and stop forming personality cults within the church. And perhaps Apollos didn't want to go to

Corinth for that very reason—he may have feared that by going to Corinth at that time, he would have only aggravated the Corinthians' tendency to form factions around certain personalities. So, though Paul urged him to go, Apollos chose not to go. Here we see one reason why Paul's personal note at the end of this letter provides a fascinating glimpse into the life of the New Testament church.

Do everything in love

Next, Paul tells the Corinthians how they should live in times of temptation and persecution:

> Be on your guard; stand firm in the faith; be men of courage; be strong. Do everything in love. (1 CORINTHIANS 16:13–14)

Paul says, "Be on your guard." In other words, be watchful and wary. Be alert to people and forces that would subvert the ministry of the church.

A number of years ago, there was a man who traveled from church to church, sharing his testimony, a story of having practiced witchcraft and Satanism. He claimed to have been a member of a secret fraternity, the Illuminati, who were plotting world domination. His story, though fantastic, was detailed and convincing. Many pastors believed him and supported him—even when he began accusing some of the world's most respected Christian leaders of being involved in a global Satanist conspiracy.

Eventually, some Christian publications, including *Christianity Today*, investigated this man's claims and found that his story was riddled with lies and inconsistencies. He was later imprisoned after being convicted of serious sex offenses. But for a long time, this man was believed and supported by many pastors and churches. They fell for his lies because they weren't on their guard.

Paul says, "Stand firm in the faith." There are many philosophies that sound reasonable and useful—Eastern religion, transcendental meditation, spiritual psychotherapy (*A Course in Miracles*), *The Urantia Book*, Unitarianism, Scientology—but these philosophies contradict biblical Christian faith. People often get hooked into false belief systems by trying to mix these beliefs with Christianity—but these false systems invariably pull the unwary away from the truth and away from a relationship with God. So Paul rightly warns, "Stand firm in the faith."

Next, Paul links courage with strength: "Be men of courage; be strong." In Scripture, courage and strength never derive from self-confidence. Our courage and strength come from our utter weakness and reliance upon the power of God. As Paul put it in his letter to the Ephesians, "Finally, be strong in the Lord and in his mighty power. Put on the full armor of God so that you can take your stand against the devil's schemes" (Ephesians 6:10–11).

Finally, Paul says, "Do everything in love." Earlier, the apostle beautifully defined love for us: "Love is patient, love is kind. It does not envy, it does not boast, it is not proud. It is not rude, it is not self-seeking, it is not easily angered, it keeps no record of wrongs. Love does not delight in evil but rejoices with the truth. It always protects, always trusts, always hopes, always perseveres. Love never fails" (1 Corinthians 13:4–8a). That's how believers are to behave toward one another in the church.

"Do everything in love." If we Christians would truly follow Paul's simple dictum to the Corinthians, we would transform lives and churches—and the wasteland of secularism that surrounds us would become a new Eden of Christian love and grace.

"In my own hand . . ."

Next, Paul writes of another group of Christian servants:

> You know that the household of Stephanas were the first converts in Achaia, and they have devoted themselves to the service of the saints. I urge you, brothers, to submit to such as these and to everyone who joins in the work, and labors at it. I was glad when Stephanas, Fortunatus and Achaicus arrived, because they have supplied what was lacking from you. For they refreshed my spirit and yours also. Such men deserve recognition. (1 CORINTHIANS 16:15–18)

Stephanas, Fortunatus and Achaicus were the ones who brought a letter to Paul in Ephesus—the letter that Paul replies to throughout much of 1 Corinthians. These three men reported to Paul on conditions of the church in Corinth and, Paul adds, they encouraged him and refreshed his spirit.

Paul remembers the faith of Stephanas and implies that we should always hold up such people as inspiring examples. Stephanas and his family, Paul says, were the first converts in Greece. That means he was probably a citizen of Athens, for that is where Paul first began to preach in Greece. Stephanas may have been converted by that remarkable message, preached in the courtyard of the Areopagus (Mars Hill), as recorded in Acts 17.

Because he was the first Greek convert, he held a special place in Paul's heart.

Paul reminds the Corinthians that Stephanas and his household have devoted themselves to the service of the saints. The original Greek word translated "devoted" conveys the idea of addiction. Paul was saying that Stephanas was a servanthood addict. Stephanas couldn't help himself—he was addicted to serving other people. Hooked on hospitality—what a wonderful addiction to have!

Notice that Paul tells the Corinthians to "submit" to Stephanas and other servanthood addicts like him. Does he mean that the Corinthians should obey Stephanas and be subservient to him? No. He is saying, "Listen to Stephanas. This humble servant has insights and wisdom you need to hear."

Paul goes on to say that he was glad when Stephanas, Fortunatus and Achaicus arrived, because "they refreshed my spirit and yours also. Such men deserve recognition." People like that make your day. When you are down, they pick you up. When you are weary, they energize your spirit. Praise God for people like these three servants of the Lord! Paul says, in effect, "Recognize them and thank them for their ministry among you! Affirm them! Let them know how God has used them in your life."

Next, Paul adds greetings from the Christians in Ephesus and the surrounding region. He writes:

> The churches in the province of Asia send you greetings. Aquila and Priscilla greet you warmly in the Lord, and so does the church that meets at their house. All the brothers here send you greetings. Greet one another with a holy kiss. (1 CORINTHIANS 16:19–20)

Paul mentions two kinds of churches here. First, there is the great Ephesian church, which is a network of churches planted by Paul in the Roman province of Asia. This church grew out of Paul's preaching ministry from a rented hall in Ephesus. Second, there is the little house church in the home of Aquila and Priscilla.

The apostle Paul mentions this remarkable couple in several of his letters. According to Acts 18:2–3, Aquila and Priscilla were tentmakers. Paul first met them in Corinth; they had originally come from Rome. Later, in the letter to the Romans, it's clear they have returned to Rome, where they again have a church meeting in their house. At the time this letter was written, they were living in Ephesus.

Paul says that the brothers in Ephesus send their greetings. Their way of greeting each other was with a holy kiss. We have gotten away from the holy kiss in our culture. We shake hands or, at most, give each other a hug. (Perhaps, in time, the holy kiss may make a comeback.)

Paul then closes with his personal greeting:

> I, Paul, write this greeting in my own hand. If anyone does not love the Lord—a curse be on him. Come, O Lord! The grace of the Lord Jesus be with you. My love to all of you in Christ Jesus. Amen. (1 CORINTHIANS 16:21–24)

This is Paul's way of authenticating his letters. Paul dictated his letters, but he had a habit of taking the pen from the secretary and adding a final greeting in his own handwriting. Many Bible scholars believe Paul was almost blind, so he wrote with large letters, scrawled across the bottom of the page.

After this greeting, Paul adds an odd parting thought: "If anyone does not love the Lord—a curse be on him." The phrase "a curse be on him" is a single word in the original Greek: *anathema*. It literally means, "Let him be damned." Paul was not cursing the lost; he was giving a warning to Christians.

When Paul speaks of those who do not "love the Lord," he does not use the Greek word *agape* ("love"). He uses the Greek word *phileo* ("affection, friendship"). If someone has no affection for the Lord Jesus, then what does he have affection for?

Paul is saying that anyone who claims to be a Christian but has no fondness for Christ and all He represents is a self-deceived fraud. He is already on his way to being damned. After all, Christianity is not just a philosophy or a set of doctrines. Christianity is a Person with whom we have a relationship. If you do not develop a *phileo* affection for this Person, then you have missed the core reality of Christianity.

Next, in a kind of a play on words, Paul follows the word *anathema* with a similar word from another language—the Aramaic word *maranatha*. This Aramaic word is translated as three English words: "Come, O Lord!" With Hebrew and Aramaic words, it's difficult to tell what tense is intended, so the word *maranatha* could mean "Our Lord has come!" or "Our Lord shall come!" or "Our Lord is coming at all times!"

I believe that a better translation might be, "Our Lord is at hand. He is present." That seems to be Paul's thought in this passage: "Jesus is not far away. He is at hand. If you don't know Him, you can settle your relationship with Him here and now, because He is available to you at this moment."

Paul closes with these words: "The grace of the Lord Jesus be with you. My love to all of you in Christ Jesus. Amen." This great letter has ended. But its truth endures to bless our hearts, enlighten our minds, stir our emotions, move our wills, and transform our lives. Such is the power of God's Word.

PART II

Standing for Truth in a World of Lies

2 CORINTHIANS

22

WHY DOES IT HURT SO MUCH?

2 Corinthians 1:1–2:4

In *Christian Discipline*, Oswald Chambers wrote, "Suffering is the heritage of the bad, of the penitent, and of the Son of God. Each one ends in the cross. The bad thief is crucified, the penitent thief is crucified, and the Son of God is crucified. By these signs we know the widespread heritage of suffering."

These are profound words! Suffering is a heritage in which we all share—and in which Jesus has shared. As we come to 2 Corinthians, Paul turns to the problem of suffering—and the opportunities that our sufferings bring into our lives. "For just as the sufferings of Christ flow over into our lives," he writes, "so also through Christ our comfort overflows."

Paul's unknown letter

The letter we call 2 Corinthians is probably the least known of all his letters. It has sometimes been called "Paul's unknown letter," because it tends to be neglected by Bible teachers and preachers. This is unfortunate, because it is the most personal and autobiographical of all of Paul's epistles.

These two letters, 1 and 2 Corinthians, are very different from each other. In 1 Corinthians, we gained a fascinating and revealing picture of the church at Corinth—a church that is much like the church in the United States today. Now, in 2 Corinthians, we get a revealing look at Paul as he opens up his life to the Corinthian believers.

We call this letter 2 Corinthians, but in reality it is 4 Corinthians. Paul wrote four letters to the church in Corinth, but only two of those letters have been preserved for us. The first and third letters were lost, and the second (1 Corinthians) and fourth (2 Corinthians) are included in the New Testament canon.

In terms of structure and theme, this letter could be divided into four parts. Here is a thumbnail sketch of 2 Corinthians:

Part I: Introduction and Salutation (2 Corinthians 1:1–11)
Paul briefly greets the Corinthians and describes hardships that he
and his companions encountered in the province of Asia.

Part II: Paul's Conciliatory Defense (2 Corinthians 1:12–9:15)
Paul's gentle and conciliatory defense of his ministry (addressed to
the majority in the church): the apostle is a minister of the new covenant; the gospel is a treasure contained in jars of clay; the ministry of
reconciliation; "hilarious" giving.

Part III: Paul's Combative Defense (2 Corinthians 10:1–13:10)
Paul's confrontational and sarcastic defense of his ministry against
the accusations of the false apostles (whom he ironically calls "the
super-apostles"); Paul's visit to heaven and his thorn in the flesh; the
marks of a true apostle; final warnings.

Part IV: Concluding Greetings (2 Corinthians 13:11–14)
Paul urges the church to practice love and peace toward one another
and to greet each other with a holy kiss.

It may be helpful to take another look at the history of Paul's relationship with the Corinthian church. He founded the church in Corinth
somewhere around 52 or 53. He stayed there for about a year and a half,
then went to Ephesus. Except for a brief trip to Jerusalem, he remained in
Ephesus for a lengthy period of time, preaching and teaching and making
converts. In Ephesus, he wrote 1 Corinthians.

We know about the first lost letter from 1 Corinthians 5:9: "I have
written you in my letter." Paul had written that first letter to warn the
Corinthians against following a worldly lifestyle. In response to that letter,
the Corinthians wrote back to him with many questions. In reply to that
letter, Paul wrote a second letter that we now call 1 Corinthians. In that
letter, Paul answered their questions and instructed them in how to walk
in power and resolve problems in the church.

The Corinthian church apparently reacted badly to that letter, because
in 2 Corinthians we learn that Paul made a quick journey to Corinth. We
know little of what Paul did and said there or how long he stayed. We
do know that it was probably an unpleasant experience for Paul and the
Corinthians, because Paul later wrote in 2 Corinthians 2:1, "I made up my
mind that I would not make another painful visit to you." Paul probably

went to Corinth with a sharp and severe rebuke, and the Corinthians may not have received it well—but we can only speculate.

After Paul returned to Ephesus, he sent another letter to Corinth. It was carried there by Titus, who was gone a long time. This was Paul's third letter to Corinth; like the first, the third letter is no longer known to exist.

Transportation and communication being slow in those days, Paul grew anxious to hear what was happening in Corinth. He became so troubled that he left Ephesus and went to Troas and then up into Macedonia to meet Titus. In the region of Macedonia, probably in the city of Philippi, Paul and Titus met. Titus brought Paul an encouraging report about the Corinthian church, and Paul responded by writing a fourth letter, which we now call 2 Corinthians.

So let's open this letter and discover what Paul has to say to the Corinthian believers—and what God has to say to you and me.

Suffering and comfort

Paul opens with a brief greeting:

> Paul, an apostle of Christ Jesus by the will of God, and Timothy our brother, To the church of God in Corinth, together with all the saints throughout Achaia: Grace and peace to you from God our Father and the Lord Jesus Christ. (2 CORINTHIANS 1:1–2)

Paul begins by emphasizing his apostleship. His authority does not come from any religious institution or governing body. It comes from the Lord Himself. The teachings of Paul were taught to him by Jesus. Paul's message comes with the full authority of the Lord Jesus.

Paul addresses this letter to "the church of God in Corinth, together with all the saints throughout Achaia." Achaia was the ancient name for Greece. All of the Greek mainland, the southern peninsula known as the Peloponnesus, and the Greek isles were part of Achaia. So this letter was addressed to all the churches in Greece.

As Paul does in all of his letters, he wishes them grace and peace. This is no empty salutation. "Grace" is a word that sums up all that God is ready to do for us and give to us. All of His supply comes to us by grace.

Next, Paul plunges into the opening theme of this letter—why Christians suffer:

> Praise be to the God and Father of our Lord Jesus Christ, the Father of compassion and the God of all comfort, who comforts us in all our

troubles, so that we can comfort those in any trouble with the comfort we ourselves have received from God. For just as the sufferings of Christ flow over into our lives, so also through Christ our comfort overflows. If we are distressed, it is for your comfort and salvation; if we are comforted, it is for your comfort, which produces in you patient endurance of the same sufferings we suffer. And our hope for you is firm, because we know that just as you share in our sufferings, so also you share in our comfort. (2 CORINTHIANS 1:3–7)

Two words, "sufferings" and "comfort," stand out. From a Christian perspective, these two words always go together. Suffering can take the form of pain, loss, pressure, stress, or trouble. It is any experience that ties our stomachs in knots and makes us feel anxious, angry, sad, or depressed. It is any experience that hurts. Christians in the first century faced tremendous suffering for living out their faith in a hostile and godless culture. Paul experienced great suffering—and great comfort from God.

What does Paul mean by comfort? He is not merely talking about a little cheeriness or friendly encouragement. The word Paul uses for "comfort" means "strengthening." When Paul suffered, he experienced the strengthening of God so that he could stand up under the pressure. The word Paul uses for "comfort" or "strengthening" is a form of the word used for the Holy Spirit when the Bible calls Him the Comforter. It would be equally accurate to call the Holy Spirit the Strengthener.

Many Christians, when they face suffering, pray to have their sufferings removed. They pray for an escape. Paul wants us to know that God has not promised us an escape from our sufferings. Rather, He promises strength and comfort for our sufferings.

A Christian lady once said to me, "I know we are supposed to suffer as Christians, but why does it hurt so much?" Paul offers four reasons why our sufferings are so painful.

First, *suffering hurts so much because that is how we learn what God can do.* How can we learn about the strengthening of God if we never undergo pain or stress? When we suffer, we discover God's resources for our trials. So don't run from suffering. Instead, look for God's comfort and strength in it.

Paul writes, "For just as the sufferings of Christ flow over into our lives, so also through Christ our comfort overflows." The strengthening we receive is equal to the pressure we experience. Our loving God is in control of our lives, and He limits our sufferings (as He promised) so that they will not be more than we are able to bear. Yet He deliberately allows suffering in our lives so that we might discover the inner strengthening that keeps our hearts at peace even under pain and pressure.

There is a phrase that appears numerous times in the King James Version of the New Testament: "And it came to pass." Someone once said that his favorite phrase in Scripture was, "And it came to pass." Why? Because it did not come to stay. It came to pass. The sufferings we experience come to pass, not to stay. When your sufferings pass, you will find yourself strengthened and encouraged.

"It is for your comfort"

Second, *suffering hurts so much because God wants to use our pain to bring healing and maturity to others.* God permits suffering in our lives for our sake and for the sake of other people. Paul tells us that God "comforts us in all our troubles, so that we can comfort those in any trouble with the comfort we ourselves have received from God." The more mature we grow as Christians, the more clearly we see this principle.

People are watching to see how we respond to life's pain and pressures. When we give way to complaining and cursing, we set a poor example of faith. We convey to those who are watching that the promises of Scripture can't be trusted.

Paul, however, is determined to use his own sufferings to minister to others. "If we are distressed," he writes, "it is for your comfort and salvation; if we are comforted, it is for your comfort, which produces in you patient endurance of the same sufferings we suffer." Moreover, because Paul has found comfort and strength in his sufferings, he is confident that the readers of this letter will also find comfort and strength. "And our hope for you is firm," he writes, "because we know that just as you share in our sufferings, so also you share in our comfort."

I often wish I could spare other people from trials and sufferings. I wish I could shield my children from hurt. I wish I could spare close friends from trials of loss, illness, financial setbacks, and other forms of suffering. But not only is it impossible for me to do so but in many cases I would be harming them if I could. God's people need to experience suffering so that they can experience His strengthening and comfort—and so that God can use their sufferings to instruct and comfort others.

That's the perspective Charles Colson has regarding his suffering and humiliation during the Watergate scandal. Colson was the chief counsel for President Richard Nixon from 1969 to 1973 and was one of seven White House officials convicted of Watergate-related crimes. Colson was accused of helping to organize a burglary of a psychiatrist's office in an attempt to discredit Daniel Ellsberg, an anti-war activist. Colson maintains that he was innocent, but in 1974 he pleaded no contest to an obstruction of justice charge in order to avoid years of costly litigation. He served seven months in the Maxwell Correctional Facility in Alabama.

For a long time, Colson struggled to understand why God put him through that experience. Then the answer came to him: He went to prison to learn what prisoners go through. There he saw the forgotten men and women of our society, and he learned of the injustice many endured in prison. Before going to prison, he never thought about what life was like for prisoners. Afterwards, it was all he could think about.

In 1979, Charles Colson found Prison Fellowship International, which is now an international ministry with branches in more than a hundred countries. Prison Fellowship supports prison chaplains, works for improved conditions in prisons, assists prisoners with medical needs, fosters victim-offender reconciliation programs, helps ex-prisoners re-enter society, and reaches out to the children of offenders through its Angel Tree Program. Colson has devoted his entire post-prison life to the needs of men and women in prison—and it never would have happened if he hadn't been imprisoned himself.

God often takes us through trials and sufferings—not only for our own sake but also for the sake of others. True Christian maturity means accepting our sufferings, rejoicing in them, and offering them back to God for the blessing of others.

Self-confidence versus God-confidence

Paul gives us another reason why we undergo affliction in the next few verses:

> We do not want you to be uninformed, brothers, about the hardships we suffered in the province of Asia. We were under great pressure, far beyond our ability to endure, so that we despaired even of life. Indeed, in our hearts we felt the sentence of death. But this happened that we might not rely on ourselves but on God, who raises the dead. He has

delivered us from such a deadly peril, and he will deliver us. On him we have set our hope that he will continue to deliver us, as you help us by your prayers. Then many will give thanks on our behalf for the gracious favor granted us in answer to the prayers of many. (2 CORINTHIANS 1:8–11)

We do not know what kind of hardships Paul went through. They may have involved illness or persecution or betrayal. Those hardships probably involved the great riot that broke out against Paul and the Christian community in Ephesus, as described in Acts 19. For a time, it appeared the whole Christian cause had collapsed in Ephesus and all of Paul's labors had come to nothing. He must have suffered great emotional stress and many physical threats.

Paul tells us, "We were under great pressure, far beyond our ability to endure, so that we despaired even of life. Indeed, in our hearts we felt the sentence of death." That is the lowest ebb a human soul can sink to. He saw no way out of his suffering and had given up hope. But, Paul concludes, "This happened that we might not rely on ourselves but on God, who raises the dead." And this brings us to our next principle.

Third, *suffering hurts so much because God wants to teach us to rely on Him, not on ourselves.* Remember that the apostle Paul was once Saul of Tarsus, a brilliant and strong-willed Pharisee, a self-reliant young man who thought he could accomplish anything by the power of his personality. Again and again God had to break Paul's self-confidence and replace it with God-confidence. The Lord had to allow Paul to despair of life itself so that he could rely on the One who brings life out of death.

Fourth and finally, *suffering hurts so much because we need to learn to rely on each other and pray for one another.* Paul writes, "On him we have set our hope that he will continue to deliver us, as you help us by your prayers. Then many will give thanks on our behalf for the gracious favor granted us in answer to the prayers of many." God sends suffering into our lives to show us that we are not isolated individuals. We are members of a body, and we need each other. When you have a difficulty or trial, share it with others so that they can pray with you. Many prayers bring great deliverance.

When we suffer, we rebel and demand that God take us out of our problems—right this instant! In our spiritual immaturity and selfishness, we feel entitled to a trouble-free life. But God knows us better than we know ourselves. He knows the experiences we need in order to become more like

Jesus. That's why Paul can say to us, even in times of suffering, "Grace and peace to you from God our Father and the Lord Jesus Christ."

When you are misjudged and misunderstood

Next, Paul turns to a painful subject. A misunderstanding has arisen between the Corinthians and Paul. In the next few verses, we see that Paul feels misjudged, and he wants to straighten out the matter:

> Now this is our boast: Our conscience testifies that we have conducted ourselves in the world, and especially in our relations with you, in the holiness and sincerity that are from God. We have done so not according to worldly wisdom but according to God's grace. For we do not write you anything you cannot read or understand. And I hope that, as you have understood us in part, you will come to understand fully that you can boast of us just as we will boast of you in the day of the Lord Jesus. (2 CORINTHIANS 1:12–14)

Paul has not yet mentioned the problem that caused the misunderstanding, though it will soon become apparent. Instead, he starts by stating that his conscience in the matter is clear. He wants the Corinthians to know that he is not merely being defensive and self-justifying but that he stands innocent before God.

When you feel that someone has misjudged you, the first thing you should ask yourself is, "Have I done something wrong? Is my conscience clear—or does my conscience convict me? What does God think about my actions?" If you feel the Spirit of God and your conscience convicting you, then confess that you have been wrong. When accused of wrongdoing, always begin with self-examination, not self-defense.

Clearly, Paul has examined himself. He has done something or said something, and the Corinthians feel offended because of it. So Paul has examined his conscience and concluded that he has done nothing wrong. "Our conscience testifies," he says, "that we have conducted ourselves in the world, and especially in our relations with you, in the holiness and sincerity that are from God."

He also adds, "For we do not write you anything you cannot read or understand." In other words, he is going to try to clear up the misunderstanding, and he hopes the Corinthians will grasp his explanation fully. He wants to have absolute clarity and truth in the relationship between himself and the Corinthians.

He says, "And I hope that, as you have understood us in part, you will come to understand fully that you can boast of us just as we will boast of you in the day of the Lord Jesus." The Corinthians have been righteously and rightfully proud of the fact that their church was planted in Corinth by the great apostle—and Paul is proud of the Corinthians, because he labored long and hard to establish them in the faith. He wants to restore the pride that he and the Corinthians had in each other.

Throughout Scripture we are taught that, as Christians, we are to settle disputes quickly and be reconciled with one another. For example, this is what Jesus taught in the Sermon on the Mount:

> "Therefore, if you are offering your gift at the altar and there remember that your brother has something against you, leave your gift there in front of the altar. First go and be reconciled to your brother; then come and offer your gift." (MATTHEW 5:23–24)

When we neglect our relationships in the body of Christ, we pave the way for division and the destruction of God's work in the church.

Plan A and Plan B

Next, Paul describes the cause of the misunderstanding:

> Because I was confident of this, I planned to visit you first so that you might benefit twice. I planned to visit you on my way to Macedonia and to come back to you from Macedonia, and then to have you send me on my way to Judea. When I planned this, did I do it lightly? Or do I make my plans in a worldly manner so that in the same breath I say, "Yes, yes" and "No, no"? (2 CORINTHIANS 1:15–17)

The problem was that Paul had previously written to the Corinthians about his travel plans, which we could call Plan A. He had intended to leave Ephesus, cross the Aegean Sea, and arrive at Corinth for a visit. From there he planned to travel through northern Greece to Macedonia, to the cities of Thessalonica and Philippi, where he had planted churches. Then he would return again to Corinth so that the Corinthians "might benefit twice" from his presence. From there, he planned to take a ship back to Israel so that he could take gifts from the churches to help the suffering saints in Jerusalem.

But Paul wasn't able to carry out Plan A. Instead, he had to resort to Plan B, as he explained in 1 Corinthians 16:5–9:

After I go through Macedonia, I will come to you—for I will be going through Macedonia. Perhaps I will stay with you awhile, or even spend the winter, so that you can help me on my journey, wherever I go. I do not want to see you now and make only a passing visit; I hope to spend some time with you, if the Lord permits. But I will stay on at Ephesus until Pentecost, because a great door for effective work has opened to me, and there are many who oppose me. (1 CORINTHIANS 16:5–9)

Plan B required Paul to go directly from Ephesus to Macedonia and work his way down the coast to Corinth. Then, after only one visit there, he wanted the Corinthians to help him make his return to Israel with the gifts for Jerusalem. It might seem like a ridiculous thing for the Corinthians to be upset about. After all, Paul could hardly have sent the Corinthians an e-mail.

Yet the Corinthians were offended by Paul's change of plans—so offended that they made strong, angry accusations against him. Titus probably brought word to Paul that some of the Corinthians now accused him of being untrustworthy or dishonest. We know there were factions in Corinth and at least one group in the church opposed Paul. These opponents were apparently quick to seize on Paul's change of plans and say, "You see? Paul can't be trusted!"

God's promises are "Yes"

Paul now explains the true situation: He writes:

But as surely as God is faithful, our message to you is not "Yes" and "No." For the Son of God, Jesus Christ, who was preached among you by me and Silas and Timothy, was not "Yes" and "No," but in him it has always been "Yes." For no matter how many promises God has made, they are "Yes" in Christ. And so through him the "Amen" is spoken by us to the glory of God. Now it is God who makes both us and you stand firm in Christ. He anointed us, set his seal of ownership on us, and put his Spirit in our hearts as a deposit, guaranteeing what is to come. (2 CORINTHIANS 1:18–22)

Notice he does not say yes or no. Is there anything wrong with saying no? No! It's a perfectly good word, and it comes in handy when you need to avoid situations that are harmful or sinful: "No, I won't do that!"

Paul means that if you promise something (yes), you should keep that promise if at all possible. Jesus made a similar statement in the Sermon on the Mount: "Simply let your 'Yes' be 'Yes,' and your 'No,' 'No'; anything beyond this comes from the evil one" (Matthew 5:37). As Christians, we must keep our word.

But Paul didn't give his word without intending to keep it. Circumstances forced him to change his plans—to cancel Plan A and follow Plan B instead. A change of plans is regrettable but not dishonest.

Paul starts by defending his actions in a specific situation involving his travel plans, then transitions to a great theological statement. He says that when he, Silas, and Timothy preached Christ, there was no uncertainty about their message—no "Yes and No," only "Yes." Why? Because Jesus is certainty itself. The Holy Spirit is in our hearts as God's own guarantee of certainty.

Paul's point is that human beings can't make absolute guarantees—but God can. God's plans are eternal, but man's plans are temporal and temporary at best. God sees all of history from Genesis to Revelation, but a man can't know when his next heartbeat might be his last. When God says "Yes," we can say "Amen" with confidence. Whatever God promises will surely come to pass.

Another important truth that emerges in this passage is that God's promises are "Yes" because they are always for blessing, never for cursing. Paul writes, "He anointed us, set his seal of ownership on us, and put his Spirit in our hearts as a deposit, guaranteeing what is to come." All of God's promises deal with blessing, healing, and salvation, never with hurting or condemnation. Jesus did not come to hurt us or condemn us but to revive us and save us. He said, "I have come that they may have life, and have it to the full" (John 10:10).

The prophet Isaiah says that God gives His children "a crown of beauty instead of ashes, the oil of gladness instead of mourning, and a garment of praise instead of a spirit of despair" (Isaiah 61:3b). God's promises are positive promises of blessing and restoration, not threats of desolation. His promises are "Yes."

The way to receive God's blessing, then, is to respond to His promise by believing Him. That's what Paul means when he says, "And so through him the 'Amen' is spoken by us to the glory of God." The Spirit of God brings God's promises home to us, makes them alive to us, and empowers us to obey them. As Paul writes, God "put his Spirit in our hearts as a deposit, guaranteeing what is to come." When we choose to obey, the Spirit of God gives us the power to carry out that choice.

Paul is not the boss

Having made this great theological point, Paul returns to the matter of the misunderstanding. He wants the Corinthians to know that there was a good reason for this change of plans: God's will. He writes:

> I call God as my witness that it was in order to spare you that I did not return to Corinth. Not that we lord it over your faith, but we work with you for your joy, because it is by faith you stand firm. (2 CORIN-THIANS 1:23–24)

Here Paul gives us one reason why his plans changed. He says, "It was in order to spare you that I did not return to Corinth." Spare them from what? He says he refrained from coming in order to preserve the Corinthians' freedom to act as they felt the Lord wanted them to act. He wanted to spare them from being intimidated and manipulated by the force of his personality.

This is an important principle. Paul challenges a misunderstanding that is widespread in churches today. Paul says, in effect, "I'm not your boss. If I had come to Corinth the way I had originally planned, after having already paid you a painful visit, my powerful personality and strong will, coupled with my authority as an apostle, would have put a lot of pressure on you to obey me—not out of conviction from God but out of intimidation by me. So I decided not to return in order to preserve your freedom and to make sure I didn't lord it over you. I'm your fellow worker, your partner, not your boss. I work with you for the sake of your joy."

One of the major problems in the church today is a misunderstanding of the nature of authority and leadership in the church. All too many Christians think that a church ought to have a boss, a CEO who calls the shots and gives the orders. They think that everyone needs to get permission from some boss before making a decision. There is no biblical support for such a view.

Christians should never have to obtain permission from the pastor or anyone else to exercise their spiritual gifts. Christians should never have to ask the pastor if it's okay to teach a home Bible study or minister to needs in the neighborhood. The pastor's job is to encourage, motivate, and liberate people to exercise their gifts—not hinder them. All governance comes from the Lord, who is the Head of the body.

280

So Paul says, "That's why I didn't come. I didn't want to preempt the Lord's authority over you. I didn't want to be your boss. You stand firm in your faith in the Lord—and I refuse to get in the way of that."

The heart of a surgeon

Paul's explanation continues on into chapter 2. He writes:

> So I made up my mind that I would not make another painful visit to you. For if I grieve you, who is left to make me glad but you whom I have grieved? I wrote as I did so that when I came I should not be distressed by those who ought to make me rejoice. I had confidence in all of you, that you would all share my joy. For I wrote you out of great distress and anguish of heart and with many tears, not to grieve you but to let you know the depth of my love for you. (2 CORINTHI-ANS 2:1–4)

Here Paul gives another reason for not coming back to Corinth a second time: The Spirit led him to see that he had already caused pain by his letters and his earlier visit. Like a surgeon, Paul had to inflict pain in order to promote healing. He had to speak painful truths in order for the Corinthians to grow in Christ. A good surgeon doesn't enjoy inflicting pain, but he cuts where he must in order to remove a cancerous tumor or an inflamed appendix.

Paul is saying, "I wrote you a sharp and candid letter. I know it was painful for you to read that letter. I didn't want to hurt you. In fact, when you are hurting, I feel great distress and anguish myself. But the pain I inflicted on you was for your healing, and it was motivated by love."

What is this painful letter Paul wrote to the Corinthians? Some Bible scholars think Paul speaks here of 1 Corinthians, Paul's second letter to that church. Others, myself included, think it was probably the third letter, which has been lost. In any case, Paul didn't want to hurt the Corinthians again. Here is a beautiful picture of Paul writing to his friends in Corinth with tears of love and deep anguish rolling down his face.

Paul opens 2 Corinthians on a note of pain—the pain of suffering, the pain of being misunderstood and misjudged. Why does the Christian life often hurt so much? Why must we suffer? Paul's reply: When suffering comes, remember that God has allowed it to enter your life for a purpose.

Times of trial bring four benefits into our lives: we have the opportunity to experience the strengthening power of God, we have opportunity to share our own comfort and strength with others, we learn to trade self-reliance for reliance on God, and we learn to lean on one another and pray for one another in the body of Christ.

And Paul teaches us by example how to respond when the pain of misunderstanding and misjudgment come our way. We see that even for the great apostle, it is painful to be criticized and misunderstood. When we feel misjudged, we are tempted to retaliate. But Paul has shown us a godly response to being misjudged: We examine ourselves to see if there is validity to the criticism. If there is, we apologize and right our wrongs. If not, we explain what happened as clearly and simply as we can. If anything painful must be said, we minimize the pain by affirming our love for the individual and our commitment to the relationship.

Life hurts, and relationships can be painful. Thank God for Paul, this godly surgeon of the soul, for pointing the way to healing and restoration amid the pain.

23

DISCIPLINE, FORGIVENESS, AND VICTORIOUS LIVING

2 Corinthians 2:5–17

Attorney Ken Sande is president of Peacemaker Ministries and author of *The Peacemaker: A Biblical Guide to Resolving Personal Conflict*. He tells the story of how God enriched the life of a church through a difficult experience of church discipline.

In a certain church there was a businessman who used his church affiliation to persuade elderly Christians to risk their savings in his questionable investment opportunities. These trusting churchgoers handed him thousands of dollars only to find out that their investments never paid off.

When the leaders of the church learned what this businessman was doing, they confronted him. He smoothly explained that the investors would all get their money back. In time, however, it became clear that he had fooled the church leaders just as he had fooled his clients. So the church leaders told the man he had to refund the money or be formally disciplined by the church. Several things happened as a result of the church's decision to discipline this man.

First, he returned the money to the investors.

Second, the businessman openly and sincerely repented of his dishonest business practices. He admitted that he had made a career of putting other people's money into high-risk ventures. At his own request, this man went before the congregation, confessed his sin, and received the forgiveness of the entire body of believers.

Third, on the day of this man's public confession, a woman stood up from the congregation after the businessman spoke. She went to the front of the church and told the entire church, "I need forgiveness more than this man does. For weeks, I've been complaining about him and attacking him in conversations I've had with many of you. You know the hatred I've expressed for this man. I have murdered him in my heart."

Then she turned to the businessman and said, "I want you to know that I forgive you. Will you please forgive me?"

Great healing came to the church on that day. Sande concludes, "That is a Sunday you want visitors present. They are seeing the gospel lived out in a powerful way. In this case the sinner was restored, the body was protected, and God was honored." Here in 2 Corinthians 2, we find Paul dealing with an issue that is as pressing today as it was twenty centuries ago: the issue of church discipline.

A three-step process

Paul writes:

> If anyone has caused grief, he has not so much grieved me as he has grieved all of you, to some extent—not to put it too severely. The punishment inflicted on him by the majority is sufficient for him. Now instead, you ought to forgive and comfort him, so that he will not be overwhelmed by excessive sorrow. I urge you, therefore, to reaffirm your love for him. (2 CORINTHIANS 2:5–8)

Here, Paul addresses a case of formal church discipline in Corinth. At first glance, you might assume that this case involved the man in 1 Corinthians 5 who was living in an incestuous relationship with his father's wife. If you think that this passage in 2 Corinthians 2 is a follow-up to the problem Paul addressed in 1 Corinthians 5, you are in good company. Many Bible scholars believe the offender in that case responded to the discipline of the church, repented, and was restored. They believe that here, in 2 Corinthians 2, Paul urges the church to forgive this man and care for him.

There are other Bible teachers, and I am among them, who believe that 2 Corinthians 2 deals with a separate and unrelated case of church discipline. The underlying causes of this second incident are different from the first. The offender in 2 Corinthians 2 appears to be guilty of rebellion against Paul's authority and stirring up dissension; there is no hint in this case of sexual immorality.

Paul writes in 2 Corinthians 2:5, "If anyone has caused grief, he has not so much grieved me as he has grieved all of you, to some extent." This suggests that the offender committed a hurtful act aimed specifically at the apostle Paul, perhaps involving slander against the apostle's reputation. Paul acknowledges that this man's actions grieved him directly, but he

284

graciously dismisses the harm to himself. Paul's words here do not fit the prior case involving incest.

Ultimately, it doesn't matter what the specific details of the case are. The only thing that matters is that we understand the principles God wants to teach us through these situations in Paul's letters. In the case before us, church discipline has been exercised, an offender has repented, and Paul urges the Corinthians to forgive and restore the repentant individual.

The process that we call church discipline was first instituted by the Lord Jesus when He said:

> "If your brother sins against you, go and show him his fault, just between the two of you. If he listens to you, you have won your brother over. But if he will not listen, take one or two others along, so that 'every matter may be established by the testimony of two or three witnesses.' If he refuses to listen to them, tell it to the church; and if he refuses to listen even to the church, treat him as you would a pagan or a tax collector." (MATTHEW 18:15–17)

The Lord Jesus outlined a practical, step-by-step process, and the believers in Corinth clearly followed this process. Those steps are:

Step 1: Privately confront the offender with his sin. If he listens and repents, there is no need for anyone else to know about the issue, and this will help to maintain peace in the congregation.

Step 2: If the offender doesn't repent, confront him again in the presence of one or two other witnesses, so that the facts of the situation can be objectively established. If the offender repents, then once again, there is no need for the issue to be publicized. Once again, the peace of the congregation is maintained.

Step 3: If the offender still does not repent, then the matter must be publicly disclosed to the church. The expectation here is that everybody in the congregation who knows the individual will plead with him to reconsider and repent, so that peace can be restored.

Step 4: If he still refuses to repent, then the church body must treat the offender as if he is not a Christian. The offender is self-deceived in calling himself a Christian, since he refuses to live by Christian principles.

The church in Corinth had evidently reached the third step after the offender had resisted correction in steps 1 and 2. Now the matter had been told to the church, and as Paul writes, the "punishment inflicted on him by the majority" has had its effect: The offender has repented.

Some people might ask, "Why is step 3 necessary? Why expose the offender's sin in public?" Paul explains why in verse 5: "He has grieved all of you, to some extent." Sin hurts the entire church. We like to think that our sins are private matters that hurt no one else. But the effects of sin always radiate out to others. As the poet John Donne reminds us, "No man is an island." When there is unhealed strife between two fellow believers, the poison spreads, infecting others. Schisms and factions form, leading to division. I have seen this tragic scenario play out many times.

Here in Corinth, the individual was publicly disciplined—and the disciplinary process was effective. The man has demonstrated the mark of true repentance, which is sorrow. So Paul urges the congregation to forgive the repentant man and welcome him back into the fellowship "so that he will not be overwhelmed by excessive sorrow."

It's important to understand that not everyone who says "I'm sorry" is expressing true sorrow over sin. Some people, when caught in a sin, say, "I'm sorry," but they clearly feel they have a right to be forgiven. Their attitude seems to be, "I *said* 'I'm sorry'! What more do you want? Get off my back!"

A person who is genuinely sorrowful over sin does not feel entitled to forgiveness—quite the opposite! Such a person usually says, "I don't deserve to be forgiven." That's the mark of genuine repentance. If a person does not express deep remorse and sorrow, then we should question whether there is genuine repentance.

This Corinthian man had expressed true sorrow for what he had done, so it was time for the disciplinary process to end. After all, the purpose of church discipline is to bring the offender to that point, so that he can experience recovery and healing. The moment he reaches that point, all sanctions and pressure must cease. It's time for grace to begin. So Paul writes, "I urge you, therefore, to reaffirm your love for him."

How to forgive

Next, Paul explains to us what a restorative process involves:

> The reason I wrote you was to see if you would stand the test and be obedient in everything. If you forgive anyone, I also forgive him. And what I have forgiven—if there was anything to forgive—I have forgiven in the sight of Christ for your sake, in order that Satan might not outwit us. For we are not unaware of his schemes. (2 CORINTHIANS 2:9–11)

There are three key ingredients of restoration in this paragraph. First, restoration begins with faithful confrontation. Paul says, "I wrote ... to see if you would stand the test and be obedient in everything." Obedient to whom? Not to Paul—to the Lord! Paul was not giving orders to the Corinthians. He was merely reminding them of what the Lord had said. Paul didn't see himself as a boss; he was a brother.

The Corinthians responded in obedience to the Lord. They followed the process Jesus set forth in Matthew 18. It was a painful, difficult process for them to follow, but they obeyed the Lord.

One reason there are so many problems in churches today is that so few churches obey the Lord's command regarding discipline. In our litigious and fractious society, obedience takes courage. When we have practiced biblical church discipline at Peninsula Bible Church, our elders and I have been threatened with lawsuits and even bodily harm. It takes courage to obey the Word of God—but that same Word promises,

The fruit of righteousness will be peace;
> the effect of righteousness will be quietness and confidence
> forever.   (ISAIAH 32:17)

If you act obediently and courageously, the ultimate result will be peace. Cowardice in the face of sin will only embolden offenders and destroy the ministry of the church.

It's amazing to see how freely Paul forgives the man who apparently defamed him: "If you forgive anyone, I also forgive him. And what I have forgiven—if there was anything to forgive—I have forgiven in the sight of Christ for your sake."

Paul doesn't take an "I'll forgive you but I can't forget" attitude. When we authentically say, "I forgive you," we are making a promise to the offender: "The offense is put aside forever. I will never mention it again—not to you and not to anyone else. From now on, I will relate to you as if this never happened. I also promise that whenever this incident comes to mind, I will instantly put it out of my thoughts."

Some people will say, "But I can't do that! The offender asked my forgiveness, but the hurt is just too deep." If that is your attitude, then you don't understand forgiveness. Your basis for forgiving others is the fact that God has forgiven you. If you cannot forgive, it's because you've forgotten that you were forgiven. As Paul told the Ephesians, "Be kind and compassionate to one another, forgiving each other, just as in Christ God forgave you" (Ephesians 4:32).

Paul then reminds us that we must forgive in order to prevent Satan from gaining an advantage over us. He writes, "And what I have forgiven—if there was anything to forgive—I have forgiven in the sight of Christ for your sake, in order that Satan might not outwit us. For we are not unaware of his schemes." Satan keeps reminding us of past wounds, making it difficult for us to forgive. He wants to gain a foothold in our lives, so that he can keep us in a state of resentment and bitterness.

Satan continually plots to destroy us. "But," Paul says, "we are not unaware of his schemes." When an arsonist is loose in the city, you can expect fires. Buildings will burn all over town. That is what Satan is like—a scheming arsonist who goes around setting fires of anger and bitterness. He seeks to burn down lives, relationships, families, and churches—burn them right to the ground. He wants to set off grudges and fights and divisions. He is scheming against us all the time.

How do we defeat Satan's schemes? By loving and forgiving one another. By healing broken relationships. By letting go of resentment and bitterness. That is how we keep Satan from gaining an advantage over us. That is how we repel his attacks.

No peace of mind

Next we come to a parenthesis in Paul's letter—a digression from the grand themes of suffering, discipline, and forgiveness that mark the opening paragraphs of 2 Corinthians. Here Paul recalls his journey to Macedonia:

> Now when I went to Troas to preach the gospel of Christ and found that the Lord had opened a door for me, I still had no peace of mind, because I did not find my brother Titus there. So I said good-by to them and went on to Macedonia. (2 CORINTHIANS 2:12–13)

Paul left Ephesus and proceeded to Troas in northwestern Asia (modern-day Turkey) next to the Aegean Sea (Troas is the region where the ruins of ancient Troy are located). His goal was to preach the gospel and plant new churches in Troas; nothing gave Paul more joy than preaching the good news of Jesus Christ.

While Paul journeyed to Troas, his friend and ministry partner, Titus, went to Corinth. The plan was for Titus to join Paul in Troas—but when Paul arrived in Troas, Titus failed to show up. Still, Paul found a great door of ministry open for him. The people responded to his message, and many were saved.

Even though Paul experienced great success in Troas, his heart was troubled. He was anxious for news from Corinth—and news of his missing friend, Titus. His spirit was so disturbed that he found he could not minister in Troas. He had to leave.

Why was Paul troubled about the situation in Corinth? He was worried about the divisions there, the lax attitude toward sin, and the other problems in the Corinthian church. He had founded the church and was worried that all of his labors might come to nothing. His anxiety was so great that he couldn't minister in Troas, despite the success he was having. He was worried sick about the Corinthians and his friend Titus. So Paul proceeded to Macedonia, hoping to locate Titus there.

Can you identify with Paul's anxious mood? I can. I remember times when I had to preach the Word of God while my heart was so distressed that I hardly knew what I was saying. You have probably had similar experiences yourself. So I think we can understand how Paul felt.

Later in this letter, Paul tells us he was joined by Titus at Philippi in Macedonia, and that Titus brought a favorable report from Corinth. In response to the good news from Corinth, Paul wrote the letter we know as 2 Corinthians.

The fragrance of the gospel

Paul's next words are astounding:

> But thanks be to God, who always leads us in triumphal procession in Christ and through us spreads everywhere the fragrance of the knowledge of him. (2 CORINTHIANS 2:14)

A personal note: This is my favorite verse in all of Scripture! It's a statement of immense gratitude to God for a powerful and effective ministry. Amazingly, this shout of triumph comes immediately after Paul has confessed his failure, anxiety, and despair. Why does Paul make this sudden reversal?

Humanly speaking, the apostle's circumstances were discouraging. But spiritually speaking, Paul knew that God was at work and even the difficult circumstances he encountered were brimming with ministry possibilities. So Paul could rejoice that God was leading him in a "triumphal procession."

Paul had in mind an image of the Roman victory parades. Whenever a Roman general returned from a successful military campaign, the Roman senate would grant him a triumph—the Roman equivalent of a ticker-tape parade. The general would pass through the streets of Rome in his chariot, preceded by pagan priests swinging censers of fragrant incense (which is why Paul writes of spreading the fragrance of the knowledge of Christ).Behind the conquering general would come the captives—prisoners of war bound in shackles and chains. The people would cheer their victorious army.

Now, this is a strange image, because Paul suggests here that Jesus Christ is the conquering general and he, Paul, is the prisoner in shackles and chains. Paul is saying that while he was in Macedonia, feeling depressed, anxious, and discouraged, he was like a prisoner in chains. But even though he was a prisoner of his loneliness and depression, the Lord was leading him around in a triumphal procession and using him to spread the fragrant knowledge of Christ wherever he went.

What an amazing juxtaposition! Paul was depressed and suffering, but God was glorified! Paul expands on this metaphor in the next verses:

> For we are to God the aroma of Christ among those who are being saved and those who are perishing. To the one we are the smell of death; to the other, the fragrance of life. And who is equal to such a task? (2 CORINTHIANS 2:15–16)

In the Roman triumph, the fragrance of incense was in the nostrils of all, the conquerors and the conquered, the victors and their victims. The prisoners were being marched to their enslavement or execution, so as they trudged along in chains, the fragrance of the incense was an odor of death. But to the general, his army, and the citizens of Rome, the incense was a sweet fragrance of life.

Paul applies this analogy to himself. He says that as he preaches this good news, the fact that Jesus lives and delivers people from sin and death is a fragrance of life for all who believe. God breathes in the sweetness of His Son in everything Paul does and says.

Moreover, Paul's message is a fragrance of Christ to those who receive it. But to those who responded to Paul's message with anger and opposition, the message of Christ meant death and judgment. Paul's opponents wanted nothing to do with the Savior—so they were lost in their sins. They not only resented the gospel story but also hated the messenger who brought it to their ears—the apostle Paul.

As Paul traveled the Roman Empire, preaching the message of Jesus, he often met indifference and even persecution. Paul frequently experienced frustration and depression. But even in his discouragement, Paul knew that he was being led in triumph by Jesus Christ. The fragrance of Christ was going out around the world. People were being set free. So Paul was able to shout, "Thanks be to God, who in Christ always leads us in triumph!"

The victorious Christian life

When Paul sees God's triumphs in his own defeats, he is properly describing the victorious Christian life. We often hear that phrase today, but I think it's rare that the victorious Christian life is described accurately and biblically. Some preachers proclaim a victorious Christian life in which God shields us from life's problems, guarantees our continual health, and showers us with wealth and blessing, so that we sing and rejoice all day long. This false teaching may fill the collection plate, but it sets the hearers up for disillusionment when they don't experience this victory in their own lives.

Some Christians view the victorious life as living in Disneyland. If you've ever visited the Pirates of the Caribbean attraction at Disneyland, then you surely recall the experience: You step aboard a boat that takes you through a dark tunnel. Soon you are surrounded by enemies. Pirates leap out of the darkness at you, brandishing swords and firing pistols right in your face. Cannons fire and cannonballs splash the water on either side of your boat. A city burns down before your eyes. It seems as though you are in mortal danger every moment of the ride—yet you sit there unafraid. You are amazed and amused, but you are never in fear of being captured, harmed, or killed. You feel safe because, after all, this is Disneyland.

Many people view the Christian life as a Disneyland attraction—full of thrills and exciting things to see. "But," they think, "I'm a Christian. God will protect me from any real dangers. He won't let anything hurt me." If that's your view of the victorious Christian life, I want you to know that it was certainly not Paul's view. He didn't know anything about such a life, because his life was filled with pressure, suffering, and testing.

Paul's letters cry out with pain and despair—yet they also shout with triumph! Paul never expected God to take him out of his sufferings, but he always knew that God would take him through his sufferings and bring ultimate victory out of despair.

Next, Paul summarizes his ministry in the final verse of chapter 2:

Unlike so many, we do not peddle the word of God for profit. On the contrary, in Christ we speak before God with sincerity, like men sent from God. (2 CORINTHIANS 2:17)

Paul says in effect, "Some act like sidewalk vendors. They take attractive little trinkets out of the Word of God and peddle them just to make a buck. I don't do that. Christ has called me, God has sent me, and I speak the truth of God with sincerity."

Then as now, there were religious racketeers. In the first century, they probably stood on street corners. In the twenty-first century, they have TV and radio shows and Internet Web sites. They find attractive little trinkets in the Word of God—tongues, healing, prophecy, miracles, the prosperity gospel—and they make a fortune. Paul says, "I don't sell God's Word for a profit. I speak the truth with total sincerity."

Paul describes three keys to understanding his ministry: First, his ministry is sincere. He practices what he preaches, and he believes it with all his heart. Second, his ministry is in Christ. He says, "in Christ we speak"—that is, he declares the gospel with the authority of Christ. Third, his ministry is purposeful. He says he speaks as one who is sent from God and commissioned by God. He has a goal to achieve, a mission to accomplish. His mission is to proclaim the gospel "so that we may present everyone perfect in Christ" (see Colossians 1:28).

And what a great responsibility Paul has! That's why he says, "And who is equal to such a task?" Jesus confronted His disciples with the question: "Can you drink the cup I am going to drink?" In their ignorance and arrogance, his disciples answered, "We can." Then Jesus said, "You will indeed drink from my cup" (see Matthew 20:22–23). By this He meant that there would be danger, opposition, and death—but they would see the power of God released through their trials and suffering.

The victorious Christian life is not a thrill ride at Disneyland, exciting but safe. No! The victorious Christian life often feels like defeat. But God is in the business of bringing triumph out of defeat, of bringing the fragrance of life out of tragedy and death.

That's the true victory of the victorious Christian life.

24

THE GLORY AND THE VEIL

2 Corinthians 3

Who was the apostle Paul? What qualified him as God's choice to write almost half of the entire New Testament canon?

Paul spent much of his ministry in prison. He had no permanent residence. He earned his living not as an author or speaker but as a tentmaker. He admitted having an unimpressive appearance. In short, Paul didn't fit the image of a dynamic Christian leader! No wonder some of the Corinthians questioned whether he was truly an apostle. In 2 Corinthians 3, Paul writes:

> Are we beginning to commend ourselves again? Or do we need, like some people, letters of recommendation to you or from you? You yourselves are our letter, written on our hearts, known and read by everybody. You show that you are a letter from Christ, the result of our ministry, written not with ink but with the Spirit of the living God, not on tablets of stone but on tablets of human hearts. (2 COR-INTHIANS 3:1–3)

It's amazing that anyone in Corinth would think that Paul needed a letter of recommendation when he returned. He had led them to Christ and founded their church—yet at least some of them felt that Paul should bring a letter of recommendation when he returned, perhaps from Peter or James or another apostle. So Paul replied, in effect, "*You* are my letter of recommendation! Christ has written the letter on your hearts!"

How did the Lord write the letter on their hearts? By transforming their lives, delivering them from sinful habits, healing their hurts, and removing their guilt. The Holy Spirit was the ink, writing a message of power and love upon their hearts.

Ministers of a new covenant

Next, Paul presents us with a powerful and life-changing truth:

> Such confidence as this is ours through Christ before God. Not that we are competent in ourselves to claim anything for ourselves, but our competence comes from God. He has made us competent as ministers of a new covenant—not of the letter but of the Spirit; for the letter kills, but the Spirit gives life. (2 CORINTHIANS 3:4–6)

I believe that, aside from the deity of Christ, this is the most important truth in all of Scripture: You and I are ministers of a new covenant. Under the old covenant, people were required to keep the rules and rituals of the Law. Under the new covenant, people are empowered to live by God's grace. As ministers of the new covenant, we do not have to be self-sufficient, because God is our sufficiency.

As you read through the writings of Paul, Peter, James, and John, you see that they never take credit for anything. These are men of great ability, yet they always say, as Paul writes in Galatians 2:20, "I no longer live, but Christ lives in me." They deny that their ability and power comes from their own humanity, and they give total credit to God. Paul and the other apostles are not merely being modest. They know for a fact that they do not have the power to cause the church to spread so rapidly in such a short span of time. It could only be the power of God working through them.

The old covenant involved human beings doing their best and working their hardest to please God. The new covenant is God doing His work through obedient human beings. What a difference that is! That's the great truth we need to learn.

Understand, Paul was not an incompetent nobody. He had marvelous spiritual gifts. He had a keen intellect and a powerful personality. He could trace his ancestry all the way to Abraham, so he had a tremendous religious and cultural heritage in the Jewish world. He had an impeccable record of religious orthodoxy, being, as he said in Philippians 3:5, "a Hebrew of Hebrews; in regard to the law, a Pharisee." His moral life was blameless.

But Paul had learned that his abilities, traits, talents, and achievements weren't worth a snap of the fingers before God. No human being can do God's work. Only God, working through people, can do the work of transforming lives and building new communities of faith. If human beings try to do God's work, relying on their own strength and wisdom, the work will be wasted. All around us we see the wreckage of ministries that tried to do God's work through human effort.

The old covenant says, "Here's the standard; do your best to live up to it." The new covenant says, "Say yes to God. Let Him work through you and leave the results to Him. You won't get credit for it. You're not supposed to. All credit is His alone."

When Paul tells the Corinthians that they are a letter from Christ, written upon human hearts, we hear echoes of the ancient prophecy of Jeremiah:

> "The time is coming," declares the LORD,
> "when I will make a new covenant
>> with the house of Israel
>> and with the house of Judah. . . .
> I will put my law in their minds
>> and write it on their hearts.
> I will be their God,
>> and they will be my people." (JEREMIAH 31:31, 33B)

God had long ago promised to write His laws on the hearts of the people instead of merely writing them on tablets of stone. Under the old covenant, God's law was an external demand. Under the new covenant, God's law becomes an internal desire.

The new covenant transforms the way we live our lives. Instead of living by the letter of the Law, we live by the Spirit. Paul writes, "For the letter kills, but the Spirit gives life." Have you ever noticed how the demand of a law destroys your motivation for obedience?

A young man once told me this story: One morning, he decided to do something to show his dad how much he loved him. He made up his mind that right after breakfast, he would go out and mow the lawn and wash the car without his dad having to tell him.

The young man went down to breakfast—and there was his dad. Before the young man could say a word, his dad said, "Son, I'm going out for a few hours. While I'm gone, I want you to mow the lawn and wash the car. Make sure you get it done—I'd better not come back and find the grass high and the car dirty."

"That changed the whole picture," the young man concluded. "Before, I was eager to do those chores to show my dad I appreciate him. But after he told me I had to do it, I lost all my motivation. I mowed the lawn and washed the car—but I hated every minute!"

The external law makes demands and kills motivation. The internal law, written by the Spirit upon our hearts, makes us eager to please God.

Glory that fades, glory that lasts

Next, Paul contrasts the old covenant versus the new:

> Now if the ministry that brought death, which was engraved in letters on stone, came with glory, so that the Israelites could not look steadily at the face of Moses because of its glory, fading though it was, will not the ministry of the Spirit be even more glorious? If the ministry that condemns men is glorious, how much more glorious is the ministry that brings righteousness! For what was glorious has no glory now in comparison with the surpassing glory. And if what was fading away came with glory, how much greater is the glory of that which lasts! (2 CORINTHIANS 3:7–11)

Paul says there is a kind of attractive glory about the old covenant, symbolized by the brightness of Moses' face when he came down from the mountaintop with the tables of the Law. God made his face shine.

But God also made it fade, because He wanted to teach the people an important truth: The glory God gave to Moses, the glory of the old covenant, was a fading glory. The glory of the new covenant, the ministry of the Spirit, would be an unfading glory. Paul calls the old covenant "the ministry that condemns men," because the law of the old covenant brings guilt upon us. The result of trying to meet God's standards by our own resources is condemnation.

But the new covenant is a much more glorious ministry, Paul says—"the ministry that brings righteousness." Righteousness means being fully accepted by God. It means that God has given us a standing of worth. We don't have to earn our sense of worth; God gives it to us by His grace. God tells us, "I love you. I forgive you. I have cleansed you. I have adopted you as my beloved child. Your life is significant."

Psychologists tell us that people need a sense of worth, approval, and significance in order to function. We need to know that we are accepted, loved, and cherished—and that is what the new covenant does for us. It gives us our sense of being accepted by God. We can't gain God's acceptance by earning it; we can only gain it by receiving it as a free gift of His grace.

Unfortunately, many Christians have the idea that God wants us to feel worthless and unacceptable. People have come to me after church and said, "That was a great sermon, pastor! I feel so guilty and worthless! God really used you to get to me today!"

That's the worst thing I've ever heard! I don't want my congregation to feel that way—and neither does God. Authentic preaching begins with God's love, not our own wretchedness. When we truly hear what God is saying to us, our hearts should be full of joy. We shouldn't feel worthless; we should realize the worth and significance we have as God's beloved people.

With unveiled faces

Next, Paul teaches us an important truth, using the symbol of a veil:

> Therefore, since we have such a hope, we are very bold. We are not like Moses, who would put a veil over his face to keep the Israelites from gazing at it while the radiance was fading away. (2 CORINTHIANS 3:12–13)

God loves to teach in visual symbols, and Paul here uses the veil of Moses as a symbol. The veil Moses wore is a symbol of the old covenant, the Old Testament law, with its demands and standard of behavior. When Moses came down from the mountaintop, his face was shining—a symbol of the attraction and glory of the law of God. We've all felt that attraction at times. We want to show God that we can please Him, that we are good people, that we can meet the Law's demands. We don't like to think that we are helpless and lost in our sin.

The glory of the Law, Paul says, is a fading glory. There is something more glorious, more lasting, and more attractive than the Law. It is the new covenant, which God has provided for us through Christ. The new covenant gives us a right relationship with God through Christ. We can't earn this relationship; it's a free gift. This gift gives us a new kind of hope.

Paul says, "Since we have such a hope, we are very bold." Boldness is the mark of somebody who has placed his trust in the new covenant. He becomes bold and confident. He becomes transparent and has nothing to hide. As Paul goes on to say, "We are not like Moses, who would put a veil over his face to keep the Israelites from gazing at it while the radiance was fading away."

Paul refers to the story found in Exodus 34. There, Moses brought the Ten Commandments down from the mountain, and his face shone like the sun. It was such a strange sight that people fled from Moses. He called them back and gave them the words of God—then he covered his face with a veil. Moses wouldn't remove the veil unless he went into God's presence to speak with Him.

Why did Moses veil his face? I doubt that he understood the symbolic significance of the veil that Paul brings to light in this passage. In fact, it's hard to know what the motive of Moses was. Some Bible commentators suggest that Moses felt that if the people saw that the radiant glory of Moses' face was fading, they would not pay attention to the Law. Others suggest that Moses was trying to preserve his own status as a special mediator between God and Israel.

One thing is clear: In veiling his face, Moses was not acting boldly or confidently. He acted out of fear and an attempt to hide something from the people. Next, Paul contrasts his own boldness and confidence with the fear and concealment of Moses:

> But their minds were made dull, for to this day the same veil remains when the old covenant is read. It has not been removed, because only in Christ is it taken away. Even to this day when Moses is read, a veil covers their hearts. But whenever anyone turns to the Lord, the veil is taken away. (2 CORINTHIANS 3:14–16)

Paul is saying that those who live under the Law have their minds dulled and darkened. Their minds are under a veil, just as the face of Moses was veiled. Those who are under the Law wear the veil of the old covenant to hide the fading glory of self-effort. They do not see that their efforts to live a righteous life are doomed to end in death and futility—but this is what will inevitably happen.

To this day, the goal of Judaism is to enable people to make their own atonement for sin. The Jewish view is that human beings possess the power to atone for their own sins; the Torah (the law of Moses) provides all the guidance people need to focus their hearts and minds on righteous living. That's the old covenant. That's the veil that covers the human mind, preventing those who are under the Law from seeing that the glory of the Law is fading.

Sometimes people come into the Christian faith thinking that if they try hard enough and work hard enough and abstain from evil, then they will live lives that are pleasing to God. They may have received the gift of salvation by faith—but they quickly begin trying to keep their salvation by keeping a set of rules.

These people have misunderstood grace—and by falling into the error of trying to work their way to God, they have become locked into failure, futility, and guilt. They have lists of do's and don'ts: no drinking, no smoking, no dancing, no movies, and so forth. But these are all external trappings—they are not the reality of faith. They are the veil, not the glory.

It is hard to get people to remove the veil of the old covenant so that they can discover the freedom of the new covenant. Why is it so hard to remove their veil? Because they do not turn to the Lord for grace. They insist on working their way to God. As Paul writes, "But whenever anyone turns to the Lord, the veil is taken away." You cannot take the veil off any other way. You can't prove your self-righteousness. You must turn to the Lord and accept His righteousness.

Paul offers us a solution, a way to remove the veil and pass from the darkness of the old covenant to the light of the new:

> Now the Lord is the Spirit, and where the Spirit of the Lord is, there is freedom. And we, who with unveiled faces all reflect the Lord's glory, are being transformed into his likeness with ever-increasing glory, which comes from the Lord, who is the Spirit. (2 CORINTHIANS 3:17–18)

Where the Spirit of the Lord is, there is freedom! Paul is not confusing the persons of the Trinity. He does not mean that the Holy Spirit and Jesus the Lord are one and the same. He is saying that they are so intimately identified in purpose and function that you can exchange one for the other. To walk in fellowship with Christ is the same thing as to walk in the fullness of the Spirit.

The Holy Spirit has come to reveal the Lord Jesus. The Spirit-led life is one in which Jesus Christ is visible to our eyes. So where the Spirit of the Lord is, there is freedom. What kind of freedom does Paul refer to here? It means the freedom of being bold and transparent, of having nothing to hide. You can take an unflinching look at even your worst sins, and you can know that you have God's acceptance and approval.

You do not deserve a life of significance, but you receive it anyway as a free gift of God. You can't earn it. Your best behavior can't buy it. It's yours for free because you have turned to God and the veil of the old covenant has been taken away.

When the veil is removed a wonderful thing happens. Paul writes, "And we, who with unveiled faces all reflect the Lord's glory, are being transformed into his likeness with ever-increasing glory, which comes from the Lord, who is the Spirit." As the veil of the old covenant is removed, we reflect the unfading glory of the Lord Jesus, the lasting glory of the new covenant. We find ourselves transformed into the shining likeness of the Lord Jesus. That, after all, is God's goal for your life and mine: Christlikeness.

As Paul wrote to the Romans, "For those God foreknew he also predestined to be conformed to the likeness of his Son, that he might be the firstborn among many brothers" (Romans 8:29). It is a process that will continue throughout our lives, Paul says, "with ever-increasing glory, which comes from the Lord."

What will we look like as we become more like Christ? Paul paints a word picture of a Christlike believer in his letter to the Galatians. A Christlike person is one who increasingly exhibits the fruit of the Spirit: "love, joy, peace, patience, kindness, goodness, faithfulness, gentleness and self-control" (see Galatians 6:22–23).

The first of these qualities, of course, is love—and love is the fulfillment of the Law. Love fulfills the demand of the Law of the old covenant that is written in tablets of stone. And love fulfills the desire of the new covenant that is written upon the tablets of the heart.

While we were under the old covenant, we tried to fulfill the Law by our self-effort—and we failed. Now, under the new covenant, we are growing more and more like Christ. We are learning to live out the love, grace, and forgiveness of God—and in the process, we fulfill the same Law that we could never fulfill under the old covenant. It's a growth process. It doesn't happen in one giant leap of transformation. It happens slowly, imperceptibly, as we learn not to rely on our own effort, but on the Spirit whom God has sent. As Paul says, our growth into Christlikeness "comes from the Lord, who is the Spirit."

It is God who does the work of making us like Jesus. He has the responsibility, and He has the power. Our only responsibility is to say, "Here I am, Lord. Take me, use me, and do with me as you will."

25

LIGHT FOR OUR DARKNESS

2 Corinthians 4

Some years ago, a member of our church introduced me to an aerospace engineer. This engineer had a brilliant mind and was openly agnostic. Though he thought it was possible that God might exist, he wanted nothing to do with Jesus or the Christian gospel. At the time I was introduced to him, he had been going through a lengthy depression. His emotional problems were so pronounced that he had lost his job. He would sit at home for hours, staring at the walls. His wife threatened to take the children and leave him.

This was his emotional state when he came to my office and told me his story. I asked him what he looked forward to in life. "Nothing," he said. "I have no hope." I asked him what he believed in. "Nothing," he said. "I don't believe that Jesus ever lived, so I certainly want nothing to do with those myths about the virgin birth or His deity or the resurrection." I talked with him at length and could find no ground of faith in him.

Finally, I said, "I'm sorry. There's nothing I can do to help you—but I don't want to abandon you. In fact, I believe there's help for you. If you'll come here every week, I'll meet with you and do two things: One, I'll read the Bible to you. Two, I'll pray for you."

To my amazement, he said, "Okay. I'll do that."

So he came to my office week after week. Each time, I read a portion of Scripture, then I asked him, "Does that mean anything to you?" Each time, he'd reply, "No. Not a thing." Then I would pray for him and for his family. By this time, his wife had left him, so he was living alone.

At least eight months went by. We met faithfully every week. One day I asked him, "Isn't there anything I have read that means anything to you?"

"Well," he said, "there's one thing. This morning I was thinking about the words of Jesus in the Garden of Gethsemane: 'Not my will but thine be done.' That meant something to me."

I didn't have the nerve to ask him how that related to his life, but I said, "If that meant something to you, pray that prayer over and over. Whenever you need help, whenever you need God to act in your life, say, 'Not my will but thine be done.'"

He agreed to do so.

A few more weeks went by, and we continued our routine. One day I read a passage, and he said, "Oh, yes. That's good, isn't it?" In all the months we'd been meeting together, that was only the second time he had seized on something in the Bible as meaningful to him. I encouraged him to memorize that text, and he said he would.

More weeks passed. Another passage spoke to him. More weeks, another passage. And another. And another. The light seemed to dawn on him more frequently and with greater intensity. The truth of the Scriptures became more and more real to him.

Finally, the day came when he acknowledged Jesus as Lord of his life and he surrendered his heart to Him. From that day forward, his faith blossomed. He devoured the Word of God, reading his Bible for hours on end. Though his wife never returned, he maintained his faith and had one of the most joyful testimonies I've ever witnessed.

Here was a man who spent years in darkness. Even after I came to know him, he went for months, hearing the Word of God week after week without the slightest glimmer of light. But he and I persisted together, and that glimmer grew to a gleam, and the gleam to a glow, and that glow to the shining glory of God reflected in the face of Jesus Christ. This man is living proof of the words we now come to in 2 Corinthians, "For God, who said, 'Let light shine out of darkness,' made his light shine in our hearts to give us the light of the knowledge of the glory of God in the face of Christ" (2 Corinthians 4:6).

No deception, no distortion

The passage begins with a tremendous declaration by the apostle Paul about the ministry he has received from God:

> Therefore, since through God's mercy we have this ministry, we do not lose heart. (2 CORINTHIANS 4:1)

Paul says "we do not lose heart" in doing ministry for God. I look around at the Christian world and see many people losing heart and becoming discouraged.

I think of one pastor who has been leading a church that is widely regarded as successful. Attendance is high, finances are strong, and the church seems to be doing a great evangelistic work in the community—yet this man told me that he gets up every morning with a sense of dread and goes to bed every night with a sense of failure. He tells me he feels he's accomplishing nothing of lasting value. In fact, his depression is so deep that, were it not for the impact on his family, he would have committed suicide.

The problem isn't confined to pastors. Every believer is a minister. As Christians we are called by God to minister to people in our home, our church, our neighborhoods, our offices, and wherever else we may be. Yet many Christian laypeople are becoming discouraged. They are losing heart in the ministry and are even on the verge of quitting the work they've been doing for God.

Paul wants us to know that the new covenant, which we looked at in 2 Corinthians 3, empowers us to press on even through obstacles and opposition. Think of all the many problems Paul encountered in his ministry—the stonings, beatings, riots, shipwrecks, imprisonment, betrayal, and on and on. Yet his word to us is, "We do not lose heart." Paul shares with us the secret of persevering amid heartbreaking circumstances:

> Rather, we have renounced secret and shameful ways; we do not use deception, nor do we distort the word of God. On the contrary, by setting forth the truth plainly we commend ourselves to every man's conscience in the sight of God. (2 CORINTHIANS 4:2)

He says he has nothing to do with secret, shameful, deceptive practices. As we look around at the Christian world today, we see many so-called ministries engaging in the shameful practices that Paul here condemns. Paul refuses to employ deception.

Today, deception is widespread in the church. There are evangelists who have people planted in the audience with instructions to stand up and confess Christ or give a testimony about being healed—just to make the evangelist look good. There are ministers who have obtained phony diplomas and degrees in order to appear more learned than they are. There are some who plagiarize their sermons, taking transcripts from the Internet and delivering another minister's work verbatim instead of opening the Word and discovering what God wishes to say to that congregation.

Paul says, "Anyone who relies on deception may appear successful for a while, but it doesn't last. Sooner or later, the bottom will drop out of that man's ministry and he'll be left with nothing but shame, failure, and depression."

The apostle Paul also refuses to tamper with the truth of the Scriptures. Can you imagine anybody in the name of Jesus tampering with God's Word? Yet it happens all the time. Peter speaks of "ignorant and unstable people" who distort the Scriptures "to their own destruction" (see 2 Peter 3:16).

People sometimes imply that the revelation of the Bible is inferior to the discoveries of modern knowledge—that science has proved the Bible to be untrustworthy. Such a claim constitutes tampering with the Word of God, because nothing in the Bible has ever been proved wrong by scientific discovery.

The most common way of twisting the Scriptures is proof texting. This is the practice of going to the Bible and taking isolated passages out of context and forcing them to support your preconceived idea. It's a way of reading into the Bible what you want it to say instead of reading out of it what it says. Every pseudo-Christian cult is based on this practice—and there are a number of widely respected Christian teachers and leaders who also twist the Scriptures in this way. They are distorting the Word of God for their own ends.

Paul does not engage in these practices. Instead, he says, "By setting forth the truth plainly we commend ourselves to every man's conscience in the sight of God." That is why Paul does not get discouraged. He doesn't have to constantly think up new gimmicks to get people to pay attention to his gospel. He knows that the truth is the most exciting and attractive message in the world.

Is it true?

The test of any belief system is not whether it makes people feel good or whether it is popular. The test is "Is it true?" A belief system that does not square up with reality is worth nothing. The message of the Bible is true. It reveals life as it is.

Paul goes on to say, "We commend ourselves to every man's conscience." His message speaks not only to the intellect but also to the conscience.

Truth is addressed to the mind. God, the divine Mind that created the human mind, is concerned with the human intellect and the evaluation of truth. But behind the intellect is a faculty called the conscience. Sometimes God is able to reach a man's conscience even when his mind has rejected the truth.

C. S. Lewis, the great English scholar and defender of the faith, was a committed atheist in his early years. He believed that life was meaningless and that logic precluded the existence of a supreme Being. Once, before leaving on a train trip, the unbelieving Lewis purchased a copy of *Phantastes*, a fantasy novel by George MacDonald. The novel had Christian themes woven throughout. Something about the tale seemed to leap off the pages and, as Lewis later put it, "baptized" his imagination. The reality of the gospel bypassed Lewis's resistant intellect and reached into his conscience.

Lewis was not instantly converted—but a process had begun in his life. He began reading other Christian authors, and their worldview began to make sense to him. By contrast, the atheist writers he had always agreed with began to sound "tinny" and hollow. He became friends with Christian scholars at Oxford—men like Neville Coghill, Hugo Dyson, and J. R. R. Tolkien. He had many talks with them about faith and reality.

While riding a bus at Oxford, Lewis had a strong feeling that Someone was knocking at the door of his life. He felt he had to open the door—or lock it tightly. As he wrote in his autobiography, *Surprised by Joy*, "In the Trinity term of 1929 I gave in, and admitted that God was God, and knelt and prayed; perhaps, that night, the most dejected and reluctant convert in all England." God reached past the unbelief of Lewis's formidable intellect and touched his conscience, leading him to faith.

"We commend ourselves to every man's conscience," Paul says. In other words, "I don't rely on mere intellectual truth. When I preach the good news of Jesus Christ, I rely on God's ability to convict the human heart."

The veil of delusion

You might wonder: If that's the case, then why don't more people respond with their conscience and believe? That's the question Paul deals with next:

> And even if our gospel is veiled, it is veiled to those who are perishing. The god of this age has blinded the minds of unbelievers, so that they cannot see the light of the gospel of the glory of Christ, who is the image of God. For we do not preach ourselves, but Jesus Christ as Lord, and ourselves as your servants for Jesus' sake. For God, who said, "Let light shine out of darkness," made his light shine in our hearts to give us the light of the knowledge of the glory of God in the face of Christ. (2 CORINTHIANS 4:3–6)

Why do people perish in their sins? Because they do not believe. And why do they not believe? Because they are blinded by Satan, the god of this age, the evil spiritual being who works behind the scenes of world events. The world unwittingly pays allegiance to the god of this age, and he has deceived the worldlings into believing that illusion is reality. As a result, they don't understand and believe the good news.

This is a revealing passage. Paul tells us that Satan's tool of deception is the veil. Satan is responsible for human unbelief, and men and women are witless victims in the clutches of this demon-god. What is the veil? It's the lie that tells us, "You don't need God. You don't need anyone. You can handle life all by yourself." This veil of delusion was put into words by William Henley in his poem "Invictus." He writes:

> It matters not how strait the gate,
> How charged with punishment the scroll,
> I am the master of my fate:
> I am the captain of my soul.

The tragedy of those words is compounded by the fact that Henley penned them in Edinburgh Hospital, during one of many periods in his life when he required treatment for crippling tuberculosis of the bone. The death of his five-year-old daughter devastated him, and he died at age fifty-four, broken in soul and spirit.

Satan has veiled the minds of the people of this planet in order to keep them from seeing the death and condemnation that awaits them at the end of the fading glory of this life. If Satan has veiled their minds, how can the truth of the gospel ever penetrate their hearts? People can't remove the veil themselves. How, then, can they be saved?

The answer: Only Christ can remove the veil. And Paul says, in effect, "That's where preaching comes in. I was sent to preach Christ, so that the veil of Satan can be removed from the eyes of the people." Paul writes, "For we do not preach ourselves, but Jesus Christ as Lord, and ourselves as your servants for Jesus' sake."

There are many people in ministry these days who preach themselves, not Christ. I once heard a radio preacher say, "If you have faith in my prayers, then put your hands on the radio while I pray." That man was preaching himself, not Christ. I have heard television preachers say, "If you have faith in my ministry, send me your donations." Those men are preaching themselves, not Christ. They preach a false gospel.

Paul says, "I don't preach myself. I preach Christ. I am your servant on behalf of Jesus. I am here to minister to you and labor among you, but I'm not your boss and I'm not here to take advantage of you." The apostle is careful to make that plain.

"We preach Jesus Christ as Lord," Paul says, in effect. This is a crucial declaration. Among first-century Christians, the fundamental declaration of the good news was "Jesus is Lord." In other words, Jesus is in control; He's in charge of human history. Moreover, He is the Master of my fate; He is the Captain of my soul.

People sometimes want to receive Jesus as Savior without receiving Him as Lord, but it cannot be done. The Word of God is clear: Jesus must be your Lord, or He cannot be your Savior. Romans 10:9 and 13 tell us, "If you confess with your mouth, 'Jesus is Lord,' and believe in your heart that God raised him from the dead, you will be saved.... Everyone who calls on the name of the Lord will be saved." The Bible never teaches us to receive Jesus as your Savior; it teaches us to "receive Jesus as Lord."

The fact is, Jesus is Lord whether we know it or not, whether we receive Him or not. So it only makes sense to bow to His lordship with a willing and thankful heart.

Let there be light!

Finally, Paul says, "For God, who said, 'Let light shine out of darkness,' made his light shine in our hearts to give us the light of the knowledge of the glory of God in the face of Christ." The moment a person acknowledges that Jesus is Lord, light shines into that person's darkness. The veil is removed.

Notice that Paul ties the conversion experience to the creation. He takes us back to a time when the whole world lay in darkness. No one could dispel the darkness but God. So God said, "Let there be light! Let the light shine out of darkness!" Instantly, light exploded in obedience to the creative word of God.

Paul says that this same creative act must take place whenever a man, woman, or child becomes a Christian. God has to say that same creative word, "Let there be light! Let light shine out of darkness!" When He speaks that word, the darkness disappears. Light shines into the darkened human heart, just as it shone all around Paul at his conversion encounter on the Damascus road. Paul is saying, in effect, "The light that created the universe also broke through the darkness of my deluded heart, and I saw that Jesus was Lord."

He goes on to say that the light God shines in our hearts illuminates "the knowledge of the glory of God in the face of Christ." Where do you find the light of the glory of God? In the face of Jesus Christ! And where do you find Jesus? In the Scriptures.

The Old Testament is filled with symbols, metaphors, and prophecies that foretell His coming in the flesh. The Gospels give us the record of His amazing life on earth. The epistles explain the implications of His life, death, and resurrection. Throughout the Old and New Testaments, we learn of the hope of His glorious return. The Bible is all about Jesus. It is radiant with light for the darkened human heart.

Are you walking in darkness? Then seek the face of Christ in the pages of Scripture. Seek His face through prayer. That is where the Light shines.

Jars of clay

Next, Paul employs one of his most memorable metaphors to describe our relationship to God:

> But we have this treasure in jars of clay to show that this all-surpassing power is from God and not from us. (2 CORINTHIANS 4:7)

A jar is made to contain something. This is a beautiful image of our humanity. Paul is telling us that we were made to contain God. Our Creator designed us to correspond to His deity, so that His power and His character might be poured into us like water poured into a jar.

Paul may have been thinking of the Old Testament story of Gideon, who was called by God to deliver Israel from the Midianite invaders. Gideon was one of the most obscure members of a remote tribe of Israel. He considered himself a nobody—yet God called him to be the deliverer of Israel. After Gideon initially gathered an army of thirty-two thousand men for the battle, God whittled the number down to a mere three hundred.

At God's command, Gideon's army took earthen jars—common pots of clay—and put candles in them. During the night, they encircled the Midianite camp. Then, at a trumpet signal, the Israelites broke the pots, causing the lights to spring up on every side. The Midianites awakened and thought they were ringed by a great army. They panicked and began to kill each other—and Israel was saved.

This story tells us that if we live on the basis of the new covenant, with Jesus as Lord of our lives, we can demoralize the enemies of our faith. Though they outnumber us, they will attack one another—and the victory will be ours.

Paul then writes:

> We are hard pressed on every side, but not crushed; perplexed, but not in despair; persecuted, but not abandoned; struck down, but not destroyed. (2 CORINTHIANS 4:8–9)

I like the way this verse is translated by Bible commentator William Barclay:

> We are sore pressed at every point, but not hemmed in; we are at our wit's end, but never at our hope's end; we are persecuted by men, but never abandoned by God; we are knocked down, but not knocked out. (2 CORINTHIANS 4:8–9, BARCLAY TRANSLATION)

Here, Paul draws a vivid contrast between the clay jar and the transcendent power of God that is poured into that jar. It is a quiet power—like the quiet light of a candle in an earthen jar—yet when that quiet power is released, it accomplishes amazing things.

Paul lists all the weaknesses of the clay jar of our humanity: "We are sore pressed . . . we are at our wit's end . . . we are persecuted by men . . . we are knocked down." But each time our human clay is broken and its weakness is displayed, the power of God is released: we are "not hemmed in . . . never at our hope's end . . . never abandoned by God . . . not knocked out." That is the way God expects us to live.

We must experience the weakness in order to release the strength. That's the part we don't like. We all want to see the power of God in our lives, but we don't want to be weak. We don't want to be pressed and pushed to our wit's end. We don't want to be persecuted and knocked down. We want God's power to be released amid peaceful, pleasant circumstances.

But that's not how God works. His message to us is that same word He gave to Paul in his sufferings: "My grace is sufficient for you, for my power is made perfect in weakness" (2 Corinthians 12:9). And Paul's response must be our response: "For Christ's sake, I delight in weaknesses, in insults, in hardships, in persecutions, in difficulties. For when I am weak, then I am strong" (2 Corinthians 12:10).

This is the attitude God expects. We are not even permitted to choose the form of martyrdom we receive. We can't go down the list and say, "Very well, Lord. I'll have one 'sore pressed' and two 'wit's ends' but I think I'll pass on being 'persecuted by men' and 'knocked down.'" No, we take what God sends. Whatever He wills, we must go through.

Paul wants us to know that we are not shielded from the hard realities and suffering of life. I wish we were, but we are not. There are teachers and preachers who spread a false and unrealistic notion that if you are walking with the Lord or if you pray with enough faith, then God will keep you from all harm. If you're right with God, these preachers say, you won't even get sick. These dangerous doctrines are contradicted at every point by Scripture.

Faithful, obedient Christians sometimes get cancer. They sometimes suffer bankruptcy. Godly believers sometimes go through divorce or see their children rebel against them. They have car crashes. Some are afflicted with Alzheimer's, Parkinson's, heart disease, ALS, or a stroke. No matter how loving, faithful, and obedient they are, Christians go through suffering. We are jars of human clay—but the power and light of God is released when these jars of human clay are broken.

We have to be crucified

Earlier in this letter, Paul described a time of utter despair in his life. "We were under great pressure," he wrote, "far beyond our ability to endure, so that we despaired even of life. Indeed, in our hearts we felt the sentence of death" (see 2 Corinthians 1:8–9). But even when all hope has died, God still used Paul's sufferings to manifest the resurrection life of Jesus Christ. Paul writes:

> We always carry around in our body the death of Jesus, so that the life of Jesus may also be revealed in our body. For we who are alive are always being given over to death for Jesus' sake, so that his life may be revealed in our mortal body. (2 CORINTHIANS 4:10–11)

The life of Jesus is always connected to the death of Jesus. We must experience His death in order to reveal His life. We all want the life of Jesus, but we don't want the suffering that His death entails. Yet the resurrection life can only be unleashed amid pressures and trials. That's when the character and life of Jesus are displayed.

The death of Jesus took place on a cross. The Roman cross is a symbol of weakness and powerlessness, shame and abandonment, pain and horror and death. The cross was a place of obscurity and darkness, where the Creator of the universe went to die. Jesus, who was God in human form, lost everything when He was nailed to the cross—and He trusted the Father to restore to Him all that He had lost, including His life, and to make His sufferings meaningful and significant.

Are you willing to carry in your body the death of Jesus? Are you willing to go to the place of obscurity and darkness? Are you willing to lose everything, trusting God to restore your life and to make your sufferings meaningful and significant? Are you willing to be nailed to whatever cross God sets before you? Once you are willing to be obedient to the death of the cross, God's life can be revealed through your mortal body.

This is where we struggle, isn't it? I struggle here, the same as you. We want the power of God, but we don't want the cross. We want the power, but we don't want the obscurity and suffering. We want the power—but we also want to get some credit, some glory. We want the life of Jesus, but we also want to satisfy our own flesh.

We have to be crucified. We have to die. We have to come to the end of our dependence on ourselves and rest upon the power of God at work in us, quietly changing us, inside and out, until we are like Jesus. If you are willing to be nailed to that cross, then you are ready to have the life of Jesus revealed in you. As Paul goes on to write:

> So then, death is at work in us, but life is at work in you. It is written:
> "I believed; therefore I have spoken." With that same spirit of faith we
> also believe and therefore speak, because we know that the one who
> raised the Lord Jesus from the dead will also raise us with Jesus and
> present us with you in his presence. All this is for your benefit, so that
> the grace that is reaching more and more people may cause thanksgiv-
> ing to overflow to the glory of God. (2 CORINTHIANS 4:12–15)

Paul quotes Psalm 116:10, where the psalmist declares by faith that his trials and pressures will be used to bless the lives of others: "I believed; therefore I said, 'I am greatly afflicted.'" The psalmist didn't know how God would use his affliction, but he believed God and he knew it would come to pass. In the same way, Paul says, "I believe with the same faith that was expressed by the psalmist. I believe that God, who raised Jesus from the dead, will raise me—and He'll raise you in His presence. As a result, you will benefit—and the message of God's grace will go out to more and more people all around you. And the result will be that the praise and thanksgiving of many people will overflow—and God will be glorified even through our present sufferings."

That is the nature of the body of Christ. We share His life with one another, and as we lose ourselves in costly service, His life becomes visible in other people. His saving resurrection grace spreads from one person to the next. As we endure the long, lonely hours of praying for one another, of faithfully upholding one another, of carrying one another's burdens, the life of Christ is revealed in the body.

"All this is for your benefit," Paul writes, "so that the grace that is reaching more and more people may cause thanksgiving to overflow to the glory of God." The power of God is unleashed when the people of God go through sorrow and sufferings while giving thanks and glory to Him. It's an amazing blessing to meet a believer who demonstrates joy, peace, and thanksgiving in the midst of trials.

Many years ago, I clipped and saved a testimony that was published in Billy Graham's *Decision* magazine. I don't know whether it was written by a man or a woman, because no byline was given. This anonymous person wrote:

> For a long time I had been bitter about life. It seemed to have dealt me a dirty blow, for since I was twelve years old I have been waiting for death to close in on me. It was at that time I learned I had muscular dystrophy.
>
> I fought hard against this disease and exercised hard, but I only grew weaker. All I could see was what I had missed. My friends went away to college, then got married and started having families of their own. When I lay in bed at night thinking, despair would creep from the dark corners to haunt me. Life was meaningless. In March of last year my mother brought home from our public library Billy Graham's book *World Aflame*. I started reading it, and as I read I realized that I wanted God. I wanted there to be a meaning to life. I wanted to receive this deep faith and peace.
>
> All I know is that my life has changed and I now have joy in living. No longer is the universe chaotic. No longer does life have no goal. No longer is there no hope....
>
> I continue to grow weaker. I am close to being totally helpless and am in pain most of the time, but sometimes I am so glad I am

alive that it is hard to keep myself from bursting at the seams. I can see for the first time the beauty all around me, and I realize how very lucky I am.

This is a person who carries in the body the death of Jesus so that the life of Jesus might be revealed. This is the note of joyful thanksgiving amid trials that truly glorifies God. May God give us the mind of the One who said, "Not my will but thine be done."

26

BEYOND THE END

2 Corinthians 4:16–5:17

The most important question we all face in the privacy of our own thoughts is, "What is waiting for me when I die?" The answers to that question fall into three categories.

First, some say that nothing happens to you after you die. When you're dead, you're dead. Your consciousness ceases to exist. There is no heaven, there is no hell, there is simply . . . nothing. This view leads to despair.

There is no hope for lasting meaning in life if all of our hopes and dreams come to an abrupt and permanent end. The Old Testament book of Ecclesiastes articulates this point of view:

> Man's fate is like that of the animals; the same fate awaits them both: As one dies, so dies the other. All have the same breath; man has no advantage over the animal. Everything is meaningless. All go to the same place; all come from dust, and to dust all return. (ECCLESIASTES 3:19–20)

A noted Christian philosopher and theologian, Dr. William Lane Craig, wrote in *Reasonable Faith*, "Sartre observed that death is not threatening so long as we view it as the death of the other, from a third-person standpoint, so to speak. It is only when we internalize it and look at it from the first-person perspective—'my death: I am going to die'—that the threat of non-being becomes real."

Second, some say that when you come to the end of your life, anything can happen. You plunk down your soul and take your chances. The trouble with this view is that it is based on wishful thinking, not reality.

This "anything can happen when we die" view may even be based upon the uncertain and controversial experiences of people who claim to have died and been resuscitated—what are called near-death experiences (NDEs). There are indications that some of these experiences may be due to oxygen deprivation in the brain; others may involve delusions sent by

314

deceitful spirits—that is, demons. In any case, it hardly seems wise to base your worldview on the testimony of people whose bodies were shutting down and whose minds were not in touch with reality.

Third, some say that when you come to the end of your life, you face the spiritual reality that is detailed for us in the Word of God. There is only one man in history who ever returned from death and reported on his findings, and that man is Jesus. He promised that a whole new plane of existence—eternal life in new resurrection bodies—awaits those have placed their trust in Him.

Outwardly perishing, inwardly renewed

Here Paul transitions from the issue of suffering in this life to the hope of glory in the life to come. He writes:

> Therefore we do not lose heart. Though outwardly we are wasting away, yet inwardly we are being renewed day by day. For our light and momentary troubles are achieving for us an eternal glory that far outweighs them all. So we fix our eyes not on what is seen, but on what is unseen. For what is seen is temporary, but what is unseen is eternal.
> (2 CORINTHIANS 4:16–18)

Paul repeats the statement he made in 2 Corinthians 4:1: "Therefore . . . we do not lose heart." Earlier, Paul said he did not lose heart in the face of suffering and persecution. Here he says he does not lose heart even in the face of death. He explains, "Though outwardly we are wasting away, yet inwardly we are being renewed day by day."

It's true, Paul says, that the outward man is perishing. What is the outward man? Paul refers to our physical bodies and our minds, which age and deteriorate over time. This is the part of us that finds it harder with each passing year to roll out of bed, climb stairs, or read newspaper print.

Paul says, in effect, "I don't get discouraged over the deterioration of my outward man, because the inner man is being renewed day by day." The inner me, of course, is the real me. It's the human spirit within that has its conscious expression in the soul. The combination of soul and spirit marks humankind as different from the animals, and it is our inner self that is made new every day. Our inner selves are being prepared for something wonderful to come. That's the hope of the believer.

Do you meet each new day with that hope? Have you learned to rise above your circumstances with that sense of inner renewal? Are you able

315

to remain joyful even in the shadow of death because the Spirit of God renews your inner life every day?

The weight of glory

Paul goes on to say, "For our light and momentary troubles are achieving for us an eternal glory that far outweighs them all." The King James Version put it this way: "For our light affliction, which is but for a moment, worketh for us a far more exceeding and eternal weight of glory" (2 Corinthians 4:17 KJV).

Every now and then, you encounter a verse of Scripture that is so full of possibilities and meaning that you could contemplate it for hours. This, to me, is such a verse. What does Paul mean when he writes of "an eternal glory that far outweighs them all" or "a far more exceeding and eternal weight of glory." And isn't it amazing that Paul links this weight of glory directly to the afflictions and struggles of our present life?

Paul is telling us that there is a direct connection between the suffering and the glory. The suffering prepares us for the glory. The glory inspires us to endure the suffering. Paul puts it this way in his letter to the Romans:

> Now if we are children, then we are heirs—heirs of God and co-heirs with Christ, if indeed we share in his sufferings in order that we may also share in his glory. (ROMANS 8:17)

No matter how great our trials may seem, two things are always true.

Compared with the eternal glory to come, our present trials are momentary. Eternity lasts forever; suffering eventually comes to an end. What is a year compared with eternity? Or a century? Or even a billion years? The longest span of time you can imagine is a blink of an eye compared with eternity.

Compared with the eternal glory to come, our present trials are light. What does Paul consider a light trial? He was beaten with fists, beaten with rods, stoned, shipwrecked, and imprisoned. He endured hunger and thirst and many other forms of suffering and pain. His life was constantly in danger. Yet, compared with the weight of glory that awaited him in eternity, Paul thought these trials scarcely worth mentioning.

In *The Weight of Glory*, C. S. Lewis writes:

> The door on which we have been knocking all our lives will open at last. . . . And to be at last summoned inside would be both glory and honor beyond all our merits and also the healing of that old ache. . . .

We do not want merely to see beauty, though, God knows, even that is bounty enough. We want something else which can hardly be put into words—to be united with the beauty we see, to pass into it, to receive it into ourselves, to bathe in it, to become part of it. . . .

We cannot mingle with the splendors we see. But all the leaves of the New Testament are rustling with the rumor that it will not always be so. Some day, God willing, we shall get in.

But how do we know that this hope of an eternal weight of glory is true? Paul writes, "So we fix our eyes not on what is seen, but on what is unseen. For what is seen is temporary, but what is unseen is eternal." It's hard to believe in things we do not see. Science tells us that the universe is made up of atoms, and we accept it as true. But we do not experience atoms, and they are not part of our daily experience, so we don't really think about the fact that our chairs, food, and bodies are made up of atoms.

Yet Paul says that we must "fix our eyes" on the unseen spiritual realities. We must think seriously and continually about realities that are beyond our comprehension. Our minds grasp what Paul is telling us, but our emotions struggle with it. Why should we "fix our eyes" on the unseen realities? Because the visible realities are passing away; only the unseen realities are eternal. As we approach the end of life, the unseen realities of eternal life grow more and more significant.

As evangelist D. L. Moody lay dying, his last words were, "Earth is receding. Heaven is approaching. This is my crowning day." At that moment, Moody saw reality with absolute clarity—and what he saw was glorious.

An earthly tent, a heavenly dwelling

In chapter 5, Paul goes on to describe this "weight of glory" in greater detail. In words that brim with confidence and certainty, he writes:

Now we know that if the earthly tent we live in is destroyed, we have a building from God, an eternal house in heaven, not built by human hands. Meanwhile we groan, longing to be clothed with our heavenly dwelling, because when we are clothed, we will not be found naked. For while we are in this tent, we groan and are burdened, because we do not wish to be unclothed but to be clothed with our heavenly dwelling, so that what is mortal may be swallowed up by life. (2 COR-INTHIANS 5:1–4)

317

Paul speaks here of our resurrected body—the body we will receive when "what is mortal" is "swallowed up by life." The resurrection body is the body that will be ours in that moment Paul described in 1 Corinthians:

Listen, I tell you a mystery: We will not all sleep, but we will all be changed—in a flash, in the twinkling of an eye, at the last trumpet. For the trumpet will sound, the dead will be raised imperishable, and we will be changed. For the perishable must clothe itself with the imperishable, and the mortal with immortality. (1 CORINTHIANS 15:51–53)

That is the body we have to look forward to—imperishable, immortal—and we will receive that body in a twinkling of an eye on the day of resurrection. Our present body, Paul says, is like a tent. A tent is temporary, and it's uncomfortable. I once visited a family who had to live in a tent while their permanent home was being finished. They couldn't wait to move out of their tent and into their permanent dwelling.

I truly feel that my own body is a tent—a sagging, drooping tent that has been patched too many times. It's not a very comfortable tent—but I know that I have a permanent dwelling place waiting for me. With every day that passes, I become more and more convinced of this fact: If we truly understood how limited our present bodies are compared with our resurrection bodies, we wouldn't fear death. We would eagerly look forward to moving day!

Notice that Paul tells us that our heavenly bodies are not merely a future hope—they are waiting for us now. He writes, "We have a building from God, an eternal house in heaven, not built by human hands." He doesn't say "we will have." He says "we have."

Paul chooses his words very carefully in this passage. He says, "We do not wish to be unclothed but to be clothed with our heavenly dwelling, so that what is mortal may be swallowed up by life." In other words, "We don't want to float off to some disembodied existence. We don't want to be ghosts and spooks, haunting cemeteries to frighten people. We want to have bodies—real, substantial, eternal, immortal bodies."

Deceitful spirits want us to believe that when we die, we become ghosts and disembodied spirits that roam the earth or haunt houses. The reality is that this kind of activity is demonic activity. When mediums summon what they think are "spirits of the dead" or when people think they see a ghost, they are seeing demons impersonating the dead.

Paul tells us that a resurrected body is a real body. Life after death is not a disembodied state but the state of being eternally embodied. That is why he speaks of our mortality being "swallowed up by life." Think about what a startling statement that is! When you die in Christ, your mortality is swallowed up—not by death but by life! A ghostly existence would be a deathly existence—but Paul tells us that, for us, life after death will be life indeed, a life so real and substantial that this mortal life seems like an insubstantial dream by comparison.

The question naturally arises: Where are we during the time between death and resurrection? The scriptural answer: The moment we die, we are instantly with the Lord.

Paul writes:

> If I am to go on living in the body, this will mean fruitful labor for me. Yet what shall I choose? I do not know! I am torn between the two: I desire to depart and be with Christ, which is better by far. (Philippians 1:22–23)

To be in the body is to be absent from the Lord. To be absent from the body is to be home with the Lord. This view is affirmed by the fact that, as Jesus was being crucified, He told the repentant thief, "I tell you the truth, today you will be with me in paradise" (see Luke 23:43).

But how can that be? If we receive our resurrection bodies on the day of the Lord's return, how can we be present with the Lord at the very moment we die? Some people suggest that we receive temporary bodies to use until we receive our resurrection bodies—but there is not a single verse of Scripture to support that idea.

I believe there is only one possible answer: When we leave our earthly bodies, we also leave time. We are used to thinking in terms of sixty-minute hours and twenty-four-hour days, because that is all we know. That's the only kind of time we have ever experienced. So we tend to think of eternity as time that goes on and on and on. But eternity is not time. Eternity is timeless.

The evidence of Scriptures is that when we die, we exit time and enter a timeless eternity, so that there is no sense of waiting or time passing between the moment we die and the moment we receive our resurrection bodies. From our perspective, it will be as if we close our eyes in death—then open our eyes in our new resurrection bodies. This will be true for all the saints who have ever passed through death—those who died five seconds ago and those who died five millennia ago.

319

Paul goes on to say:

> Now it is God who has made us for this very purpose and has given
> us the Spirit as a deposit, guaranteeing what is to come. (2 CORIN-
> THIANS 5:5)

That refreshing and renewing daily experience of the Holy Spirit in
our lives is our guarantee of the coming resurrection. Our mortal life is
deteriorating. The outward man is falling apart—but praise God! Our
inner man is growing more mature, richer in character, more loving and
forgiving with every passing day. Day by day, the Spirit is working within
us, making us more and more like Jesus Christ.

We live by faith, not by sight

We open our newspapers and are confronted with natural disasters, global
warming, terrorism, nuclear proliferation, biological weapons, wars, and
rumors of wars. What is the world coming to? The same thing it's always
been coming to! The daily news in Paul's day was every bit as depressing
as it is today. There were natural disasters, civil uprisings, Roman oppression, government corruption, slavery, famine, plague, persecution, wars, and
rumors of wars. And remember, in Paul's day there was little or nothing in
the way of sanitation, health care, transportation, education, or entertainment. The average life expectancy was around forty years.

Life in Paul's era was stark and often bleak—yet when you read the
New Testament, you never see a sense of despair. Instead, you hear shouts
of triumph and hope. We especially see Paul's hope and confidence in these
verses:

> Therefore we are always confident and know that as long as we are at
> home in the body we are away from the Lord. We live by faith, not by
> sight. We are confident, I say, and would prefer to be away from the
> body and at home with the Lord. (2 CORINTHIANS 5:6–8)

The key, of course, is that little word *therefore*. Paul says, in effect, "In
view of what I have just been saying, we are always confident, we are of
good courage." Throughout this passage, Paul has been talking about the
power and availability of God. That's the basis for the Christian hope.
That's the answer to an age of despair. No matter how much tragedy there
is in the world, God is at work. He will act.

Paul adds, "We live by faith, not by sight." We can't see God. Nevertheless, we have His presence with us. We do not see Him, but we believe in Him and we know Him, because we live by faith, not by sight.

The Lord Jesus put it this way when He comforted the disciples in the upper room before the crucifixion. "Do not let your hearts be troubled," He told them. "Trust in God; trust also in me." He was teaching them to live by faith, not by sight.

"We are confident, I say," the apostle repeats, "and would prefer to be away from the body and at home with the Lord." Christians should always look ahead. We should always be optimistic. We should be like children who are looking forward to Christmas. Our eyes should be wide with delight and the expectation of future joy.

Notice again Paul's beautiful phrasing: For now, he says, we are "at home in the body." But we would prefer to leave this life and be "at home with the Lord." It's true that you feel at home in your body right now. It doesn't feel strange or unnatural to be in your body. In fact, it would be very strange to *not* have your body.

But then Paul uses the same phrase, "at home," to speak of being in the presence of Jesus: "at home with the Lord." When this life is over and we enter into our resurrection life, it will seem even more natural to be "at home with the Lord." In fact, we will wonder how we were ever able to stand living in those dilapidated bodies that were dying and falling apart while we were still using them.

We were created to be at home with the Lord. That was the life we were meant to experience in Eden. When we are finally at home with the Lord, we will no longer live by faith alone. We will see Him face to face. As the apostle Peter observes,

> Though you have not seen him, you love him; and even though you do not see him now, you believe in him and are filled with an inexpressible and glorious joy. (1 PETER 1:8)

So we are confident because we are heading into light instead of darkness. We know that we will one day be home with the Lord.

The judgment seat of Christ

Next, Paul writes:

> So we make it our goal to please him, whether we are at home in the body or away from it. (2 CORINTHIANS 5:9)

This is an eternal principle. Our reason to be here on earth is to please God. That will not change when we are at home with the Lord. Our goal will still be to please Him. Paul continues:

> For we must all appear before the judgment seat of Christ, that each one may receive what is due him for the things done while in the body, whether good or bad. (2 CORINTHIANS 5:10)

Many Christians are frightened and troubled by this verse. The concept here is often misunderstood. Paul speaks of a judgment seat, and that word strikes terror to our hearts. Unfortunately, we tend to identify this judgment seat with the imposing scene in Revelation 20 where all of the dead stand before the "great white throne" of God. There the books are opened and lives are reviewed—and eternal destinies are settled. It's a sobering scene—but that's not what Paul writes about here.

The judgment seat of Christ is not a judgment to settle an individual's eternal destiny. Instead, it is a personal evaluation given to each individual by the Lord regarding his life. It is as though you and the Lord walked together through all the scenes of your life and he pointed out to you the real nature of what you did, what you said, and what motivated your words and deeds.

The essential characteristic of the judgment seat is that it's a time when the secret, silent reaches of our hearts will be disclosed to ourselves—and to others. Paul writes, "We must all appear." In the original Greek, he literally says, "We shall all be manifested" or "We shall all be unveiled." In other words, our innermost motives will be revealed in the sight of all. This is the moment Jesus spoke of when He said,

> There is nothing concealed that will not be disclosed, or hidden that will not be made known. What you have said in the dark will be heard in the daylight, and what you have whispered in the ear in the inner rooms will be proclaimed from the roofs. (LUKE 12:2–3)

Paul also refers to this judgment in his previous letter to the Corinthians:

> Therefore judge nothing before the appointed time; wait till the Lord comes. He will bring to light what is hidden in darkness and will expose the motives of men's hearts. At that time each will receive his praise from God. (1 CORINTHIANS 4:5)

Notice that this judgment is about our motives, not our actions. God is not as concerned with what we do as with why we do it. Yes, there are some areas of clear-cut sin, and these actions do displease the Lord. But we do many right things for the wrong motives—and these motives are also displeasing to the Lord.

If you make a large donation to the church, or pray in public, or preach a sermon, or write a Christian book, or help a needy child, people will think you've done a good thing. But people look at your actions from the outside. God knows your heart. He knows if you did that good thing out of faith, love, and obedience—or if you did it in order to gain glory or fame or to make yourself look good. Your motive is more important than the deed. Your motive will be revealed before all at the judgment seat of Christ.

"Without faith it is impossible to please God," the Bible tells us (see Hebrews 11:6). Faith must be the driving force behind everything we do or our actions cannot please Him. Paul wants to make sure that when he goes before the judgment seat of Christ, he will experience joy, not shame. It will be a time of disclosure and evaluation, when we learn for the first time the truth about ourselves and our hidden motivations.

If the judgment seat of Christ worries you, there is something you can do to affect the Lord's evaluation of your life—and you can do it right now. Paul wrote:

> But if we judged ourselves, we would not come under judgment.
> (1 CORINTHIANS 11:31)

In a real sense, the judgment seat of Christ has already begun. By means of His indwelling Spirit, the Lord continually points out to me my wrong attitudes and wrong motives. I think I am doing God's work according to God's will—and then I discover that my good works were motivated by religious pride or a desire to be noticed. I learn that what I thought was genuine humility was really conceited false modesty. If I unflinchingly face the truth about myself now, then I'll have one less unpleasant truth to learn about myself on that day.

I know that God has dealt with my sin on the cross of Christ. I know that He loves me, He's forgiven me, and He has given me the free gift of His righteousness. When I stand at the judgment seat of Christ, I will not have to fear eternal punishment. I will not be judged for my sins; Jesus has already taken that judgment upon Himself.

But I don't want to see a look of disappointment on my Lord's face. When He evaluates my life, I want to hear Him say, "Well done, good and faithful servant! Come, Ray, and share your master's happiness!" (see Matthew 25:21).

You should not think of the judgment seat of Christ as a place where the Lord gives you the bad news about your life. It will also be a time of encouragement. Remember, Paul says, "At that time each will receive his praise from God." Won't it be wonderful to hear God's praise for your life!

Love compels us

Paul goes on to say:

> Since, then, we know what it is to fear the Lord, we try to persuade men. What we are is plain to God, and I hope it is also plain to your conscience. We are not trying to commend ourselves to you again, but are giving you an opportunity to take pride in us, so that you can answer those who take pride in what is seen rather than in what is in the heart. If we are out of our mind, it is for the sake of God; if we are in our right mind, it is for you. (2 CORINTHIANS 5:11–13)

What does Paul mean when he speaks of the fear of the Lord? Paul is not saying that he preaches fire-and-brimstone sermons in order to frighten people into the kingdom. The fear of the Lord is not a sense of terror; rather, it's the respect and awe we feel when we recognize that our God is a God of truth. We can't escape the truth about ourselves that He will reveal.

Paul is saying, in effect, "I know that God will deal fairly with me at the judgment seat of Christ—but He will reveal the truth of my life. So I don't want to waste my life. When God unveils the truth about my life, I want it to be a truth that pleases Him, not a truth that makes me ashamed."

He also says, in effect, "I want you to be able to be proud of me. I want you to be able to answer the critics who have been attacking me. You know what my critics have been saying: 'Paul is out of his mind! How can you listen to anything he says? He claims Jesus spoke to him on the Damascus road! He claims that his teachings come straight from Jesus Himself!' Well, if I'm crazy, then I'm crazy for God's sake. And if I behave sanely, then I'm sane for your sake. I'm crazy for God, I'm sane for you. But sane or insane, everything I do is motivated by love."

Paul goes on to add:

> For Christ's love compels us, because we are convinced that one died
> for all, and therefore all died. And he died for all, that those who live
> should no longer live for themselves but for him who died for them
> and was raised again. (2 CORINTHIANS 5:14–15)

The apostle's first great motive for ministry is a desire to please God
at the judgment seat of Christ. His second great motive for ministry is the
love of Christ. "For Christ's love compels us," he says. The Greek word
translated "compels" is a strong word. Paul is saying that the love of Christ
drives him and urges him onward.

Love is a wonderful motivator. It is one thing to be driven by threats or
fear of punishment or the promise of financial gain. But love is the greatest
motivator of all. The love of Christ refreshes our spirits and energizes us to
go the extra mile. When we know that Jesus loves us and believes in us, our
confidence soars—and so does our incentive.

Paul says, "We are convinced that one died for all, and therefore all
died. And he died for all, that those who live should no longer live for
themselves but for him who died for them and was raised again." I continually hear people talking about "my needs," "my rights," and "what's in it
for me." Paul wants us to know that the death of Jesus sets us free from the
need to live for our selfish wants and needs. Jesus gave up His rights and
died for us—and He set an example of unselfish sacrifice for us to follow.

Christ died for all, and therefore all died. This means that we look at
people differently than before. Paul writes:

> So from now on we regard no one from a worldly point of view.
> (2 CORINTHIANS 5:16a)

We do not look at others the way we once did. We are not impressed
by power, money, fame, or achievement—nor do we look down upon those
who are powerless, poor, and obscure. We see people from God's perspective, and we acknowledge that the greatest of all and the least of all are
equal in God's sight. So we treat everyone with respect and compassion—
and we never forget that everyone needs to hear the good news of Jesus
Christ. Paul goes on to say:

> Though we once regarded Christ in this way, we do so no longer.
> (2 CORINTHIANS 5:16b)

In other words, Paul once viewed Christ from a worldly point of view. He once thought of Jesus as a worthless rabble-rouser, a tub-thumping street preacher from Nazareth. Jesus had no family position, no higher education, and no political connections. From a worldly point of view, Jesus was a troublemaker who claimed to be something He was not.

But though Paul once regarded Christ from a worldly point of view, he does so no longer. He now sees Christ for who He truly is: the Lord of glory, the King of the ages, the Prince of life, the God-Man, the Word made flesh. Paul now preaches about the very Christ he once persecuted. And Paul has been liberated from his prejudices. He now treats kings and beggars with equal respect, for both kings and beggars need a Savior.

A new creation

Next Paul makes this uplifting and oft-quoted statement:

> Therefore, if anyone is in Christ, he is a new creation; the old has gone, the new has come! (2 CORINTHIANS 5:17)

What does Paul mean? He is telling us that there is hope for everyone! No matter how vile and sinful we were, God can transform us. No matter how resistant we have been to the gospel, God can reach us.

No one is beyond the reach of God's grace. He can take the vilest, most repulsive specimen of humanity on the planet and transform him into a shining saint. There is always hope because God doesn't just make us better; He makes us new. When God begins a work, He finishes it. You and I may write people off as hopeless, but God never does. If you are in Christ, you are a new creation.

A businessman once put a warehouse up for sale. As he took a prospective buyer around the warehouse, he pointed out the building's flaws. "The place has been vacant for a while," he said. "Vandals broke out the windows and kicked in the doors, but we'll make those repairs. Don't worry about the roof—we'll take care of those holes. Oh, and we'll clean up all this trash and paint over the graffiti and—"

"Don't say another word," said the buyer. "You don't have to fix the place up. I don't want the structure. I just want the site. I'm going to remove this warehouse and put up a brand-new building."

That's what God does in our lives. He doesn't patch us up, fix us up, or paint us over. When He comes in, the old is gone and He makes everything new. What a wonderful hope we have!

27

THE MINISTRY OF RECONCILIATION

2 Corinthians 5:18—6:10

On April 18, 1942, just four months after the Japanese attack on Pearl Harbor, General Jimmy Doolittle led a squadron of sixteen B-25 bombers off the deck of the carrier *Hornet*. Their target: Tokyo. One of the airmen on that mission was bombardier Jacob DeShazer, a corporal in the United States Army Air Corps. He flew in plane No. 16, the last plane off the deck. After Jake DeShazer and his crew successfully bombed a factory and oil storage facility, they became lost in dense fog and were forced to parachute over China in total darkness.

As DeShazer was falling to earth, he wondered if he should pray. He had been raised in a Christian home but had drifted away from his faith during his high school years. As he fell, he decided it would be hypocritical to pray now after spending years away from God. Yet, at that very moment in a small Oregon town, his mother awakened suddenly from a dream in which she was dropping through the air in the dark. She wasn't even aware that Jake was on a dangerous secret mission, but she prayed for him until her burden lifted.

DeShazer and the other men came down over Japanese-occupied China and were captured. Three were executed on the spot; the rest were imprisoned, beaten, tortured, and starved. Jacob DeShazer endured forty months in a prison camp. Most of the time he was alone in a 5–by–8–foot cell with a small slit in the door. That cell was an oven in the summertime, a walk-in freezer in the winter. He was often sick, and at times his body was covered with boils like Job's.

Jake recalled, "My hatred for the enemy nearly drove me crazy." A fellow captive, Lieutenant Robert J. Meder, told him, "Jesus Christ is the key to getting through all this." A few days later, Lieutenant Meder died of malnutrition.

DeShazer asked his captors for a Bible and was allowed to have a Bible for just three weeks in 1944. He read that Bible through and committed as much as he could to memory, including the Sermon on the Mount and the entire epistle of 1 John. He was amazed at how clearly the Old Testament prophecies depicted the life of Christ. One sentence from the Gospels had a profound impact on his life—Jesus' prayer from the cross: "Father, forgive them, for they know not what they do."

Jake DeShazer renewed his commitment to Jesus Christ as Lord and Savior—and his hatred was replaced by Christian love. "I realized that these people did not know my Savior," he recalled. "If Christ is not in a person's heart, it's natural to be cruel. I was afraid I was going to die, and I told God, 'I don't want to come to you with empty hands. I want to do something for Jesus before I die.'"

The ministry of reconciliation

One of the guards delighted in beating and kicking DeShazer for every infraction. On one occasion, the guard slammed the iron door on Jake's foot because he didn't think Jake was moving fast enough. The pain was incredible. Remembering the Sermon on the Mount, he wondered, "How could Jesus expect me to love my enemies and pray for those who persecute me?" But he knew God was calling him to do exactly that.

The next morning, when the guard came by the cell, Jake stood on his throbbing foot, put his face to the slit in the door, and said, "Good morning!" in Japanese. Jake continued to show kindness to the guard—and within a few days, the guard stopped beating him and started bringing him extra food.

On August 10, 1945, Jacob DeShazer sensed God calling him to pray for peace. He had no way of knowing that days earlier, two Japanese cities had been leveled by atomic bombs. For several hours, DeShazer prayed. Five days later, Japan surrendered. Jake and his fellow captives were set free.

DeShazer attended college and seminary, and he wrote a Christian tract, "I Was a Prisoner of Japan," that was distributed throughout postwar Japan. Three days after Christmas 1948, Jacob DeShazer arrived in Japan as a missionary. When the Japanese people asked him why he came back to the country that had imprisoned him, he told them about the love of Jesus.

Soon after his arrival, Jake was introduced to Mitsuo Fuchida, the Japanese pilot who had led the attack on Pearl Harbor on December 7, 1941.

Fuchida had read DeShazer's tract and received Jesus as his Lord and Savior. DeShazer and Fuchida became close friends, and Fuchida spent the rest of his life as an evangelist, spreading the gospel throughout Asia.

The Japanese people were amazingly responsive to the gospel in those early postwar years. "The people wanted to know the truth," DeShazer recalled. "They had been taught that the emperor of Japan was a god. After the war, when the emperor admitted he was just a human being, a lot of Japanese young people lost all faith and committed suicide. When we came to Japan and told them about the Lord, they said, 'We've never heard anything like this before!'"

Jacob DeShazer spent thirty years as a missionary in Japan, living out what Paul calls "the ministry of reconciliation." Paul describes the ministry of reconciliation in 2 Corinthians 5:

> All this is from God, who reconciled us to himself through Christ and gave us the ministry of reconciliation: that God was reconciling the world to himself in Christ, not counting men's sins against them. And he has committed to us the message of reconciliation. We are therefore Christ's ambassadors, as though God were making his appeal through us. We implore you on Christ's behalf: Be reconciled to God. (2 CORINTHIANS 5:18–20)

We need to understand the ministry of reconciliation very clearly, because God has called each of us to this work.

Five facets of our ministry

In this passage, we find five facets of this ministry that we should notice.

First, *this ministry was given to us by God; it originates with Him.* "All this is from God," Paul writes, "who reconciled us to himself through Christ and gave us the ministry of reconciliation." If this ministry comes from God, then you and I are responsible to God, not to anyone else, to carry out this ministry. When Paul went around the Roman world, preaching the gospel and planting churches, he did not have to check in with the apostles in Jerusalem to get permission. He was not commissioned by any human authority but by God.

I have visited churches where it is clear that the pastor thinks it's his responsibility to control what goes on in the congregation. Before church members can do ministry of any kind, they must get permission from the pastor or the board. They can't even have a home Bible study without official clearance. While I would agree that a church member should seek help, counsel, and support from the church leaders when starting a ministry, that church member is not responsible to anyone but the Lord.

God has given us the ministry of reconciliation, so we should conduct this ministry as unto Him. God gave you the ministry of reconciliation when He reconciled you to Himself through Jesus Christ. You are the world's greatest authority on what God has done in your life; no one can say, "You're doing it wrong," because it's your ministry, your message, your experience. Only you can tell the story of how God has reconciled you, enfolded you in His loving arms, and forgiven you by His divine grace. That's the message of reconciliation that you and you alone can share with the world.

Second, *God uses us to spread the message of reconciliation by which He is reconciling the world to Himself.* Paul writes that God "gave us the ministry of reconciliation: that God was reconciling the world to himself in Christ, not counting men's sins against them." This is the message the world needs to know.

People everywhere live apart from God, having no sense of acceptance or self-worth. They feel estranged from God. They live in a universe that does not belong to them. They did not make it. They do not run it. They do not feel at home in it. Alienation is the supreme problem of our day, as any psychiatrist will tell.

When I attended seminary, I was taught that my job as a preacher was to make people aware of sin and God's eternal judgment. I was taught that you have to frighten people with the fires of hell before they will repent and turn to Christ for salvation. But the more I read the Scriptures and counseled parishioners, the more I realized I didn't have to make people aware of their sin—they knew they were sinners. They were already afraid of God's judgment. All I needed to do was tell them about a loving Father who wanted to heal them, forgive them, and reconcile them to Himself.

When God looks upon the human race, He sees people who have been broken by sin. So He comes to humanity with a message of love that says, "I know you can't make it through life on your own—but I've taken care of the sin problem. Put your trust in My Son Jesus; then let's talk about having a relationship that will go on forever."

You do not have to tell your neighbors, "You're living an immoral life. You're sinning." In fact, if you go to them with an attitude of moral superiority, you will probably not have a ministry of reconciliation. So your message should be, "I'm no different from you. You've sinned, I've sinned, we have all been estranged from God. But let me tell you what I've discovered: God reached out to me even in my sin! He bridged the gap and drew me to Himself, even though I didn't deserve it."

Isn't that an appealing message of hope? And isn't that the truth of your life?

Third, *God's message of reconciliation requires voluntary acceptance.* Paul writes, "We are therefore Christ's ambassadors, as though God were making his appeal through us. We implore you on Christ's behalf: Be reconciled to God." The Lord doesn't force reconciliation on anyone. People are free to accept this message—or reject it. That's why God does not make demands. Instead, speaking through Paul, God makes an appeal. He implores, He urges—but He does not insist.

When we share this message of reconciliation, we go as Christ's ambassadors. An ambassador is a diplomat, a representative. He conveys the message he was sent to convey, and he seeks to be persuasive, but he can't force others to obey him. People must respond voluntarily to this message in order to be reconciled to God.

This passage makes it clear that there is no universal salvation. Many people claim that a loving God would never send anyone into eternal punishment, but Paul makes it clear that the message of reconciliation must be received and accepted or reconciliation can't take place. This truth is heartbreaking but undeniable.

Fourth, *reconciliation can be achieved only through the righteousness of God, not through human effort.* Paul writes:

> God made him who had no sin to be sin for us, so that in him we might become the righteousness of God. (2 CORINTHIANS 5:21)

People want to be right with God, but they don't know how to achieve it. Most people naturally assume that the righteousness must come from their own good works. But human works can never produce reconciliation with God. Only the righteousness of God can make a person right with God.

Have you ever noticed how people desperately need to be right? The quickest way to offend someone is to say, "You're wrong!" We hate to be wrong! As soon as we are accused of being wrong, we try to justify ourselves. It's no coincidence that the Bible uses this very concept—*justification*—to describe the precondition to being reconciled to God. As Paul wrote to the Romans:

For all have sinned and fall short of the glory of God, and are justified freely by his grace through the redemption that came by Christ Jesus. (ROMANS 3:23–24)

Justification is that mysterious transaction that took place on the cross when Jesus, the sinless One, suffered and died for all of our sins. Jesus took our place on the cross, and God agreed to it. God sent His Son into the world to become sin for us; that is how we were justified. Now that we are justified, God is able to reconcile us to Himself.

Fifth, *God now calls us to live reconciled lives that proclaim God's reconciliation to the world*. Paul makes this point in the opening verses of chapter 6 (the chapter division at this point is misleading). Paul writes:

As God's fellow workers we urge you not to receive God's grace in vain. For he says,

"In the time of my favor I heard you,
and in the day of salvation I helped you."

I tell you, now is the time of God's favor, now is the day of salvation. (2 CORINTHIANS 6:1–2)

What does Paul mean when he says, "We urge you not to receive God's grace in vain"? The term "God's grace" refers to all that God has done for us in Christ. Paul uses this term in reference to being reconciled to God. He's speaking to those who have already been reconciled to God: "Don't let your reconciled relationship with God come to nothing. Don't let it be in vain. Build on this relationship, live accordingly, live a life that is worthy of one who has been reconciled to God."

Paul is not suggesting that a saved and reconciled believer can lose his salvation. Other Scripture passages make it clear that this is not possible. Paul is saying that once we received Christ as Lord, He lives in us to show us right from wrong, and He gives us the power to do right and reject wrong. But we need to listen to Him and obey Him. Otherwise, we have received the grace of God in vain. If we receive the salvation of Christ but we live as if we never did, then it's as if we do not even have Him in our lives.

So Paul implores us to live worthy of the grace we've received. When should we begin obeying God? The hands on God's clock only point to one time: NOW. Paul writes, "Now is the time of God's favor, now is the day of salvation."

Now is the only time you may ever have. You don't have yesterday. You may not have tomorrow. So don't wait. Live now. Be reconciled now.

God looks out over a dying, despairing world, and He weeps over the lost and the lonely. His appeal to us is, "Take my message of reconciliation and share it with the world. There's no time to lose. Do it now."

Do you have to be a fanatic?

Next, Paul writes:

> We put no stumbling block in anyone's path, so that our ministry will not be discredited. Rather, as servants of God we commend ourselves in every way: in great endurance; in troubles, hardships and distresses; in beatings, imprisonments and riots; in hard work, sleepless nights and hunger; in purity, understanding, patience and kindness; in the Holy Spirit and in sincere love; in truthful speech and in the power of God; with weapons of righteousness in the right hand and in the left; through glory and dishonor, bad report and good report; genuine, yet regarded as impostors; known, yet regarded as unknown; dying, and yet we live on; beaten, and yet not killed; sorrowful, yet always rejoicing; poor, yet making many rich; having nothing, and yet possessing everything. (2 CORINTHIANS 6:3–10)

Having just urged the Corinthians to make sure that they didn't receive the grace of God in vain, Paul now describes his own life, showing us what the committed Christian life looks like. He speaks of intense persecution, enduring hunger and sleeplessness, maintaining pure character and a sincere love, putting up with slurs against his reputation, rejoicing in sorrows, and more—all for the sake of spreading the message of reconciliation far and wide. He is living out the ministry of reconciliation to the full.

Now I ask you: Does this man sound like a fanatic to you? Is his commitment to Christ a bit over the top? Does it seem as if he takes his religion a little too far? There were people in Paul's day who thought so.

Paul was often accused of being not just fanatical but downright crazy. People heard the story of his remarkable conversion on the Damascus road. They saw his intense dedication to evangelism and church planting—even to the point where he lost sleep and denied himself most of the comforts and pleasures of life. The book of Acts records that the Roman governor Festus told him, "You are out of your mind, Paul! Your great learning is driving you insane" (see Acts 26:24).

So as we read this passage, we ask: Do you have to be a fanatic to be a Christian? To understand what God is truly saying to us through Paul, let's break this passage down into three divisions.

First division, verse 3

In verse 3, Paul says he is very careful how he speaks and acts before men. The ministry of reconciliation that God has given us requires that we maintain a faithful testimony and a reputation that is above reproach.

Paul writes, "We put no stumbling block in anyone's path, so that our ministry will not be discredited." Paul was aware that he was a role model, a representative of his Lord, and he was careful not to do anything to bring discredit upon the gospel.

Did people find fault with him? Absolutely. All the time. He was often accused of being a deceiver, a phony, a false apostle, an arrogant and prideful man. If you set out to do anything important for God, you will make enemies, you will be accused, you will be criticized. Every great and godly leader suffers attacks—and the greatest of all, Jesus of Nazareth, suffered the worst and most unfair attacks, including crucifixion. Paul expected to be unfairly criticized—but he was determined not to give anyone a legitimate reason to accuse him. He would put no stumbling block in anyone's way.

Elsewhere, Paul wrote:

For the appeal we make does not spring from error or impure motives, nor are we trying to trick you. On the contrary, we speak as men approved by God to be entrusted with the gospel. We are not trying to please men but God, who tests our hearts. You know we never used flattery, nor did we put on a mask to cover up greed—God is our witness. We were not looking for praise from men, not from you or anyone else. (1 THESSALONIANS 2:3–6)

One of the great tragedies of the church is the number of prominent Christian leaders who have brought discredit on the gospel through financial misconduct, sexual misconduct, or making public statements that needlessly offend people. These leaders not only ruin their own reputations but also bring discredit on the gospel and the church.

Paul lived with a continual awareness that he was being closely watched by both believers and unbelievers. So he was careful to make sure that no fault could be found in his ministry. If anyone was going to accuse Paul of wrongdoing, it would have to be a false accusation, because Paul refused to compromise his integrity.

Second division, verses 4–7

In verses 4 through 7, Paul makes the point that the ministry of reconciliation he has received from God is approved by God. Having endured much and suffered greatly, he maintains his godly character and his righteous way of life.

Paul writes, "Rather, as servants of God we commend ourselves in every way: in great endurance; in troubles, hardships and distresses; in beatings, imprisonments and riots; in hard work, sleepless nights and hunger; in purity, understanding, patience and kindness; in the Holy Spirit and in sincere love; in truthful speech and in the power of God; with weapons of righteousness in the right hand and in the left."

Endurance is the key. God is pleased and glorified by the fact that no matter what happens in Paul's life, he perseveres. He endures. The mark of Christian maturity is the ability to maintain a walk with God even under pressure. Paul lists the pressures he has endured in three groups of three. Those three categories of pressure might be called tough circumstances, tough opposition, and tough commitments.

First, he endured troubles, hardships and distresses. We know what Paul is talking about. "Troubles" can involve marital problems, parenting problems, in-law problems, disappointments, setbacks, and so forth. "Hardships" involve being deprived of the necessities we need in life, such a food, health, medicine, clothing, a roof over our heads, and so forth. "Distresses" are the calamities of life. The Greek word Paul uses literally means "narrow places," and it speaks of the times when things close in on us and we don't see any way out. Paul endured tough circumstances.

Next, Paul endured beatings, imprisonments and riots. In 2 Corinthians 11:23–27, Paul tells us that by this point in his life, he had been beaten with 39 lashes—not once but on five occasions. That's 195 lashes—which means that the flesh of his back was seamed with scars. Three times he had been beaten with rods—a brutal form of punishment often called caning. He had been stoned once in the city of Lystra and left for dead. Scripture records that he was imprisoned at least three times, and he also faced angry mobs of rioters on several occasions. He faced tough opposition.

Finally, Paul endured hard work, sleepless nights and hunger. Paul was a hard-working man. He preached during the day and made tents at night in order to provide for his needs. He lost sleep and missed meals because of his intense schedule. Why did he work so hard? Because he wanted to preach the message of reconciliation to as many as he could. He endured tough commitments.

People today are so quick to buckle under the pressure. Not Paul. He wanted to please God and win His stamp of approval, so he endured. He was unstoppable.

Not only did Paul endure pressure, but he committed himself to a lifestyle of godly character. Here Paul divides character into eight distinct qualities, two sets of four qualities. The first four are consistent qualities of Paul's life: purity, understanding, patience and kindness.

Purity is at the top of Paul's list. He lived in a culture of rampant sexual immorality, yet he was determined to keep his thoughts and lifestyle pure. Like many people who travel a great deal because of their work, he could have gone to a strange city and said, "Here's my chance to do what I've always wanted to do—and no one will ever find out." But Paul guarded his purity.

Understanding comes next. As he told the Christians in Rome, Paul continually renewed his mind (see Romans 12:2) so that he could test and prove God's will for his life. He continually bathed his mind in Scripture so that he could always be reminded of God's view of reality.

Then comes patience. Paul was patient with his difficult circumstances, patient with people, and patient with God. It's hard to wait for trials to pass. It's hard to wait for people to develop spiritual maturity. It's hard to wait for God to answer prayer. But Paul had learned the spiritual discipline of waiting.

Then there is kindness. Paul practiced thoughtfulness and courtesy toward people. He conveyed warmth and caring through his words and his tone of voice. If we want to demonstrate that the message of reconciliation has truly transformed our lives, then we should demonstrate kindness.

Paul then lists a second set of four qualities—and now he goes deeper, demonstrating the resources he relies upon in order to be a man of godly character.

First, "in the Holy Spirit." Jesus promised that He would ask the Father, and the Father would send the Spirit "to be with you forever" (see John 14:16). The Spirit is our greatest Resource, our constant Guide through life, our Counselor, Strengthener, and Comforter. Paul relied on this Resource more than any other.

Second, "and in sincere love." This, I believe, is a direct reference to what Paul said earlier, "For Christ's love compels us" (see 2 Corinthians 5:14). Knowing that Jesus loves us is a great motivation for ministry. If you read the stories of the great saints of history, they always say that the force that held them steady under pressure and persecution was a continual sense of the love and companionship of the Lord Jesus Christ. His love enables us to reflect Christlike love to others.

Third, "in truthful speech." Literally, this phrase is "the word of truth," a reference to the Scriptures. God's Word of truth contains the knowledge of how God sees life—which is the knowledge of how life truly is. You can't understand reality without studying your Bible. You can't be forewarned of the pitfalls of this life unless you face the truth contained in the Bible. And you can't know how to experience true meaning and joy in life if you don't learn from God's Word where they may be found. Paul spent a great deal of time studying God's Word of truth.

Fourth, "in the power of God." Paul didn't rely on his own strength but on the power of God. This is always the secret of a life that honors God—and a life that is honored by God. The power of God transforms lives, opens the doors that are shut, and shuts doors that are open. The power of God is, above all, the power to raise the dead.

Finally, Paul adds this fascinating clause: "with weapons of righteousness in the right hand and in the left." What does Paul mean? What is the right hand? What is the left? I believe that the right hand stands for the public life; Paul called for believers to make a public stand for righteousness, justice, equality, fair treatment, and peace. And the left hand, I believe, stands for one's personal life; Paul called for believers to be pure, holy, righteous, loving, honest, and honorable in their private dealings. Righteousness is a potent weapon, and Paul wielded this weapon in each hand, in his public life and in his private life.

Third division, verses 8–10

Here, Paul sets forth a series of paradoxes to show how his way of life confounds the world. Paul practices the ministry of reconciliation and preaches the message of reconciliation wherever he goes, regardless of his circumstances. He is faithful to his calling whether he receives glory or dishonor, whether his reputation is praised ("good report") or slandered ("bad report").

Sometimes Paul is honored as a genuine apostle—and sometimes condemned as an impostor. ("After all," some said, "Paul was not one of the Twelve.") Sometimes he is "the famous apostle Paul," and sometimes he is treated as an anonymous street preacher. When he was an up-and-coming young Pharisee named Saul, he made a name for himself, but Paul the apostle was a nobody in the Jewish world, a nobody in the Roman world. The only fame Paul craved was to be known in heaven and to have his name written in the Book of Life.

Paul notes that he has suffered so many attempts on his life that he should be dead—yet he lives on. He has been beaten, stoned, flogged, and caned, yet not killed. He suffers one sorrow after another—yet he is always rejoicing. He has nothing—yet his words make people spiritually rich. He owns nothing; he possesses everything.

Through all of these ups and downs, these triumphs and tragedies, he is the same apostle Paul, preaching the same gospel, practicing the same ministry of reconciliation that God gave him at the start. What a magnificent life he lived! Paul was a first-century original, and there will never be another man like him. God made one Paul—then He broke the mold.

But God doesn't need another Paul. He has you and me. We're originals, too. There will never be another me or another you—and that's just fine with God. He has given us the ministry of reconciliation and the message of reconciliation. We are Christ's ambassadors, and God is making His appeal to the world through you and me:

People of the twenty-first century, be reconciled to God!

28

CHOOSE LOVE, NOT COMPROMISE

2 Corinthians 6:11—7:1

A Christian man was invited to visit a lodge meeting to be considered for membership. This man was a church elder and strong in his faith and witness.

During the meeting, he met many of the members, all of whom were prominent in the community. At one point, the master of ceremonies took the Christian man aside and said, "We always close our meetings with a word of prayer. Some of the members asked that I invite you to give the closing prayer tonight. Would you do so?"

"I'd be honored," the Christian said.

"Good!" the master of ceremonies said. "Now, please keep in mind that we are a nonsectarian organization. Everyone here believes in God, of course, but our members come from various faith traditions. I trust you'll keep that in mind as you pray."

"I certainly will," said the Christian.

A few minutes later, the master of ceremonies called him to the front to give the closing prayer. So the Christian man prayed—and throughout the prayer, again and again, he referred to Jesus. He spoke of "the cross of our Lord and Savior, Jesus Christ." He thanked God the Father for sending "your Son Jesus to die for our sins." He spoke of "the resurrected Lord" and "Jesus the coming King" and "the Lamb of God who takes away the sin of the world." Throughout his prayer, this man heard people coughing nervously. Finally, he concluded, "We ask these things in the name of your Son, Jesus. Amen."

Afterwards, the master of ceremonies leaned over and, with obvious annoyance, said, "I thought I made myself clear! Some of our members do not believe in Jesus Christ! We pray to God—but we never use the name of Jesus! Your constant references to that name were offensive to some of our members!"

"Sir," the Christian said, "I didn't wish to offend anyone. But if I can't mention the name of my Lord and friend Jesus Christ in this place, then I won't be coming back." He left that night and never returned.

This man made a decision to honor a principle that we are about to explore in 2 Corinthians 6: "Do not be yoked together with unbelievers."

Obstacle No. 1: Withholding affection

Paul has just been discussing the ministry of reconciliation he has received from God. Now he is going to turn to the problems and obstacles that easily get in our way in the Christian life. If we fail to confront these problems squarely and courageously, they will defeat us morally and spiritually.

In this passage, Paul confronts two obstacles that often block our path and prevent us from achieving Christian maturity. They are withholding affection from other believers and compromising with the world. Paul writes:

> We have spoken freely to you, Corinthians, and opened wide our hearts to you. We are not withholding our affection from you, but you are withholding yours from us. As a fair exchange—I speak as to my children—open wide your hearts also. (2 CORINTHIANS 6:11–13)

Paul had a great affection for the people in Corinth, and he manifested his affection toward them in at least two ways. First, he said, "We have spoken freely to you." He communicated with them. He told them, candidly and transparently, what was taking place in his own life. He shared his feelings, his struggles, his failures, his pressures, and his problems.

We take a chance whenever we open our lives to other people. Our openness can be abused, exploited, and used against us—but authentic Christlike love is willing to take that risk. To love someone is to be vulnerable. To shut down communication is to withhold love.

This is a major problem in churches today. Christians think it is right and healthy to be closed, private persons, unwilling to communicate who they are and how they feel and where they struggle in their lives. That's a worldly attitude. The world teaches us to be private and closed. In the body of Christ, we belong to one another and must learn to be open and vulnerable with one another.

Paul loved the Corinthian believers. "We have spoken freely to you, Corinthians," he says, "and opened wide our hearts to you. We are not withholding our affection from you." Paul has opened himself to them; he has hidden nothing. Now he wants them to return his affection, not merely for his benefit but for theirs.

When Paul says that he opened his heart wide to the Corinthians, he means he showed no favoritism. His heart took in everyone, the whole congregation—not just the nice people, but the difficult ones, the hard-to-get-along-with ones. He accepted them all—but they were not loving him in return.

Love requires a response, yet the Corinthians were unresponsive. They withheld their affection. They imprisoned themselves within the narrow boundaries of their selfish lives, and they were not experiencing the richness that the Christian life has to offer.

So Paul pleaded with the Corinthians: "We are not withholding our affection from you, but you are withholding yours from us. As a fair exchange—I speak as to my children—open wide your hearts also." This is one of the most important lessons we can learn in life. Love must respond. As C. S. Lewis observed in *The Four Loves*:

> To love at all is to be vulnerable. Love anything, and your heart will certainly be wrung and possibly be broken. If you want to make sure of keeping it intact, you must give your heart to no one, not even to an animal. Wrap it carefully round with hobbies and little luxuries; avoid all entanglements; lock it up safe in the casket or coffin of your selfishness. But in that casket—safe, dark, motionless, airless—it will change. It will not be broken; it will become unbreakable, impenetrable, irredeemable. The only place outside Heaven where you can be perfectly safe from all the dangers and perturbations of love is Hell.

Over the years, I have met many Christians who have locked up their hearts in a casket. They go to church, sit in the back of the church, then leave without speaking to anyone. Perhaps they have been wounded and are protecting themselves against being hurt again. But they are shutting out love, and God did not send His Son to die in order that the world would be filled with cold, stone-walled churches filled with cold, stone-faced Christians.

Love is attractive. The world is looking for love, and if there is one place that the worldlings should be able to find it, it's in the church, which proclaims that God is love. Congregations that are open, warm, and loving are exciting and attractive. They draw people in. That's what the apostle Paul wants the Corinthian church to be.

Love cannot increase in the church unless people respond to love with love. That means we must respond to God's love by loving God—and loving one another. Jesus said that these are the two greatest commandments in Scripture: "'Love the Lord your God with all your heart and with all your soul and with all your mind.' This is the first and greatest commandment. And the second is like it: 'Love your neighbor as yourself'" (Matthew 22:37–39).

God has loved us and displayed His love in providential care. He gave us food, shelter, clothing, family, friends, and all the richness of life. He sent His Son to save us from sin, guilt, emptiness, and feelings of worthlessness. He has placed us in a family of faith and has given meaning and purpose to our lives. All of these blessings are gifts of His love. Our lives should be a response of love to His amazing love.

Obstacle No. 2: Compromising with the world

Next, Paul focuses our attention on the problem of compromising with the world—compromises that defile us and destroy our usefulness to God. He writes:

> Do not be yoked together with unbelievers. For what do righteousness and wickedness have in common? Or what fellowship can light have with darkness? What harmony is there between Christ and Belial? What does a believer have in common with an unbeliever? What agreement is there between the temple of God and idols? For we are the temple of the living God. As God has said: "I will live with them and walk among them, and I will be their God, and they will be my people."
>
> "Therefore come out from them
>   and be separate,
>   says the Lord.
> Touch no unclean thing,
>   and I will receive you."
>   "I will be a Father to you,
>   and you will be my sons and daughters,
>   says the Lord Almighty."
>
> (2 CORINTHIANS 6:14–16)

Paul writes here of becoming involved with unbelievers in such a way that these associations limit us, drag us down, and keep us from being what we ought to be in Christ. Paul says, "Do not be yoked together with unbelievers."

What is a yoke? In the culture of Paul's day, a yoke was a familiar implement of agriculture. It is a wooden frame or bar with loops at either end, fitted around the necks of two animals to tie them together and cause them to work as a team. That's what Paul speaks of here. He's thinking of a passage from the Old Testament law that says, "Do not plow with an ox and a donkey yoked together" (Deuteronomy 22:10).

This may seem like a strange command, but God had good reason for instructing Israel not to tie together two animals of a different nature. I have never seen an ox and a donkey yoked together, but once, while I was traveling in the Middle East, I saw a farmer plowing his field with a camel and a donkey under the same yoke. It would have been comical if it hadn't been sad. The camel was much taller than the donkey, and his legs were longer. Because the camel's stride was long, the little donkey had to run to keep up. The farmer let the camel set the pace, and he beat the donkey to force him to go faster. Both animals were miserable because they were unequally yoked.

That's what the Law and the apostle Paul tell us: It's cruel, inefficient, and foolish to yoke together two creatures of very different natures. The principle is obvious and makes perfect sense. Christians and non-Christians are very different creatures and should not be yoked together. When we try to put Christians and non-Christians together under a common yoke, the result is misery, pain, and the hindering of God's work.

"For what do righteousness and wickedness have in common?" asks Paul. "Or what fellowship can light have with darkness?" He sets forth pairs of polar opposites: righteousness and wickedness, light and darkness. We easily forget that the unbelievers around us are in darkness. This is not to say that a believer is superior to an unbeliever. Christians are in the light—but only because of the grace of God, not because of any innate righteousness on their part. Before Christians came to know Christ, they were unbelievers and lived in darkness, too.

In Scripture, light is a symbol of understanding, of an awareness of true reality. Imagine someone who sees life clearly, from God's point of view, yoked to someone who is in darkness, whose worldview is an unreal fantasy, whose reason for existing is not godliness but selfishness. That's a formula for disaster.

Paul continues, "What harmony is there between Christ and Belial? What does a believer have in common with an unbeliever?" Belial is another

343

name for Satan; the name means "worthlessness." That's what Satan does. He turns things of value into objects of worthlessness and futility. He takes human lives and destroys whatever potential for good there might be in those lives.

"What agreement is there between the temple of God and idols?" Paul asks. "For we are the temple of the living God. As God has said: 'I will live with them and walk among them, and I will be their God, and they will be my people.'" This is a powerful description of the glory of Christianity—the fact that God dwells within His people. Our bodies are the temples of God.

Now imagine a person who, as a temple of God, is joined to a person who is the temple of an idol. If you do not worship the true God, you worship a false god; behind every false god there are demons. So if you link the worship of God to the worship of idols, you join God worship and demon worship together. This is an unthinkable thing—a horror, a blasphemy. That's why Christians are warned against such associations.

What is a yoke?

The great unanswered question, then, is, "What is a yoke?" Is a business partnership a yoke? Is union membership a yoke? Is marriage a yoke? Is a date with a non-Christian a yoke?

We have to be careful in interpreting this metaphor. Some have taken it as a justification for complete withdrawal from the world and from all contact with non-Christians. That's not what Paul is saying. After all, just a few verses earlier, he told us we are ambassadors for Christ (see 2 Corinthians 5:20)—and you can't be an ambassador if you have no contact with the world.

God wants us to rub shoulders with the people of the world. He wants us to talk to them, love them, and minister to them so that they will receive our word when we tell them, "Be reconciled unto God." You cannot reach people from the opposite side of the Grand Canyon. You have to move among people and draw them into your life.

Jesus said, "I am sending you out like sheep among wolves" (see Matthew 10:16). That's where God expects Christians to be. We are not to withdraw from the world. We are to be in it—but not of it.

So what is the kind of yoke we should avoid? Not all associations with unbelievers are yokes. A genuine yoke has two identifying characteristics.

The first mark of a yoke: *A yoke is not easily broken*. It is a long-term or even permanent relationship. When you yoke two animals together, they cannot separate themselves. They are bound together, and they have no choice in the matter. That's why the church has always interpreted this passage as referring especially to marriage. Matrimony is a relationship that is not easily broken because the law and the state are involved in making the marriage binding. That's why this "little piece of paper" (the marriage license) is so significant. That legal document defines the binding terms of a marriage relationship.

"A woman is bound to her husband as long as he lives," Paul writes in 1 Corinthians 7:39. It's perilous and foolish to enter into a lifelong bond with an unbeliever. If a person is already in such a relationship, the bond should not be broken. But if a believer and an unbeliever are contemplating marriage, they should be warned. Paul's point is that we should not form unequal yokes; we should not enter into binding relationships that require compromise with the world and with people of unbelief.

It's easy to be drawn into such relationships. Romantic attraction is strong. Our emotions easily overpower our Christian values and principles. When we are emotionally attracted to someone, it feels right even if it's not right—and we rationalize and say, "Yes, I know that in general it is wrong to be unequally yoked. But this is different! This is real love! I can feel it!" Months or years later, what felt right turns out all wrong. The warnings of Scripture are revealed to be wise and true.

We should always obey God's Word. Feelings come and go. Emotions can trick us into making terrible decisions. Everyone who ever entered into an unequally yoked relationship against the counsel of Scripture did so because it felt right, because the people involved thought, "Our love is different." When we give more weight to emotions than to God's Word, we set ourselves up for tragedy and lifelong regret.

A young woman once wrote this prayer in her diary on her wedding day:

> Dear God,
>
> I can hardly believe that this is my wedding day. I know I haven't spent much time with you lately with all the rush of getting ready. I suppose I also feel a bit guilty because John isn't a Christian.
>
> But God, I love him so much! What else can I do? I couldn't give him up! I know you will save him somehow. You know how much I've

prayed for him and witnessed to him. Of course, I didn't want to seem too religious—I didn't want to scare him off!

John really isn't opposed to you. He just doesn't feel that he needs religion in his life right now. But I'm sure he'll change someday.

Dear God, please bless our marriage. I don't want to disobey you, but I do love him. Be with us today, and please don't let anything spoil my wedding day.

This young woman's rationalizations are obvious to everyone but herself. Her prayer could be paraphrased this way:

Dear God, I don't want to disobey you, but I must have my own way at all costs. I want what I want, even though you've told me it's wrong and it will hurt me. Please be a good God and do what I say. All I ask is that you deny your Word, step down from the throne, and let me take over. Is that too much to ask? If you can't do that, then at least don't ruin my wedding day. My will be done!

The second mark of a yoke: *A yoke constrains us.* It does not permit independent action. It forces you to comply whether you like it or not. Any relationship that does not permit a believer to follow his Lord is a yoke.

A friendship can be a yoke. Sometimes a friendship can become a possessive relationship where you feel you can't do what God wants you to do because you will offend or anger your friend. That kind of yoke must be broken. God must have first place.

A business partnership can be a yoke. Christian businesspeople sometimes find that they have unwisely entered into a relationship with people who don't respect Christian ethics and values. When you try to make Jesus the Lord of your business life and your partner is continually undermining that goal, you are unequally yoked.

There are many other examples I could cite, but the principles are clear: A yoke is any relationship that binds you and is hard to break and constrains you and limits your freedom to follow your conscience and follow your Lord. If you are involved in any relationship of this kind with an unbeliever, you will regret it one day.

Be separate

Finally, Paul tells, "'Come out from them and be separate,' says the Lord. 'Touch no unclean thing, and I will receive you. I will be a Father to you, and you will be my sons and daughters, says the Lord Almighty.'"

God is saying to us, "I love you, I want to make you my royal son, my royal daughter. I want to be a Father to you—a tender, loving Father. I can't do that while you are giving all your affection to my enemy. I can't lead you into my light while you choose the darkness. I can't lead you into my righteousness while you choose evil. I want to bless your life, but I can't do that while you choose to be yoked to everything that is opposed to me."

In the first verse of the next chapter, Paul makes this appeal:

Since we have these promises, dear friends, let us purify ourselves from everything that contaminates body and spirit, perfecting holiness out of reverence for God. (2 CORINTHIANS 7:1)

We must purify ourselves. We must throw off everything that contaminates us. We must break the yoke that weighs us down. God will not take it away from us against our will. We must willingly turn our backs on darkness and face His light.

Finally, don't make the mistake that some people make when they read this passage. They think that turning away from all the unclean things in life will make us holy. We can't make ourselves holy. Authentic holiness is a gift that God gives us at the beginning of our Christian life. As Romans 12 tells us, "I urge you, brothers, in view of God's mercy, to offer your bodies as living sacrifices, holy and pleasing to God."

We are already holy because the sacrifice of Jesus on the cross has made us holy. But our holiness is made visible and tangible when we live lives that manifest the holiness of God. That's the appeal that Paul makes to us here.

And that's what this world is waiting to see.

29

THE JOY OF REPENTANCE

2 Corinthians 7

In C. S. Lewis's fantasy novel *The Lion, the Witch and the Wardrobe* we meet a sullen and resentful boy named Edmund Pevensie. He follows his sister Lucy through the magical wardrobe into the enchanted land of Narnia. There he meets the evil White Witch, who has decreed that it is always winter in Narnia but never Christmas.

The White Witch tempts Edmund with an addictive candy called Turkish Delight. She promises him all the Turkish Delight he wants if he will bring Lucy and his other siblings to her castle. Edmund doesn't know that the witch plans to kill them all to prevent an ancient prophecy from being fulfilled.

Soon Edmund realizes that he has betrayed his siblings and allied himself with evil—but it's too late. The ancient law of Narnia gives the Witch the right to execute traitors. And Edmund is a traitor. Edmund symbolically represents all of us as human beings, lost in sin, condemned by the law.

There are also strong similarities between Lewis's tale and the gospel story. One obvious similarity is the parallel between the traitor Edmund in Lewis's story and Judas Iscariot, who betrayed Jesus.

But Lewis is careful to show that human beings always possess a thing called free will, the power to make moral choices. Our fate is not predetermined. Judas betrayed Jesus—then he committed suicide. Edmund betrayed his siblings—then he experienced redemption. How was Edmund redeemed? He did something Judas did not do: He repented.

We have all sinned. We have all broken God's law. We have all hurt others and ourselves by our actions. Because we have sinned, we need to repent.

Paul's affirming approach

Repentance is the act of changing your mind, your actions, and your life. When you repent, you take responsibility for your sin, you admit guilt and express remorse for your sin, and you resolve not to repeat the sin. Whenever possible, genuine repentance also includes making restitution for the harmful effects of your sin.

In Old Testament Hebrew, repentance was expressed by two verbs, *shuv* and *nicham*, meaning "to return" and "to feel sorrow." In the New Testament, the Greek word for repentance is *metanoia*, from *meta*, meaning "after," and *noeo*, meaning "to think." *Metanoia* suggests that a person has come to a place where he thinks differently after committing a sin and therefore changes his mind, his consciousness, his heart, and his way of life. A genuinely repentant person is one who has turned his life around and now proceeds in a new and changed direction.

In 2 Corinthians 7, Paul makes an appeal to the Corinthian Christians to repent. In the process, he shows us how all such appeals should be made:

> Make room for us in your hearts. We have wronged no one, we have corrupted no one, we have exploited no one. I do not say this to condemn you; I have said before that you have such a place in our hearts that we would live or die with you. I have great confidence in you; I take great pride in you. I am greatly encouraged; in all our troubles my joy knows no bounds. (2 Corinthians 7:2–4)

Notice Paul's affirming approach. He does not condemn, nor does he accuse. Instead, he does three positive things.

First, Paul states that he himself has a clear conscience: "Make room for us in your hearts. We have wronged no one, we have corrupted no one, we have exploited no one." There had probably been murmured accusations about Paul, and he makes it clear that he has never done the things he's accused of.

If Paul is guilty of any wrongdoing, then that is where he should begin—with honest confession and repentance on his own part. But Paul has searched his own conscience, and it is clear. He has established the truth of the matter, and he states that he has wronged no one.

Second, Paul states that he does not condemn the Corinthian believers. He writes, "I do not say this to condemn you; I have said before that you have such a place in our hearts that we would live or die with you." The apostle Paul is a great student of human nature. He knows that when calling someone to repentance, the worst thing you can do is lash out with condemnation. When people feel attacked, they naturally defend themselves. It's impossible to be repentant and defensive at the same time.

349

So Paul says, in effect, "I'm not attacking you; I'm not condemning you. I'm on your side. I'm so committed to you that I would willingly live or die with you." That's an extravagant statement of affection. Who could feel attacked or condemned after hearing such words? Who could feel defensive? No one.

Third, Paul strongly affirms the Corinthian Christians. "I have great confidence in you," he writes. "I take great pride in you. I am greatly encouraged; in all our troubles my joy knows no bounds." This is a resounding statement of affirmation and encouragement. Paul reassures the Corinthians that his pride in them is undiminished, his confidence in them is strong, and he encourages them to go further.

This is important: If you have to tell someone he is wrong, start out with something right. Encourage him. Affirm your love and commitment to the relationship. Show your strong and unshakable support.

If you love, you level

The apostle goes on to show the Corinthians how he identified with their hurts:

> For when we came into Macedonia, this body of ours had no rest, but we were harassed at every turn—conflicts on the outside, fears within. But God, who comforts the downcast, comforted us by the coming of Titus, and not only by his coming but also by the comfort you had given him. He told us about your longing for me, your deep sorrow, your ardent concern for me, so that my joy was greater than ever. (2 CORINTHIANS 7:5–7)

Paul's reason for writing this letter was his distress and anxiety for the Corinthians as he was waiting for Titus to return from Corinth. In 2 Corinthians 2 Paul tells us he was so restless in mind and spirit that he couldn't wait at Troas for Titus but went into Macedonia to find him. There he located Titus and received good news from Corinth.

We don't know exactly what Paul means when he says, "conflicts on the outside, fears within." Perhaps there was some difficulty in Macedonia. He had been imprisoned once in Philippi; there may have been enemies there who made life difficult for him. In any event, Paul had many troubles in Macedonia. Life is frequently that way, isn't it? Troubles sometimes come in waves. Many things go wrong at once. We face external conflicts while battling internal anxieties. If you feel that way, you're treading where saints have trod.

It's comforting to know that God understands. Paul writes, "God, who comforts the downcast, comforted us by the coming of Titus." The presence of Titus made the pressure and anxiety bearable. When we find ourselves in hot water, God often uses other believers to adjust the temperature and make life bearable.

Next, Paul goes right to the heart of the matter: The need for repentance. Here, Paul begins his gentle and loving confrontation:

> Even if I caused you sorrow by my letter, I do not regret it. Though I did regret it—I see that my letter hurt you, but only for a little while—yet now I am happy, not because you were made sorry, but because your sorrow led you to repentance. For you became sorrowful as God intended and so were not harmed in any way by us. (2 CORINTHIANS 7:8–9)

This is a reference to what Bible scholars call Paul's "severe letter." Paul may be referring to the lost first letter, the lost third letter, or his second letter, which we now know as 1 Corinthians. In any case, it was a straightforward letter, and the Corinthian believers were stung by his words. Paul knew it would be a painful letter when he wrote it, and he says that when he sent it he himself was distressed ("I did regret it").

Earlier, Paul had said, "For I wrote you out of great distress and anguish of heart and with many tears, not to grieve you but to let you know the depth of my love for you" (2 Corinthians 2:4). How human the apostle Paul is! After he sent that earlier letter, he had second thoughts about it. "I don't regret it now," he says, "but I felt terrible about it at the time." Have you ever sent a letter or an e-mail like that? You knew it would cause pain, yet you felt that it had to be said. Paul knew his letter would cause pain, but he believed that it would be a surgical kind of hurt, intended to heal, not harm.

If you love someone, then speak the truth in love. You might say, "I don't want to hurt anyone's feelings!" But the truth is that you don't want to get yelled at or you just don't want to take the time. We must stop lying to ourselves and excusing our cowardly silence. When we fail to confront sin, it's not because we love the sinner too much; it's because we love too little. It's because our cowardice, laziness, or fear exceeds our love.

Once when I was in college, I did something foolish to get attention (to this day, I'm so embarrassed about it, I refuse to say what it was). Most of my friends laughed or made light of it—but one person loved me enough to privately confront me. "Ray," he said, "that was wrong. I hate to see you acting that way just to get noticed."

Oh, that hurt! I was instantly ashamed.

But I was grateful to know that I had one friend who cared enough to confront my stupid behavior for my own good. I knew that he loved me because he risked the relationship to tell me a truth I needed to hear. That incident cemented a friendship that has lasted a lifetime.

That's what Paul does here. He faithfully confronts these people whom he deeply loves. He tells them what's wrong in order to draw them to repentance.

Paul continues:

Godly sorrow brings repentance that leads to salvation and leaves no regret, but worldly sorrow brings death. (2 CORINTHIANS 7:10)

Whenever someone points out that something is wrong with your life, it hurts. You feel an emotional sting when someone makes you aware of a flaw in your character, a wrong belief, a base motive, or a hurtful action. The moment you hear it, you know it's true—but the truth hurts. Pain always produces a reaction. The pain of hearing you are in the wrong about something will cause you to react in one of two ways: godly sorrow or worldly sorrow.

If you respond with godly sorrow—"You're right, it's true, thank you for revealing this to me"—then you will go on to experience true repentance.

But all too often, instead of responding with godly sorrow, we lash out with worldly sorrow: "How dare you! You don't know what you're talking about! Mind your own business!" We know the criticism is true—but we deny the truth. We become defensive. We lash out at the one who risked and dared to tell us the truth. Instead of proceeding to repentance, we retreat into bitterness and worldly sorrow.

The result of worldly sorrow is death: the death of a friendship, the death of spiritual and emotional growth, the death of your character, the death of truth. If the painful truth you're rejecting is serious enough ("You're in a destructive relationship," "Your drinking is out of control,"

"You're drifting away from the Lord"), then worldly sorrow could even result in your physical or spiritual death.

True repentance

Jesus told a story about a man who had two sons (see Matthew 21:28–31). The man said to the first son, "Go and work in the field." The boy answered, "I will not." But later he repented—that is, he changed his mind and did as his father told him. Then the father said to the other son, "Go and work in the field." The boy said, "All right, sir, I'm going," but he did not go. Jesus asked the question, "Which of the two did what his father wanted?" The answer, of course: The one who repented.

Repentance is an action, not a feeling. Some people think that if you feel bad about what you've done, that's repentance. It's not. Feeling sorry means nothing if it doesn't change your actions. A feeling accomplishes nothing. It's the change of behavior that constitutes true repentance.

I well remember that when I was a young Christian, I had such poor self-esteem that I was extremely sensitive to the things people said to me. A little offhand remark could devastate me, sending me into a pit of self-pity for days. What I was feeling is what Paul calls worldly sorrow, the kind that produces anger, resentment, and death.

I had my moment of truth one day as I was talking with a Christian friend. She didn't confront me or criticize me. She didn't say anything about me at all. She was talking about herself—but what she said hit me right between the eyes.

"I used to get my feelings hurt all the time," she told me. "But I've learned that being hypersensitive to the things people say is nothing but selfishness."

She had no idea how those words stunned me. She had nailed my problem to the wall! Inside, I squirmed and thought, "No, it's not true!"—but I knew it *was* true. The reason I was so thin-skinned and easily offended was that I was self-centered. I hated that about myself—and I resolved to crucify my self-centeredness.

The next time somebody offended me, I told myself, "That's not his fault. He didn't mean to hurt me. I'm taking it the wrong way. I'm going to let this slide and focus on being more like Christ." I continued to take this attitude, and with each new experience, I felt greater freedom and deliverance. I stopped thinking the worst of people's intentions and started thinking the best. I moved from worldly sorrow to godly sorrow—and the change in my attitude was amazing.

That's what Paul is talking about in this passage. Godly sorrow acknowledges the truth, changes behavior, and leads to repentance and freedom. Worldly sorrow produces anger, bitterness, and self-pity. Godly sorrow leads to salvation from the self. Worldly sorrow leads to emotional and spiritual bondage.

Paul goes on to further describe and explain godly sorrow:

> See what this godly sorrow has produced in you: what earnestness, what eagerness to clear yourselves, what indignation, what alarm, what longing, what concern, what readiness to see justice done. At every point you have proved yourselves to be innocent in this matter. (2 CORINTHIANS 7:11)

Godly sorrow, Paul says, produces an earnestness and eagerness to live a righteous life, to completely clear out all the hidden corners of sinful habits and harmful attitudes. Godly sorrow makes the soul indignant over the stupidity and brutishness of the self. We see this godly indignation in the words of the psalmist:

> When my heart was grieved
>   and my spirit embittered,
> I was senseless and ignorant;
>   I was a brute beast before you. (PSALM 73:21–22)

Those who suffer from worldly sorrow are more to be pitied than condemned. Their minds and emotions are so brittle and inflexible that they can't bear to face the truth about themselves. They are condemned to emotional and spiritual immaturity—possibly for the rest of their lives. They go through life feeling resentful and angry. They blame others for their own faults. They are miserable and inwardly crippled. They will never be healed until they learn to stop denying the truth and defending the indefensible.

Complete confidence

Next, Paul writes about the joy of recovery when godly sorrow produces repentance in our lives:

> So even though I wrote to you, it was not on account of the one who did the wrong or of the injured party, but rather that before God you

could see for yourselves how devoted to us you are. By all this we are encouraged. (2 CORINTHIANS 7:12–13A)

Paul is saying, in effect, "The most important reason I wrote was not to straighten out this problem. My real objective was not to deal with who did what to whom. I wrote to remind you of the kind of people you are—that you are devoted, obedient, committed believers. And you are devoted to me as true friends! Recognizing the depth of your devotion is encouraging to me and should be encouraging to you as well." Paul wanted the Corinthians to know their own identity, their own character. He wanted them to feel comforted and encouraged, not criticized and condemned.

Next Paul vindicates his previous confidence in the Corinthians:

In addition to our own encouragement, we were especially delighted to see how happy Titus was, because his spirit has been refreshed by all of you. I had boasted to him about you, and you have not embarrassed me. But just as everything we said to you was true, so our boasting about you to Titus has proved to be true as well. (2 CORINTHIANS 7:13b–14)

All the positive, glowing things Paul had said about the Corinthians to Titus was vindicated by their action. That is one of the joyful things about repentance—it enables people to have confidence again in the good qualities they always saw in you.

Next, Paul says that repentance awakens respect and affection in others:

And his affection for you is all the greater when he remembers that you were all obedient, receiving him with fear and trembling. I am glad I can have complete confidence in you. (2 CORINTHIANS 7:15–16)

Titus was impressed by the Corinthians because of their repentance. Their earlier blindness shook his confidence in the Corinthian church—but their change of heart more than restored it.

I once felt God calling me to confront a man for a harsh accusation he made. I saw in him some of the same self-righteousness he was criticizing in another believer. When I pointed it out to him, he looked shocked and stunned. I could see the pain on his face. He wanted to defend himself and say I was wrong—but he knew it was true.

He was quiet for a long time as he thought the matter over. Then he said, "Ray, thank you for loving me enough to tell me the truth about myself. I can see that you were absolutely right."

My esteem and respect for him soared. I had always thought that he was a wise and godly man—which is why I had been disappointed to hear him criticize another brother. When he admitted his error and repented, he more than restored my confidence in him. I felt the same way of him that Paul felt toward the Corinthians: "I am glad I can have complete confidence in you."

When we repent, our joy increases. Indeed, everyone's joy increases! Godly sorrow leads to repentance, and repentance leads to rejoicing.

30

HILARIOUS CHRISTIANS!

2 Corinthians 8 and 9

Do you remember the fable of "Stone Soup"? The story is thought to have originated centuries ago near the village of Almeirim, Portugal, though versions of the story have been told for many years in villages all across Europe.

According to the story, three soldiers passed through Almeirim on their way home from fighting in a war. The soldiers asked for some food, but the villagers said, "The war has left us poor and hungry. There's not one bite of food in this entire province. If we haven't anything to feed our children, how can we feed three soldiers?"

"Never mind, then," the soldiers said. "Just lend us a large cauldron and let us have some water and three large stones. We'll make stone soup and have a great feast!"

The baffled villagers found a huge cauldron and three large stones. The soldiers built a fire in the town square, set the pot over the fire, then filled the pot with water from the well, and tossed in the stones. Soon the water began to boil. The soldiers sat around the pot and sang army songs as the villagers looked on in amazement.

"Ah!" one soldier said. "Stone soup! Have you ever smelled anything so good?"

"Oh, it smells delicious!" said the second soldier.

"It could use a little salt," said the third. "Too bad there's no salt in this village."

One of the villagers said, "I have salt!" And he rushed home to fetch it.

The soldiers continued to sniff the boiling water. "If only we had a carrot or two," said one. "Stone soup with carrots can't be beat!"

"And potatoes," said another. "Stone soup with potatoes would sure be nice."

"And cabbage," said the third. "Cabbage would make it perfect."

Different villagers took off and returned with a few carrots and potatoes and a head of cabbage. This process continued—the soldiers wishing for just one more ingredient—a soup bone, a few onions, some peas and beans, a bit of garlic or basil—and the villagers always managed to scrounge the items from a root cellar or pantry.

Finally, the soup was done—and there was enough hearty, thick soup in the cauldron for the soldiers and all of the villagers and their children. Just a couple of hours earlier, the villagers hadn't a morsel of food to spare. Now they had a feast! It happened because everybody contributed. Everybody put something in the pot.

As we come to 2 Corinthians 8 and 9, we return to a subject we previously touched on in 1 Corinthians 16—the issue of Christian giving. The amazing thing about Paul's discussion is that he spends two entire chapters talking about giving—and the word *money* isn't mentioned even once.

The privilege of giving

Paul opens with an example of giving that he encountered while in Macedonia:

> And now, brothers, we want you to know about the grace that God has given the Macedonian churches. Out of the most severe trial, their overflowing joy and their extreme poverty welled up in rich generosity. For I testify that they gave as much as they were able, and even beyond their ability. Entirely on their own, they urgently pleaded with us for the privilege of sharing in this service to the saints. And they did not do as we expected, but they gave themselves first to the Lord and then to us in keeping with God's will. (2 CORINTHIANS 8:1–5)

You'll recall from our discussion of 1 Corinthians 16 that a great famine had devastated Palestine. The Christians in Jerusalem were suffering. Paul had enlisted the cooperation of all the Gentile churches to mount a relief effort to aid the Jewish Christians. Not only would this be an expression of Christlike compassion, but it would also help break down the middle wall of partition between Jews and Gentiles in the church. When Paul mentioned the need of the Jerusalem Christians to the Macedonian churches of Philippi, Thessalonica, and Berea, the response was tremendous.

The Macedonian response shows us how God wants Christians to give. I find that few Christians understand the biblical view of giving, so these two chapters in 2 Corinthians are wonderfully instructive. Many Christians give from the wrong motives, give in the wrong way, or do not give at all—so we desperately need to be taught in this area.

First, Paul says that our giving should reflect the grace of God. "And now, brothers," he writes, "we want you to know about the grace that God has given the Macedonian churches." God's grace should be our number one motive for giving. If God has never done anything good for you, then don't give Him a dime. If He has blessed you, then pour out your gifts accordingly. That is always the argument of Scripture.

The Old Testament decreed that a tithe should be given—that is, a 10 percent religious tax. This tax was levied on the people for the support of the priesthood, people who made their living by religious service. But when you come to the New Testament, you find that the old-style priesthood is replaced by the priesthood of all believers. Every Christian is a priest. We are a royal kingdom of priests, so there is no tax to support a separate religious class.

The New Testament never legislates a tax on believers. Christians are never told to tithe in the New Testament. Many churches today teach tithing, and I am always sorry to see that. Under the new covenant, giving is not a duty or a legal requirement. Giving is a privilege we partake of to express the gratitude of our hearts for God's grace.

Why do Christians usually give? Some give to get a tax write-off. We'd rather see our money go to God than to the government, so we write a check to the church.

Others give to enhance their reputation. The very first deaths recorded in the early church occurred when a couple, Ananias and Sapphira, donated a portion of the proceeds from a real estate sale—then claimed they had given all. They sought a reputation as big donors. God dealt severely with their hypocrisy (see Acts 5:1–11).

I have known people who gave large amounts of money because they were afraid of dying and they wanted to make brownie points with God. They felt that giving hundreds of thousands of dollars might help their standing at the judgment seat.

God is very concerned about motives, and these three motives for giving are all wrong motives. The Macedonians gave for the right reason: Their hearts were moved by the grace of God. The extent of their giving is highlighted by the apostle Paul.

The Macedonians were not rich. In fact, according to Paul, the Macedonians gave "out of the most severe trial." These churches were suffering persecution. You might think this would make the Macedonians want to conserve their resources. Persecuted people never know how much they might need for their own survival. Yet, Paul says, "their overflowing joy and their extreme poverty welled up in rich generosity."

The Macedonians weren't giving spare change. They were scraping together what little they had and pooling it to produce rich generosity. They could have said to Paul, "Don't talk to us about the saints in Jerusalem. Don't pass the collection plate here. We're already starving!" But they had been touched by the grace of God. Paul says that their affliction and poverty motivated them to give. They didn't just give according to their means; they gave beyond their means. "For I testify," Paul says, "that they gave as much as they were able, and even beyond their ability."

A man was sitting in church as the offering was being taken. The usher handed the man the plate, and the man hesitated, the plate in one hand, his open wallet in the other. "Sir? Is something wrong?" the usher asked.

"I'm just trying to decide what to give," the man said. "I think I could give ten dollars and not feel it."

"In that case," the usher said, "why don't you give twenty dollars and feel it?"

Our goal should not be to give and not feel it. It is only when we truly feel it that the real blessing of giving comes upon our lives. Some say, "Give until it hurts." God says, "Give until it feels good!" That's how the Macedonians gave.

Paul writes, "Entirely on their own, they urgently pleaded with us for the privilege of sharing in this service to the saints." It seems that Paul was reluctant to tell them about the urgent needs in Jerusalem because he didn't think the Macedonians could afford to give. When they heard about the needs, they pleaded for an opportunity to contribute. One mark of a heart that's been touched by God is that it counts giving as a privilege.

Jesus became poor to make us rich

Once you have given yourself to the Lord, the rest is easy. The Old Testament mindset was "Ten percent is the Lord's, and 90 percent is mine." The New Testament mindset is "One hundred percent belongs to the Lord. I am merely a steward, holding these things in trust on behalf of the Lord."

This is not just Paul's teaching; it's the teaching of Jesus. Some people once asked Jesus whether they should pay taxes or not. He asked for a coin and held it up. "Whose image is on this coin?" he asked. The people answered, "Caesar's." Jesus replied, in effect, "Give to Caesar the things that have Caesar's picture on them, the things that belong to Caesar, but give to God the things that have the image of God upon them, the things that belong to God" (see Matthew 22:20–21; Mark 12:16–17; Luke 20:24–25).

What things have the image of God stamped on them? We do! We are made in His image. So Jesus says we are to give to God the things that are God's, the things that have His image on them. Give that and it will be enough—because it will be everything we are and have.

Next, Paul says:

> So we urged Titus, since he had earlier made a beginning, to bring also to completion this act of grace on your part. But just as you excel in everything—in faith, in speech, in knowledge, in complete earnestness and in your love for us—see that you also excel in this grace of giving.
>
> I am not commanding you, but I want to test the sincerity of your love by comparing it with the earnestness of others. (2 CORINTHIANS 8:6–8)

Paul does not use pressure or guilt. He does not manipulate the Corinthians by saying, "Let's see if you can out-give the Macedonians! We'll set up two giant cardboard thermometers, one for the Macedonians, one for the Corinthians, and make this a contest to see who can give the most!" Paul doesn't do this. In fact, he's careful to remove all pressure, saying, "I am not commanding you."

Paul's argument is, "The Macedonians gave because their love was genuine. They were moved by the grace of God. If you give on that basis, you can demonstrate that your love is as genuine as theirs." Then Paul cites the example of Jesus:

> For you know the grace of our Lord Jesus Christ, that though he was rich, yet for your sakes he became poor, so that you through his poverty might become rich. (2 CORINTHIANS 8:9)

Throughout His earthly life, Jesus was poor. When He wanted to show whose image was on a Roman coin, He had to borrow the coin. Everything Jesus used was borrowed—His food, His clothing, the donkey He rode into Jerusalem, and even the tomb in which He was buried. On one occasion, when the disciples all went to their own homes, Jesus went to the Mount of Olives because He had no home.

Here, Paul says that Jesus "was rich, yet for your sakes He became poor." When was Jesus rich? He tells us in His prayer in the upper room: "And now, Father, glorify me in your presence with the glory I had with you before the world began" (see John 17:5). He became poor when He became a human being. Why did Jesus become poor? So that we might be rich, says Paul. He made us rich by paying the debt of sin that we could never pay, and by making us heirs of the King.

According to your means

Next, Paul shares with us some practical principles of giving:

> And here is my advice about what is best for you in this matter: Last year you were the first not only to give but also to have the desire to do so. Now finish the work, so that your eager willingness to do it may be matched by your completion of it, according to your means. For if the willingness is there, the gift is acceptable according to what one has, not according to what he does not have. (2 CORINTHIANS 8:10–12)

When Titus first visited Corinth, he apparently announced the need of the saints in Jerusalem. At that time, many promised to give to that need. They promised to take up a collection, but it was never taken. Here it is, a year later, and Paul reminds them of this fact. There is a hint that some Corinthian believers were unable to give the amount they had promised, so they were waiting until they could scrape it together.

Paul says they should not delay but should give what they can. "Now finish the work," he writes, "so that your eager willingness to do it may be matched by your completion of it, according to your means." Notice that last phrase, "according to your means." God does not expect us to give out of a blessing we have not received. He doesn't expect us to deprive our own families of food and shelter in order to provide food and shelter for someone else. So Paul adds, "If the willingness is there, the gift is acceptable according to what one has, not according to what he does not have."

Again, we see that God is more interested in the motives of the heart than in the size of the gift. So give according to what you have, not according to some standard that has nothing to do with your own situation. Don't worry if you can't give as much as the next person. Just give what you can and it will be enough in God's eyes.

Another principle emerges as Paul continues:

Our desire is not that others might be relieved while you are hard pressed, but that there might be equality. At the present time your plenty will supply what they need, so that in turn their plenty will supply what you need. Then there will be equality, as it is written: "He who gathered much did not have too much, and he who gathered little did not have too little." (2 CORINTHIANS 8:13–15)

Some see Paul's use of the word *equality* as justification for socialism, a system of redistribution of wealth. Socialism says, "From each according to his ability, to each according to his need." This is not what Paul advocates. He does not say that everyone should have an exactly equal level of income and possessions. Rather, he is arguing that there should be an equality of response. In effect, he is saying, "You are supplying what they lack right now; later, perhaps, it will be your turn to receive, and they will supply what you lack in an equal fashion. This way, no one hoards a surplus, and no one suffers need. Everyone gets to give and receive."

Paul supports this teaching with a quotation from the Old Testament, where God took care of Israel by supplying bread from heaven that the people called manna. They gathered the manna every day, and it was enough to feed a crowd of two million people. The Scriptures tell us,

The Israelites did as they were told; some gathered much, some little. And when they measured it by the omer, he who gathered much did not have too much, and he who gathered little did not have too little. Each one gathered as much as he needed. (EXODUS 16:17–18)

Paul uses this event as a parable to illustrate how we should live and give.

Dr. Donald Grey Barnhouse, the great Bible expositor, was once asked a question by a skeptic, an unbeliever. "Dr. Barnhouse," the questioner said, "the Bible claims that two million Israelites lived in a desert for forty years without any way to grow crops. How did they survive?"

"God," Dr. Barnhouse replied.

That's the answer. God gives us what we need. He is the Source of life and blessing. All we have comes from Him—and He gives us the privilege and joy of thanking Him by sharing and meeting the needs of people around us.

Insuring absolute integrity

Next, Paul gives us another practical principle about giving, drawn from the example of Paul's partner in ministry, Titus:

> I thank God, who put into the heart of Titus the same concern I have for you. For Titus not only welcomed our appeal, but he is coming to you with much enthusiasm and on his own initiative. And we are sending along with him the brother who is praised by all the churches for his service to the gospel. What is more, he was chosen by the churches to accompany us as we carry the offering, which we administer in order to honor the Lord himself and to show our eagerness to help. We want to avoid any criticism of the way we administer this liberal gift. For we are taking pains to do what is right, not only in the eyes of the Lord but also in the eyes of men.
>
> In addition, we are sending with them our brother who has often proved to us in many ways that he is zealous, and now even more so because of his great confidence in you. As for Titus, he is my partner and fellow worker among you; as for our brothers, they are representatives of the churches and an honor to Christ. Therefore show these men the proof of your love and the reason for our pride in you, so that the churches can see it. (2 CORINTHIANS 8:16–24)

Here we find an important principle: Giving requires that the control of donated funds be vested in several individuals, not just one. Paul had the churches appoint other men to go with Titus to Corinth to take up the collection for Jerusalem. Paul is careful to see that this fund not be controlled by any single person. Instead, several people of proven integrity should bear this responsibility.

Three men were given the task of taking the donations from Corinth to Jerusalem. One was Titus, who went to Corinth and brought word back to Paul.

Then Paul mentions another man, though he does not give his name. This second man is described as being famous among the churches for his service to the gospel—that is, for his preaching and teaching. From these clues, many scholars deduce that this man was Luke, the beloved physician, a traveling companion of Paul's and the author of the gospel of Luke and the book of Acts.

Finally, Paul mentions another man, also unnamed, whom Paul identifies as "our brother who has often proved to us in many ways that he is zealous, and now even more so because of his great confidence in you." It is impossible to say who this might be.

We don't know why Paul didn't name these men in his letter. The important issue in this passage, however, is not their names but the principle of financial responsibility. Paul sent Titus as a steward of the donations, and the other two men were chosen by the churches. This insured that no single individual could have too much influence, and would have no opportunity to juggle the books. The Lord's money must be handled by people who are trustworthy, and they must be held accountable for their stewardship.

There is another principle embedded in this same passage. Let's look again at two of these verses:

> We want to avoid any criticism of the way we administer this liberal gift. For we are taking pains to do what is right, not only in the eyes of the Lord but also in the eyes of men. (2 CORINTHIANS 8:20–21)

Many Christian leaders today feel no need to be open and subject to scrutiny in their handling of the Lord's resources. If asked to give an accounting, they say, "Why? Don't you trust me?" Paul says that believers who bear a financial responsibility should avoid even the faintest hint of impropriety; that's why Paul says he takes pains to do what is right, not only in God's sight but also in the sight of men, in the realm of appearances.

When I was a young Christian, I attended a church where the pastor had total, unquestioned control of church finances. He was not accountable to anyone. He took the offerings and deposited them in the bank in his own name. He even owned the church building. At one point, it became clear that the pastor was mishandling church funds and appropriating money for his personal use. Before the dust settled, the church had split and the Christian witness in that community was damaged. My own faith was bruised. All this harm could have been avoided if the church had insisted on responsible checks and balances for the handling of church funds.

Hilarious giving

Next, Paul points out another reason for sending these three brothers as stewards:

> There is no need for me to write to you about this service to the saints. For I know your eagerness to help, and I have been boasting about it

to the Macedonians, telling them that since last year you in Achaia were ready to give; and your enthusiasm has stirred most of them to action. But I am sending the brothers in order that our boasting about you in this matter should not prove hollow, but that you may be ready, as I said you would be. For if any Macedonians come with me and find you unprepared, we—not to say anything about you—would be ashamed of having been so confident. So I thought it necessary to urge the brothers to visit you in advance and finish the arrangements for the generous gift you had promised. Then it will be ready as a generous gift, not as one grudgingly given. (2 CORINTHIANS 9:1–5)

Giving must not come as the result of manipulation or pressure. Paul is saying, in essence, "I sent these three brothers to you so that you would not be embarrassed at the last minute. I know you haven't had time to get these donations all together, so I sent these men so that the matter could be taken care of before I come to you."

This statement is similar to one he made in 1 Corinthians: "On the first day of every week, each one of you should set aside a sum of money in keeping with his income, saving it up, so that when I come no collections will have to be made" (1 Corinthians 16:2). The reason he doesn't want collections made when he comes is that he doesn't want people to give on the basis of his overpowering personality.

What a contrast with the pleas for donations we hear today! Many preachers do not hesitate to wring the emotions of the audience, telling sob stories and flashing photos of crying children on the PowerPoint screen—anything to manipulate people into opening their checkbooks. I'm not saying that when there are needs to be met, we should not be allowed to hear about them. I'm talking about evangelical pitchmen who put their listeners' hearts in a vise, then squeeze in order to extract as much cash as they can. That is not a Christ-honoring way to motivate giving.

Paul goes on to write:

Remember this: Whoever sows sparingly will also reap sparingly, and whoever sows generously will also reap generously. (2 CORINTHIANS 9:6)

Here Paul offers an analogy. A farmer scatters seed to plant a crop, hoping to reap a great harvest when the crop has matured. How much seed should he scatter? If he is miserly with the seed, scattering thinly, then he should not expect a generous harvest. A generous harvest is only possible when a generous amount of seed has been planted.

The meaning is clear: When we give to God's work, we should give generously if we want to see a generous harvest. A stingy investment will yield a sparse harvest.

Next, Paul stresses that giving should be voluntary. He writes:

> Each man should give what he has decided in his heart to give, not reluctantly or under compulsion, for God loves a cheerful giver. (2 CORINTHIANS 9:7)

That last phrase is fascinating. The original order of the Greek words would be transliterated, "A cheerful giver God loves." The word *cheerful* in English has a connotation of wearing an affable smile. The original Greek word *hilaros* (from which we get our word *hilarious*) is stronger than that. It has connotations of being merry, joyous, and eager. A *hilaros* giver does not merely wear a pleasant face. He's merry and joyful. He's eager to give. He has fun putting that check in the collection plate. Anytime he can give to God, it makes his day!

God really does want to see His churches filled with hilarious Christians who chuckle merrily as they write out the biggest check they can afford. He wants His churches filled with people who are glad that God has blessed them with the ability to give. He wants to see His children laughing out loud as they give to support God's work.

If people have to be shamed or cajoled into giving, they should keep their money. "Each man should give what he has decided in his heart to give," Paul says, "not reluctantly or under compulsion." God doesn't need anyone's money. He has all the money in the world. But He truly wants more hilarious Christians who get their jollies through hilarious giving!

Expectant giving

Next, Paul writes:

> And God is able to make all grace abound to you, so that in all things at all times, having all that you need, you will abound in every good work. As it is written:
>
> > "He has scattered abroad his gifts to the poor;
> > his righteousness endures forever." (2 CORINTHIANS 9:8–9)

True giving, Paul says, must be expectant giving. You are dealing with God, and He is able to give back far more than you can ever give. Many people would say, "Hold it right there! You're talking about giving out of selfish motives. You're encouraging people to give so that they can get."

There's nothing wrong with recognizing that giving brings benefits to our lives. God's Word expresses this truth in many places. Paul is not saying, "You should give a lot of money so that God can give you even more money in return." Nowhere does God say that if we give money to Him, then He will shower us with Cadillacs, mansions, big-screen TVs, and round-the-world trips. We give to further the work of God, and God blesses us to further His work. So whether we give or we receive, the focus is all on doing God's will and abounding in good works. Paul continues:

> Now he who supplies seed to the sower and bread for food will also supply and increase your store of seed and will enlarge the harvest of your righteousness. You will be made rich in every way so that you can be generous on every occasion, and through us your generosity will result in thanksgiving to God. (2 CORINTHIANS 9:10–11)

If you give to God in order that He might bless you and give you more so that you have more to give, then you are right in line with God's program. That's exactly what He wants. He doesn't want to give you more wealth to spend on yourself but to invest in the kingdom. If you give in order to have more material wealth to lavish on yourself, then you are giving for wrong reasons.

There are so-called Christian ministries on TV and radio that preach a twisted interpretation of this passage. These TV and radio preachers have figured out that the key to getting donations is to play on human greed. So they say, "You can't out-give God! If you send a hundred dollars to our ministry, then God will bless you many times over!"

A friend of mine once received a pitch like this in the mail. He wrote back and said, "I believe you when you say that we can't out-give God. So here's my suggestion. Instead of me sending you a hundred dollars and God giving it back to me seven times over, why don't you send me the hundred dollars. That way, God will give it back to you seven times over. I want you to get the bigger blessing!"

Not only did my friend not get a check from that ministry, but they took him off their mailing list. We must be careful not to twist God's Word into a kind of spiritual chain letter or pyramid scheme. When we give, God may bless us by giving us more money to give—or He may bless us in some nonmaterial way. Our motive for giving should not be greed but love for God and zeal for the work of His kingdom.

Giving is God-like!

Paul concludes his discussion of hilarious giving with these words:

> This service that you perform is not only supplying the needs of God's people but is also overflowing in many expressions of thanks to God. Because of the service by which you have proved yourselves, men will praise God for the obedience that accompanies your confession of the gospel of Christ, and for your generosity in sharing with them and with everyone else. And in their prayers for you their hearts will go out to you, because of the surpassing grace God has given you. Thanks be to God for his indescribable gift! (2 CORINTHIANS 9:12–15)

Paul says that if you give according to the law of harvest, God will give back. His giving will take several forms.

First, God will awaken gratitude in those to whom you give. God's people will overflow with expressions of thanks to God. I have seen this kind of thanksgiving many times in our congregation as people have stood up in a worship service, sometimes with tears running down their faces, rejoicing that the body of Christ has supplied something they lacked. Whenever I hear God people express thanks to God for the generosity of the body, I feel richly repaid.

Second, God will be glorified by the thanksgiving and praise of many people. It delights God to see His people respond with love and generosity to human needs—and it pleases Him to hear other people give praise for the generosity of God's people. Paul writes, "Men will praise God for the obedience that accompanies your confession of the gospel of Christ, and for your generosity in sharing with them and with everyone else."

Third, God will motivate people to pray for you. You, the giver of a gift, will become the recipient and beneficiary of other people's prayers. Paul writes, "And in their prayers for you their hearts will go out to you, because of the surpassing grace God has given you." Because people pray for you, heaven will open and pour out blessings on you in ways you never expected.

Paul concludes, "Thanks be to God for his indescribable gift!" Giving is God-like! When we give, we imitate God.

Throughout Scripture, we are reminded that we should give because we have richly received. We have been blessed to live in a land of opportunity and great wealth. There are few people reading these words who don't have wealth and possessions in excess of their basic needs—wealth that could be invested in God's kingdom.

Freely we have received. As imitators of God, let us freely give!

31

FIGHTING THE FORTRESS OF EVIL

2 Corinthians 10:1—11:15

We are about to read some of the strongest language used by the apostle Paul in any of his letters. Because his tone is so severe, some Bible scholars think that this was not originally part of 2 Corinthians but a fragment of an earlier letter that was tacked onto 2 Corinthians. Some even think that this may be the lost severe letter that Paul referred to when he wrote, "For I wrote you out of great distress and anguish of heart and with many tears" (2 Corinthians 2:4a).

I think there is a much simpler explanation for the abrupt change of tone in Paul's letter at this point. I think Paul took a break in dictation. As he traveled from place to place, he dictated his letters, usually at night. He might start dictating a new section of a letter one day or even several days after leaving off the previous section. These interruptions could explain some of the sudden changes of tone and subject that we encounter in his writings from time to time.

Chapter 10 deals with a subject different from that in chapters 8 and 9—and it is directed to a different audience. The previous section was directed at the entire church; chapter 10 is directed specifically at the false teachers in the church.

This is an instructive theme for us, because there are false teachers all around us, within and outside of the church. Some of these false teachers are easy to spot. Some are dangerously subtle. All false teachers have this in common: Whether they know it or not, they are used by Satan to derail the church and rob Christians of their liberty and joy in the Lord.

Weapons of the flesh

Paul opens chapter 10 with these words:

> By the meekness and gentleness of Christ, I appeal to you—I, Paul, who am "timid" when face to face with you, but "bold" when away! I beg you

371

that when I come I may not have to be as bold as I expect to be toward some people who think that we live by the standards of this world. For though we live in the world, we do not wage war as the world does. The weapons we fight with are not the weapons of the world. On the contrary, they have divine power to demolish strongholds. We demolish arguments and every pretension that sets itself up against the knowledge of God, and we take captive every thought to make it obedient to Christ. And we will be ready to punish every act of disobedience, once your obedience is complete. (2 CORINTHIANS 10:1–6)

False teachers are among the Corinthians, and they appear to be Christians, yet they teach destructive heresies. Paul does not normally speak so sharply. In fact, he refers to himself in the same way his enemies in Corinth described him: "I, Paul, who am 'timid' when face to face with you, but 'bold' when away!" The false teachers said, "Don't pay any attention to Paul. He's just a paper tiger. He sounds impressive when he writes, but when he comes in person, he's timid and meek."

Notice, too, that Paul links his enemies' accusation of timidity to the character of Jesus Christ: "By the meekness and gentleness of Christ." Our Lord was meek and gentle, but there were times when He spoke sharply. Paul says, in effect, "When I come to Corinth, I will act as Jesus did. Like the Lord, I may seem meek and gentle—but make no mistake, I will deal forcefully with those who corrupt the truth."

Paul goes on to write of weapons and warfare: "For though we live in the world, we do not wage war as the world does. The weapons we fight with are not the weapons of the world. On the contrary, they have divine power to demolish strongholds." At this point, I think we should note that the New International Version takes liberties with this passage. The Greek word translated "the world" here literally means "the flesh." So to be literally accurate, let's look at the New American Standard translation:

For though we walk in the flesh, we do not war according to the flesh, for the weapons of our warfare are not of the flesh, but divinely powerful for the destruction of fortresses. We are destroying speculations and every lofty thing raised up against the knowledge of God, and we are taking every thought captive to the obedience of Christ, and we are ready to punish all disobedience, whenever your obedience is complete. (2 CORINTHIANS 10:3–6 NASB)

I can understand why the NIV translators changed the wording, because the concepts of the flesh and the world are closely linked. Whenever the Scriptures refer to the flesh, there is a strong connotation of worldliness and selfishness. When a group of self-centered people form a society, they create a fleshly and self-centered society that the Bible refers to as "the flesh" or "the world."

The kingdom of God is continually at war with the kingdom of the world, the kingdom of the flesh, the kingdom of the self. So Paul says that we Christians do not war against the fleshly, worldly forces of this world with fleshly, worldly weapons. Instead, Christians employ the weapons of spiritual warfare, the weapons of the kingdom of God.

Our first weapon: God's truth

What are the weapons of the flesh? What are the weapons the world uses to solve its problems? Intimidation, coercion, pressure, and power. Whenever you see pressure groups marching and picketing, striking and boycotting, shouting and chanting slogans, you are seeing the weapons of the flesh in action. Whenever you see threats, intimidation, manipulation, wheedling, and cajoling, you see the weapons of the flesh in action.

We see weapons of the flesh used all the time in the political process, in situations of labor disputes and campus unrest and various political movements. The weapons of the flesh are unrighteous weapons. They are intended to frighten and bully and impose change by force. People who use the weapons of the flesh say, "The ends justify the means." In other words, "We are fighting for a good cause. Who cares if we are using unrighteous weapons as long as our cause is right?"

Followers of Christ always reject the weapons of the flesh. We know that the ends never justify the means. Unrighteous weapons do nothing but dishonor and invalidate a righteous cause. You cannot advance God's truth with coercion, intimidation, manipulation, or threats.

We wage war, Paul says, but we use a different order of weaponry. Our weapons have the power of God behind them, and they are capable of destroying strongholds of evil. Our weapons are able to tear down speculations and theories, ideas and ideologies that are lifted up against the knowledge of God. Our weapons can seize disobedient human thoughts and take them prisoner, forcing them to obey Christ.

Paul never states in this passage what these weapons are. Why doesn't he? Because the Corinthians already know what the weapons of righteousness are. Paul has referred to these weapons in various ways and in various places in his letters. We find references to these weapons scattered throughout Scripture.

The first weapon is Scripture—the truth of God. As Christians, we have been given an insight into reality that others do not have. We know what is at work behind the scenes of the world, and we know how to do battle in that invisible realm. As Paul wrote to the Ephesians,

> For our struggle is not against flesh and blood, but against the rulers, against the authorities, against the powers of this dark world and against the spiritual forces of evil in the heavenly realms. (EPHESIANS 6:12)

People are not our enemy. People may attack us, ridicule us, slander us, and blaspheme our Lord, but people are not the enemy. Our enemy is not made of flesh and blood. We are at war against rulers, authorities, powers, and spiritual forces of evil in the unseen realms. We are at war against Satan and his demons.

Even when people wound us and persecute us, we are not to lash back at them. Our response should be the same as the response of our Lord: "Father, forgive them, for they know not what they do." This is the truth that the Word of God reveals to us. When you understand the Word of God, you are looking at life as it really is. So our first and greatest weapon is truth—the truth of God as revealed in His Word.

Our other weapons: love, faith, prayer, and service

Again and again, the Word of God links truth with love: "speaking the truth in love" (Ephesians 4:15). Love is a powerful weapon—and it is a godly weapon, not a fleshly one. When you treat people with patience instead of anger, forgiveness instead of bitterness, then you win them over. As Abraham Lincoln once said, the best way to eliminate your enemies is to turn them into friends.

The Word of God links love with faith. Jesus said to one of the seven churches in Revelation, "I know your deeds, your love and faith" (see Revelation 2:19). And Paul told the Galatians, "The only thing that counts is faith expressing itself through love" (Galatians 5:6). Faith is not mere mental assent to a set of doctrines and creeds; rather, it is the eager expectation that God will act in our lives. It is the active belief that Jesus is the Lord of history and the Lord of our lives.

Linked to faith is prayer. We see the power of prayer throughout Scripture and throughout our daily lives. The Word of God exhorts us to pray and seek the prayer support of other believers, asking God to act and change events. For example, Paul writes to the Thessalonians, "And pray that we may be delivered from wicked and evil men, for not everyone has faith" (2 Thessalonians 3:2). Again and again the biblical and historical record testifies that events have been drastically altered by Christians who pray.

Linked to prayer is service. The Word of God says, "Do good to those who hate you . . . pray for those who mistreat you" (see Luke 6:27–28). Pray and do good. Most of us are willing to pray—but are we willing to serve? Are we willing to back up prayers with deeds? History is changed when Christians pray—and when Christians serve.

The fortress of falsehood

Paul uses vivid metaphors to describe the evils and errors of false teachings. He calls them "fortresses" (or, in some translations, "strongholds"). A fortress is a fortified castle, with walls, turrets, towers, and moats, defended by soldiers. It's difficult and dangerous to attack an enemy in his fortress. To lay siege to a fortress can take months or years and cost many lives. So this is a vivid description of the evil we face.

Why is it so difficult to defeat heresies and cults? Why are so many theories around to explain why Jesus supposedly is not God, or that He didn't die on the cross, or that He lived a life that is very different from the one described by the Gospels? Why are so many churches cherry picking the Scriptures, choosing to believe or reject various doctrines based purely on their biases? It's because evil is a fortress; error is a stronghold. False teaching is forcibly defended by the kingdom of Satan.

Paul says, "We are destroying speculations and every lofty thing raised up against the knowledge of God, and we are taking every thought captive to the obedience of Christ." The word *speculations* literally means "reasonings" in the Greek. It refers to the intellectual process of rationalizing and defending an idea.

If you have ever debated in school, you know that even falsehood can be rationally defended. On debating teams, students are taught to argue the pro side of an idea for a while, then switch sides and argue the con side. Criminal attorneys routinely defend clients who are clearly guilty—and manage to prove them innocent. Reason and logic can prove that black is white, that 2 plus 2 equal 5, and that evil is good.

It's difficult to argue with evil. Falsehood is a fortress that aggressively defends itself. If you try to attack evil and error, expect to be wounded. Expect to have your character and reputation smeared. Expect to be interrupted, shouted down, and ridiculed. You will fight fairly because you are a Christian—but your enemy will cheat, lie, threaten, and attack you in ways you can't even imagine.

Never give in to falsehood—and never take up the fleshly weapons that the fortress of evil uses against you. Stick with the weapons of God, weapons Paul says are "divinely powerful for the destruction of fortresses." Wield divine weapons of Scripture, Christlike love, bold faith, fervent prayer, and loving service to others, including your enemies.

Paul also refers to "every lofty thing raised up against the knowledge of God." What are these lofty things? If you read the writings that defend error in our day, you'll often see an arrogant statement about human ability. You'll read that human beings have a nearly god-like ability to solve problems and control human destiny. The human race is afflicted with a strange and persistent insanity that makes men think that human wisdom is equal to every challenge and problem faced by the human race.

The humanists will tell you that Christianity is an obstacle to human progress. If we could just get rid of the God myth, then war would end, poverty would disappear, and people would finally love one another. This is one of Satan's most insidious lies, and the fortress of falsehood defends it with murderous zeal.

Paul also refers to the falsehoods that arise within our own hearts and souls, saying, "We are taking every thought captive to the obedience of Christ." He uses a word that refers to the imaginings of our minds, our daydreams of power, our lust for inner satisfaction, including sexual desires that are fed by pornography and lustful thoughts. You will never win the battle against the fortress of evil as long as you willingly indulge in those kinds of imaginings. So Paul tells us we must take every thought captive and submit ourselves obediently to Christ.

Once we have made our thoughts obedient to Christ, Paul says, we must be alert to deal with any outbreak of disobedience in our thoughts. He writes, "We are ready to punish all disobedience, whenever your obedience is complete." Why do we so often struggle for years against sin without ever experiencing victory? It's because we think we can stop sinful acts without controlling sinful thoughts. As long as we permit ourselves to mentally flirt with sinful imaginings, we will be unable to control our sinful behavior.

Jesus said, "For out of the heart come evil thoughts, murder, adultery, sexual immorality, theft, false testimony, slander" (Matthew 15:19). And Proverbs tells us, "For as he thinks within himself, so he is" (Proverbs 23:7 NASB). Once we win the battle over sinful habits and thoughts, we must punish every disobedient thought that arises. If we let our guard down, if we let evil imaginings to arise and gain a toehold in our minds, we will end up enslaved once more.

Paul's credentials

Next, Paul asks the Corinthians to look beyond surface appearances and examine the evidence of Paul's own life and character. "Don't just take the word of these false teachers," he says, in effect. "Instead, test their claims against reality." He writes:

> You are looking only on the surface of things. If anyone is confident that he belongs to Christ, he should consider again that we belong to Christ just as much as he. For even if I boast somewhat freely about the authority the Lord gave us for building you up rather than pulling you down, I will not be ashamed of it. I do not want to seem to be trying to frighten you with my letters. For some say, "His letters are weighty and forceful, but in person he is unimpressive and his speaking amounts to nothing." Such people should realize that what we are in our letters when we are absent, we will be in our actions when we are present. (2 CORINTHIANS 10:7–11)

This is much-needed counsel for our own day. Though there are a number of excellent Bible teachers who use the medium of television to spread the truth of God's Word with integrity (I immediately think of Dr. Billy Graham; there are others), many well-known TV preachers spread falsehood. They may have a Bible open in their hands, but their teaching distorts God's Word beyond recognition.

Many Christians blindly follow these false teachers because they are charming, colorful, and persuasive. Well-meaning believers send large sums of money to support these false teachers. Why? Because these well-meaning people do not check what these teachers say against Scripture. They don't look beyond surface appearances. So Paul says, in effect, "Open your eyes and see what is right in front of you. Here are the marks of authentic Christian ministry. Learn to recognize them so you won't be fooled."

The false teachers in Corinth may have claimed to have known Jesus before His death and resurrection. Paul's only known face-to-face encounter with Jesus was his conversion encounter on the Damascus road. Paul's enemies might have derided his conversion encounter as nothing but a hallucination. So they claimed that their understanding of Jesus was superior to Paul's.

The apostle answered those claims by saying, "If anyone is confident that he belongs to Christ, he should consider again that we belong to Christ just as much as he." Paul insists that his relationship with Christ is valid, as the Corinthian Christians ought to know. So this is Paul's first credential: He belongs to Christ.

Paul's second credential is his authority as an apostle, given him by the Lord Himself. He writes, "For even if I boast somewhat freely about the authority the Lord gave us for building you up rather than pulling you down, I will not be ashamed of it." In other words, Paul's boast of his authority from the Lord is not an exaggeration. Paul will never have to be ashamed of making a false claim. His authority is genuine.

As we look at the many people who claim to speak for God today, we have to ask ourselves, "What is their authority?" Remember Paul's warning: "You are looking only on the surface of things." We must get beyond the superficial aspects of those who make these claims—their personal charm, their eloquent style, their winning smile, and the big Bible they wave around. We must ask ourselves: "What is the evidence of this person's life?" Jesus said that the way a person lives is testimony to his authority: "Thus, by their fruit you will recognize them" (see Matthew 7:20).

What kind of fruit should we look for? The answer is obvious: We should look for the fruit of the Spirit—love, joy, peace, patience, kindness, goodness, faithfulness, gentleness and self-control (see Galatians 5:22–23). Are the followers of this leader growing more mature and Christlike? Are they finding freedom from sin and destructive habits? Do they seek Christ—or do they seek signs, wonders, and emotional highs? Are they becoming more loving and accepting—or more rigid and prejudiced? Are the leader and his followers characterized by righteousness and integrity—or by scandal and corruption?

Godly authority is always affirmed by the fruit of the leader's life and ministry. If the fruit is bad, the tree is diseased.

Four marks of authentic ministry

Next, Paul describes four marks of a ministry that is authenticated by God:

We do not dare to classify or compare ourselves with some who commend themselves. When they measure themselves by themselves and compare themselves with themselves, they are not wise. We, however, will not boast beyond proper limits, but will confine our boasting to the field God has assigned to us, a field that reaches even to you. We are not going too far in our boasting, as would be the case if we had not come to you, for we did get as far as you with the gospel of Christ. Neither do we go beyond our limits by boasting of work done by others. Our hope is that, as your faith continues to grow, our area of activity among you will greatly expand, so that we can preach the gospel in the regions beyond you. For we do not want to boast about work already done in another man's territory. But, "Let him who boasts boast in the Lord." For it is not the one who commends himself who is approved, but the one whom the Lord commends. (2 CORINTHIANS 10:12–18)

The first mark of a ministry that is authenticated by God: The ministry does not commend itself. Paul says, "We do not dare to classify or compare ourselves with some who commend themselves. When they measure themselves by themselves and compare themselves with themselves, they are not wise."

I wince to see Christian leaders commending themselves. Their literature and Web sites announce, "Dr. Jones is a dynamic, internationally known speaker!" Or, "Rev. Smith is the universally acclaimed author of thirty best-selling Christian books!" Authentic ministry is given by God, and God's commendation is all that counts. As someone once said, "There are no great preachers. There is only a great God."

The second mark of a ministry that is authenticated by God: The ministry enters doors that God has opened. How did Paul come to Corinth, where he founded the Corinthian church? God opened the door. You can trace the story in the book of Acts.

It started back with that Macedonian call, where Paul had a vision one night from a man in Macedonia saying, "Come across into Europe and help us" (see Acts 16:9). In response, Paul went to Philippi. There he got into trouble and ended up in jail. When he got out, he went to the next city, Thessalonica. Again, his preaching met with opposition and he was driven away. He went to Berea—and again there was trouble and a riot. He went to Athens and his message was rejected.

Finally he came to Corinth, armed with nothing but the power of the Spirit of God. All alone, he preached on street corners and in the marketplace. A convert here, a convert there—and the Corinthian church was founded. This is what Paul refers to when he writes, "We are not going too far in our boasting, as would be the case if we had not come to you, for we did get as far as you with the gospel of Christ."

God closed all the doors marked Philippi, Thessalonica, Berea, and Athens—then he opened a door marked Corinth. All Paul had to do was walk through the door and start preaching. The open door of Corinth authenticated the ministry of Paul among the Corinthians.

The third mark of a ministry that is authenticated by God: Genuine ministry reaches out to the unreached.

Paul writes, "Neither do we go beyond our limits by boasting of work done by others. Our hope is that, as your faith continues to grow, our area of activity among you will greatly expand, so that we can preach the gospel in the regions beyond you. For we do not want to boast about work already done in another man's territory." Paul says that he is eager for the Corinthians to increase in faith to a point where Paul is able to move out beyond them, to regions where the gospel has never penetrated before.

Sometimes a Christian will move his membership from Church A to Church B—and the pastor of Church A will get upset and accuse Church B's pastor of sheep stealing. What a short-sighted attitude! There are thousands of unreached people around every church. Pastors should never get possessive about the sheep in their flock. Instead, they should continually increase their flocks by reaching the lost.

The fourth mark of a ministry that is authenticated by God: The minister exalts God, not himself.

Paul writes, "But, 'Let him who boasts boast in the Lord.' For it is not the one who commends himself who is approved, but the one whom the Lord commends." Paul knew he was incapable of accomplishing anything for Christ. The only that mattered was what Christ did through him. His attitude was, "I didn't do it. God did it through me. What a privilege to be an instrument in God's hands."

A simple relationship

In the opening verses of 2 Corinthians 11, Paul writes:

> I hope you will put up with a little of my foolishness; but you are already doing that. I am jealous for you with a godly jealousy. I prom-

ised you to one husband, to Christ, so that I might present you as a pure virgin to him. But I am afraid that just as Eve was deceived by the serpent's cunning, your minds may somehow be led astray from your sincere and pure devotion to Christ. For if someone comes to you and preaches a Jesus other than the Jesus we preached, or if you receive a different spirit from the one you received, or a different gospel from the one you accepted, you put up with it easily enough. (2 CORINTHIANS 11:1–4)

Paul says he feels a "godly jealousy." Can jealousy ever be godly? Yes, it can. God says, "I, the Lord your God, am a jealous God" (see Exodus 20:5). He is not willing to share us with idols, demons, material things, drugs, alcohol, sex, or any other substitute god. His jealousy over us is for our own good. If we are unfaithful to Him and worship some lesser thing, we will destroy ourselves. God's jealousy is a facet of His love.

Ungodly jealousy is selfish and envious. It wants to possess and control another person. Ungodly jealousy is domineering and demands its own way. It's one of the most destructive forces in the world today.

But Paul's jealousy for the Corinthians is like God's jealousy. It is a loving jealousy that wants only the best for the Corinthian believers. Godly jealousy is selfless and devoted. Paul likens his jealousy to that of a father who has betrothed his daughter to a young bridegroom: "I promised you to one husband, to Christ," he says, "so that I might present you as a pure virgin to him."

Now a threat has arisen that threatens the spiritual virginity of the Corinthian bride. Paul says, "I am afraid that just as Eve was deceived by the serpent's cunning, your minds may somehow be led astray from your sincere and pure devotion to Christ." The New American Standard Bible puts it this way: "I am afraid that . . . your minds will be led astray from the simplicity and purity of devotion to Christ." Simplicity and purity! There is nothing more vital than maintaining the simplicity that is in Christ.

Over the years, I've noticed that when religion becomes complicated, it has drifted away from the simple realities and centralities of faith. The Jewish religion of Jesus' day was a complex maze of rituals and rules that made no sense. For example, a man could not spit in the dust on the Sabbath, because spittle and dust together made mud, which could make bricks for building houses—so spitting in the dust was working on the Sabbath! A man had to be careful to spit only on a stone during the Sabbath. This was one of hundreds of complex rules that oppressed the people in Jesus' day.

God is the Spirit of simplicity. The faith that Jesus brought us is a simple faith. Martyn Lloyd-Jones, who ministered at Westminster Chapel in London and presided over Inter-Varsity Christian Fellowship in the United Kingdom, once observed:

> As life in general becomes more and more complex, so religion tends to be affected in the same way. It seems to be assumed that if the affairs of men are so difficult and complicated, the affairs of God should be still more complicated, because they are still greater. Hence there comes a tendency to increase ceremony and ritual, and to multiply organizations and activities.... As we get further away from God, life becomes more complicated and involved.

Paul wants the Corinthians to know that Christianity is not a creed, not a set of rules or doctrines, not a theological system or institutional structure. It is fellowship with Jesus. That's why, early in 1 Corinthians, Paul writes, "God, who has called you into fellowship with his Son Jesus Christ our Lord, is faithful" (1 Corinthians 1:9). Christianity isn't a complex system of doctrines, rituals, and observances. It's a relationship, pure and simple.

The good news is free!

Paul goes on to say, "For if someone comes to you and preaches a Jesus other than the Jesus we preached, or if you receive a different spirit from the one you received, or a different gospel from the one you accepted, you put up with it easily enough." In other words, "You are listening to other teachers, taking in everything they say without questioning. I have taught you the truth—so why are you opening yourselves up to a different teaching than the one you received from me?"

Next, Paul uses irony to make a point:

> But I do not think I am in the least inferior to those "super-apostles." I may not be a trained speaker, but I do have knowledge. We have made this perfectly clear to you in every way. (2 CORINTHIANS 11:5–6)

Paul freely admits that he is not an orator. He doesn't speak with a lofty voice. He says, in effect, "I may not be a great speaker in the grand oratorical style—but style isn't as important as content. Through my plain, untrained speaking, I impart unveiled truth." Bible scholars agree that no biblical writer communicates more knowledgably and perceptively than Paul. His writings are penetrating studies in everything from theology to sociology to psychology—all the realities of life. Paul wrestles with the tough questions of life and gives us answers that satisfy the soul.

Next, Paul deals with the charge that he didn't love the Corinthians enough to let them support him:

> Was it a sin for me to lower myself in order to elevate you by preaching the gospel of God to you free of charge? I robbed other churches by receiving support from them so as to serve you. And when I was with you and needed something, I was not a burden to anyone, for the brothers who came from Macedonia supplied what I needed. I have kept myself from being a burden to you in any way, and will continue to do so. As surely as the truth of Christ is in me, nobody in the regions of Achaia will stop this boasting of mine. Why? Because I do not love you? God knows I do! And I will keep on doing what I am doing in order to cut the ground from under those who want an opportunity to be considered equal with us in the things they boast about. (2 CORINTHIANS 11:7–12)

Paul had taught the Corinthians that those who preach the gospel have a right to live by the gospel. He had taught them the Old Testament proverb, "Do not muzzle an ox while it is treading out the grain" (Deuteronomy 25:4). Yet when he came to Corinth, he refused to accept their support. Instead, he made tents to support himself.

There were times when tent making didn't cover Paul's living expenses, because he says, "When I was with you and needed something, I was not a burden to anyone, for the brothers who came from Macedonia supplied what I needed." He barely made ends meet and had to accept support from the Macedonian Christians—but he refused to be a burden to the Corinthians.

Paul was careful not to exploit the Corinthians for profit. But in the process of being so conscientious, Paul opened himself up the opposite criticism. The false teachers in Corinth said, "You know why Paul didn't accept support from you? Because he's an inferior apostle! He's not a 'super-apostle' like us! And he doesn't care about you. By refusing your donations, he was insulting you!"

No matter what Paul did, people criticized him. There was nothing Paul could do to please his critics.

Paul adds, "And I will keep on doing what I am doing in order to cut the ground from under those who want an opportunity to be considered equal with us in the things they boast about." In other words, Paul says, "I refuse to change just to please my critics. I refuse to let these false teachers claim they work as we do. They're leeches, making their living off of you—then they turn around and falsely claim that they live like the apostle Paul!"

Blunt words

Next, Paul exposes these false teachers in blunt, harsh, candid words:

> For such men are false apostles, deceitful workmen, masquerading as apostles of Christ. And no wonder, for Satan himself masquerades as an angel of light. It is not surprising, then, if his servants masquerade as servants of righteousness. Their end will be what their actions deserve. (2 CORINTHIANS 11:13–15)

Paul strips the masks from these imposters. "They're phonies!" he says. "They're deceivers, pretending to be apostles of Christ—but they weren't sent by Christ, and they don't teach the truth. Just as Satan masquerades as an angel of light, they pass themselves off as God's servants—but they're storing up future judgment for themselves!"

Does this seem overly harsh? Do you wish Paul would be a bit more diplomatic? We tend to soft-pedal the truth in churches today—and that's one reason so many churches have fallen into error. We think that, as Christians, we're obligated to be nice to everyone—even the servants of Satan. Paul speaks bluntly because only blunt talk will do. He represents the Lord Jesus, who called the Pharisees "snakes" and "dead men's tombs full of rotting bones" (see Matthew 23:27).

False teachers can do a lot of damage—but their fate is inevitable. "Their end will be what their actions deserve," Paul says. They will fall victim to their own lies. They will lose the ability to tell truth from error. While seducing the church with their false teachings, they may gain worldly power and possessions. But as Jesus said, "What good is it for a man to gain the whole world, yet forfeit his soul?" (Mark 8:36).

May God give us wisdom to know the truth and courage to oppose Satan's lies. May He grant us the simplicity of knowing Christ and experiencing daily fellowship with Him. Let's take every thought captive to the obedience of Christ, that we may tear down the fortress of evil and error.

32

STRONGEST WHEN WEAK

2 Corinthians 11:16—12:10

Paul bothers people. He annoys his enemies. He even makes his friends uneasy.

I've known a number of earnest Christians who have said, "Pastor, I know I shouldn't feel this way, but I just can't stand the apostle Paul! He seems so conceited. Imagine telling people, 'Imitate me as I imitate Christ.'"

I am always amazed by this criticism. As I study the letters of Paul, I am continually struck by the genuine humility of this wonderful servant of God.

Having said that, I have to acknowledge that in the passage we are about to examine, we will hear Paul make some extravagant boasts—

But we will also understand why he speaks that way. Believe me, boasting and arrogance were repugnant to Paul. The boasting Paul does in this letter is designed to make a point, and it's aimed at a specific segment of Paul's audience. If you are one of those who say, "I just can't stand the apostle Paul!" then take a closer look—

And you might learn to love this fascinating and surprising apostle.

Under the spell of false teachers

As we have previously seen, false teachers had come to Corinth from Jerusalem, claming to be apostles and boasting of their supposed accomplishments for Christ. As a result, the Corinthians were in danger of following these false teachers rather than listening to the apostle who had won them to Christ and nurtured their faith.

So Paul employs an interest technique. He reasons that, since the Corinthians seem to be impressed by boasting, he will boast, too. Paul adopts a tactic of sinking to the level of his opponents and boasting of his own accomplishments—to make a point. Keep these facts in mind as you read.

I repeat: Let no one take me for a fool. But if you do, then receive me just as you would a fool, so that I may do a little boasting. In this self-confident boasting I am not talking as the Lord would, but as a fool. Since many are boasting in the way the world does, I too will boast. (2 CORINTHIANS 11:16–18)

Do you see how reluctant Paul is? Boasting goes against the grain of this humble man's character. He says, "In this self-confident boasting I am not talking as the Lord would, but as a fool." In other words, it's wrong for a Christian to talk this way, but to show the Corinthians how foolish these boastful false teachers are, Paul will speak boastfully and foolishly himself. He continues:

You gladly put up with fools since you are so wise! In fact, you even put up with anyone who enslaves you or exploits you or takes advantage of you or pushes himself forward or slaps you in the face. To my shame I admit that we were too weak for that! (2 CORINTHIANS 11:19–21A)

Such righteous sarcasm! "You Corinthians are so wise," he says, in effect, "that you'll tolerate any amount of foolishness! If people enslave you, lie to you, make fools of you, cheat you, take your money, advance their own interests at your expense, insult you, and slap you silly, you just grin and ask for more abuse! Well, you're better men than I am, because I could never put up with such abuse! I'm too weak for that! I salute you for being so wise, tolerant, and strong!"

Paul is trying to verbally shake the Corinthians out of the spell that these false teachers have cast over their minds. When people are being insulted, abused, and enslaved and they don't even know it, something is desperately wrong. You may think, "Who in their right mind would ever put up with being abused by a false teacher?" Surprisingly, a lot of people would.

Years ago, I traveled out of state and attended a large church service. There were about a thousand people in the audience, most in their twenties or thirties. The pastor had quite a following. I sat down and prepared to hear what this man had to say.

A few minutes into his sermon, the pastor stopped and looked at a woman who was sitting near the front. "Young lady," he said, "why are you fussing with your hair? This is a Bible study, not a beauty parlor. That's the trouble with you flaky females! And flaky is a good adjective for females.

You can't sit still and be serious for one hour and learn from the Word!" He ripped into her for a minute or so while she sat with her head down, red-faced and embarrassed, saying nothing. No one said a word in her defense.

Finally, the pastor resumed his study. I followed along with the study, and I could see that his teaching was seriously flawed. He would yank passages of Scripture out of context and twist their meaning out of all recognition.

Before long, the pastor spotted a man near the back of the room, thumbing through his Bible, cross-referencing something the pastor had said. "There's a man back there who's not reading where the rest of us are," the pastor said. "He's not following along in the study."

I was sitting fairly close to the man, and I knew he had been following the study intently—yet the pastor had singled him out for a reprimand.

"Sir," the pastor continued, "you appear to be looking up something in the Old Testament while the rest of us are in the New Testament. If you aren't interested in following along with the rest of us, you can just get up and leave."

The congregation sat frozen. No one said a word. Apparently this kind of intimidation was normal behavior for this pastor. I was amazed to see the arrogance, insult, and abuse the audience would endure while under the spell of a false teacher.

That's what was happening in Corinth. The people were under the spell of false teachers, and they were putting up with abuse and insult. To shake them out of their dazed, zombie-like state, Paul stepped out of character and used a series of extravagant boasts to make a point.

Paul's "foolish boasting"

Paul goes on with his tactic of extravagant boasting:

> What anyone else dares to boast about—I am speaking as a fool—I also dare to boast about. Are they Hebrews? So am I. Are they Israelites? So am I. Are they Abraham's descendants? So am I. (2 Cor-
> inthians 11:21b-22)

Many people put a lot of stock in their pedigree. Some feel superior to others because their ancestors came over on the *Mayflower* or fought in the American Revolution. Well, it's nice to be aware of one's family heritage, but as Abraham Lincoln once observed, "I don't know who my grandfather was; I'm much more concerned to know what his grandson will be." We are each responsible to make what we can of our own lives.

Paul knows that it's foolish to boast of one's ancestors. However, he says, "What anyone else dares to boast about—I am speaking as a fool—I also dare to boast about." He doesn't want anyone to take his boasting seriously. But he's very serious about the point he's making, which could be stated this way: "If these false teachers dare to boast about their ancestry, fine! So will I—and I have more to boast of. They say they're Hebrews, Israelites, Abraham's descendants? Well, so am I. This whole subject is silly—but the fact is, I can make the same claims."

I've heard Christians boast of their spiritual pedigrees: "I was raised in the First Church of the Highfalutin!" "I've been listening to Dr. Knowitall's preaching for twenty years!" "I graduated from Divinely Inspired University!" "I'm a fourth-generation Orthodox Unreformed Antidenomination-alist—and proud of it!" Some Christians boast of their religious lineage as if it makes them part of a spiritual aristocracy. With scathing satire, Paul shows that such boasting is the height of foolishness.

What about boasting of our own accomplishments? Paul writes:

> Are they servants of Christ? (I am out of my mind to talk like this.) I am more. I have worked much harder, been in prison more frequently, been flogged more severely, and been exposed to death again and again. (2 CORINTHIANS 11:23)

With tongue firmly planted in cheek, Paul boasts of being a servant of Christ—then he says he's not merely talking like a fool but a madman. "I am out of my mind to talk like this," he says. He goes on to satirically brag about his hard work, his time spent in prison for Christ, the floggings and the times he was close to dying. If these false teachers want to brag about all they've done for Christ, Paul, though he feels like a lunatic for saying so, can out-brag them at every point. He goes on to list other trials he has endured as a servant of Christ:

> Five times I received from the Jews the forty lashes minus one. (2 CORINTHIANS 11:24)

Here Paul describes a Jewish form of punishment. The law of Moses prescribed that for certain offenses you could be publicly whipped with forty lashes. But it also prescribed, according to the rabbis, that if more than forty strokes were inflicted, the man who did the whipping would receive forty lashes. So, to be on the safe side, the man who administered the punishment gave his victim thirty-nine lashes—or, as Paul says, "forty lashes minus one." Many prisoners died in the course of these floggings—yet Paul endured this punishment on five different occasions. He continues:

> Three times I was beaten with rods, once I was stoned, three times I was shipwrecked, I spent a night and a day in the open sea. (2 CORINTHIANS 11:25)

Beating with rods was a Roman punishment. Paul was a Roman citizen, and although the law of Rome decreed that no citizen should be beaten with rods, he had suffered three such beatings. We should note that the book of Acts records an incident in which Paul was beaten with rods—a fourth beating, since it would have occurred after this letter was written. Evidently, Paul's message was so offensive to some that the law was disregarded and Paul was illegally punished.

He was also stoned by a mob, dragged out of the city, and left for dead. This incident is recorded in Acts 14. It took place in the city of Lystra, the place where Paul met young Timothy on his first missionary journey. When Paul was dumped outside the city, bloodied and unconscious, he appeared dead—yet God restored him to life and enabled him to continue his ministry.

Paul mentions three shipwrecks, plus a night and a day adrift at sea— he probably used a plank or some other piece of wreckage as a flotation device. There is an account in Acts of a shipwreck; since that would have occurred after this letter was written, Paul must have been shipwrecked on at least four separate occasions. He continues:

> I have been constantly on the move. I have been in danger from rivers, in danger from bandits, in danger from my own countrymen, in danger from Gentiles; in danger in the city, in danger in the country, in danger at sea; and in danger from false brothers. I have labored and toiled and have often gone without sleep; I have known hunger and thirst and have often gone without food; I have been cold and naked. (2 CORINTHIANS 11:26–27)

I look at that list and ask myself, "What have I ever endured for Christ?" I've never been flogged or shipwrecked. I've hardly suffered anything for Christ but some verbal attacks. When I read these words, I'm profoundly impressed with what Paul went through as a minister of the gospel. Though Paul is bragging only to make a point, I think he has truly earned his bragging rights.

Paul's love and empathy

Next, Paul writes of his feelings of worry and concern for the churches:

> Besides everything else, I face daily the pressure of my concern for all the churches. Who is weak, and I do not feel weak? Who is led into sin, and I do not inwardly burn? (2 CORINTHIANS 11:28–29)

What motivated Paul to endure this life that was so filled with sorrow, anxiety, peril, pressure, hardship, and suffering? What motivated him to persevere in loving the Corinthian believers when they were on the verge of turning against him and following false teachers? The answer, which he gave earlier in this letter: "the love of Christ constrains me" (see 2 Corinthians 5:14 KJV).

The love of Jesus flowed through Paul's life. I have often said to young people, "In life, you'll have some true friends and some false friends. You can always tell true friends from false by this: Those who endure through tough times, conflict, trials, and sorrows are true friends. Those who fall away were never really friends to begin with."

The apostle Paul was a true friend to the Corinthians. A false apostle would never have put up with their waywardness. Jesus said:

> "I am the good shepherd. The good shepherd lays down his life for the sheep. The hired hand is not the shepherd who owns the sheep. So when he sees the wolf coming, he abandons the sheep and runs away. Then the wolf attacks the flock and scatters it. The man runs away because he is a hired hand and cares nothing for the sheep." (JOHN 10:11–13)

The Corinthians have been listening to a confusing babble of voices, all claiming to be true apostles. Paul wants them to know where the truth lies and which voice they can trust. So he has been using satirical boasting in order to make his voice heard.

A "basket case"

Now Paul turns to the things that Christians can authentically boast about:

> If I must boast, I will boast of the things that show my weakness. The God and Father of the Lord Jesus, who is to be praised forever, knows

that I am not lying. In Damascus the governor under King Aretas had the city of the Damascenes guarded in order to arrest me. But I was lowered in a basket from a window in the wall and slipped through his hands. (2 CORINTHIANS 11:30–33)

Paul reaches back twenty years into the past, recalling a remarkable incident shortly after his conversion. He says, "If I must boast, this is the kind of thing I'll boast of." What is this incident about? Paul's weakness! "If I must boast," he writes, "I will boast of the things that show my weakness."

In essence, Paul places his hand on a Bible and affirms that he is telling the truth: "The God and Father of the Lord Jesus, who is to be praised forever, knows that I am not lying." Then he relates one incident that stands as the epitome of his life. It was a time of complete failure and humiliation. It's a time when he was forced to crawl into a basket and be lowered from an opening in the wall as if he were a helpless kitten.

Remember all of Paul's talk of beatings, hardships, dangers, and shipwrecks? He now dismisses all of that with a wave of his hand. He says, "The thing I want to be known for is the time I became a 'basket case.' When you think of me, think of weakness, think of helplessness."

We find this account in Acts 9. After Paul's conversion, he went into the wilderness of Arabia. There he studied the Scriptures and tried to understand how he had failed to recognize Jesus as the promised Messiah. As he studied, he found Jesus on every page—in the prophecies of Isaiah 53 and Psalm 22, in the arrangement of the tabernacle of Exodus, in the system of sacrifices in Leviticus—in verse after verse, line after line. Everything pointed to Jesus.

Paul returned from his wilderness experience with two burning convictions in his heart: First, the Old Testament proved that Jesus of Nazareth was the promised Messiah. Second, God had chosen Paul to be an apostle to Israel. So Paul began his ministry by going to the synagogues and demonstrating from the Scriptures that Jesus was the Messiah. He had some success, but he also faced opposition and persecution.

At one point, while he was in Damascus, the governor, at the instigation of the Jews in Damascus, sought to seize Paul and put him to death. Guards were posted at all the city gates to kill him, but Paul's friends heard of the plot, and they let him down in a basket through an opening in the wall.

Looking back on that adventure, Paul says, "That's what I will brag about—that I went to Damascus, planning to convert the city to Christ, and I ended up hiding out, fearing for my life, and being lowered in the basket so I could slink away like a thief. I will brag that I am weak, and that I can't do anything in my own strength. I will brag that the only power in my life is the power of God alone."

Paul exemplified the secret Jesus taught His disciples: "Apart from me you can do nothing" (John 15:5). This is the secret we must all learn. Only when we reach the end of our own strength is God's power manifested.

The third heaven

Paul's boasting continues into chapter 12—and here Paul reveals an incident in his life that sounds like it is truly worth boasting about:

> I must go on boasting. Although there is nothing to be gained, I will go on to visions and revelations from the Lord. (2 CORINTHIANS 12:1)

Here we see the basis of Paul's claim to be an apostle. According to Scripture, an apostle had to be an eyewitness of the resurrected Lord. Paul was not one of the original Twelve, but he had seen Christ on the Damascus road. Now he goes on to tell us that there were other occasions when he had visions of the Lord.

What is a vision? It's not a dream, a hallucination, or a fantasy. A vision, in the sense that Paul means here, is an actual appearance of the Lord. Paul saw Jesus, and Jesus personally taught him. It's important to remember that the Lord instructed Paul, and that is why Paul speaks with authority in Scripture.

Paul goes on to describe the most dramatic of these visions. Notice as you read that Paul speaks of himself in the third person:

> I know a man in Christ who fourteen years ago was caught up to the third heaven. Whether it was in the body or out of the body I do not know—God knows. And I know that this man—whether in the body or apart from the body I do not know, but God knows—was caught up to paradise. He heard inexpressible things, things that man is not permitted to tell. (2 CORINTHIANS 12:2–4)

I'm not sure why Paul writes as if he is speaking of some other man, but later, in verse 7, Paul makes it clear that "this man" is Paul himself. There he writes, "To keep me from becoming conceited because of these surpassingly great revelations." Paul does not give us much detail about the life beyond, but several things are clear.

First, Paul's experience took him beyond this present life. He entered the "third heaven" or "paradise." The "third heaven" refers to the ancient Jewish belief regarding the structure of the universe. According to this view, there were three heavens. The first was the atmosphere around the earth, the realm of the winds and clouds. Beyond that was the second heaven, the realm of the sun, moon, and stars. Beyond that was the third heaven, the invisible realm of paradise, the place of God's throne.

Second, Paul tells us when this vision occurred. It took place fourteen years before he wrote this letter. That would place Paul's vision at about the time he came from Tarsus and returned to Antioch, about ten years after his conversion.

Third, Paul tells us that the body was rather unimportant to this experience. If he was in the body, he was not aware of it; if he was out of the body, he didn't miss it. This suggests to me that going to be with the Lord will not be as strange an experience as we might think. Remember that Paul previously referred to heaven as being "at home with the Lord" (see 2 Corinthians 5:8). Perhaps the reason Paul gives this account in the third person is because it seemed like it happened to someone else, and he was not aware of whether his body was involved or not.

Fourth, Paul heard things he could not speak about. He must have heard some marvelous truths that contributed greatly to his understanding of life and reality. These insights enabled him to better grasp what God is doing in human history, yet he was not able or not allowed to describe these insights in words.

When you read the Old Testament prophets and Revelation, you see that people who had visions of heaven could not adequately express in words what they saw. That's why such visions are usually expressed in symbols. Ezekiel saw wheels within wheels and creatures with four faces. Daniel's descriptions and John's in Revelation are similarly symbolic. These visions suggest that when we are with the Lord, our knowledge will be vastly increased. We will know secrets that cannot be put into language.

Paul's "thorn in the flesh"

Next, Paul returns to the problem of these false teachers and their boasting:

> I will boast about a man like that, but I will not boast about myself, except about my weaknesses. Even if I should choose to boast, I would not be a fool, because I would be speaking the truth. But I refrain, so

no one will think more of me than is warranted by what I do or say. (2 CORINTHIANS 12:5–6)

Paul says that his vision of heaven was an astounding experience; if he were inclined to boast, as the false teachers do, he would boast of his vision. But Paul is not trying to impress anyone. He goes on to say:

To keep me from becoming conceited because of these surpassingly great revelations, there was given me a thorn in my flesh, a messenger of Satan, to torment me. Three times I pleaded with the Lord to take it away from me. But he said to me, "My grace is sufficient for you, for my power is made perfect in weakness." Therefore I will boast all the more gladly about my weaknesses, so that Christ's power may rest on me. (2 CORINTHIANS 12:7–9)

This, Paul says, is the only thing he will boast about: his weakness.

And out of the most amazing, awe-inspiring experience imaginable—his vision of heaven—came the most debilitating agony of his life. He refers to this problem as "a thorn in my flesh, a messenger of Satan, to torment me." We don't know what this thorn was. It might have been his poor eyesight, which we have evidence of in that he signed his signature in large letters (see Galatians 6:11).

When I traveled with Dr. H. A. Ironside, he suffered from cataracts, and when he wrote in longhand, he wrote with very large letters. I often thought of Paul when I saw Dr. Ironside's handwriting.

Some Bible commentators think that Paul may have had a speech impediment because he mentions having difficulty saying what he wishes to say. Others have suggested that Paul had been married once and had a nagging wife. Since Paul says it was "a thorn in my flesh," I think it more likely that Paul's thorn was a physical ailment.

It is interesting that Paul attributes this thorn to both God and Satan. He refers to the fact that God had a reason for giving him this thorn and not removing it: "To keep me from becoming conceited because of these surpassingly great revelations." Yet Paul also called it "a messenger of Satan." Whatever this thorn was, it bedeviled him. He hated it—but he could do nothing about it. So he humbly accepted it, blaming Satan for the pain it caused while crediting God for the character growth it produced.

Paul was a mighty man of prayer, so it was natural for him to ask God to take this thorn away from him—but God's answer was clear: "My grace is sufficient for you, for my power is made perfect in weakness." God said it was more important for Paul to be humble than comfortable, so He permitted the thorn to remain.

So Paul comes to this conclusion:

> That is why, for Christ's sake, I delight in weaknesses, in insults, in hardships, in persecutions, in difficulties. For when I am weak, then I am strong. (2 CORINTHIANS 12:10)

This is the paradox of spiritual warfare. When is the devil being defeated? Not when we feel confident. Not when all is well. Not when we feel strong and victorious. The devil is being defeated when we feel weak and helpless, oppressed and attacked. The devil is being defeated when we go to the Lord, pleading for the strength to fight for one more day.

I once received a letter from a missionary in New Guinea. He wrote:

> It's great to be in the thick of the fight and to draw the old devil's heaviest guns! He comes at you with depression and discouragement, slander and disease! He doesn't waste time on a lukewarm bunch, but he hits good and hard when a fellow is hitting him.
>
> You can always measure the weight of your blow by the one you get back. When you're on your back with fever and at your last ounce of strength, when some of your converts backslide, when your mail gets held up and some don't bother to answer your letters, is that time to put on mourning? No sir! That's the time to pull out the stops and shout hallelujah! The old fellow's getting it in the neck and hitting back!
>
> Meanwhile, heaven is leaning over the battlements and wondering, "Will he persevere—or run away? Does he know that God has unlimited reserves that he can access through prayer?"
>
> Glory to God! We will not retreat!

This man understands the triumphant shout of the apostle Paul: "When I am weak, then I am strong!"

Like Paul, we will boast of only one thing: Our weakness. We delight in persecution and hardship, suffering and helplessness, because this is where the power of God is unleashed. This is where the grace of God is released.

When we are weak, we are strong!

33

THE MAKING OF AN APOSTLE

2 Corinthians 12:11—13:4

The apostles were the specially called and gifted men to whom Jesus entrusted the mysteries of God. They were called to go into the world in the name of Jesus, preach in the name of Jesus, establish the church in the name of Jesus, and die in the name of Jesus.

Foremost among the original twelve apostles who walked with Jesus was Simon Peter. He was a fisherman from Bethsaida in Galilee when the Lord called him. Peter led the Jerusalem church for many years and later went to Rome where, tradition says, he was martyred under Nero, the Roman emperor who publicly declared himself an enemy of God. When Nero condemned Peter to be crucified, the apostle asked that his cross be turned upside-down, saying, "I am unworthy to die in the same manner as my Lord."

And what of the other apostles?

Andrew, Peter's brother, was also a fisherman. Andrew was nailed and bound to an X-shaped cross; his death was slow, and he preached the gospel of Christ to his executioners until his last breath.

James and John were fishermen and sons of Zebedee. Jesus called them "the Sons of Thunder," and they were two of the three apostles who witnessed the transfiguration of Jesus (the third was Peter). James was martyred by beheading in Jerusalem. John, believed to be the only apostle to die a natural death, was exiled to the isle of Patmos, where he had his vision of the Revelation.

Philip of Galilee took the gospel into Syria, Greece, and the province of Asia. He was crucified in Phrygia, in Asia Minor.

Bartholomew took the gospel as far east as India. Tradition records that while in Armenia, the apostle Bartholomew was executed by being flayed alive, then crucified without his skin.

Thomas Didymus (doubting Thomas) is said to have carried the gospel to the East Indies, where he was martyred by being impaled by a spear.

James the son of Alphaeus (or James the Younger) was taken by a mob and thrown from a high pinnacle of the temple in Jerusalem. He was found on the pavement, broken but alive, crying out, "I forgive you!" Someone in the mob beat him with a club until his cries of forgiveness were silenced.

Matthew the tax collector was executed with a sword in Ethiopia.

Simon the Canaanite (Simon the Zealot) is believed to have taken the gospel to Britain, where he was martyred by means of a saw.

Jude (also known as Thaddaeus) took the gospel to Syria, Libya, and Mesopotamia. In Persia (now called Iran) he was hacked to death with an axe.

Matthias, who replaced the traitor Judas Iscariot as one of the Twelve, was martyred in Jerusalem. He was stoned by an angry mob—and when the mob found that he still lived after the stoning, he was beheaded.

And finally there was Paul, the thirteenth apostle. Dionysius, bishop of the church in Corinth about a century after Paul's death, wrote that both the apostle Peter and the apostle Paul, "having planted the church at Corinth, likewise instructed us; and having in like manner taught in Italy, they suffered martyrdom about the same time." Other church historians, including Tertullian and Caius, record that Peter and Paul were both executed at around the same time in the city of Rome under emperor Nero. Eusebius writes that Paul was "said to have been beheaded at Rome."

Clearly, the apostles were called by the Lord to live for Him and die for Him. In Paul's day, as in our own day, there were many people who tried to lay claim to the title of apostle. In this passage, however, Paul points out that not everyone has the right to say, "I am an apostle." Only those special few who bear the marks of an apostle have a right to wear that title.

The signs and wonders of a true apostle

In the closing verses of 2 Corinthians 12 and the opening verses of chapter 13, Paul sets forth some of the marks which identify a true apostle of Jesus Christ. He writes:

> I have made a fool of myself, but you drove me to it. I ought to have been commended by you, for I am not in the least inferior to the "super-apostles," even though I am nothing. The things that mark an apostle—signs, wonders and miracles—were done among you with great perseverance. How were you inferior to the other churches, except that I was never a burden to you? Forgive me this wrong! (2 CORINTHIANS 12:11–13)

Paul seems surprised and wounded that the Corinthians did not defend him when the false teachers arrived on the scene. Couldn't they tell a true apostle from phonies? Because they were so easily deceived, Paul found it necessary (in an embarrassed way) to defend himself. He begins by setting forth the marks of a true apostle.

Earlier in this book, we defined this word *apostle*, but it might be helpful to do so again. The word *apostle* comes from the Greek word *apostolos*, meaning "someone sent forth to carry out a mission." The original twelve apostles were hand-picked by Jesus. The Scriptures list several qualifications of an apostle: For example, an apostle must have seen the Lord and must be an eyewitness that He is risen (the original eleven faithful disciples saw Him in His earthly flesh and His resurrection body; Paul saw the resurrected Lord in his Damascus road conversion and in a series of visions). In Acts 1:22, Peter says that an apostle must be an eyewitness to the reality of the resurrection.

I believe that there are no successors to the original New Testament apostles. There are many today who claim to be apostles, but I do not believe the church needs apostles today. Jesus chose the apostles to lay the foundations of the church; those foundations were laid long ago and remain strong. The church has no need of new apostles—in large part because the original apostles are still with us. They continue to teach the church through their inspired letters—the letters of Paul, John, Peter, James, and others. Moreover, since Peter has said that an apostle must be an eyewitness to the resurrection, there cannot be any authentic new apostles in our own era.

When we hear people claiming to be apostles, claiming to have new revelations of the mind of God that are outside of Scripture, we must ask ourselves: What are the authenticating signs of a true apostle? If those who claim to be apostles cannot demonstrate the marks of an apostle, we have no reason to accept their word.

In this passage, Paul says that some of the authenticating marks of an apostle are signs, wonders, and miracles. A true apostle has power from God—power to do things that ordinary people cannot do, power to do signs, wonders, and miracles. Signs are works that have a significant or symbolic meaning (the ability to speak in a tongue is a sign). Wonders are amazing demonstrations of the power of God—startling displays that grab our attention. Miracles are acts that can be accomplished only by the power of God, such as physical healings.

In his letters, Paul rarely refers to signs, wonders, or miracles in his ministry. The book of Acts refers to several miraculous events in Paul's ministry, but Paul hardly mentions them. Nevertheless, Paul does mention them here, and I believe it is helpful to examine these three marks of a true apostle in light of the words of Jesus in Mark 16.

As we noted earlier in our study of 1 Corinthians 12, there is some debate among Bible scholars regarding Mark 16:9–20. The earliest and best Greek manuscripts of Mark do not contain those verses, and scholars generally agree that those verses were tacked on later. This doesn't mean that Jesus never spoke the words that are quoted in that passage. It means that we don't know the original source of that text or how it came to be incorporated in Mark's gospel. In that passage, Jesus says:

> "And these signs will accompany those who believe: In my name they will drive out demons; they will speak in new tongues; they will pick up snakes with their hands; and when they drink deadly poison, it will not hurt them at all; they will place their hands on sick people, and they will get well." (MARK 16:17–18)

Note this statement: "These signs will accompany those who believe." Clearly, Jesus didn't mean that signs, wonders, and miracles would accompany every believer. This would be in conflict with Paul's statement that signs, wonders, and miracles are the marks of a true apostle. If all believers performed signs, wonders, and miracles, then these acts would certainly not mark an apostle as anyone special.

Yet some people have misunderstood Jesus' words in Mark 16. They interpret these words as saying that miraculous signs will accompany every person who believes the gospel. But if you look at the context of these words in Mark 16, it becomes clear that Jesus is speaking of the apostles. Just a few verses earlier, we find this statement, describing Jesus' appearance to the eleven apostles shortly after the resurrection:

> Later Jesus appeared to the Eleven as they were eating; he rebuked them for their lack of faith and their stubborn refusal to believe those who had seen him after he had risen. (MARK 16:14)

Jesus rebuked the eleven apostles! He didn't rebuke anyone else, just the apostles. What did he rebuke them for? "Their lack of faith and their stubborn refusal to believe those who had seen him after he had risen." He rebuked them for not believing in the resurrection, even though Jesus had promised to rise again, and even though they had ample evidence that He had done as He promised. In fact, Jesus was standing before them, and some of them *still* doubted.

Then Jesus gave them the Great Commission, after which He said, "And these signs will accompany those who believe" (see Mark 16:17). In other words, "If you will stop doubting the resurrection and believe that I have truly risen as I promised, then you, the apostles, will be accompanied by these miraculous signs." Then Jesus went on to list the same marks of an apostle that Paul listed, a series of signs, wonders, and miracles. The apostles would drive out demons, speak in new tongues, pick up snakes with their hands, drink poison without being harmed, and heal the sick.

It's interesting to note that each one of these signs that Jesus predicted (except drinking poison without being harmed) was specifically fulfilled by events recorded in the book of Acts—and in each case, these signs and wonders accompanied the ministry of an apostle. Speaking in tongues accompanied the ministries of Peter (Acts 2; 10:46) and Paul (Acts 19:6). Evil spirits were driven out and the sick were healed by Paul (Acts 19:12). In Acts 28:3–5, a snake fastened itself to the hand of the apostle Paul, but he shook it off and was unharmed. So, just as Jesus promised and just as Paul says in this passage, the signs of a true apostle were done among the people in Acts.

Clearly, the signs listed in Mark 16 are the authenticating signs that indicated that the original eleven apostles, plus Paul, were genuinely sent from the Lord. This is further demonstrated by the closing statement of Mark 16:

> Then the disciples went out and preached everywhere, and the Lord worked with them and confirmed his word by the signs that accompanied it. (MARK 16:20)

Jesus in Mark 16 and Paul in 2 Corinthians 12 speak with one voice on this subject: A true apostle is authenticated by supernatural manifestations that accompany his ministry. As Paul points out, Paul had performed signs, wonders, and miracles among the Corinthians—yet when these false teachers came into the Corinthian church, the believers there began to question Paul's apostleship.

The humility of a true apostle

Supernatural manifestations have accompanied Paul's ministry in Corinth—but signs, wonders, and miracles are not the only authenticating marks of an apostle. As we continue exploring this passage, we will see several other identifying marks by which the Corinthian believers should have known that Paul was a true apostle:

First, *Paul was humble*. A true apostle demonstrates Christlike humility. We see Paul's humility:

> I have made a fool of myself, but you drove me to it. I ought to have been commended by you, for I am not in the least inferior to the "super-apostles," even though I am nothing. The things that mark an apostle—signs, wonders and miracles—were done among you with great perseverance. How were you inferior to the other churches, except that I was never a burden to you? Forgive me this wrong!
> (2 CORINTHIANS 12:11–13)

There is a remarkable paradox embedded in verse 11. Paul says he is not inferior to these false "super-apostles"—yet at the same time he says, "I am nothing." We tend to think that the only way we can serve Christ is by being somebody, by accomplishing great things for Christ. Paul says we serve Christ best by being nothing. Christ does His greatest work through humble nobodies. If we supply the humility and the obedience, Christ will supply the power—and there's no limit to what He can do through us.

If we insist on being somebody instead of nothing, then Christ can't work through us. We might put on a good religious show and fool many people, but nothing of eternal value is ever accomplished through human effort.

Paul goes on to say, in effect, "While I was with you, signs, wonders and miracles accompanied my ministry among you. My apostolic credentials were on full display among you for a long time, and I treated the Corinthian church as fully equal to all the other churches in the region—except for one thing: I didn't take your money. Now you say I insulted you by refusing to let you support me financially! Well, forgive me for 'wronging' you by not taking your money!"

You may recall that in 2 Corinthians 11:9, Paul wrote, "And when I was with you and needed something, I was not a burden to anyone, for the brothers who came from Macedonia supplied what I needed. I have kept myself from being a burden to you in any way, and will continue to do so."

The false teachers who had infiltrated the Corinthian church were telling the people that Paul had insulted the Corinthians by refusing their support. "He let the Macedonians support him while he was in Corinth," they said, "and he even supported himself as a tentmaker. But he wouldn't let you support him! Why? Because he thinks that you Corinthians are inferior to the believers in other churches!"

Paul responds sarcastically, "Well, excuse me for 'wronging' you by not taking your money!" He's showing the Corinthians how silly it sounds for them to be offended because Paul wanted to ease their burden.

As an apostle and a minister of the gospel, Paul had every right to financial support. But to avoid seeming to exploit the Corinthians, Paul worked doubly hard, preaching the gospel by day and making tents at night. This was tiring work, and Paul sacrificed his own comfort and sleep so that no one would accuse him of exploiting the Corinthians.

What does this say about Paul? Once again, it is proof of the apostle's humble spirit. Humility is an authenticating mark of an apostle—and humility deeply marked the life of the apostle Paul.

The love of a true apostle

Second, *Paul exhibited Christlike love.* A true apostle loves people the same way Jesus loved people. Paul writes:

> Now I am ready to visit you for the third time, and I will not be a burden to you, because what I want is not your possessions but you. After all, children should not have to save up for their parents, but parents for their children. So I will very gladly spend for you everything I have and expend myself as well. If I love you more, will you love me less? (2 CORINTHIANS 12:14–15)

Paul saw himself as a loving parent and the Corinthians as his children. He had led them to Christ. He loved them. As a parent, he was responsible to provide for his children—not the other way around. One mark of a true apostle is that he lavishes love upon those under his care. He does not ask anything from them. Paul expresses the love of a true apostle in these words: "What I want is not your possessions but you." Paul's fatherly love contrasts sharply with the grasping and selfish hearts of the false apostles.

A false apostle expects to be ministered to. He expects money, gifts, praise, and adulation. False teachers are in ministry to receive, not give. They have a narcissistic need to be loved and supported and told how important and wonderful they are. They feel entitled to gifts and financial support in return for their ministry.

What a contrast is Paul's attitude! He says, "So I will very gladly spend for you everything I have and expend myself as well. If I love you more, will you love me less?" Paul had lavished love on the Corinthians, but they were not responding with love. Instead, they had turned away from Paul and given their love to these false teachers. They had believed lies that the false teachers told about Paul. How did Paul respond? Not with anger, but with the wounded love of father responding to a wayward child.

You can hear the hurt in Paul's words: "If I love you more, will you love me less?" After all he had done for the Corinthian believers, they had rejected his love in order to follow false teachers. But even though the Corinthians had taken the wrong path, Paul, like all loving parents, continued to lavish his love on them: "So I will very gladly spend for you everything I have and expend myself as well."

A mother once sat down to breakfast and found, next to her plate, a bill from her thirteen-year-old son. It read:

For Services Rendered:

Mowing the lawn	$ 2.00
Drying the dishes	1.00
Raking leaves	3.00
Cleaning the garage	4.00
Total owed	$10.00

She didn't say anything about the bill to her son. The next day, when the boy came home from school, he found a plate of milk and cookies on the table. Next to the plate was a bill that that read:

Dear Son:

For ironing clothes	no charge
For mending socks	no charge
For cooking meals	no charge
For bandaging knee	no charge
For baking cookies	no charge

Love, Mom

That's Paul's attitude. He loves the Corinthians and expects nothing in return. That kind of selfless, big-hearted, unqualified love is the mark of a true servant of Christ. That's the test we should apply to those who claim to be apostles. Do they truly love God's people, expecting nothing in return—or are they in ministry for personal gain?

The selflessness of a true apostle

Third, *Paul was selfless.* A true apostle thinks of others and forgets himself. Paul writes:

> Be that as it may, I have not been a burden to you. Yet, crafty fellow that I am, I caught you by trickery! (2 CORINTHIANS 12:16)

This translation makes Paul sound sarcastic—and the apostle has certainly used biting irony at times throughout this section. But I don't think that in the original Greek, Paul was conveying sarcasm here. I think he is continuing the tone of feeling wounded by the Corinthians' rejection. He tried not to be a burden—but instead of appreciating Paul's sacrifice, the Corinthians believed the false teachers who claimed Paul was seeking to exploit them in other ways. Here is the same verse in the Revised Standard Version:

> But granting that I myself did not burden you, I was crafty, you say, and got the better of you by guile. (2 CORINTHIANS 12:16)

Paul is saying, "Some of you claim that by not burdening you with my living expenses when I was among you, I was taking advantage of you in a sneaky, underhanded way. You claim, 'Well, Paul's only refusing our support in order to allay our suspicions. When he has won our trust—*wham!* He'll *really* take advantage of us!'"

The apostle responds to this charge:

> Did I exploit you through any of the men I sent you? I urged Titus to go to you and I sent our brother with him. Titus did not exploit you, did he? Did we not act in the same spirit and follow the same course? (2 CORINTHIANS 12:17–18)

In other words, "I challenge you to name even one time when I ever exploited you in any way! Did my ministry partner Titus take advantage of you? Or the other Christian brother I sent with Titus? Didn't my partners and I make sure that we were never a burden to you? We poured our lives

404

into you and never took anything from you! How, then, can you accuse me of even thinking of taking advantage of you?" I like to think that this argument effectively silenced Paul's opposition in Corinth.

An apostle answers to God, not men

Fourth, *an apostle answers only to God.* A true apostle does not answer to men, nor does he feel obligated to defend himself before men. Paul writes:

> Have you been thinking all along that we have been defending ourselves to you? We have been speaking in the sight of God as those in Christ; and everything we do, dear friends, is for your strengthening. For I am afraid that when I come I may not find you as I want you to be, and you may not find me as you want me to be. I fear that there may be quarreling, jealousy, outbursts of anger, factions, slander, gossip, arrogance and disorder. I am afraid that when I come again my God will humble me before you, and I will be grieved over many who have sinned earlier and have not repented of the impurity, sexual sin and debauchery in which they have indulged.
>
> This will be my third visit to you. "Every matter must be established by the testimony of two or three witnesses." (2 CORINTHIANS 12:19–13:1)

A true apostle answers to God, not to a congregation, not to critics, not to false teachers. A true servant of Christ does not need to justify himself or defend himself. If a servant of Christ has God's approval, no other opinion matters.

From the reports Paul has received, he expects to find many problems in Corinth when he arrives. He fears he will encounter quarreling, jealousy, anger, factions, slander, gossip, arrogance, and disorder. In other words, Paul fears that he will find that the Corinthian church is just like so many churches today! Why are so many churches afflicted with selfish behavior and sinful attitudes? I believe it's because we ignore what God's Word tells us about how to treat one another in the body of Christ.

The Bible tells us that if someone offends us, we should go to that person and gently confront him in private. All too often, however, we respond with gossip, complaining, and bitterness. We call ourselves Christians—but we behave just like worldlings, running the church as if it were a secular business, playing hardball politics, demanding our way, and intimidating those who disagree with us. These actions destroy the testimony of a congregation.

The apostle Paul has heard that such things are taking place in the Corinthian church, so by the authority of an apostle, he says, in effect, "When I come I will deal with these problems in the church. Because I'm an apostle, I do not require your approval, so I can deal bluntly with the problems I find there."

Not only were there divisive, worldly attitudes in Corinth, but there was also sinful conduct. Paul says he fears he will be grieved to find "impurity, sexual sin and debauchery"—sins that Paul had already confronted in the Corinthian church but that people still practiced without repentance. Paul has written letters to the church and has sent emissaries on his behalf. He has gone to Corinth, and now he is going again. When he arrives, he will deal with the sins that continue to infect the church. He will do so because a true apostle is answerable to God and not to men.

Will Paul come into the church and punish sinners left and right? No, when he confronts sin, he will do so in a fair and biblical fashion. He quotes Deuteronomy 19:15: "Every matter must be established by the testimony of two or three witnesses." Secrets will be pried open, sins will be exposed, and wrongs will be set right—but all will be done according to biblical rules of evidence and fairness.

The power source of a true apostle

Fifth, *a true apostle relies on the power of God.* Twice in the next passage, Paul speaks of "the power of God." Let's see what God's power means in his life. He writes:

> I already gave you a warning when I was with you the second time. I now repeat it while absent: On my return I will not spare those who sinned earlier or any of the others, since you are demanding proof that Christ is speaking through me. He is not weak in dealing with you, but is powerful among you. For to be sure, he was crucified in weakness, yet he lives by God's power. Likewise, we are weak in him, yet by God's power we will live with him to serve you. (2 CORINTHIANS 13:2–4)

Paul had already warned those who rebelled against his authority as an apostle, and now he warns them again. Just as Jesus was crucified in weakness and raised by God's power, so Paul would come to Corinth in human weakness but act by God's power. Paul probably refers to the fact that he intends to take the final step of church discipline that Jesus refers to in Matthew 18:15–20.

The discipline process begins when you go to someone and quietly tell him his fault, between you and him alone. If he will not hear you, take one or two witnesses and try to resolve the problem. If he still will not repent, then there comes a time when the matter must be told to the church. That is what Paul talks about here.

When Paul comes to Corinth, he will tell the matter to the whole church and the church will seek to bring the individual to repentance. If the offender will not hear the church, then the Lord says, let him be unto you as a tax collector and a sinner. In other words, regard him no longer as a Christian; let him go his way.

Nothing further is required, for the power of God will begin to work on that person's life. As Paul says, Jesus Christ "is not weak in dealing with you, but is powerful among you. For to be sure, he was crucified in weakness, yet he lives by God's power. Likewise, we are weak in him, yet by God's power we will live with him to serve you." Paul relies on the power of God to bring about the results.

Many years ago, Peninsula Bible Church went through the painful experience of having to discipline a prominent church member. The nature of his sin need not be mentioned here. What is important is that we followed the biblical process of church discipline. We started by trying to counsel him privately, but he resisted the counsel of the church.

Eventually, we had to take the step of reporting the matter to the church in the manner that our Lord prescribed. I grieved for this brother who had fallen away from fellowship with the Lord. We felt powerless to reach this man. But there was One who had the power we lacked: Jesus.

Several years after we disciplined this man, I had the joyful privilege of standing before the congregation and reading a letter from him, which I've condensed here:

My fellow Christians,

Several years ago the church took public action against me in accordance with Matthew 18:15–20. I cannot reverse history and relive the events that led me to my downfall. Because I was an outspoken, prominent member of the Christian community, my sins were all the more deplorable and horrendous.

In time I became self-deceived and arrogant. Twice I went through the horror of manic-depressive psychoses (as Nebuchadnezzar did), so that I might learn that God resists the proud but gives grace to the humble. I came close to suicide and should have died in disgrace except for the Scripture which says, "Do you show your wonders to the dead? Do those who are dead rise up and praise you?"

I need your forgiveness, for I have wronged you all. I need your prayers for wholeness and deliverance. It's impossible for me to retrace my footsteps and right every wrong. However, I welcome the opportunity to meet and pray with any individuals who have something against me that needs resolution. I am looking for the further grace and mercy of God. I now know your actions were done in love for my own good and that of the body of Christ.

Our church loved him and welcomed him back—and we took the Lord's parable of the loving father and his prodigal son (see Luke 15) as our model for restoring our beloved brother. In the story, after the son returned, the father said, "Quick! Bring the best robe and put it on him. Put a ring on his finger and sandals on his feet. Bring the fattened calf and kill it. Let's have a feast and celebrate. For this son of mine was dead and is alive again; he was lost and is found."

Instead of a robe, we bought our brother a new sport coat. We put a gold ring on his finger, and we barbecued a fatted calf. We welcomed him home, and he has remained in our church family ever since.

But the pastors and members of the church could never have engineered this man's restoration. Nothing but the power of God could bring our brother back to his senses. When we welcomed him home, he told us some of the experiences God had taken him through during the years he was away. God dealt with him in ways that were ruthless yet loving. God put him through hell to bring him to heaven.

That's what the apostle Paul is saying to the Corinthians and to us: Our Lord Jesus "is not weak in dealing with you, but is powerful among you. For to be sure, he was crucified in weakness, yet he lives by God's power. Likewise, we are weak in him, yet by God's power we will live with him to serve you."

That is both a sober warning and a wonderful promise. Thank God for this man Paul, an authentic apostle of the Lord Jesus Christ.

34

THE END

2 Corinthians 13:5–14

We come now to The End.

Paul has said almost everything he can say. The church at Corinth, after reading this far, must surely have repented and changed its attitude toward him. I like to think that when he went in person to the church, Paul had much to rejoice about.

There may have been a handful of people who stubbornly insisted on following the false apostles rather than Paul. There may have been a few who chose to live in licentiousness and open immorality even after Paul had warned them and called them to repentance. Paul told them there would be public exposure for rebels and unrepentant sinners when he came. Perhaps Paul did have to cleanse the Corinthian church upon his arrival. We can only speculate. History does not record the response of the Corinthian believers to this strong letter.

Before we leave 2 Corinthians, let's take one more overview of the structure of the letter. The message of this letter could be divided into four parts:

Part I: Introduction and Salutation (2 Corinthians 1:1–11)
Paul briefly greets the Corinthians and describes hardships that he and his companions encountered in the province of Asia.

Part II: Paul's Conciliatory Defense (2 Corinthians 1:12–9:15)
Paul's gentle and conciliatory defense of his ministry (addressed to the majority in the church): the apostle is a minister of the new covenant; the gospel is a treasure contain in jars of clay; the ministry of reconciliation; "hilarious" giving.

Part III: Paul's Combative Defense (2 Corinthians 10:1–13:10)
Paul's confrontational and sarcastic defense of his ministry against the accusations of the false apostles, whom he ironically calls "the

super-apostles"; Paul's visit to heaven and his "thorn" in the flesh; the
marks of a true apostle; final warnings.

Part IV: Concluding Greetings (2 Corinthians 13:11–14)
Paul urges the church to practice love and peace toward one another
and to greet each other with a holy kiss.

Am I a true Christian—or a counterfeit?

As we come to the closing lines of this letter, Paul confronts the Corinthian
church with a final question that he hopes will change hearts and minds:

> Examine yourselves to see whether you are in the faith; test yourselves.
> Do you not realize that Christ Jesus is in you—unless, of course, you
> fail the test? And I trust that you will discover that we have not failed
> the test. (2 CORINTHIANS 13:5–6)

Is Jesus Christ in you? Paul wants every individual in the church to ask
himself that question. Through these two letters, 1 and 2 Corinthians, Paul
has repeatedly dealt with problems of sin and error in the church—and in
the lives of Christians. When we, as Christians, do not live according to
Christian standards, we need to ask ourselves, "Am I a true Christian, or
am I a counterfeit?" As Paul says, "Examine yourselves to see whether you
are in the faith."

A Christian is not simply a person who joins a church. There are millions of church members in the world today who are not Christians. Doing
good works does not make you a Christian. Adhering to a moral standard
doesn't make you a Christian. Reading and memorizing the Bible doesn't
make you a Christian. There is only one thing that truly marks you as a
genuine Christian: Jesus Christ living in you. If He does not dwell in your
life, then you are not a Christian.

Let's put Paul's question another way: "Are you really born again?" This
term has been greatly misused in recent years. Many people think that a
born-again Christian is anyone who belongs to a fundamentalist, evangelical, or Pentecostal church. Again, we have to remember that the spiritual
reality of being born again is not an outward matter of church membership. It's an inward reality; it's Christ living within us.

In John 3:3, Jesus told a man named Nicodemus, "I tell you the truth,
no one can see the kingdom of God unless he is born again." In other
words, no one is truly a Christians unless Jesus Christ has come to dwell

within that person. You may ask, "How can I know that I've been born again? How can I know that Christ lives in me?"

We find the answer in several places throughout Scripture. The Bible speaks of an inner witness that we belong to God. Paul writes:

> For you did not receive a spirit that makes you a slave again to fear, but you received the Spirit of sonship. And by him we cry, "Abba, Father." The Spirit himself testifies with our spirit that we are God's children. (ROMANS 8:15–16)

There is an inner testimony, a sense of identity with God as our loving Father. Our spirits want to cry out, "Abba, Father!" *Abba* is an intimate Aramaic term that could best be translated "Daddy" or even a toddler's cry of "Da-Da!" The Spirit testifies within us that God is no longer our Judge, waiting for an opportunity to condemn us. Instead, we see God as a patient, gentle Father, our heavenly Daddy whose arms are wrapped around us in a loving embrace.

I had the joy of leading my barber to Christ. Once, while I was having my hair cut, he told me about the changes in his life as a result of giving his life to Christ. Before he said a word about his newfound faith to anyone, his friends began telling him, "You're so positive and confident all of a sudden. What happened to you?"

"They don't understand what I feel within," he told me. "It's hard to put into words. The only way I can explain it is that I have a deep sense that my heavenly Daddy is with me all the time."

I had never explained those verses in Romans 8 to him. The sense that God was his heavenly Daddy was something he felt within. That's the witness of the Spirit, and it is one of the signs that Christ is in us, and that we are genuine Christians.

Scripture also speaks of a sense of inner peace. In Romans 5, Paul writes:

> Therefore, since we have been justified through faith, we have peace with God through our Lord Jesus Christ. (ROMANS 5:1)

Our conflict with God is over. We are no longer at war with Him. We are no longer alienated from God by sin. The work of Christ has satisfied His justice, so we are at peace with Him. Inner peace is one of the marks that signifies that Jesus Christ is in us.

A hunger for the Word

Scripture also speaks of new desires that are born in the heart of a new Christian. The apostle Peter tells us:

> Like newborn babies, crave pure spiritual milk, so that by it you may grow up in your salvation. (1 PETER 2:2)

One of the marks of authentic born-again believers is that they have a thirst for the Word of God—a hunger to be fed the truth of God. The Bible is a fascinating book that speaks with relevance and power to the core issues of our lives. There should be a hunger to know this book—a hunger that continues throughout our lives.

In the 1970s, Ron Rhodes was part of a family singing group. He toured the country with his six brothers and sisters, making personal appearances from California to New York. They appeared on TV with Merv Griffin, Dinah Shore, Jackie Gleason, Dick Clark, Jerry Lewis, Sammy Davis Jr., and many other stars. Once, Ron and his siblings shared a stage at Disneyland with Pat Boone and his family. After one performance, Pat's wife, Shirley, spent time backstage with young Ron Rhodes and his family, telling them about her faith in Jesus Christ.

"It's the first time I ever saw tears of joy in someone speaking about Jesus," Ron later recalled. "That got my attention. Within a month, I became a Christian, and my whole life changed! After I became a Christian, I had a hunger for God's Word that wouldn't quit."

As Ron continued touring from city to city with his family, he kept his Bible by his side. The long drives gave him plenty of time to read, and he read the Bible through several times during his teenage years. He not only had a hunger for reading the Bible, but he read as many books about the Bible as he could find.

After his touring and performing days ended, Ron went on to college and later enrolled at Dallas Theological Seminary, where he earned master's and doctoral degrees. His wife, Kerri, recalls, "I thought I was marrying a rock star, and I got a seminary student instead!" Today, Ron is a Bible teacher and the author of dozens of books, including *Christianity According to the Bible.*

If Christ is in us, our lives will be marked by a desire for God's Word. Does Jesus live in you?

We have looked at several inner evidences—the inner testimony of the Spirit, a sense of identity with God as our loving Father, an inner sense of peace with God, and an inner hunger for God's Word. These are subjective evidences.

But there is also objective, outward evidence that Jesus lives in us. An inner change, if it is genuine, will produce an outward change. Outward change is objective evidence, verifiable by the people around us. People should be able to answer the question of whether Jesus Christ lives in us merely by observing our lives.

New Christians almost always manifest a strikingly different attitude toward things they once viewed as normal. People who have been living sexually promiscuous or perverted lives suddenly see their old lifestyle as detestable. What was once pleasurable becomes painful and disgusting. No one has to say, "Now that you're a Christian, you have to stop living that way." They simply don't want to live a sinful life anymore.

I'm not saying that new Christians don't have any struggles with old sins. Struggles and temptations are common to all believers. But new Christians suddenly hate the things they once loved. Liars, thieves, and alcoholics find Christ—and suddenly they cannot tolerate their old habits of lying, stealing, and getting drunk. Their attitude has changed. Their behavior is visibly changing. This is because Christ lives in them, and they are aware that light can have no part in darkness.

Inner change produces outward change—but if we are honest, we have to acknowledge that many Christians seem to have lost that outward difference. At some point, the newness of their Christian experience wears off and they begin drifting back into old patterns. When this happens, the question that Paul asks becomes all the more crucial: "Examine yourselves to see whether you are in the faith; test yourselves. Do you not realize that Christ Jesus is in you—unless, of course, you fail the test?"

There are people around us who are looking at our lives and asking that very question: "Is he in the faith? Does he not realize that Christ lives within?" Or, when people look at our lives, do they conclude that we fail the test?

We need to continually ask ourselves if we are living out our faith. Our behavior tells the story. If we believe that Jesus is Lord and lives within, our lives will be different from the lives of the worldlings around us.

Is Paul for real?

Paul has urged the Corinthians to examine themselves to see whether they are in the faith, whether Christ lives in them or not. But then he goes a step further and adds, "And I trust that you will discover that we have not failed the test."

The Corinthians have been doubting Paul and asking, "Is Paul really an apostle? Should we believe him? Should we believe these other teachers who claim to be apostles? They claim that Paul is a false apostle. Who are we to believe?" So Paul says, in effect, "First examine yourselves to make sure that Christ truly lives in you. Then examine me. Look at the evidence of my life. If you can answer this question about your own life, you will clearly see the answer in my life. If you are real Christians, if you pass the test, then you will know that I pass the test as a true apostle."

Paul goes on to explain:

> Now we pray to God that you will not do anything wrong. Not that people will see that we have stood the test but that you will do what is right even though we may seem to have failed. For we cannot do anything against the truth, but only for the truth. We are glad whenever we are weak but you are strong; and our prayer is for your perfection. This is why I write these things when I am absent, that when I come I may not have to be harsh in my use of authority—the authority the Lord gave me for building you up, not for tearing you down. (2 CORINTHIANS 13:7–10)

Paul says he is not looking for an opportunity to come and demonstrate his authority as an apostle by judging them. He takes no delight in flexing his apostolic muscle. He does not enjoy being tough on the Corinthians. He would prefer that they judge themselves and stop their errant behavior, so that he could come and rejoice with them. If the Corinthians would deal with their own problems, Paul wouldn't have to.

The apostle makes it clear that true authority in the church is to be used constructively and redemptively. The Lord gave him his authority as an apostle, he says, "for building you up, not for tearing you down." In other words, church authority and power should never be used to boss people around.

I once heard of a church where the elders had decided that a certain woman was not being appropriately submissive to her husband, so they imposed a sanction on her: For the space of a year, she could not leave her apartment building without written permission from the elders. On one occasion, her mother became seriously ill, and she wanted to go visit and care for her mother—yet she was unable to contact the elders, so she couldn't leave her home. This is an abuse of church authority; nowhere do you see this kind of church authority upheld; throughout Scripture, it is condemned. The authority of the church is intended to build people up, not tear them down.

Twenty centuries later

In closing his letter, Paul appeals to the Corinthian brothers to support one another and live in harmony together:

> Finally, brothers, good-by. Aim for perfection, listen to my appeal, be of one mind, live in peace. And the God of love and peace will be with you. Greet one another with a holy kiss. All the saints send their greetings.
>
> May the grace of the Lord Jesus Christ, and the love of God, and the fellowship of the Holy Spirit be with you all. (2 CORINTHIANS 13:11–14)

Paul closes on a note of peace. As we have seen, the church in Corinth was fragmented and rocked by scandal and division. Yet Paul was able to look beyond all of these problems and see the basic unity of the Corinthian church. God created that unity, and the unity of the Corinthian believers remained there in spite of the quarreling, jealousy, and division in the assembly.

Christians belong to each other. They are part of the family of God, and they ought to act that way, he says. The unity of the Spirit exists whether we are aware of it or not, whether we are practicing it or not. Even when two Christians are at odds with each other, arguing and struggling with each other, the same Spirit of unity is within each of them. Our job is to listen to the urgings of the Spirit and live worthy of His presence within us. That's why Paul told the Ephesians,

> Make every effort to keep the unity of the Spirit through the bond of peace. (EPHESIANS 4:3)

When we heal our differences and restore our wounded relationships, then we are able, as Paul says, to "greet one another with a holy kiss." In our culture, we might greet each other with a holy hug instead, but the meaning is the same. Paul wants us to visibly, outwardly express Christian love, affection, and acceptance to one another in the body of Christ.

I was once driving down the freeway and a car cut in front of me. I had to brake hard and swerve to the side to keep from hitting it. The driver continued weaving from lane to lane, cutting off other drivers just to gain a few car lengths of advantage, probably because he was late to some appointment. I noticed that the offending vehicle had a bumper sticker that read: THE DIFFERENCE IN ME IS JESUS. I was not very impressed with the difference I saw. The world is not impressed by Christians who behave like everyone else and, on occasion, *worse* than everyone else.

If Jesus Christ lives within us, there should be a difference between us and the world around us. There should be a difference that makes people take notice and ask why we are different. We should be more positive, more optimistic, more friendly, more open, more accepting, more loving, and more forgiving than the people around us.

We should be full of grace and love. We should demonstrate to the world what true fellowship and Christian community should look like. So Paul closes with this blessing—which also serves as a reminder of the kind of people God wants us to be: "May the grace of the Lord Jesus Christ, and the love of God, and the fellowship of the Holy Spirit be with you all."

We live under Corinthian conditions, surrounded by a pagan culture that is drenched in sin and false beliefs. We are called to live lives that are distinct and different from the dying culture around us. If Jesus truly lives among us and within us, we cannot be the same kind of people we once were.

Twenty centuries have come and gone since Paul wrote these two letters to the Corinthian church. History doesn't tell us how the believers in Corinth responded to these letters—but that doesn't matter. Today, there's only one important question:

How will you and I respond?